State, Capitalism,
and Democracy
in Latin America

State, Capitalism, and Democracy in Latin America

Atilio A. Boron

LYNNE
RIENNER
PUBLISHERS

BOULDER
LONDON

To Maria
To Gabriela and Pablo
To Lucia, Tomás, and Andrés
For all the hours and days I took away from them

Published in the United States of America in 1995 by
Lynne Rienner Publishers, Inc.
1800 30th Street, Boulder, Colorado 80301

and in the United Kingdom by
Lynne Rienner Publishers, Inc.
3 Henrietta Street, Covent Garden, London WC2E 8LU

Library of Congress Cataloging-in-Publication Data
Boron, Atilio.
   [Estado, capitalismo y democracia en América Latina. English]
   State, capitalism, and democracy in Latin America / Atilio A.
Boron.
     p. cm.
   Includes bibliographical references and index.
   ISBN 1-55587-508-4 (alk. paper)
   1. Latin America—Politics and government—1948–
2. Democracy—Latin America. 3. Authoritarianism—Latin America.
4. Capitalism—Latin America. I. Title.
JL952.B6513 1995
320.98'09'049—dc20   95-8987
                                           CIP

British Cataloguing in Publication Data
A Cataloguing in Publication record for this book
is available from the British Library.

Printed and bound in the United States of America

5 4 3 2 1

Contents

Preface

I wrote this book while living in Mexico, returning to my native Argentina, and frequently lecturing in the United States and England, but it addresses one basic theme: the possibilities and limits of democratic capitalism in Latin America.

The first two chapters are an exploration of the tensions and contradictions between capitalism and democracy and of the doctrinal basis that, in neoliberal thought and free-market economics, leads to the justification of the "historical mission" of despotic regimes. The next two chapters deal with the overwhelming role played by the state in modern capitalist societies: Chapter 3 is a reflection spurred by Tocqueville's insights on the deep-seated tendencies of the capitalist state toward bureaucratic hypertrophy and on the contradictions of a neoliberal discourse that glorifies the market yet is viciously addicted to the state; Chapter 4 deals with the autonomy of the capitalist state, the problem of "stadolatry," and the prospects and limits of "state-centered" approaches in political science.

Chapters 5 and 6 deal with the critical issues of social reform and democratic consolidation—as distinct from democratic endurance—in Latin America and the deleterious impact of the economic crisis during the "lost decade" of the 1980s. Chapter 7 examines the prospects of democratization in Latin America at the beginning of the 1990s, and Chapter 8 explores the crisis of Marxist political theory and the possibilities of its eventual reconstitution.

Because this book was written over a period of years, the topics and concerns examined in it clearly reflect the change in the intellectual and political atmosphere in Latin America and, more generally, in the West. The historical period dealt with is circumscribed by two events to which Hegel would not hesitate to assign a historical-universal significance: the first is the U.S. defeat in Vietnam—the only defeat ever suffered by the United States—which symbolizes the beginning of the slow but unconcealable decline of U.S. hegemony. The other event is the fall of the Berlin Wall—a symbol of the collapse of the "really existing socialism" of Eastern Europe and of the exhaustion of the Russian Revolution. It is within this epoch-making time frame that the history of the military dictatorships of the 1970s, the triumph of the Sandinista revolution in Nicaragua, the fall of the Shah of Iran, the long agony of Francoism in Spain, perestroika, the explosion of the Latin American foreign debt, the rise and fall of "Euro-Communism," the neoconservative offensive, the Malvinas War, and democratic reconstruction in Latin America are inscribed.

This period encompasses twenty years of dense and dramatic history, when the volatility of events undermine the accuracy of many analyses and predictions. The arguments of this book express an intense debate: viewed from the mid-1990s, some of them look like burned, ash-covered coals—put out forever?—of a moment when historical developments seemed to allow the boundaries of the possible to expand. Yet, the corrections made to the original versions of these chapters did not modify their fundamental theses. Both accurate predictions and historical refutations will easily be seen throughout the book. My pessimism regarding the future of democracy in Latin America might seem unwarranted today. Yet, I believe that the persistence of democratic governments in our dependent and peripheral capitalisms has weak foundations, and should not be interpreted as being a genuine democratic consolidation. Quite the contrary, in Latin America the promise of democracy has been diminished by being emptied of its ethical content and divorced of all aspirations for justice. The reenfranchised masses have been demoralized by democratic regimes whose governmental performance has been less than mediocre, promoting crude skepticism and cynicism among the citizenry. In short, there seems to be an attempt—marked by a phenomenal shortsightedness—to capitalize on popular disappointment and disillusionment in order that neoliberal governments may rule without being challenged by high popular expectations or working-class militancy, transferring to the market and to individual citizens the responsibilities of attaining the goods and services that, in mature democracies, are delivered by sound governmental performance. As the cases of Peru and Venezuela have dramatically shown in recent times, there are reasons to be concerned with the detrimental impact of neoliberal ideas on the future of Latin American democracies.

*   *   *

Every book is a social product, and this is not mere rhetoric. Endless discussions and arguments with friends, colleagues, and students in a variety of countries constitute the basis of this book. In addition, some institutions provided particularly important encouragement for my research and writing. First of all I should mention FLACSO in Santiago, Chile, where I went to do my graduate studies as a young Argentine sociologist, only to be trapped by the irresistible attraction that political developments in Chile of the late 1960s—leading to the presidential election of Salvador Allende in

1970—exerted on an entire generation of Latin Americans. I must also express my gratitude to the Mexico City branch of FLACSO, the Centro de Estudios Latinoamericanos (CELA) of the Facultad de Ciencias Políticas y Sociales, the Division of Graduate Studies of UNAM, the Centro de Estudios Internacionales of El Colegio de México, and the Centro de Investigación and Docencia Económicas (CIDE), which offered me their generous hospitality. These institutions allowed me to use their resources to develop a Latin American perspective regarding numerous problems that only through an excess of parochialism could be considered questions of a national nature. I must also mention the constant encouragement I received in Argentina, when I returned after almost twenty years, from colleagues and research assistants of the Centro de Investigaciones Europeo-Latinoamericanas (EURAL). Likewise I must thank the Carrera de Ciencias Políticas of the Facultad de Ciencias Sociales of the University of Buenos Aires and the Buenos Aires and Rosario offices of FLACSO. Finally, I should also thank the Institute of Latin American and Iberian Studies (ILAIS) of Columbia University and its director, Douglas Chalmers; the Department of Politics of Warwick University in England, and especially Julio Faúndez; the people of the International Studies Overseas Program (ISOP) of the University of California, Los Angeles; and the Kellogg Institute for International Studies of the University of Notre Dame and its director, Guillermo O'Donnell; for the splendid opportunity they all gave me to come into contact with outstanding students and colleagues, whose inquisitiveness, criticisms, and viewpoints have been a permanent source of inspiration for the arguments unfolded in this book.

Substantial parts of the book were written with the support of grants and donations made by the Ford Foundation, the Tinker Foundation, and the MacArthur Foundation. Special thanks should be addressed to Jeffrey Puryear, formerly at the Ford Foundation, and to Joan Dassin and Cynthia Sanborn; to Martha Muse and Renata Rennie, of the Tinker Foundation; and to Kate Early, of the MacArthur Foundation. I am grateful to Sonia Mazzeo for her assistance in the initial translation of this book, and to Merchy Puga Marín for having relieved me of most of my administrative duties as director of EURAL while I worked on the book. I want also to thank Lynne Rienner for accepting the book for publication; the anonymous reader whose keen comments and suggestions greatly served to improve and clarify my arguments; and, finally, Gia Hamilton and Phil Murray, for the Sisyphus-like job of converting my rather rudimentary English into a fluent, pleasant, and, I hope, convincing prose.

My intellectual and affectionate debt to so many teachers, friends, colleagues, and students in Latin America, the United States, and Western Europe is so great that I could not do justice with a long enumeration of their names. However, it would be unfair not to underline the crucial role that Harvard University played in my theoretical development. The influence exerted by its outstanding faculty in government, sociology, history, and economics in the mid-1970s and the literary treasuries kept in the Widener Library have been crucial and pervasive. Many teachers at Harvard contributed decisively, with penetrating criticism and friendly comments, to helping me to spell out the full implications, merits, and shortcomings of Marxist political theory. Even at the risk of unjustly neglecting other influential teachers, to this day my intellectual debt to Karl Deutsch, Gino Germani, Alexander Gerschenkron, Louis Hartz, and Barrington Moore is incommensurable, and my recognition goes beyond what my words could possibly express. Others, such as Hayward Alker, Perry Anderson, Norberto Bobbio, Fernando H. Cardoso, Umberto Cerroni, Agustín Cueva, Robert A. Dahl, Torcuato S. Di Tella, Pablo González Casanova, Juan Linz, Guillermo O'Donnell, Claus Offe, Adam Przeworski, Adolfo Sánchez Vázquez, Alfred Stepan, and Göran Therborn have honored me with their friendship and counsel. I am sure that they will recognize themselves, and our dialogues, in the pages of this book. I take this opportunity to publicly manifest my gratitude for the patience, understanding, and intelligent comments of these friends on some of the ideas in this book. Naturally, they are not to be blamed for the errors and shortcomings surely existing in this book. These are due to my own limitations and, sometimes, to my incorrigible stubbornness.

—*A. A. B.*

Between Hobbes and Friedman: Liberalism, Dictatorship, and Democracy in Recent Latin American History

Think of all this and you will comprehend why in this unspeakable, uproarious confusion of fusion, revision, prorogation, Constitution, conspiracy, coalition, emigration, usurpation and revolution the bourgeoisie madly snorts to this parliamentary republic: "Rather an end with terror than a terror without end!"
— K. Marx, *The Eighteenth Brumaire of Louis Bonaparte*

The recent history of Latin America has been a fertile testing ground for contemporary social sciences. The patterns of capitalist accumulation, the diversity of state forms and political regimes, and the variety of social movements and political parties have provided telling examples against which to test some crucial theoretical formulations. Little wonder that two originally typical Latin American "themes," dependency analysis and the question of the state, were first discussed in the region and then exported, in the 1970s, to North American—and, to a lesser extent, Western European— scholarly debates, where they soon acquired enduring and pervasive influence.[1]

One of the issues of major practical and theoretical concern since the end of World War II in Latin America has been the possibility of setting up a long-lasting democratic capitalism. As leading Italian political theorist Norberto Bobbio persuasively argues, the study of the intricate and contradictory relationship between capitalism as a mode of production and democracy as a political regime "constitutes the most obscure and difficult chapter" of modern democratic theory.[2] The argument presented in this chapter, based on the analysis of the 1970s and early 1980s in Latin American history, attempts to suggest some guidelines for fruitful understanding of this complex problem.

The situation of Latin American societies in the early 1970s disclosed the extreme frailty of their democratic institutions. This feebleness was not a passing disturbance but the manifestation of a deep-seated chronic shortcoming, and for this reason it reappeared once again during the democratic wave of the 1980s (as we shall discuss later in this book). This alarming institutional weakness was revealed even in countries like Chile and Uruguay, which until the late 1960s were regarded by mainstream political science as shining examples of the feasibility of bourgeois democracy in peripheral capitalism. From a theoretical viewpoint, therefore, the problem should be posed in the following manner: from the mid-1960s on, the deepening and continuation of capitalist development in a significant number of Latin American countries have proven to increasingly require the systematic dismantling of institutions, practices, and values traditionally associated with capitalist democracy.[3] An apparent paradox immediately arises: the progress of some fast-growing capitalist economies seemed to have rested on the systematic violation of the political institutions, values, and ideology considered by many as the most genuine products of the capitalist spirit. To the astonishment of many observers, the Latin American authoritarian outburst in the 1970s served to unveil the intimate connection linking economic liberalism and political despotism, thus destroying the illusions that capitalist development would finally succeed in eradicating the chronic authoritarian plagues of the region's political life (attributed precisely to the weakness of the capitalist impulse) and in securing bourgeois democracy once and for all. These optimistic expectations—an appalling boast of economicism, which was regarded by many to be the exclusive inheritance of the left but was predominant in the wisdom of conventional social sciences in the late 1960s—were ruthlessly demolished by the military dictatorships that mushroomed in the region in the 1970s.

This "developmentalist optimism," à la Lipset, was hard hit by the actual course of history. There was indeed capitalist development in Latin America—Brazil became one of the ten largest economies of the world, Mexico and Venezuela consolidated their economic development, and the rest of Latin America kept growing, with few exceptions, at high rates—but the feeble democratic regimes that existed in the region were wiped out and despotic rule was more widespread than ever. By comparison with the calculated barbarism of the new dictatorships of the 1970s, the classical pantheon of old Latin American dictators—admirably portrayed by many Latin American novelists and in other times held as supreme exponents of an unsurpassable repressive ferocity—was reduced to a collection of small autocratic patriarchs and dilettantes of authoritarianism.

Latin America's historical drama in those days teaches that the praxis of liberalism was trapped in an apparently unsolvable dilemma: the adoption of liberal economic policies called for the constitution of a political order in which preexisting democratic institutions—where they existed—would vanish into thin air. The state would thus take on the apocalyptic overtones envisaged by Hobbes, wielding absolute power to ensure the unquestioning obedience of the underlying population. The leviathan, sea monster of biblical tradition, is evoked by Hobbes to categorically point out the only escape from the sinister labyrinth of the "state of nature"—that is, the war of all against all. The metaphor was not inspired in Hobbes's vision of imaginary worlds, but in the much more concrete and close experience of the English civil war, in the seventeenth century, that would crown the triumph of the emerging bourgeois society. It was this protracted conflict, in fact, that was responsible for the constant fear of violent death under which daily life of the kingdom unfolded. Hobbes summarizes his allegation with a vivid description of human life in the anarchy of civil war: "continual feare, and danger of violent death; And the life of man, solitary, poore, nasty, brutish, and short." The cure against these evils, bitter but necessary, was a strong dose of state despotism clothed in messianic guises.[4]

An indisputable similarity exists between Hobbes's frightful view of the England that had just beheaded Charles I and the view of the Southern Cone of the 1970s, with its heartbreaking scores of dead, disappeared, kidnapped, and tortured. In these countries a "state of nature" was experienced that was similar to if not exactly like the one described by Hobbes in the convulsed England of his time. When political mobilization and class confrontations reached critical levels that were perceived by elite groups as threatening the stability of bourgeois society, the dominant classes prompted the advent of a series of de facto governments aimed at "solving" the crisis—that is, unraveling it in the terms most favorable to their own interests by simultaneously resorting to both state despotism and the supposedly automatic market mechanisms. But the contradiction is flagrant: the invisible hand that regulates the market—that fetish so dear to the whole liberal tradition—requires the iron fist of the Hobbesian state. Thus, an apparently unresolvable conflict is created between the disciplinary imperatives rooted in the sphere of capitalist production and a democratic order that, in times of crisis, becomes an unbearable burden from which the bourgeoisie strives to free itself as soon as possible.

The following pages will mainly, although not exclusively, refer to the way in which this dilemma was constituted in the Latin America of the 1970s. The special emphasis placed on certain Southern Cone countries is justified by the fact that the history of the 1970s shows, with unique clarity, profound tendencies that nonetheless operate in all capitalist societies. In other words, the goal here will be to observe how in the face of the unavoidable need for structural reorganization experienced by global capitalism at several stages of its development—which throughout this century has witnessed the rise and fall of socialist states, the collapse of the old colonial empires, the occurrence of two profound economic depressions, and the outburst of two world wars—it has become necessary to redefine and qualify the scope and limits of democratic conceptions that, in a not distant past, were claimed as the bourgeoisie's lofty contributions to the constitution of modern society. This need originated in the fact that refounding a liberal economic order—one that would give free rein to the most dynamic and concentrated segments of capital—demands an increasingly authoritarian political order not only in the capitalist periphery but also in its developed core. This situation explains the insistence with which, since the mid-1970s, a host of distinguished neoconservative intellectuals started to argue in favor of the curtailment of certain citizens' rights and the reshaping of the state-market-civil society balance, and to pose the question of the "crisis of democracy." Yet, it should be asked: which democracy? Given that democracy is not a geometrical concept, a pure political form, or a system of abstract rules deprived of—or indifferent to—any substantive meaning, a correct response to that question requires one to place this problem under a totalizing perspective, which necessarily leads one to examine the links between capitalism and democracy.[5]

The Relationship Between Capitalism and Democracy: Theoretical Arguments

In the history of political theory, Rousseau's forceful arguments illustrate with unsurpassed clarity the fracture that would irreversibly divide the two paths that democratic ideas were to follow after the French Revolution: a timorous and colorless proclamation of a rising bourgeoisie, or a radical banner of plebeian barricades. In any case, in order to understand the historical meaning of democracy one must examine its relation to the issue of property. At the beginnings of the second part of his *Discourses on the Origins of Inequality Among Men,* Rousseau launches a devastating attack on the traditional framework within which the relationship between property and democracy was being discussed in the first half of the eighteenth century. In a manner that remains impressive more than two hundred years later, Rousseau writes,

> The first man, who after enclosing a piece of ground, took it into his head to say, *this is mine,* and found people simple enough to believe him, was the real founder of civil society. How many crimes, how many wars, how many murders, how many misfortunes and horrors, would that man have saved the human species, who pulling up the stakes or filling up the ditches should have cried to his fellows: Beware of listening to this impostor; you are lost, if you forget that the fruits of the earth belong equally to us all, and the earth itself to nobody.[6]

Rousseau's words thrust a dagger into the very heart of the "common sense" of the bourgeoisie, whose phlegmatic and parsimonious expression had been laid down in John Locke's *Second Treatise.* Locke asserts that "the reason why men enter into society is the preservation of their property."[7] Property, as Rousseau asserts, assumes a markedly distinct role: it is in private property that the origins of the misfortunes suffered by the noble savage should be sought, thus being the ultimate cause of human misery. It is precisely in this early critique of property as the foundation of good government that one can discover the premises of the socialist doctrine of democracy, which the Marxist classics would partly elaborate later on.[8]

The liberal tradition, on the contrary, remained loyal to the essence of Locke's thought, by keeping clear of the itching questions contained in Rousseau's theoretical discourse. Issues such as equality, popular sovereignty, and direct democracy (just to mention a few of the most distinguished) had no room in a political argument founded on the inexorable permanence of class inequalities and the legitimacy of a government based on quite a restricted franchise. The consequence of this neglect was the construction of a "possessive" theory of politics and democracy, the premises and implications of which are rightly criticized by C. B. Macpherson in a deservedly celebrated work.[9] The final stroke of this process is found in the contemporary versions of liberalism and in some expressions of mainstream political science that emptied democracy of its substantive contents and reduced it to a method solely for the constitution of public authority.

It is true that throughout this secular history liberalism incorporated into its discourse some of the themes proper of Rousseau's or Paine's radical democracy. Notwithstanding, it is also true that this process allowed only for a mechanical juxtaposition of heteroclite elements that could hardly be assimilated into the essential corpus of the classic liberal theory. This process gave way to a selective appropriation of certain contents of the democratic proposal that, as expected, were immediately reconverted when they came into contact with a doctrinal apparatus that was profoundly foreign to them. Equality became "equality of opportunities," with a complete disregard of initial conditions and minimum necessary endowments; and direct democracy and popular sovereignty quietly withered away, their place occupied by a "representative democracy" in which lobbies and interest groups are far more important than the common people, while a complex set of legal and bureaucratic procedures effectively tended to discourage popular participation in public affairs. This is why the synthesis between liberalism and democracy proved to be so difficult to attain: it is a volatile and cumbersome mixture of contradictory principles regarding the constitution of political power that are unable to beget an integrated and coherent discourse, thus leading to the chronic instability of democratic liberalism. This blatant evidence, however, is insufficient to dissuade the legion of ideologues who feel authorized to predicate the existence of an unbreakable nexus between liberalism and democracy.

An unsurpassed example of this predication is supplied by Milton Friedman in his famous *Capitalism and Freedom*—a book that has become a liberal gospel for an entire generation of orthodox economists and neoliberal policymakers. The book summarizes the fundamental principles of modern liberalism and provides the blueprint for most of the social and economic policies applied in Latin America in the last twenty years.[10] In this work, Friedman asserts that there exists "an intimate connection between economics and politics, that only certain combinations of political and economic arrangements are possible, and that in particular, a society which is socialist cannot also be democratic, in the sense of guaranteeing individual freedom."[11] He concludes his argument by assuring that "the kind of economic organization that provides economic freedom directly, namely, competitive capitalism, also promotes political freedom because it separates economic power from political power and in this way enables the one to offset the other."[12]

Thus, by means of a rather simple manipulation of complex historical categories—such as competitive capitalism and democracy—Friedman ends in the reciprocal assimilation of both terms. The historical and theoretical problem of the relationship between capitalism and democracy, which Bobbio finds so worrisome, is thus "solved" by way of a tautology: democracy simply becomes the political organization proper of capitalism—competitive *ex definitione*—and capitalism is posited as the sole structural support congruent with the specific needs of a democratic state. This sophistic operation is far from being an extravagant turn of Friedman's ideas: in one way or another the diverse expressions of the "established" political thought regularly assert this substantial identity between capitalism and democracy, not to mention the innumerable works of sociology and political science that dully reproduce the most insignificant precepts of the dominant ideology. Neither is Max Weber, unquestionably the summit of twentieth-century "bourgeois" social science, free from such statements, however subtle or elaborate his versions may be.[13]

It is not the purpose of this chapter to carry out a theoretical critique of the fallacies underlying these arguments. That task has already been brilliantly accomplished by the socialist tradition following the tracks of Marx's early critique of Hegel's legal and political philosophy. Suffice it to say that the red thread that unifies the thoughts of the major socialist thinkers in a coherent theoretical discourse is the identification of the class essence of the state. Accordingly, those thinkers reject as liberal rhetoric any attempt to posit the historical and theoretical problem of "democracy" without asking at once: for which class? Furthermore, Friedman's theses—true quintessence of contemporary bourgeois thought—were knocked down by Macpherson, whose ideas will be discussed later.[14]

The goal here is to analyze liberalism's theoretical discourse in the real historical terrain, not as if it were an isolated doctrinal system that undauntedly flows above history. It is important to evaluate liberalism's concrete implications for social struggles and the changing modalities of political domination in capitalist societies, both in the core and in the periphery. For this reason this chapter will deal strictly with the study of capitalist democracy, leaving aside a comparative examination with respect to the theory and practice of socialist democracy, understood as the maximum development of democracy and as the self-government of producers, a leap that finally accomplishes the reabsorption of the state in civil society. For the purposes of this work it is enough to point out that Umberto Cerroni's observations regarding this issue are valid, especially in relation to the unresolvable limitations inherent in liberal democracy and the representative state.[15]

As a starting point for these reflections, it is appropriate to recall the existence of an insurmountable gap between traditional conceptions of democracy and the contemporary liberal reformulations. There seems to be enough evidence to assert that the essential content of democracy—that egalitarian kernel found in Aristotle's and Rousseau's writings, for example—was abandoned and replaced by a formalistic argumentation that favors the procedural aspects of the political process and of the governmental apparatus at the expense of the substantive attributes of citizenship.[16] In this way, a point is reached where the egalitarian and "subversive" character of democracy is dissolved into a lukewarm and unappealing doctrinal proposal rightly called "elitist democracy."[17] It is another economist, this time Joseph A. Schumpeter, who bluntly advocates this process of theoretical debasement of democracy when he asserts, that "democracy is a political *method,* that is to say, a certain type of institutional arrangement for arriving at political—legislative and administrative—decisions and hence incapable of being an end in itself, irrespective of what decisions it will produce under given historical conditions. And this must be the starting point of any attempt at defining it."[18] It is therefore not surprising that Schumpeter winds up his argument by saying that "democracy means only that the people have the opportunity of accepting or refusing the men who are to rule them," a rather discouraging proposal.[19]

In this context it is interesting to compare Schumpeter's thesis with Aristotle's views on the matter. In fact, in one of his most illuminating passages the Greek philosopher states, "The really distinctive characteristics of Democracy and Oligarchy are poverty and wealth; and it is a necessary law that wherever wealth constitutes the title to rule, whether the rulers are a minority or a majority, the polity is an Oligarchy, whereas, if the poor are rulers, it is a Democracy."[20] Aristotle defines democracy as "the rule of the many for the good of the poor."[21] This assertion could never be found in contemporary versions of democratic theory because the substantive meaning of democracy evaporated when it was reduced to (1) a sole procedural political routine, stripped of all concrete content, and (2) a mere ideology that conceals the supremacy of capital. Throughout this long process—throughout which democratic ideology accommodated the liberal demands of a rising bourgeoisie that was busy building its own hegemony—democracy slowly lost its egalitarian character, as forcefully stressed by Alexis de Tocqueville, and degenerated into a formal mechanism for the constitution and organization of political power.[22] What formerly had been a condition of citizenship distinguished by the radical equality of the constituency became an abstract architectural design of the political process. In this way, bourgeois ideology could afford to call democratic such regimes as the one in Victorian England, where hardly 10 percent of adult males enjoyed political rights. This type of democracy was certainly compatible with capitalism's social order because, as Marx notes, it served only to determine which members of the dominant classes were to be in charge of administering the dictatorship of capital over the rest of the population.

The causes of this gradual disappearance of the revolutionary and liberating contents of the democratic ideas are accurately pointed out by historian Edward H. Carr when he asserts that, in Europe,

> before 1848 nobody had doubted that *political democracy* (one man, one vote) carried with it *social democracy* (equality or the levelling of classes), and that the progressive middle class which wanted universal suffrage was therefore fighting the cause of the masses. . . . [But] from 1848 onwards . . . political democracy ("liberal democracy") and social democracy ("socialism" or "communism") were to be found throughout Europe on opposite sides of the barricades.[23]

Thus, the gradual acceptance of democracy by organic intellectuals and political representatives of the propertied classes constitutes a belated phenomenon in the history of capitalism, the origins of which can be traced to the late nineteenth century. Carr assures one that "in England, where there had been no 1848 . . . the word democracy long remained in bad odour with the English ruling classes."[24] Carr's observation fully agrees with the results of a study carried out by Göran Therborn proving that even "a broad-minded liberal as John Stuart Mill remained a considered opponent of democracy" until the end of his days, supporting plural votes for capitalists and their foremen-lieutenants as a means to prevent the advance of a proletarian-inspired "class legislation."[25]

Therefore, the correspondence between democracy and capitalism is a novelty of the twentieth century made possible largely—but not exclusively, as will be shown in the following chapters—by the reduction of the former to a mere procedural arrangement. In addition, when bourgeois hegemony succeeded in introducing into the consciousness of the subordinated classes the ideological justifications of its class domination, the democratic state could coexist—without having to resort to "excessive" and/or constant repression—with an economic regime that, despite being based on the exploitation of a vast mass of expropriated producers, loudly proclaimed the "equality" of its citizens. When bourgeois hegemony was not achieved, the faulty constitution of democratic capitalism rapidly gave way to fascism or dictatorship.

The Relationship Between Capitalism
and Democracy: Historical Evidence

It is worth investigating whether historical evidence justifies what the previous section deems unacceptable from a theoretical point of view, that is, the assertion that capitalist development and democracy are no more than two sides of the same coin. To be sure, there is a concordance between the two processes. Yet the explanation to which Milton Friedman resorts appears to be purely ideological and lacking much scientific value. Methodologically speaking, there is a substantial difference between coincidence—or concomitant variation—and causation. Macpherson is right in rejecting Friedman's argument that the economic freedoms were the agents that brought about political democracy in the West. In Latin America, for instance, the liberal oligarchic state—as a concrete expression of political freedoms socially and economically circumscribed to a tiny section of the population—was formed before the constitution of the capitalist market and with the explicit purpose of creating the external conditions necessary for the maximum development of bourgeois social relations. Macpherson concludes,

> The liberal state which had, by the mid-nineteenth century in England, established the political freedoms needed to facilitate capitalism, was not democratic: that is, it had not extended political freedom to the bulk of the people. When, later, it did so, it began to abridge market freedom. The more extensive the political freedom, the less extensive the economic freedom became. At any rate, the historical correlation scarcely suggests that capitalism is a necessary condition for political freedom.[26]

Of course, it is necessary to recognize that the bourgeoisie had to confront the enormous task of creating a state in congruence with the specific modalities best suited to its class domination. Both the feudal and absolutist states interposed objective obstacles to the ruling classes' need to construct a historical block under their hegemony. Even the absolutist state, a transitional form in which the interests of the rising bourgeoisie found vivid expression, was too impregnated by feudal classes and institutions to adequately promote the accomplishments necessary for the full consolidation of capitalism as a mode of production.[27] The bourgeoisie required a complete separation between the direct producers and the owners of the means of production in order to create a free proletariat ready to sell its labor power. It is fundamental to remember that this was not merely a political or ideological demand of the rising entrepreneurial classes, but a structural need originated in the very entrails of the productive process. The bourgeoisie also needed a complete separation between the state and civil society, the destruction of all remaining feudal social relations, and the termination of the asphyxiating patrimonialism and its costly and intolerable remnants of real privileges and monopolies. In other words, for the bourgeoisie, commodifying

the labor force and the means of production—including land, of course—
was an iron necessity. To that effect it was necessary that the political order
juridically sanction, and effectively guarantee, the equality of individuals
and their right to sell their labor power, trade their properties and posses-
sions, and sign contracts.

To that end a capitalist state that was bourgeois and liberal, although not
necessarily democratic, was needed. Its progressive democratization was the
result of a long and rather violent process of expanding civil, political, and
social rights, which ensured the freedoms required for peaceful political
competition and the construction of a democratic regime. Nevertheless, it
must be highlighted that that extension of civil, political, and social rights
was not a benevolent concession "from above." On the contrary, it was the
mounting political mobilization of the subordinate classes, with their
demands and struggles, their parties and unions, that forced the democratization of the liberal state.[28] Accordingly, the popular classes should be cred-
ited with the accomplishments of democratization. If the bourgeoisie and its
allied classes and fractions agreed on introducing some progressive political
reforms, they did so only after the mobilization of the working class—sometimes in conjunction with the peasantry, the petit bourgeoisie, or sections of
the middle classes—seriously threatened the stability of bourgeois domination, or when the ruling classes perceived such activation as a potential
threat. In other words, the history of bourgeois democracy is much shorter
than the history of the bourgeoisie, and the driving forces that pushed
democracy forward are found not within the bourgeois camp but rather in
the tumultuous expression—many times inorganic and chaotic, but always
profoundly democratic—of the popular classes. Thus, Therborn is clearly
right when he states,

> In the history of democratization, two features are striking by their
> absence. Firstly, the fact that none of the great bourgeois revolutions actu-
> ally established bourgeois democracy. It is not only of the early Dutch and
> English revolutions that this is true: the democratic constitution produced
> by the French Revolution remained a dead letter from beginning to end of
> its brief existence. The July Revolution did not even manage to draft one,
> although it did stimulate the development of a male democratic movement
> in Switzerland. The international popular upsurge of 1848 was rapidly sti-
> fled by feudal-dynastic reaction—and also by the bourgeoisie itself. . . .
> The American republic was established by white propertied gentlemen, and
> the only blacks enfranchised by the Civil War were male northerners.
> Unified Italy took over the extremely narrow franchise of the Kingdom of
> Sardinia. And when, despite the misgivings of the bourgeois liberals,
> Bismarck introduced universal male suffrage in Reich elections, a régime
> of parliamentary democracy was neither the object nor the outcome of the
> measure.[29]

In other words: bourgeois revolutions did not produce by themselves
bourgeois democracy. What they did succeed in creating was a liberal state,

invariably founded on an extremely narrow electoral franchise, the expansion of which was always forced by popular agitation and lower-class unrest. Bourgeois revolutions were something quite different from what many contemporary liberal theorists would lead one to believe. Were it not for the popular mobilizations and workers' struggles, the democratic accomplishments would not have been possible, and the bourgeois state would have crystallized as a sheer oligarchical domination barely disguised under some restricted liberal institutions (especially in the economic domain) and some boisterous but rather empty legal guarantees. It was the prolonged contestation and rebellion of the laboring classes—in the majority of the cases fostered by socialistic or left-wing ideas—that democratized the capitalist state.

It is instructive to consider the "absences" pointed out by Therborn. To the one mentioned above—the nondemocratic outcome of bourgeois revolutions—Therborn adds another: in the history of bourgeois democracies, there is not "a steady, peaceful process accompanying the development of wealth, literacy and urbanization."[30] This fact warns against optimistic hopes: increases of wealth, literacy, and urbanization do not in themselves guarantee the stability of democratic achievements. Democratic progress in bourgeois societies is anything but irreversible, and capitalist rule has no preferential affinity with democracy. Capitalist rule is highly flexible and adaptable, and it is almost always able to mix quite efficiently with alternative forms of political domination, ranging from bourgeois democracy to fascism, including traditional dictatorships, the Latin American "military state" of the 1970s, and Bonapartism. Therefore, in capitalist societies there are no checks that prevent a reversion to despotic forms of bourgeois domination, nor any institutional safeguards against the constitution of a reactionary coalition aiming at "settling accounts" with the subordinate classes.

In order to ponder the historical relationships between democracy and capitalism, it is worthwhile to glance at the process of their international expansion. This will prove that the constitution of bourgeois democracy in industrialized nations was the result of intensified domestic contradictions accompanying the development and consolidation of capitalism on a global scale from the second half of the nineteenth century to World War I. The prevailing conditions in the periphery of the system, however, did not reproduce that original combination of social forces, historical legacies, and structural processes that—in just a handful of countries—led to the establishment of bourgeois democracy. On the contrary, the penetration of capitalism in some backward areas (including under this generic denomination certain European latecomers) failed to repeat either the economic forms or the political institutions of the countries of original development.[31] It is appropriate to explore the reasons for these shortcomings.

In the countries of early capitalist development, democratization was the consequence of the fusion of two factors: on one hand, a complex set of economic and social changes had revolutionized preexisting social relations of production and climaxed in the industrial revolution; on the other hand, a no less multifarious collection of historical legacies had guaranteed (well before the full predominance of capitalist relations of production) certain civil and political freedoms to some significant sections of the population. Therefore, bourgeois democracy is the culmination of a secular process in which a unique amalgam was forged between the social and political mobilization of the subordinate classes—which provided the democratic impulse from below—and a liberal, pluralist, and tolerant tradition that was slowly being formed in some European countries since the times of the Reformation and the Renaissance. If the end result of this complex amalgam was capitalist democracy, that was largely due to the fact that this felicitous synthesis took place in the competitive or liberal phase of capitalism. The emergence of monopolies and the inauguration of the imperialist stage of world capitalist development abruptly reduced the possibilities of a bourgeois democratic transformation in those countries that began their capitalist development later. It is for this reason that the extreme fragility exhibited by bourgeois democracy in Germany and Italy up to the middle of the twentieth century was no surprise, not to mention the cases of countries such as Spain, Greece, and Portugal in which the political superstructure of capitalism took root in a historical structural terrain saturated with feudal and absolutist elements filled with antidemocratic contents.[32]

A quick glance at those nations considered "democratic" by liberal theorists proves what this chapter has noted. Despite the tremendous global expansion and penetration of the capitalist mode of production, accountable progress to the credit of capitalist democracy has been insignificant.[33] Were one to compare the nations that James Bryce considered "democratic" after World War I with the list of mid-1970s "polyarchies" prepared by Robert Dahl, one would arrive at a disappointing conclusion: after more than half a century, only a few countries could be added to Bryce's short enumeration.[34] Bryce, who finished his book *Modern Democracies* in December 1920, identifies the following nations as fully deserving the adjective *democratic:* "the United Kingdom and her self-governed dominions, France, Italy, Portugal, Belgium, Holland, Denmark, Norway, the United States, Argentina and, perhaps Chile and Uruguay."[35] He excludes from his list both Austria and the new German Republic of the time, for which he declares that "it was too early to talk."(His caution was to be tragically confirmed by the subsequent history of fascism.) Bryce also excludes Switzerland because of the several discriminations and restrictions that prevailed in its electoral legislation. Furthermore, among the nations that Bryce considers democratic, there were several that left the path of capitalist democratization and underwent long periods of fascism and dictatorship, such as Italy, Greece, and Portugal.

In Latin America, the diagnosis—and the subsequent optimistic forecast made by Bryce—was mercilessly disproved by history. The significant advance that bourgeois democracy had made in Argentina beginning in 1912 ended in 1930. For more than fifty years, state life oscillated between failed attempts to reconstruct a bourgeois democratic political order—always unstable and fragile—and the recurrent downfalls of various types of military dictatorships. This phase appeared to be over with the democratic restoration of 1983.

The Chilean and Uruguayan democracies suffered a similar fate. In Chile it should be noted that the process of massive broadening of the social bases of the state was a phenomenon that began in the late 1950s in response to a formidable rise in the militancy of the popular classes and the intensification of class struggle. This mobilization was first expressed, rather imperfectly, in the establishment of a Christian Democratic government that was driven by a timid reformist vocation. The climax of this workers' and peasants' mobilization was reached in the general elections of 1970, when Salvador Allende became the first Marxist president to be popularly elected. Allende set forth an ambitious project of transition toward socialism that was drowned in blood by internal reactionary forces in alliance with U.S. imperialism. This coalition was able to inscribe on its banners the same slogan that the French bourgeoisie waved before Louis Bonaparte: "legality is killing us." Despite their continuous public statements in favor of democracy and constitutional rule, the coalition's most prominent members played a key role in facilitating the installation of Pinochet's dictatorship. The Uruguayan case reveals the narrow limitations of a bourgeois democracy for which the feasibility was structurally conditioned by the need to channel popular demands through an archaic and profoundly oligarchic bipartisan system. The traditional party system of Uruguay had been completely overwhelmed by the development of popular mobilization since the beginning of the 1960s, provoking a political crisis of unprecedented magnitude in the heart of the state. To resolve this crisis the bourgeois block was forced to eliminate the last remnants of democratic institutions that were still standing in 1973. The great expansion in the number of democratic polities had to wait until the third democratic wave of the mid-1980s.[36]

Consequently, by the mid-1970s none of these Latin American countries maintained sufficient credentials to be admitted to the exclusive club of bourgeois democracies. And from the comparison between Bryce's and Dahl's lists, one can infer how meager the advances of democratization have been in the capitalist world. Dahl finds twenty-nine polyarchies, and three special cases among them—Chile, Switzerland, and the United States—in which there were some electoral restrictions that inhibited full-fledged democracy. There are six other countries that Dahl places in a separate category he calls "quasi-polyarchies."[37] However, not all of the thirty-five countries belonging to this list (which was prepared in the late 1960s) could ten years later be regarded as still fulfilling Dahl's criteria. Of the twenty-six "pure" cases of polyarchy, Lebanon, the Philippines, and Uruguay by the end of the 1970s could no longer qualify. Of the three special cases, Pinochet's Chile would hardly satisfy any of the specific democratic standards. And regarding the quasi-polyarchies, only Venezuela continued to meet the proper standards. In short, Dahl's list is primarily composed of the old countries selected by Bryce: the United Kingdom and its independent dominions, such as Australia, Canada, and New Zealand; some other European countries (including Germany and Austria, which were politically reorganized as a result of their defeat in World War II); Japan, where bourgeois democracy was forcefully introduced through MacArthur's troops; and, finally, the rather exceptional case of Israel, where the agreement of old colonialist powers allowed for the constitution of a bourgeois democracy on a territory partly taken away from another oppressed nation.

Therefore, the history of democratic capitalism from the end of World War I up to the mid-1970s shows that the only cases of "successful" democratization were those of Costa Rica, India, Jamaica, and Trinidad and Tobago; if the standards are lowered somewhat, one can add Turkey, Colombia, Venezuela, and the Dominican Republic, which had just been rescued from fifty years of Trujillo's rule. It is unnecessary to stress the alarming fragility of most of these additions to the universe of capitalist democracies, which in many cases bear little resemblance to the state forms that predominate in the industrialized democracies. The dreadful misery of hundreds of millions of "citizens" in India; the dark prospects cast over Jamaica (under intense "destabilizing" imperialist pressure) and Colombia, where the practical dismantling of a state that appears to have lost its capacity to retain a monopoly on violence is indisputable; the repressive character of the "strong governments" of Turkey; and the inevitable uncertainty that surrounds the first steps of the Dominican democracy are enough to illustrate the extreme weakness of the liberal thesis that unifies the development of capitalism with the consolidation of democracy in a single historical process.

The documented evidence shows that the penetration of capitalism into the periphery of the world economy did not reproduce the democratic political institutions characteristic of the countries of original development. Therefore, the dissolution of the precapitalist modes of production and the all-embracing imposition of capitalism configured an incomplete process given that the democratic superstructure of the core did not accompany the expansion of capital throughout the world. That is why the diffusion of capitalism in the periphery failed to become the prelude to bourgeois democracy. Rather, as of the mid-1970s the rule seemed to be that the continuation of capitalist development favored the establishment of dictatorial and repressive regimes that bore some resemblance to the fascist regimes of the interwar period. If the development of capitalism in the most advanced nations created the conditions that made the democratic revolution possible, historical and comparative evidence seems to suggest that capitalist development in the periphery played the opposite role: it actually reduced the few possibilities that might have existed for bourgeois democratic developments.

This is not all that surprising if one recalls that, even in Europe, countries such as Germany and Italy had to experience the horrors of fascism before establishing solid grounds for a stable bourgeois democratic state; whereas others, such as Greece, Spain, and Portugal, in the 1970s began to travel on the ever harsher road of capitalist democratization. The military defeat of fascism opened up the doors of democracy to the conquered nations: this was especially true in the cases of Japan and (to a lesser degree) Germany, in which the regimes were not challenged by any organized opposition. The Italian experience was different; the downfall of fascism was primarily the outcome of an antifascist struggle of profound revolutionary and anticapitalist content. Therefore, in the Italian case, capitalist democracy was first and foremost an accomplishment of the popular resistance and the *partigiani,* whereas in Germany and Japan the endogenous drive in the direction of democracy was nil.

Whereas in the countries of original capitalist industrialization—as well as its "fragments" outside of Europe: Australia, Canada, New Zealand, and the United States—capitalist democracy was the plebeian crowning of the bourgeois revolution, in the latecomers it was constituted only after a historical tragedy (such as a dictatorship or war) and was largely an imposition of the conquerors. This conclusion is not surprising if one considers that the latecomers were in fact the countries where capitalist development took hold without a bourgeois revolution. In other words, capitalism's advancement and consolidation was the product of a "revolution from above," or of what in Gramscian analysis is subsumed under the category of "passive revolution," which left alive many of the bulwarks of precapitalist reaction.

Finally, among the nations that constitute the third industrializing wave, it is noteworthy that capitalist dynamics has established restrictive limitations to the process of democratization. In addition, at least in the periphery, the new structural tendencies of contemporary bourgeois society seem to favor the constitution of dictatorial regimes that are the purest embodiment of antiliberal and antidemocratic practices. Lenin once noted that democracy belongs to competitive capitalism whereas political reaction belongs to monopoly. If competitive capitalism created the conditions that enabled the advent of the era of "democratic revolution," it now looks like the "age of imperialism" brought with it the rigors of dictatorship for peripheral societies. It also favored the noticeable authoritarian involution observed in mature bourgeois democracies, reflected in the neoconservative reduction of the scope and limits of the democratic project and democratic expectations.[38]

Capitalism and Democracy in Latin America:
Oligarchy, Populism, and Military Rule

The establishment of capitalism in Latin America precipitated substantial changes in the region's social formations. This section will sketch the political transformations that took place as a result of the integration of some South American countries into the expansive world market during the end of the twentieth century, as well as the implications of this process on the democratization of these societies.

The oligarchic state was the capitalist state form that corresponded to the period when the primary-export economy predominated. It consecrated the unquestioned supremacy of the coalition of classes and class fractions linked to the world market either as exporters of raw materials and food-stuffs or as importers of manufactured goods, big bankers, financiers, and merchants involved in international trade.[39] This specific form of the capitalist state expressed itself through a variety of political regimes, but its historical task was to clear the way for the establishment and extension of capitalist relations of production. Moreover, the dominant classes in this state form were clearly of bourgeois nature, even when in appearance they exhibited certain precapitalist features and attributes that reflected the historical and structural complexities of social formations in which archaic social relations survived subordinated to the dominant capitalist mode of production. Hence, many times an agrarian bourgeoisie appeared or behaved—superficially speaking—as if it were a decadent landowning aristocracy. Furthermore, the entire social structure and the culture, the state and ideology, showed the powerful influence that traditional social relations had on rising capitalism. The strength of those manorial and feudal components is unequivocally shown by the lengthy persistence of the belief that what existed in Latin America was feudalism and not capitalism, a belief that was too widespread at times and that blurred not a few analyses conducted by the left.

The constitution of the oligarchic state was a necessary stage for the advancement of capitalism, given that the latter required certain conditions that could be met only through the organization of a centralized administrative and coercive apparatus of national reach. These tasks, usually included under the misleading name of "external conditions of production," overwhelmed the weak and tottering states that arose after the wars of independence. Thus, the creation of a state apparatus more in tune with the tasks to be carried out became one of the main structural imperatives in order to guarantee the development of capitalism in those regions. The oligarchic state assumed various regime forms: the highly centralized Mexican Porfiriato (1876–1910) contrasted with Brazil's loosely interconnected República Velha (1889–1930) almost as much as the Chilean parliamentary republic (1891–1920) differed from the presidential regime of Argentina between 1880 and 1930. These peculiarities reflected the context in which the different oligarchic pacts between bourgeois fractions, the precapitalist landowning strata, and imperialist capital were established. Such coalitions were defied by democratic forces of a plebeian nature—artisans, small businesses, the embryonic nucleus of the proletariat, and the peasantry—who upheld a multiform and obstinate resistance to the projects of the new power bloc with varying degrees of success. At the same time, this new ruling coalition had its share of internal, although nonfundamental, contradictions clearly reflected in the terms under which the different sections of the dominant classes had negotiated their integration into the dominant pact.

These two circumstances—the antagonism (latent or open; violent or peaceful) of the subordinate classes and the internal contradictions within the dominant bloc—largely explain the diversity of political regimes that embodied the oligarchic domination in Latin America. This heterogeneity not only is a reflection of significant national peculiarities but also reveals the extent to which the new pact was able to establish its hegemony over the society as a whole. To be sure, in Argentina and Uruguay, for example, the predominance of this alliance was manifest in the ability of the oligarchy to build a solid and long-lasting hegemonic system. This system allowed the ruling classes to enjoy the benefits of the moral and intellectual direction exerted over the subordinate classes, thus giving rise to a diffuse mass consensus that provided the plutocratic sector with an enviable political stability. In other countries, as in prerevolutionary Mexico, the supremacy of oligarchic interests instead assumed the form of "dictatorship," harshly subduing the popular classes rather than carrying out their subordinate integration into the development of the new hegemonic alliance.[40]

The oligarchic state illustrates with unsurpassed eloquence the hiatus between liberalism and democracy. Although at the level of juridical organization and of ideological discourse this state form was liberal (sometimes fanatically), its concrete practices showed consistent contempt for democratic participation and popular culture. The oligarchic state was liberal to the extent that it sanctioned the equality of its citizens; guaranteed on paper basic freedoms (of thought, speech, association, etc.); created—or rather, transcribed—codes, laws, and constitutions of enlightened liberal credentials; guaranteed individual property; fought against the anachronistic privileges of the Church and confiscated its lands; declared the division of public powers and solemnly adopted the principles of the democratic republic; abolished slavery and servitude, thereby creating a market of free individuals; and, finally, endorsed science and positivism and made secularism one of its most aggressive banners in its fight against precapitalist and clerical obscurantism. Nevertheless, all these liberal, and sometimes Jacobin features were in direct conflict with the exclusivist and oligarchic domination of the class alliance formed by several agrarian fractions, the *comprador* bourgeoisie, and imperialist capital. Some of the agrarian groups were

decidedly bourgeois, whereas others were backward landowners and therefore closer to the character of an old feudal class.) Still, it would be a mistake to consider this liberalism as a mere outward appearance that concealed
an oligarchic essence with which it related in a mechanistic and external
way. As one scholar on the subject correctly points out, liberalism and oligarchy are two aspects that "although never with the same weight were both
fundamental" in the constitution of the oligarchic state.[41] Irrefutable proof
of this notion can be observed in the crises and decomposition of the oligarchic state: in the junctures of that state's dissolution, popular struggles
questioned in a single process both agrarian-based exclusivism and "enlightened" liberalism.

The oligarchic state thus embodied the dialectical unity between a type
of society that was torn apart by profound class contradictions and a set of
liberal, and sometimes democratic, political and juridical institutions that
were as imposing as they were phantasmagoric and that on paper alone
evoked a substantial democratization of social relations. On the other hand,
the populist state that followed the defunct oligarchic regimes was the
expression of a society in which the popular classes had achieved—in some
cases, as in Argentina more than in Chile or Brazil, for instance—certain
advances in "fundamental" or substantive democratization (in the factory, in
politics, in daily life) while rejecting the validity and historical legitimacy of
the institutions of representative democracy. The recently enfranchised citizenry justly reproached the latter form of government's prolonged and open
identification with the "elitism" of oligarchic domination.[42] Hence, Latin
American political life swung between a "democratic" oligarchic form,
stripped of its real substance and devoid of any root in concrete ongoing
social relations, and the repudiation of the democratic "formalities" just
when the nature of social relations experienced an inorganic and tumultuous
yet real democratization.

The prolonged dissolution of the material and ideological bases of the
liberal oligarchic state took place along a variety of routes that will not be
discussed here.[43] What is important to keep in mind is that, sooner or later,
the attempts of the democratic forces to construct a stable bourgeois democratic regime were frustrated. The crisis of oligarchic hegemony—for which
the 1929 crash was the equivalent of the death knell—was temporarily
resolved by the rise of the populist state, not by the constitution of a full-
fledged capitalist democracy. In fact, as Octavio Ianni accurately asserts,
Peronism, Varguism, and the Chilean popular front were Bonapartist interludes between the crisis of oligarchic domination and the frustrated attempts
to establish bourgeois hegemony in those societies.[44] This effort encountered enormous obstacles given that the bourgeoisie was confronting a formidable dilemma. The bourgeoisie either (1) resolutely entered the thorny
path of a democratic revolution and thus finally resolved the pending tasks

that inhibited capitalist development (in particular the agrarian question and the liquidation of the material bases of the "creole" junkers' domination), or (2) resigned itself to achieving its economic predominance under the protection of a Bonapartist alliance, condemning the industrial interests to bind their fate to the decadent agrarian classes, the authoritarianism and short-sightedness of the military corporation, and the arrogance of imperialist capital.

This highly unstable situation of "shared hegemony" consecrated the survival of traditional and backward-looking classes and fractions antagonistic to any democratization project. The bourgeoisie, in no condition to challenge them, was then forced to strike a deal with them. The potential threat of a fervent popular mobilization, be it imminent or latent, did the rest. Later on, when the Bonapartist alliance—which guaranteed the political passivity, or at least the acquiescence, of the proletariat—started to crumble, the bourgeoisie, loyal to its ancestral traditions, preferred to yield to the dictates of a new reactionary coalition rather than confronting the risks of establishing its own domination by antagonizing its most recalcitrant allies. What Engels has to say regarding the English bourgeoisie is also true of Latin American countries: the bourgeoisie had "not yet succeeded in driving the landed aristocracy completely from power when another competitor, the working class, appeared on the stage."[45] With the entrance of the industrial working class as a protagonist in the class struggles, the cycle of the bourgeois revolutions was closed, and a new one, that of the socialist revolutions, appeared on the scene. The Latin American bourgeoisies were to react accordingly.

The Bonapartist regimes, for which national differences were no less sharp than those that in the past distinguished the oligarchic predecessors, carried out decisive tasks in the new phase of capitalist development that began after the Great Depression of 1929. They facilitated the economic ascent of a national bourgeoisie by neutralizing (without eliminating) that group's oligarchic enemies and by establishing a complex set of institutions aimed at controlling the labor movement through various tactics, incorporating it into the state, co-opting its leadership, and guaranteeing minimum levels of material well-being to the popular masses.

In accordance with the Keynesian revolution going on elsewhere, the structure and function of the capitalist state in Latin America were profoundly reorganized, its apparatuses diversified and expanded to unprecedented levels. The state thus assumed an unheard-of political and economic influence in this new phase, becoming a crucial actor in the promotion of industrialization and inward-oriented growth. The diverse governments of the region put into effect a wide variety of macroeconomic policies, such as the control of foreign trade and of interest and exchange rates; the creation of state agencies for the planning, promotion, and financing of economic development; the establishment of a few big industrial complexes under the direct control of the government; and the design of a severe tariff policy that tended to protect the nascent national industry.

Later on extensive programs for nationalizing foreign-owned large assets in the services area—mainly railways, ports, telephones, urban transportation, etc.—were also adopted. In the countries where industrial development had advanced more resolutely (Argentina, Brazil, Chile, Mexico, to mention the most important cases), these policies were accompanied by others aimed at creating large state-owned industrial complexes and/or large public enterprises controlling a key export resource, like oil in Mexico and Venezuela and copper in Chile. Once again, these policies reproduced quite closely some dominant features of postwar Europe and reflected quite clearly the Keynesian consensus that, in those days, prevailed in the West. The other side of the developmentalist policies promoted by the populist state were a series of measures targeted to produce some redistribution of incomes and wealth in favor of the urban popular classes and to help reduce the prevailing levels of social inequality. These redistributionist policies were also instrumental in enhancing the strength of the populist coalition, reinforcing the legitimacy of governments for which relationships with the dominant classes were seldom smooth.

Of course, the extent and depth of these policies were largely the result of the intensity of the "pressures from below," and in this regard the Latin American experience was variegated: in some countries, especially Argentina, popular pressures combined with the initial bitter confrontation between the populist regime and the establishment, and the result was an aggressive social policy that, for a while, significantly improved the material well-being of the populace. This result was achieved through a wide range of policies that included minimum wages, labor legislation, price controls, and the expansion of social security and of government spending in health, education, and housing. In other countries, such as Brazil and Chile, the impact of the populist redistributionist policies was far less important, and the legacies of populism withered away much more rapidly and without leaving profound tracks.[46]

However, the populist regimes eventually found themselves caught in an irreconcilable contradiction: the policies conceived to stimulate capitalist accumulation and the development of productive forces—that is, the consolidation of a project calling for an autonomous, vigorous, and expansive national capitalism—proved to be incompatible with the maintenance of the governmental initiatives that tended to ensure the integration of the popular classes, especially the industrial proletariat, into the market and the state. If the decay of the primary-export growth model had irreparably corroded the economic basis of oligarchic domination, the Bonapartist coalitions soon began to realize that the material basis on which they rested had begun to crumble. The exhaustion of import-substitution industrialization, the slowing down of economic growth, and, in particular, the stagnation of the agrarian sector—the inviolability of which was never questioned during the populist phase—undermined these regimes.

On the other hand, the diminishing effectiveness of political manipulations by the populist coalition, combined with the extraordinary impact of the Cuban revolution on the entire continent, unleashed an unexpected new wave of political mobilization, in which wide sectors of the popular classes and growing segments of the middle classes succeeded in articulating new demands that went far beyond the limited scope of populist politics and prevented the continuation of the class conciliation policies that constituted its fundamental essence. The populist alliance promptly fell apart, and the subsequent political crisis—the seriousness of which posed threats of various degrees of importance to those countries' dominant classes—was "solved" through some short-lived and rather unstable democratic experiments (as in Chile and to some extent in Argentina and Brazil) that in due time broke down and enabled the inauguration of a new form of "exceptional" capitalist state. In fact, despite the solid presence of the military in the state apparatuses, the new military regimes that mushroomed in Latin America in the 1970s cannot be identified with the "classical" military dictatorship. Neither can they be likened to fascist dictatorships in spite of the systematic use of terroristic methods of political control.[47]

It is not the goal here to consider the numerous theoretical problems posed by the emergence of this new form of capitalist dictatorship. It is important to emphasize, however, that this new form closely corresponded to the need for a profound reorganization of the productive apparatus imposed by the rising mode of capitalist accumulation. However, this argument should not be carried so far as to conclude that these new forms of bourgeois despotism were the sheer mechanical and linear impacts of the economic base on the state and political processes. Warning against conceptual simplifications, Marx observes that "the same economic basis" is affected by "innumerable different empirical circumstances, natural environment, racial relations, external historical influences, etc.," all of which cause the "infinite variations and gradations in appearance" that characterize real-world capitalist societies.[48] Failing to realize the complexity of the causal links among economy, society, and politics would make one lose sight of the fact that those "last instance" economic determinants are only efficient through multiple mediations—social, political, ideological, and cultural—that establish the specific form and degree through which the structural features of a society condition the state and the political process. Therefore, even though authoritarian and repressive aspects seem to be built into the new mode of capitalist accumulation—as illustrated by the cases of the Southern Cone countries—there are important national variations that should not be underestimated. It is of the utmost importance to recall the existence of some pronounced "deviations" from the general trend. The cases of Mexico, Venezuela, and Colombia prevent one from concluding that restructured capitalist economies inevitably bring about political authoritarianism.

Now that this brief methodological warning has been established, it is appropriate to consider the political requisites of the economic projects that South American dictatorships were carrying out in the 1970s and how they reveal the limits within which the refoundation of capitalist democracy in this region should be posed in the future.

For instance, one may consider labor policies. The restructuring of capitalism, both in the center and in the periphery, calls for drastic changes in the forms of organization of the productive apparatus pointing toward a significant devaluation of the labor force. The economy experiences acute processes of concentration and centralization of capital, and monopolistic firms predominate almost unfettered in the markets. Gigantic transnational corporations not only possess capital, but also control the technology, the financial infrastructure, and the operational resources, which guarantees the corporations' overwhelming preponderance in the markets. The transnationalization and denationalization of peripheral economies are therefore two aspects of a single process of internationalization of capital, the most visible consequences of which are the vanishing national autonomy of formerly sovereign national states, the irrepressible progression of Latin America's foreign debt, sharpening disparities in income distribution, and intensified exploitation of wage labor.

One of the implications of this complex process of internationalizing capital in the new conditions of capitalist accumulation was the freezing of wages and salaries, which made the labor force the only commodity that the state was interested in maintaining at a low price. The blatant class bias of liberalism is revealed in the fact that whereas the prices of almost all the goods and services are fixed by the market, the price of the labor force is coercively established by the government. In consonance with the liberal proposals to solve the general crisis of capitalism by abandoning Keynesian "interventionist" policies and by returning to automatic market mechanisms, these authoritarian regimes expressed an unresolvable contradiction of capitalist economies. The market is expected to assign society's economic resources rationally and efficiently, free from distortions caused by the "interference" of the state or of elements that are "foreign" to the economy. Yet this free-market proposal assumed the previous condition of authoritarian neutralization of the workers' capacity to resist and maintain their incomes. The labor force needs to be tamed or harshly repressed and its price fixed near subsistence levels through repression and the systematic disorganization of its corporative structures.

Consequently, real wages fell and the standard of living of the popular classes was depressed to levels that had few precedents in the history of Latin America. As shown in a source as free of suspicion as a study carried out by a Swiss bank in 1977, it is perfectly understandable that "if an average worker in Buenos Aires has to work 482 hours per month—sixteen hours seven days a week—to earn what is needed to pay for the bare essentials of urban life," this orthodox solution to the problems of capitalist accumulation could hardly be obtained in a democratic regime, where labor can protest and rebel, go on strike, agitate public opinion, demand the intervention of the parliament, rally the press, and mobilize the popular strata against such policies.[49]

The case of Chile reveals that these orthodox economic policies had a similar effect on the standard of living of the masses, and both the government and Milton Friedman himself justified those measures by arguing that the "normalization" of the economy required freeing the market from all types of government intervention. In this way, business could obtain high profits that would encourage further investments, thus ensuring the continuation of capitalist development. The result of this sequence of fallacious reasonings could not be more deplorable: according to official statistics, between 1972 and 1974, wages fell from 62.3 percent to 42.2 percent of the national income, while real wages (with a base of 100 in 1970) fell during the same years from 111.2 to 60.0.[50] The Brazilian case shows a similar tendency, although less abrupt: real wages in São Paulo and Guanabara also fell after the 1964 coup. These wages declined 25 percent during the first three years, whereas in Argentina or Chile the decline was 50 percent after only one year.[51]

Unemployment figures reveal an equally alarming tendency: in Chile, the unemployment rate remained stable at near 20 percent of the total economically active population,[52] whereas in Argentina and Uruguay the figures were much lower. This led some ideologues in these regimes to argue that economic reconversion took place without the costs of mass unemployment. However, the statistics conceal a crucial fact: these countries experienced significant population losses because of the unprecedented numbers of working-age people who were forced to emigrate as a result of political persecution or prolonged unemployment. Some estimates point out that some 25 percent of the economically active population abandoned Uruguay after 1973, and highly conservative estimates indicate that about 350,000 emigrated from Argentina in the 1970s. Given such a loss in the size of the labor force, it is natural that unemployment statistics do not show the full impact of the capitalist adjustment. Moreover, it is no secret that the amazing "definitional elasticity" of those state agencies that were in charge of producing these statistics poorly reflects the real level of unemployment.[53]

Much more evidence could be added to support this interpretation: the evolution of state expenditures shows that there have been drastic cuts in health, education, and housing budgets; the number of commercial bankruptcies has reached unprecedented levels; and innumerable small and medium-sized businesses have been either absorbed or simply displaced from the market. However, it is not the intent here to take inventory of all the economic and social implications that originate in this conservative modernization of Latin American capitalism in the 1970s. Instead it is important to highlight that this process is based on the need to reintegrate peripheral economies into the new international division of labor generated by the exhaustion of the post–World War II Keynesian boom. The dictatorships of the Southern Cone are both a condition and a consequence of this epochal change, and the intensifying exploitation of the labor force is not a transient circumstance of this new capitalist mode, nor is it solely limited to Latin America. On the contrary, the attack on labor is the cornerstone on which the neoconservative reconversion of capitalist economies is founded. These policies have been implemented, with various degrees of success, in many capitalist countries, advanced and dependent. Think of the "conservative revolution" brought about by the rise of Reaganism in the United States or the impact of Thatcherism, the influence of which is felt far beyond the United Kingdom. These two governments set the tone of the bourgeois response to the crisis, fostering the adoption of policies of "fiscal austerity" and "structural adjustment" for which the concrete implications were the sharpening of class inequalities and the regressive reconstitution of advanced capitalist societies.

Prospects for the Future

The argument and evidence presented in this chapter suggest some conjectures regarding the prospects of bourgeois democracy in contemporary capitalism.

It seems beyond any reasonable doubt that the public policies implemented by Latin American dictatorships are designed to produce profound modifications of the social and economic structures of the region. Authoritarianism and repression seem to have become integral components of these restructuring policies. The question then arises: will it be possible to continue applying governmental programs that follow the same neoconservative inspiration without severely violating the human, civil, and political rights of the population? Perhaps there may be a change in the way these abuses trample upon human dignity, but the essence would remain unaltered. If capitalist development in Latin America was incapable of constituting a stable and legitimate bourgeois democratic regime, its achievements in the 1970s and early 1980s seem to have been the creation a new form of dictatorship based on the unprecedented intensification and diversification of state coercion. Repression has become an essential feature, not an ephemeral excess of the new economic order. For this very reason, the struggle for democracy (even for the modest achievements of capitalist democracy) entails dismantling the mode of accumulation installed by the dictatorships; a meaningful democratization of Latin American societies would hardly be possible without a substantial modification of the economic and social policies put forward by the dictators.[54]

However, the issue that emerges from the above assertion is highly complex. In fact, what are the existing democratic and capitalist alternatives? Or to put it in more comprehensive terms: would it be possible, in the dependent social formations of Latin America, to articulate a capitalist and democratic project that runs counter to the most profound tendencies prevailing in the international capitalist economy? Unfortunately, the answer is no. A glance at cases such as those of South Korea, Taiwan, the Philippines, the Shah's Iran, and Brazil of 1968 to 1973 shows that high rates of capital accumulation and the rapid development of the productive forces went hand in hand with state forms that were consistently despotic and coercive and therefore incompatible with bourgeois democracy. If there were still any possibilities for a capitalist development that would also deepen the democratization of our societies, where are the concrete examples? As shown earlier in this chapter, no such cases are yet to be found.

Therefore, it is not by chance that at the beginning of the 1960s an insightful scholar of the history of capitalism contended, "One thing, however, emerges clearly from the subsequent analysis: the development of democracy in the nineteenth century was a function of an unusual configuration of historical circumstances which cannot be repeated. The Euro-American route to democracy is closed. Other means must now be devised for building new democratic states."[55]

Notwithstanding, these new bourgeois roads have not yet been found, and it is quite likely that they will never be. They seem to belong to a bygone chapter in the history of capitalism. Instead, the authoritarian threat has acquired the character of an endemic disease in these types of societies, exacerbated by the general crisis and by the mere existence of what could losely be called the "socialist camp." And it is precisely the recognition of this situation that drives Trilateral Commission theorists to sound the alarm and rally the efforts of the dominant classes of mature capitalism to ward off the danger of the "democratic crisis." This constitutes an explicit confession in the sense that the changes observed in the international system and the delegitimation and overburdening of democratic governments have to be met with a strategy aimed at defusing the problems posed by "democratic excesses." Not in vain does Samuel P. Huntington conclude his chapter on the United States in the Trilateral's report on the governability of democracies with a devastating critique of what he considers democratic "romanticism." Quoting former presidential candidate Al Smith, who once said that "the only cure for the evils of democracy is more democracy," Huntington bluntly retorts, "Our analysis suggests that applying that cure at the present time could well be adding fuel to the flames. Instead, some of the problems of governance in the United States today stem from an excess of democracy. . . . Needed, instead, is a greater degree of moderation in democracy."[56]

After citing John Adams and his radical pessimism regarding democracy—"It never lasts long; democracy soon wastes, exhausts, and murders itself. There never was a democracy yet that did not commit suicide"—Huntington ends his analysis by arguing that "a value which is normally good in itself is not necessarily optimized when it is maximized. We have come to recognize that there are potentially desirable limits to economic growth. There are also potentially desirable limits to the indefinite extension of political democracy. Democracy will have a longer life if it has a more balanced existence."[57]

These thoughts regarding the future of bourgeois democracy in the most advanced capitalist countries nicely close the circle that the first pages of this chapter began to draw: the coexistence of democracy and capitalism is unlikely and conflictive not only at an abstract theoretical level. Historical praxis shows the difficulty in guaranteeing the continued existence of a bourgeois democratic regime even under the far better conditions prevailing in advanced capitalism. The "excesses of democracy" do not conform to the needs of the enlarged reproduction of capital, and the short historical cycle in which capitalism appeared to have adopted the political forms of bourgeois democracy seems to have reached its end. Marxist analysis is not alone in arriving at this conclusion; other theorists share this diagnosis, thereby generalizing a pessimistic perspective regarding the narrow limits of capitalist democratization. This perspective concerns both capitalist potential to develop the productive forces without destroying its very natural conditions of existence as well as its capacity to construct a democratic polity and an egalitarian society. In short, it is the explicit recognition that, in the face of the political crisis that undermines the governability of democracies, it will not be the bourgeoisie who will take on the task of democratically reconstructing the state.

The necessary discussion regarding capitalist democracy in Latin America should not be carried out in abstract terms, that is, in the ideological sphere of capitalist ideology. Therefore, the proliferation of formulas such as the "recovery of democracy," "the expansion of democracy," "the profoundization of democracy"—quite widespread in social science these days—systematically overlook the class nature and the insurmountable limitations of bourgeois democracy, something that even an author as unsuspicious of dogmatism as Gramsci never failed to do. The abstract reasoning that does not call into question "democracy for which class?" splits the analysis of the social totality into its economic and political components, reifying them as isolated "parts," reducing the political to a procedural question and reproducing the world vision consecrated by bourgeois ideology. Capitalist exploitation is conveniently hidden, thus allowing all kinds of benevolent speculations on the future worlds of "democracy"—affecting people in their sole capacity as voters—while piously disregarding all the restrictions that originate in the laws of motion of capital and that oppress people in the name of the free market. The entire rationale of this argument is trapped in the ideological universe of bourgeois thought.

In his controversy with Norberto Bobbio, Umberto Cerroni sharply remarks,

> In countries such as Italy political democracy is defended and expanded principally thanks to the socialist movement. In their anticapitalist struggles the socialists must face an antifascist battle while simultaneously promoting political democracy. This means, on the one hand, that the supersession of capitalism appears as a *necessary* condition for the development of political democracy; it also means the *possibility* of furthering the advancement of socialism hand in hand with democracy.[58]

This assertion is entirely valid in the Latin American context, no matter how much it may distress the good souls who still embrace the hopes for a full-fledged democratic capitalism in the Southern Cone and the illusions of a democratic reconstruction disassociated from an attack against the insolvable injustice of capitalism. Cerroni's reasoning refers one back to this chapter's initial discussion regarding the crucial role the popular classes carried out in the constitution of bourgeois democracy in advanced capitalist countries. Once again, the popular classes are the fundamental social forces that can democratize the state, and they may offer a progressive and civilized solution to the political crisis that affects capitalism. The true characteristics that define today's struggle for democracy in Latin America—the conquest of equality, freedom, and participation—are just multiple aspects of a unified struggle against capital that creatively recovers even the most "formal" aspects of bourgeois democracy when the bourgeoisie itself qualifies these formal rights as "subversive." The democratization of the capitalist state will be the people's victory. It will not, as in the past, be a process of filing down the exclusivist and authoritarian edges of bourgeois domination. Rather, it should accelerate the transition toward superior forms of political organization, the integral and substantive democracy of socialism. Consequently, there is no possible separation, in the real history of the Latin American people, between the struggle for democracy and the practical—as well as theoretical—critique of capitalism.

Notes

1. This issue is explored in detail in Chapter 4 of this book.
2. Bobbio, Norberto, *Política e cultura* (Milan: 1955), pp. 148 and ff., quoted in della Volpe, Galvano, *Rousseau y Marx* (Barcelona: Martínez Roca, 1969), p. 40. The relationship between Rousseau and Marx is masterfully explored in della Volpe's work. See also Cerroni, Umberto, *La libertad de los modernos* (Barcelona:

Martínez Roca, 1972), pp. 194 and ff.; Gerratana, Valentino, *Investigaciones sobre la historia del marxismo* (Barcelona: Grijalbo, 1975), Vol. 1, pp. 21–95; and Colleti, Lucio, *From Rousseau to Lenin* (London: New Left Books, 1972).

3. This is the major thesis of Guillermo O'Donnell's seminal work, *Modernization and Bureaucratic Authoritarianism* (Berkeley: Institute of International Studies, 1973).

4. Hobbes, Thomas, *Leviathan* (Middlesex: Penguin Books, 1974), p. 186.

5. See also Chapter 7.

6. Rousseau, Jean Jacques, "Discourse on the origin and foundation of inequality among mankind," in *The Social Contract and Discourse on the Origin of Inequality* (New York: Washington Square Press, 1967), pp. 211–212. This text was originally written in 1754 and was dedicated to the Republic of Geneva.

7. Locke, John, "An essay concerning the true origins, extent and end of civil government (second treatise on civil government)," in Barker, Sir Ernest, ed., *Social Contract* (New York: Oxford University Press, 1962), p. 127.

8. Cf. della Volpe, *Rousseau;* and Cerroni, *La libertad.*

9. Macpherson, C. B., *The Political Theory of Possesive Individualism,* Oxford, 1962.

10. Friedman, Milton, *Capitalism and Freedom* (Chicago: The University of Chicago Press, 1962). Friedman has been one of the main sources of inspiration (perhaps the most important) of the orthodox economic policies implemented by several Latin American dictatorships. His influence was particularly evident in the first years of Pinochet's rule in Chile, where Friedman's disciples (the so-called Chicago boys) repeatedly invited the economist to visit the country and lecture in favor of the "shock treatment." Friedman's influence was also significant in the United States at the beginning of the Reagan administration and in the great "monitoring" agencies of the international capitalist system, such as the International Monetary Fund, the World Bank, and others. Even if his stark policy recommendations were almost never strictly followed, it is beyond question that Friedman's ideas lie at the bottom of the market-oriented approach that since the 1980s had prevailed as unchallenged "common sense" all around the globe.

11. Ibid., p. 8.

12. Ibid., p. 9.

13. Weber, Max, *Economy and Society* (New York: Bedminster Press, 1968), Vol. 2, Ch. 9. On this subject see Georg Lukács's sharp observations in *El asalto a la razón* (Mexico: Grijalbo, 1967), pp. 492–493.

14. Macpherson, C. B., "Elegant tombstones: A note on Friedman's freedom," in *Democratic Theory: Essays in Retrieval* (Oxford: Oxford University Press, 1973), pp. 143–156.

15. See Umberto Cerroni's enlightening discussion on this topic in *La libertad,* Ch. 6. In a later work Cerroni carries out a provocative reconstruction of the development of the socialist theory of democracy in classical Marxist thought. Even though I hasten to point out my dissatisfaction with the treatment of some particular aspects of this very complex subject, it would be unfair to disavow the singular merit of Cerroni's work as a whole. See his *Teoría política y socialismo* (Mexico: ERA, 1976). In this connection I must also mention the controversy aroused by the publication of two brilliant theoretical articles by leading Italian political philosopher Norberto Bobbio. See Bobbio, Norberto, et al., *Il Marxismo e lo stato* (Rome: Quaderni di Mondoperaio, 1976).

16. Cerroni, *La libertad,* pp. 182–194.

17. Bachrach, Peter, *The Theory of Democratic Elitism: A Critique* (Boston: Little, Brown and Co., 1967), and Connolly, William E., ed., *The Bias of Pluralism* (New York: Atherton, 1969).

18. Schumpeter, Joseph A., *Capitalism, Socialism and Democracy* (New York and Chicago: Harper, 1942), p. 242 (italics in original).

19. Ibid., pp. 284–285.

20. Aristotle, *Politics* (London: MacMillan, 1897), pp. 121–122.

21. Ibid., p. 120.

22. Tocqueville's ideas on this regard are discussed at length in Chapter 3.

23. Carr, Edward H., *The Soviet Impact on the Western World* (New York: MacMillan, 1947), pp. 8–9.

24. Ibid., p. 9.

25. Therborn, Göran, "The rule of capital and the rise of democracy," *New Left Review* 103 (May–June 1977), pp. 3–4. In this article Therborn provides a brilliant comparative analysis of the historical formation of bourgeois democracy in advanced capitalist countries.

26. Macpherson, "Elegant tombstones," p. 148.

27. On the absolutist state see Perry Anderson's already indispensable work *Lineage of the Absolutist State* (London: New Left Books, 1974). For an evaluation of the role of feudal estamentalism in the formation of the bourgeois modern state, see Gilbert, Felix, ed., *The Historial Essays of Otto Hintze* (New York: Oxford University Press, 1975). A discussion regarding states in transition toward capitalism can be found in Poulantzas, Nicos, *Political Power and Social Classes* (London: New Left Book Press, 1973). An excellent analysis on the problem of the survival of ancien régime characteristics in the world organized by the bourgeoisie can be found in Arno Mayer's outstanding book *The Persistence of the Old Regime* (New York: Pantheon Books, 1981).

28. An outstanding analysis of the bourgeois revolutions is to be found in Moore, Barrington, *Social Origins of Dictatorship and Democracy: Lord and Peasant in the Making of the Modern World* (Boston: Beacon Press, 1966). Moore's masterpiece helps one understand the difference between a bourgeois liberal state and what is known as bourgeois democracy. The latter assumes the integration of the popular masses into the state through universal suffrage as well as their representation through the ensemble of state institutions. In this sense, Victorian England was a liberal state, but it was never a bourgeois democracy. In England, a bourgeois democracy was established after World War I. For a discussion of the different forms of the capitalist state see Therborn, "The rule."

29. Therborn, "The rule," pp. 17–19.

30. Ibid., p. 19. A different approach can be found in Stein Rokkan, *Citizens, Elections, Parties* (New York: McKay, 1970).

31. The term *latecomers* refers to the countries where the establishment and predominance of the capitalist mode of production were achieved in the final decades of the nineteenth century, coinciding with the dawn of the imperialist age. Outstanding examples are Germany, Italy, and Japan.

32. When he contrasts the English and French juridical tradition with the German one, Frederick Engels poignantly observes that the historical foundation of the German law is "nothing but the passive centuries-old process of the decay of the Middle Ages, spurred on mostly from the outside and still far from completed; an economically backward society still haunted by the ghosts of the feudal Junker and guild craftsman searching for a new body; a legal system in the fabric of which arbitrary police despotism still tears one hole after another every day, despite the disappearance of princely cabinet justice in 1848." Based on this historical legacy, Engels concludes that it was difficult for Germany to build a bourgeois democracy more or less similar to those in England and France. See *The Role of Force in History* (New York: International Publishers, 1968), p. 103.

33. It should be noted that I am referring to the period that preceded the so-

called third wave of democratization. Cf. Huntington, Samuel P., *The Third Wave: Democratization in the Late Twentieth Century* (Norman and London: University of Oklahoma Press, 1991).

34. Bryce, James, *Modern Democracies* (New York: MacMillan, 1921), Vol. 2, and see also Vol. 1, p. 22; Dahl, Robert, *Polyarchy* (New Haven and London: Yale, 1971), pp. 246–249. Dahl defines *polyarchy* as those political regimes that were substantially "popularized," that is, open to the participation of its citizens, and "liberalized," meaning that these regimes are the result of a political competition that is both recognized and encouraged by the prevailing rules of the game (ibid., pp. 7–8).

35. Bryce, *Modern Democracies,* p. 22.

36. A comprehensive discussion of these problems regarding the development of bourgeois democracy may be found in Therborn, Göran, "The travail of Latin American democracy," *New Left Review* 113–114 (January–April 1979), pp. 71–109. I have examined the Chilean case with a certain degree of detail in "Notas sobre las raíces histórico-estructurales de la movilización política en Chile," *Foro Internacional* 16(1) (Mexico: 1975). On the new democratic wave see Huntington, Samuel P., *The Third Wave;* Schmitter, Philippe C., "Cinco reflexiones sobre la cuarta onda de democratizaciones," in Solano, Carlos Barba, José Luis Barros Horcasitas, and Javier Hurtado, *Transiciones a la democracia en Europa y América Latina* (Mexico: Miguel Angel Porrúa, 1991), pp. 101–117. Some of these issues are examined at length in Chapter 7 of this book.

37. Complete polyarchies: Australia, Austria, Belgium, Canada, Costa Rica, Denmark, the Federal Republic of Germany, Finland, France, Iceland, India, Ireland, Israel, Italy, Jamaica, Japan, Lebanon, Luxembourg, the Netherlands, New Zealand, Norway, the Philippines, Sweden, Trinidad and Tobago, the United Kingdom, and Uruguay. Special cases due to voting restrictions: Chile, Switzerland, and the United States. "Quasi-polyarchies": Colombia, Cyprus, Dominican Republic, Malaysia, Turkey, and Venezuela.

38. The relation between the stages of capitalist development and state forms is one of Lenin's standing concerns, which can be seen in his various works written on the eve of the 1917 revolution. See especially his "A caricature of Marxism and imperialist economism," in *Selected Works in Twelve Volumes* (Moscow: Progress Publishers, 1976). This text, written between August and October 1916, is of great importance in part because in it Lenin proposes a radical revaluation of bourgeois democracy and asserts that "triumphant socialism can not consolidate its victories and lead mankind to the withering away of the state without achieving the most complete democracy first." On the "revolution from above" and its antidemocratic connotations, see Antonio Gramsci's classic articles on this topic as well as Barrington Moore's *Social Origins,* Ch. 7. The idea of the existence of political "ages"—elitist or democratic—finds its followers not only in the theoretical field of socialism. Conservative authors, such as R. R. Palmer, also harbor that line of historical interpretation. See his *The Age of Democratic Revolution: A Political History of Europe and America, 1760–1800* (Princeton: Princeton University Press, 1959). On the pessimism regarding democracy in mature capitalism see Crozier, Michel J., Samuel P. Huntington, and Joji Watanuki's "neoconservative manifesto" in their work *The Crisis of Democracy* (New York: New York University Press, 1975). In a similar pessimistic vein, although grounded in a social democratic terrain, see also the last article of the late Gino Germani's "Autoritarismo e democrazia nella societá moderna," and the very interesting subsequent discussion, in R. Scartezzini, L. Germani, and R. Gritti, eds., *I limiti della democrazia* (Napoli: Liguori Editori, 1985).

39. Regarding the oligarchic state in Latin America see, among others, Bagú, Sergio, "Tres oligarquías, tres nacionalismos: Chile, Argentina, Uruguay" in

Cuadernos Políticos 3 (Mexico: January–March, 1975); Cueva, Agustín, *El desarrollo del capitalismo en América Latina* (Mexico: Siglo XXI, 1976), Ch. 7 and 8; Leal, Juan Felipe, *La burguesía y el estado Mexicano* (Mexico: El Caballito, 1972), and *México: Estado, burocracia y sindicatos* (Mexico: El Caballito, 1975); Uricoechea, Fernando, *O minotauro imperial* (São Paulo: DIPEL, 1978); Cotler, Julio, *Clases, estado y nación en el Perú* (Lima: IED, 1978); Cavarozzi, Marcelo, "El Estado oligárquico en Chile," *Historia y Sociedad,* segunda época, 19 (Mexico: Fall 1978); and my unpublished doctoral dissertation, *The Formation and Crisis of the Liberal State in Argentina, 1880–1930,* (Cambridge, MA: Harvard University, 1976).

40. On the crisis of oligarchic domination see the large collection of articles on this topic gathered by Zenteno, Raúl Benítez, ed., *Clases sociales y crisis política en América Latina* (Mexico: Siglo XXI, 1977), and Casanova, Pablo González, ed., *América Latina en los años treinta* (Mexico: UNAM, 1977).

41. Leal, *México,* p. 11.

42. For the meaning of "fundamental democratization" and its relevance to the contemporary analysis of democratic systems, see Mannheim, Karl, *Freedom, Power and Democratic Planning* (New York: Oxford University Press, 1950), and his *Man and Society in an Age of Social Reconstruction: Studies in Modern Social Structure* (New York: Harcourt, Brace & Co., 1967)

43. Cf. on this regard Cueva, Agustín, *El desarrollo.*

44. Ianni, Octavio, *La formación del estado populista en América Latina* (Mexico: ERA, 1975).

45. Engels, Friedrich, *Socialism, Utopian and Scientific* (New York: International Publishers, 1935), p. 26.

46. Regarding Latin American populism see Ianni, Octavio, *La formación;* Germani, Gino, Torcuato S. Di Tella, and Octavio Ianni, *Populismo y contradicciones de clase en Latinoamérica* (Mexico: ERA, 1973); Quijano, Aníbal, and Francisco Weffort, *Populismo, marginalización y dependencia* (San José, Costa Rica: EDUCA, 1973); Cueva, Agustín, *El desarrollo,* Ch. 11; Cardoso, Fernando H., and Enzo Faletto, *Dependencia y desarrollo en América Latina* (Mexico: Siglo XXI, 1969).

47. See a lengthy discussion of this issue in my "El fascismo como categoría histórica: En torno al problema de las dictaduras en América Latina," in *Revista Mexicana de Sociología* 39(2) (April–June 1977), pp. 481–528.

48. Marx, Karl, *Capital* (New York: International Publishers, 1974), Vol. 3, pp. 791–792.

49. *Miami Herald,* February 27, 1977. Cited in NACLA, *Report on the Americas* 12(2) (New York: March–April 1979), p. 26. Nevertheless, experience teaches that within the framework of processes of democratic reconstruction, adjustment policies of a neoliberal character were also adopted. These policies place the entire weight of the crisis on workers and consumers, thus further depressing the standard of living of those individuals. In these cases, protests were not enough to force the ruling class to change the course of action. However, the neoliberal continuity that ties the economic policies of dictatorships to those of newly reborn democracies did take its toll on governments, which were defeated one by one at the ballot box. That is the history of Belaúnde, Sanguinetti, Alfonsín, Sarney, and others. Another lesson that can be learned from these years is the following: was there not an excess of optimism in terms of the capacity of democratic political institutions to influence the decisions of the governments? The need to rely on a certain degree of popular consensus does not seem to be too serious a motive in determining a government's economic policies, not even on the eve of elections. It is evident that the

gravitation of business lobbying is infinitely more powerful. All of this forces one to seriously reconsider some of the most common ideas regarding the functioning of "truly existent democracies."

50. Fortín, Carlos, "Sobre el estado y la acumulación del capital," *Chile-América* 52–53 (Rome: March–April–May 1979), p. 20.

51. Figures for Brazil were taken from Serra, José, "El milagro económico brasileño: Realidad o mito," *Revista Mexicana de Sociología* 2 (April–June 1972). For Chile see Fortín, C., "Sobre el estado." Figures for Argentina were taken from Abalo, Carlos, "Un proyecto económico cada vez más discutible," *Comercio Exterior* (Mexico: November 1977), p. 131. Friedman's argument in favor of "shock treatment" can be found in *Milton Friedman en Chile,* proceedings held at the Diego Portales building, Santiago, 1975.

52. Fortín, C., "Sobre el estado," p. 21.

53. NACLA, *Report,* p. 27. In some Latin American countries, for instance, a person who has worked just two hours in a whole week is considered employed.

54. As will be shown in later chapters, the experience of the years of democratic transition proved these expectations to be unwarranted. See Chapter 7.

55. de Schweinitz, Karl, Jr., *Industrialization and Democracy: Economic Necessities and Political Possibilities* (Glencoe: The Free Press, 1964), pp. 10–11.

56. Huntington, Samuel P., "The United States," in Crozier, Michael, Samuel P. Huntington, and Joji Watanuki, *The Crisis of Democracy,* p. 113.

57. Ibid., p. 115.

58. Cerroni, Umberto, "Esiste una scienza política marxista?" in Bobbio, Norberto, et al., *Il Marxismo,* p. 47 (my translation).

2

Market, State, and Democracy: Observations on the Political Theory of Monetarism

Milton Friedman's ideas have become a standard reference in many debates on the nature of the situation of the capitalist economies and their various strategies of recomposition since the mid-1970s. Extraordinarily exalted in international public opinion after he received the Nobel Prize in Economics in 1976, he is almost unanimously recognized as one of the leading authorities of "orthodox" neoliberal economics and "anti-Keynesian" reaction in general. He is also regarded as one of the staunchest defenders of free-market economics, the solitary voice of which was raised periodically during the Keynesian years. In the neoconservative 1980s, monetarism, Friedman's child, became a major source of inspiration for the economic policies adopted by several countries, in particular by the Reagan administration, Thatcher's government, and, in Latin America, during the first years of the Pinochet regime.

As is well known, this trend has prevailed in a variety of governments that intended to undertake a holy crusade against the so-called democratic excesses and state hypertrophy, which according to Friedman's disciples and popularizers bear the responsibility for progressively stifling the creative and liberating potential of the market. Monetarism has thus profited from the conservative—and sometimes reactionary—ideological climate that engulfed the West, especially when the "stagflation" that followed the oil crisis proved enduring. Nowadays the inflationary threat seems to be over, but slow growth, recessive trends, and high unemployment still remain as the dominant features of most capitalist economies in the core of the system. This enduring combination of circumstances allowed the monetarist current, which had been lowly regarded, to considerably increase its social import, both in the advanced capitalist nations and in the periphery of the system. As the recession of the 1970s greatly discredited Keynesian ideas—now vituperated as statist, collectivist, and demagogic—monetarism emerged as a plausible replacement for the worn-out formula. On the shoulders of an abrupt swing toward the right that reverberated throughout the whole international system, monetarism was able to articulate a series of economic policies, most of them deceptively simple, that implicitly refer to a political theory that is not only false but also profoundly antidemocratic. This ideological offensive stripped Keynesian politics of the privileged status it enjoyed since the post–World War II period—when it had become the common sense of the most successful period in the entire history of capital—and placed neoliberalism in a paramount position not only in contemporary economic thought but also in the practical principles and policies carried out by many governments. In fact, prevailing neoliberal orthodoxy—doggedly sponsored and enforced by the World Bank and the International Monetary Fund—is largely based on Friedman's ideas.

It is an indisputable fact that Friedman's theses represent an effort that goes far beyond the strictly academic realm. His laborious exegesis of the theories of Adam Smith, his vindication of late eighteenth-century liberalism, and his firm attachment to the magical thought of the period—which can be seen in the animistic belief that an invisible hand regulates the actions of individuals and exerts a benign influence on the market—take on a new value when projected onto the political scene of core capitalist states. Were it not for this practical success, it is unlikely that his ideas would command much attention, considering that most of them had been deemed as belonging to the prehistory of economic science more than a century ago. Therefore, what places Friedman's thoughts at the center of the contemporary debates is his practical influence in times of crisis and conservative capitalist recomposition. Therefore, the predominance of Friedman's ideas comes from the fact that the fundamental precepts—rule of the market, exaltation of private firms, the dismantling of the welfare state, and the curtailment of the democratic advances and their impingement on the markets—are at the core of the prevailing neoliberal orthodoxy and have been the rationalizing principles of neoconservative governments all around the world.

This chapter will explore Friedman's conceptions of state and democracy—which are usually implicit in his works—and identify their major arguments. The central axis of his discourse and the starting point of all his political and economic assertions is the notion of the market, from which paradigm one can deduce a rigorously limited role for the state and infer the limits and possibilities of a capitalist democracy. The unchallenged supremacy assigned to the market and the theoretical conception derived from this premise result in a theoretical and practical position that makes Friedmanism—and with it the entire neoliberal dogma—an apologetic ideology of the authoritarian restructuring of the capitalist state. Classical liberalism, which was originally a bourgeois program aimed at curtailing the abusive powers of the absolutist state and establishing a certain degree of democratic and pluralistic competition among the elites, deplorably reaches the end of its road by embracing neoconservative discourse and practice. Once its pseudolibertarian rhetoric is removed, its proposal seems to be exhausted in the legitimation of the growing state despotism demanded by the coercive imposition of the laws of the market.

An Idealized Reconstruction of the Market

The assertions in *Free to Choose* are a reiteration of what Milton Friedman develops in *Capitalism and Freedom,* a book published in 1962.[1] Almost twenty years later, Friedman's argument remains essentially unaltered, unruffled by the abundance of studies that have challenged its main tenets. Only specific examples were changed: in *Free to Choose* there is a stronger emphasis on the analysis of inflation, which is essential given the juncture predominant in the mid- and late 1970s. The result is a popularized edition—coauthored with his wife and written in a plainer, less technical fashion—of the subjects and rationale of his earlier book. The launching of *Free to Choose* was greatly supported and promoted by an effective worldwide advertising campaign—very unusual for the work of a scholar—which made the publishing of this book a major international political and literary event. The formidable propaganda, intended to foster the worldwide dissemination of this new liberal manifesto, points to the powerful coalition of economic interests that endorses and supports Friedman's work, as well as the scope of the ideological offensive launched by big capital and its allies.

The key argument of this "new economic liberalism" can be summarized as follows:

> The basic problem of social organization is how to co-ordinate the economic activities of large numbers of people. Even in relatively backward societies, extensive division of labor and specialization of function is required to make effective use of available resources. In advanced societies, the scale on which co-ordination is needed, to take full advantage of the opportunities offered by modern science and technology, is enormously greater. Literally millions of people are involved in providing one another with their daily bread, let alone with their yearly automobiles. The challenge to the believer in liberty is to reconcile this widespread interdependence with individual freedom.[2]

Once it has been established that the problem of freedom is posited and resolved in the realm of the economy, and not in the polis, Friedman concludes his reasoning by saying, "Fundamentally, there are only two ways of co-ordinating the economic activities of millions. One is central direction involving the use of coercion—the technique of the army and of the modern totalitarian state. The other is voluntary co-operation of individuals—the technique of the market place."[3]

In other words, there are two major strategies to solve the basic problem of how to coordinate productive activities: (1) a "political" way that implies coercion and is effected through the oppressive presence of the state, and (2) another, of an "extrapolitical" character, that does not require the intervention of any force extraneous to the market and is instead based on the voluntary cooperation of individuals motivated by expectations of mutual benefits. It is only fair to acknowledge that Friedman points out that in reality these two modalities are relatively intermixed and never found in their pure forms. Nevertheless, the movement of the economy is dominated by one of two logics: whereas in the West the market was able to subdue political commands, in the Soviet Union just the opposite took place, and the political commands prevailed over the market freedoms. The subdued modality still persists in both cases, although in varying degrees. In the United States and the rest of the Western world, there is also some economic planning, whereas in the Soviet Union and other socialist countries, political mandates coexisted with more or less sizable remnants of the market.

The underlying conception of social order in Friedman's analysis is thus reduced to the following: in all social formations it is possible to find two fundamental and opposed principles that express alternative modalities of organization of the productive process and social life. One of these, the market, is based on voluntary cooperation among individuals; it is an extrapolitical modality fully compatible with the liberal ideal of least government and individual autonomy. The other is based on coercion and commands, and it necessarily implies the strengthening of a specialized apparatus in charge of directing and planning economic activities: the state.

Accordingly, the market and the state are antagonistic and irreconcilable principles of social organization: not only is the former important in terms of economic performance but it is also the fundamental sanctuary that preserves economic and political freedoms. The latter is, or at least tends to be, the depositary of coercion and authoritarianism; it is the cradle of oppression, as much as the market is the cradle of freedom. Therefore, the struggle for freedom is a tug-of-war between two colossuses: the market and the state. Inasmuch as the market prevails over the state, it will ensure the full enjoyment of worldly goods to civil society without any coercive interference. It has to be recalled that this type of intervention originates in the political sphere and that the market is, by Friedman's definition, a prepolitical artifact. When the market is defeated by the state, individual freedoms are suffocated at their inception.

Starting with these initial premises, expressed vaguely in the first pages of *Free to Choose* and more systematically in *Capitalism and Freedom,* it becomes evident that the fundamental problem of the Friedmans' entire theoretical construction rests in their theory of the market. If this theory is both logically and empirically correct, then a discussion of the merits of the political argument constructed on the basis of this model is in order. However, if their conception proves to be wrong, the entire conceptual edifice will collapse under the weight of its own inconsistencies, with devastating theoretical and practical impacts on the theory.

It is therefore appropriate to look into the crucial question: what is the market? For monetarism the market is a noncoercive form of organization, based on bilateral voluntary transactions established among equally informed individuals who also are equally incapable of controlling either the global output or the prices of the different goods and services traded in the market. Friedman develops his argument as follows:

> In its simplest form, such a society [competitive capitalism] consists of a number of independent households—a collection of Robinson Crusoes, as it were. Each household uses the resources it controls to produce goods and services that it exchanges for goods and services produced by other households, on terms mutually acceptable to the two parties to the bargain. . . . The incentive for adopting this indirect route is, of course, the increased product made possible by division of labor and specialization of function. Since the household *always* has the alternative of producing directly for itself, it need not enter into any exchange unless it benefits from it. Hence, no exchange will take place unless both parties do benefit from it. Co-operation is thereby achieved without coercion.[4]

Friedman is aware that this simplified model—"à la Robinson," as Marx used to characterize this type of imaginary construction—cannot be applied as is to the analysis of contemporary capitalism, because the division of labor and functional specialization seem to have upset certain idyllic aspects of that heavenly market of Robinson Crusoes. But what are these unsettling modifications resulting from the advent of modern society? Friedman points out two: (1) the appearance of large economic enterprises, and (2) the introduction of money. Modern firms carry out an intermediary role among individuals involved in a myriad of daily economic transactions; money, on the other hand, replaces bartering, making possible the separation of buying and selling transactions into two independent parts. Yet, as Friedman points out,

> Despite the important role of enterprises and of money in our actual economy, and despite the numerous and complex problems they raise, the central characteristic of the market technique of achieving co-ordination is fully displayed in the simple exchange economy that contains neither enterprises nor money. As in that simple model, so in the complex enterprise and money exchange economy, co-operation is strictly individual and voluntary *provided:* (a) that enterprises are private, so that the ultimate contracting parties are individuals and (b) that individuals are effectively free to enter or not to enter into any particular exchange, so that every transaction is strictly voluntary.[5]

According to Milton Friedman, therefore, the simplified model of a competitive capitalist economy contains the fundamental elements that characterize the functioning of developed capitalism. The validity of this extrapolation, however, depends on two provisos: one pertaining to the firms, which must in the final analysis be the property of private individuals, and the other regarding the freedom that each individual has in deciding whether to participate in a given economic exchange. Friedman contends that these two conditions are fully realized in contemporary capitalism, and this is why he perfunctorily concludes that contemporary capitalism is ruled by the market's laws.

Having "proved" this, Friedman must still establish the superiority of the market over other, "coercive" forms of economic coordination. For this, Friedman resorts once again to Adam Smith in order to recover what he considers to be the "axial idea" of *The Wealth of Nations:* "if an exchange between two parties is voluntary, it will not take place unless both believe they will benefit from it."[6] That is, the market is conceived as a set of positive-sum games in which the two parties can benefit at the same time. Although it is easy enough to picture this possibility for a simple mercantile economy—such as the one of the diligent Robinson Crusoes that serves as a basis for the model of the market—it becomes much more complicated to do so for the modern complex capitalist economy. Friedman then sets out to explore the ways in which economic agents—who live in disparate parts of the world—could coordinate their economic activities with the purpose of promoting their respective interests.

> The price system is the mechanism that performs this task without central direction, without requiring people to speak to one another, or to like one another. . . . Adam Smith's flash of genius was his recognition that the prices that emerged from voluntary transactions between buyers and sellers—in short, in a free market—could coordinate the activities of millions of people each seeking his own interest, in such a way as to make everyone better off.[7]

The price system, set by the intersection of supply and demand, fulfills certain tasks that allow one to assert the superiority of the market over the models of coordination "by command." What are these tasks? In the first place, the market transmits accurate information to the economic agents through the price of the different goods and services traded in the economy. In this way, it indicates with precision the movement and prospects of supply and demand, issuing trustworthy signals for the guidance of economic actors. Second, free-market prices—quickly and efficiently transmitted—constitute a powerful incentive for producers. An increase in demand will encourage the producers to respond with augmented output by introducing technological innovations aimed at boosting productivity and by offering higher wages in order to attract the necessary labor power. Third, the free market wisely distributes incomes in the form of profits, rents, and wages and salaries. Governmental policies intended to override the distributional outcomes of free markets are condemned to failure because—according to Friedman—they artificially separate the distributive functions from the other functions performed by the price system in free markets: the transmission of information and the generation of production incentives.[8]

In short, the price system is the cybernetic nerve of the market and allows the market to assign productive forces in the most efficient manner. It encourages production wherever needed and discourages it when it is superfluous. It motivates entrepreneurs and workers to maximize their income. And as if all this were not enough, it distributes profits according to the "objective and spontaneous" parameters fixed by the market forces.

Aside from these fundamentally technoeconomic reasons, Friedman offers others of a more general nature. The market disperses economic power, thereby inhibiting any economic actor from possessing much more power or information than the rest. Because the market assumes free competition, without restrictions for the admittance of new participants, no one would be in the position to fix prices unilaterally without the complicity of the government. In Friedman's view, a monopoly is an aberrant collusion between private interests and the state for the purpose of flagrantly violating the rules of the market. Accordingly, this monopolistic threat can succeed only if the government refuses to follow the sensible policy in these cases: not to lend itself to those manipulations and instead to encourage competition. There is another type of monopoly, known as "technical," that occurs when it is more efficient for just one enterprise to be in charge of the supply of certain services to a community. A typical example is the case of telephone communications. However, if the government adopts a noninterventionist policy and encourages competition, not even these technical monopolies will be in a position to fix prices unilaterally and thus break the rules of the game. The market has at its disposal an enormous capacity of self-regulation to free itself from the distorting action of monopolies. Notwithstanding, for such self-regulation to operate, the government must refrain from meddling in the functioning of the market.[9]

But the market has other virtues as well: it reduces social and political tensions because it does not demand collective acquiescence to decisions or preferences over which individuals disagree. The use of political procedures tends to deteriorate social cohesion and to impose an opinion that is not necessarily that of the majority, much less one that commands unanimous acceptance. The market—an extrapolitical space par excellence—exempts society from the conflicts inherent in decisionmaking in social conditions marked by a plurality of antagonistic situations and preferences (ethical, religious, cultural, economic, political, etc.). To the extent that the market consolidates itself as the forum in which individuals decide their common affairs, the possibility for governmental intervention and the imposition of partial and/or sectoral preferences will be reduced. Only the market can guarantee unanimity; consequently, a society in which most collective concerns and public choices are processed through mercantile institutions will have a greater probability of building a solid consensus and fully enjoying individual freedoms. If, on the contrary, the community's affairs are decided within the inherently authoritarian sphere of the state, dissension and conflict will be the unavoidable price that society must pay. In other words, the market embodies social harmony, consensus, and freedom, whereas the state—and politics in general—represent the sphere of imposition and conflict.[10]

The Manichaeanism of this theorization is more than evident. But even after one ponders the seriousness of the authoritarian threat posed by the state, monetarism says that there is still hope. The endless competition proper of the market exerts a positive impact on both the state and democracy. This benign influence reveals itself in two ways. Thanks to its greater efficiency in optimizing economic resources, the market becomes a formidable obstacle for the uncontrolled expansion of state activities. Its strong presence, therefore, is an indispensable requisite for attaining the much desired least government and avoiding the frequent and harmful intrusion of the state into society's "private" concerns. This situation has a second advantage that is also highlighted in Friedman's writings: by limiting governmental expansion the market prevents the concentration of political power in the hands of a few, thereby indirectly but efficiently favoring democracy. By virtue of being a game of variable positive sums, the market stimulates the proliferation of multiple competitive centers of economic power; the state, on the other hand, is the monopolistic sphere of coercion, a true zero-sum game chronically inclined toward concentrating political power and inhibiting competition.[11]

The conclusion that emerges from Friedman's interpretation is crystal clear: not only is the market superior in terms of the pure logic of economic efficiency, but it is also much better at checking the expansive trends of the state and at clearing the ground for the constitution of a modern democracy. In short, the market is the true nucleus of freedom in modern society, held back in its libertarian expansion by the ill-fated progressive intrusion of the state, bearer of coercive and authoritarian values and practices. The struggle for freedom is thus reduced to a war without quarter against the state.[12]

This attempt to recount Friedman's political thought would be incomplete without taking into account the conception of government that residually appears in his theoretical model. A liberal is not an anarchist—Friedman warns—and the government has important functions to perform in a "system of natural freedom." But, he adds, "to Smith and Jefferson, the government's role was an umpire, not a participant."[13] However, in addition to being the umpire, the government must also establish the rules of the game and ensure their compliance, given that the market cannot by itself take on these tasks. What are the proper functions of the state? The Friedmans refer to the response offered by Adam Smith more than two hundred years ago—when the world was certainly quite different from ours—to the same question:

Every man, as long as he does not violate the laws of justice, is left perfectly free to pursue his own interest his own way. . . . The sovereign is
completely discharged from a duty . . . of superintending the industry of
private people, and of directing it towards the employments most suitable
to the interest of the society. According to the system of natural liberty, the
sovereign has only three duties to attend to; three duties of great importance, indeed, but plain and intelligible to common understandings: first,
the duty of protecting the society from the violence and invasion of other
independent societies; secondly, the duty of protecting, as far as possible,
every member of the society from the injustice or oppression of every other
member of it, or the duty of establishing an exact administration of justice;
and, thirdly, the duty of erecting and maintaining certain publick works and
certain publick institutions, which it can never be for the interest of any
individual . . . to erect and maintain.[14]

To these three basic duties of the government the Friedmans add one
more: the duty of protecting those members of the community who cannot
be regarded as responsible individuals.[15] At any rate it is clear that this narrow conception of the role of government (stacked in what Gramsci calls its
rather rudimentary "economic-corporative" phase), the obligations of which
were in practice limited to ensuring "law and order," is typical of the liberal thought of the late eighteenth and early nineteenth centuries. It would be
a useless endeavor to try to find in the Friedmans' work any indication pointing to the belief that the government has any other social "responsibility"
beyond the traditional ones. An examination of a more comprehensive and
less generic list of governmental activities, such as was proposed in
Capitalism and Freedom, would reveal that one is basically confronted by
the same conception of the "State = *veilleur de nuit.*" In fact, in that book it
is established that

a government which maintained law and order, defined property rights,
served as a means whereby we could modify property rights and other rules
of the economic game, adjudicated disputes about the interpretation of the
rules, enforced contracts, promoted competition, provided a monetary
framework, engaged in activities to counter technical monopolies and to
overcome neighborhood effects widely regarded as sufficiently important
to justify government intervention, and which supplemented private charity and the private family in protecting the irresponsible, whether madman
or child—such a government would clearly have important functions to
perform. The consistent liberal is not an anarchist.[16]

Any attempt to trespass these "reasonable" limits of state action would
set in motion another hand, now visible and of a quite different nature.
Instead of transforming private vices into public virtues, the visible hand of
the state behaves perversely. The eagerness to promote public interest artificially by fostering state interference in the workings of markets and civil
society would serve to benefit only private interests while damaging the
general well-being.[17]

The corollary to this argument is transparent: it is necessary to watch the state, prevent its expansion, and control its potential encroachments over society and markets at all costs. Even though the state may be led by noble and democratic individuals, justice loving and eager to preserve free institutions, the state is the irreconcilable enemy of the market and therefore of freedom. The famous "new class" of progressive politicians and intellectuals—so successfully despised by neoconservative publicists—is leading the West toward servitude by the road of a growingly collectivist welfare state.[18]

Consequently, the dismantling of hypertrophied state apparatuses is an imperative if freedom is to be preserved. In this way, the dubious democratic convictions of eighteenth-century liberalism—of which Friedman is today's most relevant prophet—are silently filed away waiting for better times. In his pilgrimage toward the sources of liberalism, the ideologue of monetarism meets the somber specter of Hobbes.

On Really Existing Capitalist Markets

The beginning of this chapter pointed out that the theory of the state and democracy underlying Friedman's thoughts—though in rudimentary form—rests exclusively on its conception of the market. It is the market that defines the nature of the political game and the role played by political factors. Therefore, a critical evaluation of the notion of the market is called for in order to consider the more properly political aspects of monetarist theory. In relation to Friedman's conception of the market, I will examine two fundamental aspects: (1) the logical consistency of the theoretical model, and (2) the model's relevance for the study of contemporary capitalism, that is, its empiric congruence regarding the actual functioning of the capitalist economies of our time.

The premise of Friedman's argument is a model of a simple mercantile economy based on direct producers, who because of the control they possess over their means of production are free to choose between production for the market or for self-consumption. The incentive for the former option is given by the greater social product fostered by the social division of labor, which means that through mercantile exchanges the producers will be able to consume a larger amount of goods than if they chose to provide only for their own subsistence. Given that Friedman posits the existence of these two alternatives—it should be remembered that he maintains, as noted previously, that producers *always* have the option to produce for themselves—he can easily conclude that cooperation is reached without coercion: if there is exchange, it is because both parties will benefit. In this model the agents are profit maximizers, and they engage in a transaction only because they both obtain benefits; no one has been coerced to resort to the market to trade their products. Cooperation is strictly voluntary, and the absence of coercive mechanisms consecrates the unrestricted triumph of personal freedom.[19]

This abstract theoretical model is hypostatized by Friedman as if it were the historical reality of competitive capitalism: its crucial features are already observable in the exchanges established among those industrious Robinson Crusoes. Nevertheless, Friedman is aware that his extrapolation would be exceedingly coarse—and therefore theoretically unsustainable—if he did not include some qualifications designed to "adapt" the model to contemporary capitalism whenever it exhibits two great innovations that were absent in its original version: the emergence of the capitalist enterprise and the appearance of money as the universal means of exchange. Inasmuch as the enterprises are privately owned (that is, that their owners are ultimately individuals) and the producers retain their freedom to enter the market or not, the market model, Friedman argues, will maintain its full force, and the transactions that take place within it will by definition be noncoercive.

One may leave aside for the time being his appreciation of what characterizes "modern capitalism" as somewhat different from its predecessor and earlier precapitalist economic forms, as well as his highly questionable assumptions regarding the "individual" ownership of gigantic multinational corporations. What is truly decisive in Friedman's market model—and which allows him to equate the market with freedom—is not that individuals are free to participate in a given mercantile transaction or not, but rather that they retain the option of whether they wish to integrate themselves into the market. This is the sole condition that allows Friedman to argue that his Robinson Crusoe freely decided, without any type of compulsion, to enter the market. Consequently, Friedman's conflation of market and freedom are valid only if the producer has the real option of making two alternative decisions: to participate in the market or to remain outside of it. Once producers have chosen the former, the freedom they will enjoy will be of a qualitatively different (and lower) order: that of selecting with whom to carry out specific transactions, naturally submitting to the laws of the market. They are therefore free only to select their mercantile counterparts. And although this freedom may still be of some import, it is not the same type of freedom of those who may decide whether it is convenient to satisfy their needs via the market.

The logical inconsistency of the argument resulting from posing the question of freedom *after* the producer is incorporated into the market—not *before*—allows Friedman to arrive easily at an outcome that is congruent with his ideological premises. Unfortunately for his theory, fallacies do not produce compulsive evidence. The problem of freedom cannot be reduced to the existence of alternative buyers and/or sellers in the market, eager to exchange their goods and services with other direct producers. The problem of freedom precedes that commercial moment, when individuals decide—or rather, are forcefully compelled—to integrate themselves into the market. Faced by that dilemma, do these producers have a real, not merely illusory, option? Friedman incorrectly says that they do, that the Robinson Crusoes could decide, if they wish, to return to their practices of self-subsistence.

It does not take a wizard to realize that Friedman's reconstruction is a fable that bears no relation to the real history of capitalism, which categorically belies the fantastic reasoning of the father of monetarism. What Friedman characterizes as the two "novelties" of modern capitalism—the corporation and the use of money—refer to a much more profound process that could not have escaped Friedman's attention: the violent separation of direct producers from their means of production. The massive expropriation of men and women in precapitalist social formations that took place during the process of "primitive accumulation" left them barely equipped with their sole labor power. Dispossessed, they were compelled to sell their labor power in the market in order to acquire the means necessary for their mere subsistence, independent of their wishes. In no country of the world was this process carried out through peaceful and democratic procedures. No one was ever asked if they wanted to enter the capitalist market. It was a cruel process accomplished mercilessly, as has been thoroughly documented in the standard literature on the issue.[20]

However, for Friedman's model the massive, painful, and prolonged dislocations produced by the constitution of capitalist markets seem to be superfluous anecdotes deprived of any theoretical meaning. In addition, Friedman does not seem interested in distinguishing between the situations of someone who enters the market to sell labor power and someone who just goes to buy power to make profit. The blind anonymity of that idol compensates everything. The fact that the dispossession of producers cruelly imposed an option is knowingly concealed, and according to liberal political philosophy—so frequently invoked in *Free to Choose*—where there is imposition there is no freedom. Therefore, the decision to enter the market was as "free and voluntary" as that of the person who hands over a purse to thieves in exchange for his or her life.

Marx convincingly explains that the constitution of capitalism presupposes a prior encounter in the market of two types of commodity owners: on the one hand, those who have money and the means of production; and on the other, the propertyless, who possess only their labor power after having been stripped of their means of production and independent subsistence. In this way, money and the means of production are converted into capital, and former direct producers become the "free" wage earners needed by capitalism. "The so-called primitive accumulation, therefore, is nothing else than the historical process of divorcing the producer from the means of production."[21] One of the most salient features of this divorce was its extraordinary level of violence, both in the colonial periphery of the rising capitalist system and in its European core. The establishment of the market, so idyllically described in Friedman's pages, was a process marked by merciless coercion and the imposition of new relations of production that, as Marx points out, were always carried out employing "the power of the State, the concentrated and organized force of society, to hasten, hothouse fashion, the process of transformation of the feudal mode of production" and the creation of the capitalist market.[22] Once the separation between direct producers and their means of subsistence was accomplished, the selling of their labor power in the market should be conceived not as an expression of their freedom but as the final act of their subjugation. There is no sense in speaking of the "freedom to survive." The Friedmans' praise of the market as the natural sphere of freedom is similarly unfounded. The historical origins of real-world markets reveal that the subordination of independent producers was a process marked by cruelty on a scale that was seldom seen before. It was a violent imposition supported by state force and not the result of the calculations of a number of Robinson Crusoes who decided to enter the capitalist market in search of a Paretian optimum for their profits.

Friedman's reasoning thus illustrates the decadent history of an entire line of interpretation that Marx, in his times, accurately called "vulgar Political Economy." Marx's remarks warrant being quoted at length not only because they illuminate the involution of some currents of modern economic thought but also because they highlight the corrosive features of the relationship between political power and social theory:

> By classical Political Economy, I understand that economy which since the time of W. Petty, has investigated the real relations of productions in bourgeois society, in contradistinction to vulgar economy, which deals with appearances only, ruminates without ceasing on the materials long since provided by scientific economy, and there seeks plausible explanations of the most obtrusive phenomena, for bourgeois daily use, but for the rest, confines itself to systematising in a pedantic way, and proclaiming for everlasting truths, the trite ideas held by the self-complacent bourgeoisie with regard to their own world, to them the best of all possible worlds.[23]

It is evident that for the Friedmans the capitalist society is the best of all possible worlds. Their admiration for the feats of the bourgeoisie is so great that, in their enthusiasm, they forget some elementary rules of scientific logic and respect for the most elementary empirical data. One example concerns their attitude toward the problem of monopolies. When speaking on this subject, Friedman is much more concerned with what he regards as "monopolistic practices" among the workers—that is, the unions with their alleged control over labor supply and its price—than with business monopolies, for which he maintains "the most important fact about enterprise monopoly is its unimportance from the viewpoint of the economy as a whole. . . . In almost any industry that one can mention, there are giants and pygmies side by side."[24] Those who believe that the predominance of monopolies has eliminated competition in the contemporary capitalist market are mistaken. It is the efforts of the working class to organize itself and to oppose capitalist exploitation that, according to Friedman, have interfered in the normal functioning of a healthy regime of economic competition.

Therefore, Friedman's diagnosis is ideologically blindfolded and incredibly inaccurate: "In one respect, there is an important difference between labor and enterprise monopoly. While there seems not to have been any upward trend in the importance of enterprise monopoly over the past half-century, there certainly has been in the importance of labor monopoly."[25]

Thus, with the stroke of a pen, Friedman simply excludes from his analytical horizon the numerous empirical studies that have produced irrefutable evidence regarding the growing control of monopolies over the modern capitalist economies on a global scale. On this point his assertions—and those of the whole monetarist current in general—are so coarse that little effort is required to show their inaccuracy. Monetarism's doctrinal character is as evident as its lack of academic rigorousness. It is worthwhile to consider the opinion of a distinguished economist, John K. Galbraith, referring to the extent of the monopolistic concentration during the same years in which Friedman failed to notice any "upward trend" of enterprise monopoly:

> In 1969, the five largest industrial corporations, with combined assets of $59 billion, had just under 11 percent of all assets used in manufacturing. The 50 largest manufacturing corporations had 38 percent of all assets. The 500 largest had 74 percent. . . . In the same year corporations with assets of more than a billion, 87 in all, had 46 percent of all assets used in manufacturing; . . . and 2,593 firms with assets of more than $10 million had 86 percent of all assets. In 1967 . . . four corporations accounted for 21 percent of all industrial research and development expenditure (the great bulk paid for by the government). . . . In 1969 the three largest industrial corporations, General Motors, Standard Oil of New Jersey, and Ford, had a gross income of $54 billion. This exceeded (by about $2.7 billion) the total income, including government payments, of all the farms in the country. In 1968, General Motors, with gross revenues of $22.8 billion, had more than a hundred times the total revenue of the state of Nevada, more than three times the total revenue of the state of New York, and about one-eighth of the total receipts of the federal government.[26]

This critical perspective is further expanded in the central argument of *Monopoly Capital,* the classic piece by Baran and Sweezy. These authors acknowledge that competition was the predominant form of market relations in the nineteenth century; however, since then there has been a steady transformation in the direction of an ever-growing oligopolistic logic, to the point that economic analysis based on the premise of the competitive market is obsolete.

> Today the typical economic unit in the capitalist world is no longer the small firm producing a negligible fraction of a homogeneous product for an anonymous market, but a large-scale enterprise producing a significant share of the output of an industry, or even several industries, and able to control its prices, the volume of its production, and the types and amounts of its investments.[27]

One of the outcomes of this increased presence of big oligopolistic firms was the progressive disarticulation and fragmentation of markets as the organizing mechanisms of capitalism's economic life. Prices of most of the critical goods are no longer set in its realm; instead, they are administered by a handful of very large corporations. Therefore, the signals transmitted by the market through the price system show with ever-growing intensity the gradual extinction of competition and its replacement by corporatist forms of peak business organization that are a far cry from that peaceful strife between a myriad of anonymous producers enshrined in liberal teachings about the market.[28] Most modern megacorporations have much more information at hand than any other economic agents and the state. Most of them also have unmatched productive capacities that place them in a situation to determine the total output of each industrial branch. These disproportionate advantages in information and production would have been considered abhorrent pathologies in Smith's classical model, incompatible with the system of natural freedom that the Glasgow philosopher and economist sponsored in his work. Nevertheless, what Smith could not anticipate has become a reality that no impartial observer can ignore, unless he or she suffers from an ideological obfuscation incongruous with the canons of scientific practice.

It is relevant to consider some elementary figures that could not have passed unnoticed by the Friedmans. How is it possible to talk about "competitive markets" and the benign effects of the "invisible hand" when, according to conservative estimates, between 35 percent and 45 percent of the total output of the U.S. private sector in 1973 was produced by a small number of firms that had almost complete control over their respective industrial branches?[29] Or when a study requested by the government of the United States shows that 78 of 185,000 corporations controlled 43 percent of all industrial assets and distributed among themselves 49 percent of the total profits produced by the U.S. manufacturing sector in 1968?[30] Any person objectively informed on the actual workings of the U.S. economy knows that monopolies predominate there, as they do in Western Europe, in Japan, and throughout the entire international capitalist economy. It is well known that a vast number of studies and investigations are available to anyone interested in this subject.[31] It is easy to understand why the Friedmans and their contemporary monetarist disciples—so excited about the progress of "liberal economic reforms" in the new democracies—prefer to ignore this information, pretending that the world is as their archaic prejudices tell them. The data in Table 2.1 serve to illustrate succinctly the incurable error underlying the liberal theses on the capitalist markets.

Therefore, the dynamics of the market forces lead to oligopolistic concentration and the progressive suppression of competition. Of course, the nature of this process is not equal in all markets, but the tendency of the "winners" to voraciously augment their control of the marketplace is impos-

Table 2.1   Industrial Branches in Which Leading U.S. Companies Retain an Overwhelming Influence in the Market (circa 1970)

Industrial Branch	Number of Leading Companies	Approximate Control in the Respective Market (in %)
Telephone equipment	1	80–90
Computers	1	70–80
Canned soups	1	90
Photographic material	1	60–70
Heavy electrical equipment	2	70–80
Cereals	2	60–70
Airplane engines	2	90–100
Metallic containers	2	80–90
Aircrafts	3	80–90
Aluminum	3	80–90
Automobiles	3	90–100
Copper	3	60–70

Source: Shepherd, William, *Market Power and Economic Welfare* (New York: Random House, 1970), pp. 152–153.

sible to conceal. Counter to Smith's optimism, Marx insightfully points out the relative and transient character of competition in capitalist markets. Competition cannot be conceived as an "eternal" attribute of that mode of production but rather as the distinctive feature of a specific phase in the development of mercantile economy. Marx asserts the dialectic and contradictory nature of historical development, which allows him to postulate the existence of a growing tendency toward the centralization and concentration of capital: capitalist competition generates its opposite, that is, monopoly.[32] Starting with these observations on the general law of capitalist accumulation, Lenin arrives at his famous conclusions regarding the passage of competitive capitalism to its "higher" stage, imperialism:

> Economically, the main thing in this process is the substitution of capitalist monopolies for capitalist free competition. Free competition is the fundamental attribute of capitalism, and of commodity production generally. Monopoly is exactly the opposite of free competition; but we have seen the latter being transformed into monopoly before our eyes, creating large-scale industry and eliminating small industry . . . leading to such a concentration of production and capital that monopoly has been and is the result.[33]

Contrary to what the Friedmans and their disciples believe, the rise of monopolies is far from being a "false problem," a mere ideological artifact of a certain pessimistic worldview of society and history. Marx, in his famous letter to Weydemeyer, says that some bourgeois economists discovered the existence of social classes and their struggles in modern society long before Marx did; the same can be said of Lenin on the problem of monopolies. Lenin's originality stems from reinterpreting what many others—especially Hobson and Hilferding—had observed, capturing the constituent and unique essence of the phenomenon. Placed in this perspective, imperialism appears not only as a circumstantial political deformation of capitalism but as its higher stage, one in which free competition is replaced by oligopolistic accommodations.

Even though the Friedmans' analysis of contemporary capitalism is wrong, it is fair to ask the extent to which their observations are adequate for a correct understanding of the functioning of capitalism in its former competitive phase. Even here, the Friedmans are wrong. The conception of the self-regulated market is justly considered by economic historian Karl Polanyi as "one of the economic superstitions of 19th Century."[34] Contrary to the belief quite widespread in nineteenth-century liberal thought, markets were not the result of a "spontaneous and natural" development that began with the expansion of the barter system. This naturalist and evolutionist interpretation is unsustainable in light of the historiographic evidence available for more than fifty years, which no serious scholar, much less a Nobel laureate such as Milton Friedman, can ignore. Polanyi asserts that "Western European domestic trade was, in fact, created by state interventions," given that its scope was traditionally limited to the narrow confines of medieval cities or, otherwise, to long-distance commerce. In addition, merchants who were integrated into these two commercial circuits were strictly separated from each other and were unable to trade with laborers and peasants.[35] These medieval cities, which were the political-administrative expression of the markets, erected all types of obstacles for the formation of an internal market: the spontaneous preoccupation of these "market forces"—and the merchants' guilds before anyone else—was to ensure the noncompetitive and monopolistic character of municipal and long-distance commerce. The new absolutist state was called on to break that decaying traditional particularism, destroying the barriers that separated local from long-distance commerce, thereby clearing the way for the formation of the internal market. This policy ended up eradicating the differences between the countryside and the city, as well as those among the different provinces and regions that were rigorously isolated.

Thus, it was state intervention that made possible the constitution of a relatively competitive national market. The elimination of the traditional systems of guilds and municipal corporations, and of fragmented political authorities—with their multiple permissions and prohibitions, levies, taxes, and restrictions—did not lead to the creation of that mythological self-regulated market on which the entire economic and political thought of liberalism rests. Polanyi rightfully quotes Montesquieu's observation in *The Spirit of Laws*—"The English constrain the merchant, but it is in favor of commerce"—to add evidence to his conclusion that "although the new national markets were, inevitably, to some degree competitive, it was the traditional feature of regulation, not the new element of competition, which prevailed."[36] Consequently, the formation of a capitalist market with its relative degree of competitiveness was not a natural and spontaneous result of the free play of market forces. This naturalist illusion, which permeates nineteenth-century liberalism, is complemented by a sort of conspiracy theory that asserts that the obstacles for the development of the market arose as a corollary to a demonic agreement between the enemies of freedom nested in the state. As Marx states with regard to vulgar economy,

> The economists have a singular manner of proceeding. There are for them only two kinds of institutions, those of art and those of nature. Feudal institutions are artificial institutions, those of the bourgeoisie are natural institutions. In this they resemble the theologians, who also establish two kinds of religion. Every religion but their own is an invention of men, while their own religion is an emanation from God. . . . Thus there has been history, but there is no longer any."[37]

The truth is that neither naturalist illusion nor the conspiracy theory can resist even the most perfunctory analysis. The English historical experience—true motherland of laissez-faire—fully proves this point. The 1830s and 1840s witnessed not only decisive attacks against the restrictive regulations of free trade (such as the abolition of the Poor Law Amendment in 1832, the 1844 Peel Bank Law, and the repeal of the Corn Law in 1846) but also the significant increase in the administrative functions of the state, equipped with an expansive central bureaucracy in charge of carrying out the enlarged tasks demanded by the complete mercantilization of social relations. The mechanism implicit in the apparently simple exhortation of Adam Smith to found a "system of natural freedom" required the development of important state functions and the subsequent expansion of public administration. In no other way could the highly intricate provisions established by the innumerable Enclosure Laws be addressed. These administrative procedures were much needed to guarantee the functioning of the capitalist market, because they granted the dispossession of direct producers and their transformation into proletarians as well as the full mercantilization of the land. Similarly, the Poor Law Amendment required the creation of a vast bureaucratic organization in order to "regulate" the industrial reserve army to be used to depress the value of the labor force in the "free market."

All of this leads to a conclusion, paradoxical only in appearance. In fact, and contrary to all expectations, the introduction of free markets, far from doing away with the need for control, regulation, and intervention, enormously increased their range. . . . Administrators had to be constantly on the watch to ensure the free working of the system. Thus even those who wished most ardently to free the state from all unnecessary duties, and whose whole philosophy demanded the restriction of state activities, could not but entrust the self-same state with the new powers, organs, and instruments required for the establishment of *laissez-faire*.[38]

The myth of the self-regulated market, that ideological artifice at the service of capital, collapses before historical evidence that proves (1) that the market concentrates capital, power, and information, and that because of its laws of motion the market transforms its primitive competition into the primacy of oligopolies; and (2) that markets have always required the assistance of the state, and whereas in their primitive phase their selective affinities were congruent with liberal democracy, today, in their monopolistic and imperialist stage, these affinities push them toward political despotism. Contrary to the claims of liberal theorists, markets require constant state support for the dominant classes that play the supposedly "neutral" game of the market with a stacked deck. It is therefore not true that the market is a sphere in which everyone wins. Instead, in social terms, in the marketplace a few gain at the expense of the many who lose.

In other words, only in rare instances does the market assume the form of a positive-sum game; its spontaneous tendency is to constitute itself as a zero-sum game.[39] The wealth appropriated by the capitalists stems from the combination of human labor and nature, yet the distribution of the rewards that the market carries out "naturally" is extraordinarily unequal, constantly reproducing class distinctions and relations of exploitation. Only the action of a democratic state has prevented these tendencies from leading to a social catastrophe of unpredictable proportions. The adjective *democratic* should be stressed because not just any capitalist state possesses the capacities necessary to mitigate and redress the painful consequences of a social Darwinism of the market. Only a state that rests on the solid grounds of popular legitimacy—and which, precisely for that reason, advances policies congruent with the citizens' demands—is capable of carrying out the task of compensating for the "civilizing barbarism" unleashed by the market. This point is brilliantly summarized by John Strachey when he observes that

in real life capitalisms it has taken the utmost efforts of the 90 per cent of the population to prevent their share of the national product from falling, and so to enable their standard of life to rise with the rise of productivity. . . . Capitalism has in fact an innate tendency to extreme and ever-growing inequality. For how otherwise could all these cumulatively equalitarian measures which the popular forces have succeeded in enacting over the last hundred years have done little more than hold the position constant?[40]

Market Crises and the
Democratization of Capitalist States

The preceding discussion clearly shows that Friedman's theory of the market—and, by extension, of the state—is profoundly mistaken. It reiterates
the standard nineteenth-century liberal discourse, by virtue of which its pro-
grammatic aspirations for least government are confused with the reality of
the liberal and exclusivist state of Victorian England. Yet, the liberal conception of the state as a diligent *veilleur de nuit* was a radical misrepresen-
tation of "really existing" capitalist states. In both the original centers and
the nations that arrived "late" to this regime of production, the role of the
state in establishing, consolidating, and reproducing capitalism was of fundamental importance, a fact that seems to be ignored by contemporary liberal theorists as well. Without the state's coercive power there would have
been no primitive accumulation, and the international expansion of capitalism would have been much slower and more problematic. Much later, without the renewed capacities of the state to articulate a social consensus
around a project of "Keynesian reformism," it is unlikely that capitalism
would have overcome the crisis of 1929. In those places where this consensus proved impossible to attain, the state adopted a ferociously repressive
strategy in order to uphold the capitalist system, as shown in the cases of
Italy, Germany, and the different versions of European fascisms. In addition,
as a host of scholars have rightly pointed out, the post–World War II period
from 1948 to 1973 will undoubtedly be remembered as the golden age of
capitalist history, and one of the key factors of this success—which liberal
authors customarily fail to underline—was the unprecedented expansion and
the greatly improved efficacy of state interventions.[41] It is not by chance that
this particular stage in the history of capitalism was also labeled as the period of state-centered growth. In short, even the most elementary understanding of the history of capitalism would prove impossible without a parallel
history of the capitalist state. The poverty of liberalism stems precisely from
its inability to reproduce, in theoretical terms, the complex but closely knit
articulation between economy and politics that has characterized the unfolding of the capitalist mode of production since its beginnings.[42]

The practical foundations of liberalism's self-serving conceptual
myopia are unveiled in a brilliant paragraph written by Gramsci regarding
"economism":

> The ideas of the Free Trade movement are based on a theoretical error
> whose practical origin is not hard to identify; they are based on a distinc-
> tion between political society and civil society, which is made into and pre-
> sented as an organic one, whereas in fact it is merely methodological. Thus
> it is asserted that economic activity belongs to civil society, and that the
> State must not intervene to regulate it. But since in actual reality civil soci-
> ety and State are one and the same, it must be made clear that *laissez-faire*

too is a form of State "regulation," introduced and maintained by legislative and coercive means. It is a deliberate policy, conscious of its own ends,
and not the spontaneous, automatic expression of economic facts.
Consequently, *laissez-faire* liberalism is a political programme, designed
to change—in so far as it is victorious—a State's leading personnel, and to
change the economic programme of the State itself—in other words the
distribution of the national income.[43]

The liberal proposals in favor of laissez-faire, laissez-passer policies are
a far cry from being the passive response of a state secluded in its aloofness.
Rather, they appear, in Gramsci's analysis, as a positive class project of the
rising bourgeoisie designed to reorganize society to suit general and long-
run bourgeois interests. An enterprise of this sort could scarcely be the
expression of irresistible market forces projected onto a phantasmagorically
empty political scenario, especially because the economism of liberal
thought—at least in its hegemonic variations—was mixed with a rather surprising cult of the state by which the latter was regarded as an almost infallible instrument to guarantee the transformation of social relations. This
"statalist" optimism on the role of the state—which contemporary advocates
of liberalism are quick to hide—is a conflicting and irritating premise that
underlies the theoretical construction of liberalism. It manifests itself in the
paradigmatic importance that Jeremy Bentham assigns to the government in
promoting material well-being. The father of utilitarianism argues that in
order to attain material well-being, three conditions are required: motivation, knowledge, and power. The individual possesses only the first, and
knowledge and power are likely to be more efficiently administered by the
public authorities. Therefore, it is the duty of the state to compile useful statistics and relevant information, to promote science and scientific research,
and to develop the administrative agencies of the government.[44]

Nineteenth-century liberalism revolved around a conception according
to which the state was perceived as an actor external to the sphere of the
social relations of production. Bourgeois thought, even in its most refined
expressions—as in Hegel, for instance—almost photographically reproduced the ideological features peculiar to the capitalist mode of production:
separation between the economy and politics; the state as a representative of
the general and universal interests of the society; and individuals separated
in an "earthly" part, the bourgeois, and a "celestial" component, the citizen.
The fallacy of this whole discourse is mercilessly exposed in young Marx's
early criticism of the Hegelian philosophy of right and the state and in
Gramsci-inspired criticisms of liberalism. In fact, by "expelling" the state
from the economy—the latter being the exclusive home of civil society and
private interests—bourgeois ideology and "vulgar political economy"
wound up blessing the social Darwinism prevailing in the marketplace.
Liberal theorists have consistently overlooked the fact that capitalist
exploitation is reproduced ceaselessly because it is upheld by a state that—

while proclaiming its neutrality in front of social struggles and raising the banner of laissez-faire, laissez-passer as a proof of its class independence—in fact intervenes through a variety of ways and means in order to stabilize capitalist rule. With the consolidation of bourgeois hegemony, the world-view and interests of the dominant classes became the universal "common sense" of a whole era, and the myth of the neutral and noninterventionist state acquired an ever-growing credibility and consistency. This situation allowed the crystallization of a model of articulation among the state, civil society, and the market based on the inconsequential equality of abstract social relations and the structural inequality predominant in concrete histor-ical practices.

In the historical bloc of liberal capitalism, the state ensured the pre-dominance of the interests of the dominant classes in two ways. First, it did so through the de facto monopoly that the bourgeoisie and its allied classes held over the upper ranks of the state apparatus and over the recruitment of its ruling cadres. The consequence of this "colonization" of the upper eche-lons of the state apparatus was that bourgeois ideology, frequently expressed by political representatives recruited from other social classes and strata, became the unchallenged ideology of the state. This greatly facilitated the traditionally smooth coordination of government's "public" policies with the bourgeoisie's "private" strategies for accumulation. This congruence was especially noticeable in key policy areas, like public finance, public budget, and taxation; foreign policy; the approach to the so-called social question; and last but not least the issue of protectionism and trade policies. The predominance of the dominant classes was further ensured by the multiple mechanisms that strictly limited the legitimate scope of state action and prevented as much as possible the invasion of the "public" into the workings of the markets. The liberal bourgeois state guaranteed—despite its various interventions in economic life—that the initiative in the fields of production, distribution, and consumption remained firmly anchored in the hands of the bourgeoisie, preventing other actors from undermining the cen-trality that this class retained in the sphere of the market. The preservation of the social order—through an efficient administration, the courts, the police, and the army—and the maintenance of an adequate financial policy were in that phase sufficient conditions for the vigorous accumulation of capital.[45]

World War I and the Russian Revolution mortally wounded that specif-ic form of bourgeois state. The precarious recovery experienced after World War I—not without surprises, such as the advent of fascism in Italy in 1922 and the German hyperinflation of 1923—served only to prolong an agony that would reach a finale with the 1929 crash. This event would mark the end of a whole phase of capitalist development as well as the beginning of a new one, pregnant with profound transformations. The prolonged and relentless struggle of the subordinate classes against capital rule and its political representatives attained a series of decisive victories in the aftermath of World War I, imposing "from below" the democratization of the liberal state. The sudden and violent incorporation of European popular masses into the war efforts required, in due course, the swift enlargement of citizenship to hitherto disenfranchised sections of the population, for whom citizenship had either been neglected or remained abstract and blurred in the anonymity of the market. Gramsci observes, with his usual lucidness, that what capitalist industrialization had not been able to achieve in its secular process of development was to be obtained by the war:

> Four years of trench warfare and blood shedding have radically transformed the psychology of the peasant. This mutation has taken place especially in Russia, and it is one of the essential conditions of the revolution. What the normal process of development of industrialism failed to bring about was produced by the war. The war has forced the nations that are more capitalistically backward, and therefore less able to make use of machinery and mechanical devices, to mobilize and enroll all available men as deep masses of living flesh to oppose the weaponry of the central Empires. For Russia the war has meant that millions of people formerly dispersed in an enormous territory got in touch for the first time; it has also meant that large human groupings were held together ceaseless for years and years in sacrifice, under the immediate danger of death and under a common and ferocious discipline. The psychological effects of these enduring conditions of collective life have been immense and rich with unforeseen consequences. . . . Solidarity links were rapidly created in the trenches, which otherwise may have been created only after decades and decades of historical experience and intermittent struggles. In four years, in the mud and blood of the trenches, a whole spiritual world emerged, and this world was ardently eager to crystallize in permanent and dynamic social forms and institutions.[46]

It was the war, that overwhelming "scene director" that Lenin recalls in his first "Letter from Afar," that vertiginously accelerated the unfolding of a profound crisis in bourgeois society and the pace of universal history. After World War I and the outbreak of the Russian Revolution, the world would change dramatically and, in many respects, irreversibly: this new political consciousness was to have immediate political—and in some cases catastrophic—consequences for the capitalist states of the period. The falls of the House of Romanov, the Austrian-Hungarian Empire, and the Hohenzollern dynasty in Germany would be only the first episodes. The various links of the imperialist chain burst one by one; the weakest went first, and the others held out a little longer.[47]

The crisis was resolved in diverse ways according to the concrete characteristics of the national struggles of that historical moment. In Russia there was a socialist revolution. In Italy the proletarian defeat gave rise to a new form of bourgeois state: fascism. In Germany it allowed the establishment of a bourgeois republic led by the social democrats. However, the Weimar Republic was never able to stand on its own, and its crisis opened the path for Hitler's legal rise to power. The stronger links of the chain profoundly readjusted to the new national and international situation without reaching such extremes: Roosevelt's New Deal, the popular fronts in France, and the rise of social democracy in Sweden are pertinent examples. However, both the traumatic cases and the more gradual ones had a common denominator: the final bankruptcy of the old liberal model that rested on the exclusion of national majorities.[48]

An underlying factor of these processes was the impetuous mobilization of the subordinate classes, which violently undermined the already corroded state structures of competitive capitalism. The abstract and inconsequential citizenship that the state guaranteed needed to be radically transformed: extending suffrage to the popular classes and strata was the first response, though it was hardly sufficient. It was not enough simply to add a wider social base—incorporated into political life by virtue of universal suffrage— to a state that preserved intact its politico-administrative apparatus, the definition of its socioeconomic role, and, more important, its traditional articulation with the classes in the civil society. The insufficiency of a merely electoral democratization that left untouched the actual models of state function was clearly proven by the fate of the weakest links of the system. Opening the political system did not mitigate the social protest that would sweep away Russian czarism, Wilhelmin's Germany, and the reactionary coalition predominant in the Austrian-Hungarian Empire. To avoid the crisis, the state not only had to incorporate demands but also had to produce— and quickly—a wide range of government policies designed to satisfy the tumultuous and long neglected popular demands. A material and concrete citizenship had replaced the formal and abstract one; this was an ever more urgent change given that after the war, the legitimacy of the bourgeois state was significantly eroded and could be salvaged only with the active consensus of the dominated masses.

Yet this new role of the state, with the inevitable consequences in terms of its structure and politico-administrative action, could not be carried out without a profound change in how the capitalist economy functioned. If in its liberal and competitive stage the role of the state had been important for regulating the tensions and antagonisms of the market, after the 1929 crisis the state became the active force behind capitalist development. The bankruptcy of the market and the incurable persistence of market failures shifted the center of gravity of the process of accumulation from the bourgeoisie to the state. Consequently, the very continuity of capitalist accumulation now greatly relied on the accuracies or mistakes of the economic policies spurred by the state.

The State, the Bourgeoisie, and the Working Class:
The Keynesian Formula for Capitalist Recomposition

The so-called Keynesian revolution produced a drastic rearticulation between the state and civil society, which in a few years eliminated the archaic models of relation inherited from the era of competitive capitalism and gave rise to a new form of capitalist state. The names utilized to designate this new form are many and diverse: "enlarged," "welfare," "interventionist," or as the Germans call it, *Sozialstaat,* the "social state." All these names highlight the growing protagonism and undisputable centrality that the state acquired to guarantee the continuity of capitalist accumulation as well as to strengthen—after not a few adaptive innovations—bourgeois hegemony. According to Buci-Glucksmann and Therborn, this massive recomposition of the capitalist state hinged on a double articulation between the state and civil society: one that established a model of accumulation and development in which the existing relations between the state and capital were redefined; and another that established a previously unheard of model of hegemony and domination centered around the relationships between the state and the popular masses, putting an end to the secular exclusion of the latter.[49]

The new model of accumulation and development aimed at politically counteracting—that is, through the active intervention of the state—the tendency toward periodic crisis that is inherent with capitalism. For this it was necessary to "organize" the anarchy of the productive process, to minimize the disorders and disruptions originated by the blind forces of the market and the so-called market failures, and to design efficient governmental instruments for their compensation. The goal was to ensure the appropriate intervention of the state in the realm of production in order to rationalize the allocation of productive resources. This was done by a variety of direct or indirect means, ranging from the impressive expansion of state enterprises to a host of indirect mechanisms such as economic controls, subsidies, tariffs, interest rates, minimum wages, and the wide range of economic policies put in effect since the Great Depression. In Keynes's original formulation, the repertoire and duration of these state initiatives were more limited than what later would prove to be the case. He was centrally concerned with remediating the crisis through specific interventions in the field of unemployment and aggregate demand, proposing the judicious use of fiscal deficits to stimulate the creation of jobs and to boost total output. The extraordinary success of his recommendations, based on his penetrating understanding that capitalism needed a "collective organizer" in order to overcome the limitations of the unrestrained egotism of the *homo economicus* so much praised in Friedman's work, conspired against some of his own ideas. This extraordinary period (1948–1973), in which the international capitalist economy grew at higher rates and for longer than in any previous period, is deservingly know as the Keynesian Era.[50]

The political motivation of this dual strategy was transparent. At the beginning of the year 1931, before publishing his famous *Treatise,* Keynes already wrote that if a country does not want to go communist, there is no other means to cope with unemployment than to seek an adequate rate of benefit for the entrepreneurs.[51] The strategy he proposed to that effect was a sort of "socialization of investments" carried out by judicious governmental authorities, which through the promotion of economic endeavors of all sorts would absorb unemployment and stimulate aggregate demand. In this way, attracted by prospective high rates of return, entrepreneurs would reinvest again and the system would have its imbalances corrected thanks to the action of this external and eminently "nonmarket" agent: the state. Yet this type of proposal relied on the continued assistance of the state in its role as overseer of the economic cycle.

The rest is well-known history: the interventionist antidote to the crisis became a true "addiction," and capitalist states have continued to this day— see, for instance, Ronald Reagan's "perverse Keynesianism"—seducing reluctant entrepreneurs through economic policies intended to guarantee high rates of profits for their investments. In this way the state became a sort of deus ex machina of capitalist development, displaying an array of initiatives by which it can appear as an investor, economic planner, entrepreneur, tax collector, promoter, and resource allocator and through which it breathed new life into the languid capitalism of the period between the two world wars. According to the prophets of neoliberalism, this frenzied multiplication of roles served only to inhibit the economic progress that naturally would have arisen from the market. Yet sober specialists agree in pointing out that these interventions were crucial for reestablishing the functioning of capitalism in the 1930s and for guaranteeing its spectacular and unprecedented growth in the golden postwar years. Already by the 1950s and 1960s the Keynesian consensus was so overwhelming that the paradigm of the British economist prevailed uncontested. Monetarism and the other variants of orthodox liberal economics, ranging from the ideas of Milton Friedman to those of Friedrich von Hayek, formed a weak intellectual and political opposition, and these dissenting voices were regarded more as diehard ideologues than as practical economists whose recommendations could be of some use in the circumstances of the time. Keynesianism became the common sense of a whole historic period.[52]

The other side of the developmentalist state was the welfare state, and it is precisely in this terrain where lies the most profoundly authoritarian component of contemporary liberalism. By revaluating the "demand side" as the main determinant of global economic activity, Keynesianism simultaneously established the legitimacy of the citizens' demands vis-à-vis the state—especially working-class demands—and the governmental responsibility in the positive treatment of these matters. It is precisely in this dialectical unit among the state, capital, and civil society that one finds the nucleus of the problems that affect contemporary capitalism. The state's capacity to successfully face the crisis depends not only on a modification of the traditional forms of relation between political power and capital but also on the state's ability to obtain the consent of the majorities. This means that the state as a crisis manager must also be a welfare state, sensitive to (and responsible for) the augmented demands of a society in which having status as a citizen—something formerly restricted to the elite—became a significant attribute to the subordinated classes. The welfare state thus rested since its inception on the doubtful compatibility of two logics: one of an economic nature, aimed at the recovery and stabilization of capitalist accumulation; and another of a political nature, concerned with warding off the dangers of revolution, ensuring social peace, institutionalizing class conflicts, and creating a stable and legitimate bourgeois order.[53]

The sudden and accelerated expansion of state interventionism that unfolded after the Great Depression counted on the support—not always publicly expressed—or at least the acquiescence of the capitalists and their political and ideological representatives. This was the case not only in Europe and the United States but also in Latin America. In fact, Keynesian anticyclical measures were a rather bitter but necessary medicine for restoring the economic normalcy that the market could no longer guarantee, and the problems facing the dominant classes were too serious to be dealt with by resorting to eighteenth-century superstitions of the self-regulated market or the so-called invisible hand. In advanced capitalist economies as well as in Latin America, the expansion of state interventionism was the work of governments that responded, with varying degrees of readiness and with different levels of efficacy and tidiness, to the demands of the capitalist class badly hit by the general crisis of capitalism. What that particular conjuncture called for was the institutionalization of a policy of "socialization of losses" in order to confront the depression. But in order for this initiative to prosper, an expanded state apparatus, capable of intervening in new and imaginative ways in the management of the economic cycle, was required, and the old laissez-faire was no longer of any help.

Nevertheless, if the readjustment of the relationship between the state and the bourgeoisie was produced as a result of the crisis, the redefinition of the relation between the state and the subordinate classes and strata arose as a corollary of a lengthy process of political mobilization and working-class activism catalyzed by the outburst of the 1929 Great Depression. The gates of the state, which had been permanently locked for subordinate groups, were opened thanks to the fear caused by the Russian Revolution, the uncertainty aroused by the fascist regimes, and the objective need to resolutely confront the recession that upset the very foundations of capitalism. The political integration of the popular sectors as effective supporters and consensual stabilizers of the new bourgeois hegemony demanded the democratization of the capitalist state. Despite its limited character, inasmuch as it did not alter the class essence of the capitalist state, that opening still was a great conquest for the dominated classes.

Hence, it would be a grave distortion to consider the welfare state and modern capitalist democracy solely as products of a demonic conspiracy of the bourgeoisie to cheat the masses.[54] Permanently integrated into the life of the state, the presence of the masses gave rise to an extraordinary expansion of all kinds of welfare services and governmental programs that, in advanced bourgeois democracies, significantly improved the lot of the popular classes. At the same time, representative institutions acquired unprecedented vigor, thus reinforcing the strength of the laboring masses at the heart of state apparatuses. This ensured that labor demands for income and wealth redistribution, supported by large organizational structures of the working class, would find a positive reception in governmental circles. To sum up: this new state form did not represent the malevolent design of an omniscient bourgeoisie but rather was the mixed result of secular popular struggles for democracy and equality. At the juncture of the 1930s, when capital was on the defensive, the historical vindications of the workers' movement crystallized in new democratic institutions that opened unprecedented possibilities for development, which only the crisis of the mid-1970s started to undermine.

Consequently, the Keynesian capitalist state—sometimes called "interventionist," though this label is incorrect because it implies that the liberal predecessor did not intervene in the "private" affairs of civil society—arose from an integral crisis that profoundly affected not only bourgeois economy but also bourgeois civilization. Fundamental landmarks of this process were World War I, the Russian Revolution, and the Great Depression of 1929. The collapse of capitalism—something many believed imminent back then—failed to materialize, yet in its place there occurred a series of transformations that significantly altered its morphology and functioning.

Keynesianism resulted from these epochal changes. The imbalances that agitated within it proved that although it did temporarily manage to conciliate the imperatives of capitalist accumulation with those of democratic legitimation, it was never able to completely suppress the contradictions.[55] Moreover, it was impossible for these contradictions not to be expressed in the state, appropriately referred to by the young Marx in *The Poverty of Philosophy* as "the official resumé of the society." Yet it was also unlikely that the social antagonisms would linearly and directly project themselves onto a sort of "state mirror," especially because the modern capitalist state, given its centrality in all spheres of modern life, has not only become more complex but at the same time has also reinforced the growing complexity of social life. This state form has developed specialized apparatuses, institutions, and agencies that allow for an unprecedented expression of class struggles and the various social contradictions that stir contemporary capitalist societies. Thus, many authors have felt confident to speak of the withering away of the class character of the state and the advent of a social and economic democracy that, with a greater or lesser degree of development, prevailed in advanced capitalist countries since the last postwar period. These authors argue that the workers' movement has attained its full integration within the system; that the socialist and communist opposition enjoys the full recognition and protection of the law; that any dissent is allowed; and that the state, now "transformed" by class struggle, has taken upon itself the task of protecting the deprived classes and strata of the population.[56]

However, this type of argument—quite widespread in European and U.S. circles and, since the recovery of democratic institutions, in Latin America as well—confuses the institutional form of the Keynesian welfare state with its class nature. Whereas the former is determined by the character of the constituent mechanisms of public authority and the "national will"—and in this sense, it is beyond any reasonable doubt that the existence of a representative democracy established a considerable degree of political equality among citizens—the class nature of the state cannot be inferred from the relative degrees of perfection of its democratic organization. Its class contents are rather shaped by the complex structural intertwining that its agencies, institutions, and governmental policies maintain with the process of capitalist accumulation. As Claus Offe and Volker Ronge rightly note, to the extent that the public authority promotes and guarantees the ceaseless reproduction of the labor force as a commodity—and of the relation of exploitation inherent in it—the state is unquestionably a capitalist state, therefore profoundly classist, even though it has a democratic, not oligarchic or exclusivist, character different from the one that historically accompanied capitalism in its competitive stage. But the capitalist state's democratic potential has quite definite limits.[57]

Some of the features proper of the democratization of the Keynesian welfare state are destined to arouse strong antagonisms among individual capitalists and various bourgeois groups against the "political government of the economic cycle." These features include (1) the fact that the welfare state's source of legitimation comes from universal suffrage; (2) the democratic character of the procedures leading to the constitution of political authority and to the elaboration of the "national will"; and (3) the quality and quantity of governmental responses to popular demands—that is, the social policies promoted by democratic governments. These sectors want a Keynesian state but stripped of its mass base, forgetting that the Keynesian state is a new and integral rearticulation between the state and civil society that is not reducible solely to its economic moment. On the contrary, it requires a dialectical amalgam between the accumulation regime and a model of hegemony. If the new regime of state-centered accumulation introduced the state as organizer, planner, and regulator of the market, the foundation of a new hegemony implicit in this gigantic "passive revolution" is unsustainable without the full integration of the masses. This unity between accumulation and hegemony cannot be broken without precipitating the profound crisis of the state. This is exactly what has been occurring since the outburst of the crisis in the beginning of the 1970s.

Despite these contradictions, the modern Keynesian capitalist state possesses a structure much more robust than the one that characterized its frail liberal predecessor. It thus expresses a higher and more complex stage of development as a form of bourgeois domination, the ethical-political moment that supersedes the crass immediatism of the old laissez-faire state stuck in the narrow defense of the property owners' economic interests. Notwithstanding, it is precisely in the upgraded soundness of the Keynesian state—a result of the integration of the popular masses—that the main potential for dialectic negation of that state lies. The popular sectors are inside the bulwarks of the bourgeois citadel, not outside as before; and though by their presence they legitimize bourgeois rule, they can also refuse to support the authorities and deprive them of the critical popular legitimacy. If to this one adds that the expansive character of democracy tends to alienate the tenuous loyalty of bourgeois sectors to this political form— because they feel threatened by popular struggles that transformed the formal and abstract citizenship of the liberal state into an attribute endowed with concrete and tangible contents—the reasons for which the conservative West has placed "the crisis of democracy" at the center of its concerns can quickly be understood.[58]

In fact, the dominant classes anxiously observe the way in which that democratism—which had once been encapsuled within the limits of the "public sphere"—vigorously expands and penetrates even the very sanctuary of the bourgeoisie: the factory. The irresistible advance of democracy now overflows the wide confines of the state to invade "private realms," which used to be safe from the irruption of the democratic element. That shift is what galvanized a strong bourgeois bloc that has damned the Keynesian state as the cause of the economic crisis and democratic "ingovernability." The democratization of the state was, by itself, already nearly intolerable. Hence, the introduction of democratic criteria into the productive process, schools and universities, the mass media, bureaucratic structures, the family, and even interpersonal relations is something that goes much beyond what the bourgeoisie and its representatives are willing to accept.[59]

It is therefore quite understandable how liberal thought has taken on— at a time when the unequaled cycle of expansion initiated in the postwar period has been exhausted—a rather apocalyptic and unmistakably reactionary tone. The crisis that capitalism is undergoing is attributed to "external" enemies and to the unruliness of a popular mobilization that, in advanced capitalism, produced the unbridled expansion of the social compromises of the state. The result of this increased social responsibility was according to its critics—the financial crisis generated by the extraordinary overburdening of demands that weigh upon the Keynesian state, which nevertheless has no means to free itself of them without losing or impairing its legitimacy. Financial disorder, they add, reinforces the state gigantism that depresses the smooth functioning of the markets, causes inflation, and tends to have negative repercussions in the social peace and discipline that private initiative needs.

In this way the final conclusion of this diagnosis is reached, shared by Friedman and other neoliberal theorists as well as their paramount policy blueprint: the return to the market requires the drastic trimming and resizing of the state. However, it should be questioned whether it is possible to carry out such modifications without seriously undermining capitalist democracy itself. Doesn't this proclaimed "return to the market" actually imply the violent restoration of a social Darwinism that—with its archaic naturalist and biological prejudices—threatens human welfare and dignity while it offends the consciousness of the citizen in the democratic state? Furthermore, to what extent are the advances of the ever-growing "social nature" required for the structure and functioning of a contemporary capitalism susceptible to reverting to a new balance resting on the capricious structures of the market? And finally, are capitalist markets in a condition to function without the assistance of a state to which they have developed a true "addiction"? Or, put differently: to what extent has the existence of a "big" state, sometimes inefficient and frequently a deficit-ridden one, been the necessary condition for the prosperity of great "private" oligopolies?

The Reactionary Outcome

The discourse of Friedman, which begins as an exaltation of the economic and political wisdom of the market—as an automatic and prepolitical mechanism capable of generating growth and fairness in distribution—winds up in a virulent antistate attack precisely when subordinate classes and groups are struggling to extend democratic conquests to other "private" realms such as factories, universities, and public spaces to deepen the democratic and representative institutions of the state. The social reception of this new orthodoxy has been impressive: publicly embraced by presidents and ministers and greeted by major mass media as the belated advent of revealed truth, these proposals represent the most serious conservative response experienced by capitalism at an international scale since 1929. The restoration of "social Darwinism" and the declared intention of dismantling the Keynesian state—aggravating the suffering of the victims of the market games and also producing the practical emasculation of that state's democratic institutions—clearly express the authoritarian vocation nested in the monetarists' seemingly innocuous and "technical" economic ideas. Actually, the other side of economic liberalism is political despotism, and contemporary history supplies unchallenged proof in this respect. Sooner or later, monetarism ends up, more or less openly, advocating a conservative—and, if needed, a reactionary—recasting of the old order.

Monetarist liberalism hopes to create a new bourgeois order that is based on a state with a shrunken social base but is bureaucratically efficient to serve capital. An eloquent example of this proposal is supplied by the Friedmans when they assert that an essential requisite to guarantee the efficiency of their miraculous cure for inflation is that the state utilize its political strength to impose the bitter medicines that the society must swallow.[60] This means simply that the adjustment program required to confront the crisis must be imposed despite the demands, opinions, and preferences to the contrary of the majority of the population, who will be affected by the program's results: recession, unemployment, and all types of physical and moral pains.

The strong government demanded by those nostalgic of the market thus appears as a sybiline apology of political despotism. The ideological formula of contemporary liberalism seems to be as follows: free market plus political despotism, or at least the subordination of the democratic ideals and practices to the market imperatives. In other words, contemporary liberalism favors freedom for the private initiative and a hard line for the management of public affairs. The alleged antistatism of the modern crusaders of neoliberalism is actually a frontal attack against the democratization that the popular classes and strata were able to construct despite the opposition of and sabotage by capitalist interests. What Friedmanites and others alike are in fact preoccupied with regarding the modern capitalist state is not its excessive size nor its deficit spending but the intolerable presence of the masses saturating all of its interstices. Governments of neoliberal inspiration have fully shown that when they carry out the recommendations of their mentors, they confirm the bourgeoisie's addiction to deficit spending and to the hypertrophied state (while cutting social expenditures, thereby suffocating the vitality of democratic institutions). It is precisely for these reasons that liberal political theory ends, both in its actions and in its discursive silences, in an antidemocratic argument.

The neoliberal proposal forces one to choose between the market and the state, as neoliberal authors suggest with unceasing insistence. Yet this is a false proposition, a mere ideological and propagandistic device that does not conform with the "statist addiction" of real-world capitalisms. Actually, neoliberalism poses a much more serious (and perhaps for this reason much less explicit) dilemma: the market or democracy. Democracy is the real enemy, lying at the bottom of the antistate criticism of neoliberalism. The attack is not against the state but against the democratic state. The option in favor of the market is simultaneously an option against the risks of democracy.

Almost five centuries ago a witness of exceptional insight, Thomas More, made some remarks concerning the convulsed transit from feudalism to capitalism being experienced by the England of his time. Already by More's time, the defenders of the emergent capitalist society appealed to abstract concepts of "order and justice" for the purpose of justifying the social calamities caused by the violent imposition of a new mode of production and the "free option for the market" made by the English. Horrified by the massive suffering of his fellow countrypeople and scandalized by the panegyrics of the bourgeoisie, More asked himself:

> For what sort of justice do you call this? People like aristocrats, gold-smiths, or money-lenders, who either do no work at all, or do work that's really not essential, are rewarded for their laziness or their unnecessary activities by a splendid life or luxury. But labourers, coachmen, carpenters, and farm-hands, who never stop working like cart-horses, at jobs so essential that, if they *did* stop working, they'd bring any country to a standstill within twelve months—what happens to them? They get so little to eat, and have such a wretched time, that they'd be almost better off if they *were* cart-horses.[61]

More's question is a very good one, and nearly five hundred years later the free-market advocates still have not been able to produce a morally satisfactory response.

Notes

1. See the prologue in Friedman, Milton, and Rose Friedman, *Free to Choose* (New York and London: Harcourt Brace Jovanovich, 1979). Milton Friedman's *Capitalism and Freedom* was originally published by the University of Chicago Press in 1962.
2. Friedman, Milton, *Capitalism,* pp. 12–13.
3. Ibid., p. 13.
4. Ibid., p. 13 (italics mine).
5. Ibid., p. 14 (italics in original).
6. Friedman, Milton, and Rose Friedman, *Free to Choose,* p. 13.
7. Ibid., pp. 13–14.
8. Ibid., pp. 32–34.
9. Friedman, Milton, *Capitalism,* pp. 119–136.
10. Ibid., pp. 22–25.
11. Ibid., p. 15.
12. See Giesbert, Franz-Olivier, "El estado es la ruina!" interview with Milton Friedman published in *Contextos* 2(19) (Mexico: May 14–20, 1981).
13. Friedman, Milton, and Rose Friedman, *Free to Choose,* p. 4.
14. Smith, Adam, *An Inquiry into the Nature and Causes of the Wealth of Nations* (Indianapolis: Liberty Classics, 1981), Vol. 2, pp. 687–688.
15. Ibid., p. 54.
16. Friedman, Milton, *Capitalism,* p. 34.
17. Friedman, Milton, and Rose Friedman, *Free to Choose,* pp. 4–7.
18. Friedman, Milton, *Capitalism,* pp. 201–202. This argument was originally

posited by Friedrich A. Hayek in *The Road to Serfdom* (Chicago: University of Chicago Press, 1944). On neoconservative political thought see also my "La crisis norteamericana y la racionalidad neoconservadora," *Cuadernos Semestrales* 9 (Mexico: CIDE, First semester, 1981), pp. 31–58.

19. See Friedman, *Capitalism,* p. 13. The brilliant critique of this argument by C. B. Macpherson has inspired much of my work on this matter. See his *Democratic Theory: Essays in Retrieval* (Oxford University Press, 1973), pp. 145–147.

20. See, among others, Polanyi's classic work *The Great Transformation: The Political and Economic Origins of Our Time* (Boston: Beacon Press, 1944).

21. Marx, Karl, *Capital* (New York: International Publishers, 1974), Vol. 1, p. 714.

22. Ibid., p. 751.

23. Ibid., p. 81.

24. Friedman, Milton, *Capitalism,* p. 121.

25. Ibid., p. 124.

26. Galbraith, John K., *The New Industrial State* (Boston: Houghton Mifflin Co., 1971, Second Edition, Revised), pp. 74–76.

27. Baran, Paul, and Paul Sweezy, *Monopoly Capital* (New York: Monthly Review Press, 1966), p. 6.

28. Cf. Altvater, Elmar, "Il capitalismo si organizza: Il dibattito marxista dalla guerra mondiale alla crisi del '29," mimeo (Rome: 1980).

29. Edwards, Richard C., "The impact of industrial concentration on the economic crisis," in URPE, *Radical Perspectives on the Economic Crisis of Monopoly Capitalism* (New York: 1975), p. 41.

30. Ibid., p. 42.

31. Block, *Post-Industrial Possibilities: A Critique of Economic Discourse.* (Berkeley and Oxford: University of California Press, 1990).

32. Aguilar, Alonso, *Teoría leninista del imperialismo* (Mexico: Nuestro Tiempo, 1978), pp. 105–121.

33. Lenin, V. I., "El imperialismo, fase superior del capitalismo," in *Obras escogidas en tres tomos* (Moscow: Progreso, 1961), Vol. 1, p. 764.

34. Polanyi, Karl, *The Great Transformation,* p. 56.

35. Ibid., p. 63.

36. Ibid., p. 66. Max Weber makes similar remarks in *Economy and Society: An Outline of Interpretative Sociology* (Berkeley: University of California Press, 1978).

37. This passage is quoted by Marx from his earlier *The Poverty of Philosophy* (1847) and reproduced as a footnote in *Capital,* Vol. 1, p. 81.

38. Polanyi, Karl, *The Great Transformation,* pp. 140–141.

39. Lester Thurow's analysis on the imbalances and readjustments of the U.S. economy demonstrates that this is not only a perversion limited to peripheral capitalist economies. See his *The Zero-Sum Society* (New York: Basic Books, 1980).

40. Strachey, John, *Contemporary Capitalism* (London: Gollanez, 1956), pp. 150–151, quoted in Miliband, Ralph, *The State in Capitalist Society* (New York: Basic Books, 1969), pp. 28–29.

41. See, for instance, Huntington, Samuel P., "The United States," in Crozier, Michael, Samuel P. Huntington, and Joji Watanuki, *The Crisis of Democracy: Report on the Governability of Democracies to the Trilateral Commission* (New York: New York University Press, 1975).

42. On state-centered models of economic development in Latin America, see, among others, Paramio, Ludolfo, "El final de un ciclo y la crisis de unos actores: América Latina ante la década de los 90," and Cavarozzi, Marcelo, "Beyond transitions to democracy in Latin America," papers submitted to the Fifteenth World

Congress of the International Political Science Association (Buenos Aires, July 1991). See also Lagos, Ricardo, "Crisis, ocaso neoliberal y el rol del Estado," *Pensamiento Iberoamericano* 5a (January–June 1984), pp. 163–188.

43. Gramsci, Antonio, "Some theoretical and practical aspects of 'economism,'" in *Selections from the Prison Notebooks* (New York: International Publishers, 1971), pp. 159–160.

44. Cited in Polanyi, Karl, *The Great Transformation,* p. 139.

45. See Offe, Claus, *Lo stato nel capitalismo maturo* (Milan: Etas Libri, 1977), pp. 38–39.

46. Gramsci, Antonio, *La questione meridionale* (Rome: Editori Riuniti, 1972), pp. 65–66 (translation mine).

47. Therborn, Göran, "The rule of capital and the rise of democracy," *New Left Review* 103 (London: May–June 1977), pp. 2–41.

48. A clarifying discussion of Europe after World War I can be found in Maier, Charles, *Recasting Bourgeois Europe* (Princeton: Princeton University Press, 1975).

49. Buci-Glucksmann, Christine, and Göran Therborn, *Le défi social-démocrate* (Paris: François Maspero, 1981), pp. 115–137.

50. Both Marxist scholars and the most enlightened liberal thinkers (among whom the most distinguished is unquestionably Lord John Maynard Keynes) agree that capitalist economies need an "ideal collective capitalist"—which is none other than the state. Regarding this matter, see the interesting work of Altvater, Elmar, "Il capitalismo si organizza," and Negri, Antonio, *La classe ouvrière contre l'état* (Paris: Galilée, 1978), especially his chapter entitled "Keynes and the capitalist theory of the state in 1929," which from a leftist perspective opens a highly sugestive dialogue with the ideas that Keynes presents in his *General Treatise.* Of course I must also include in this list the convergent interpretations arrived at by Karl Mannheim from a sociological perspective in his *Man and Society in an Age of Reconstruction* (New York: Harcourt, Brace & World, 1973). This book, originally published in Holland in 1935—that is, a year before the publishing of Keynes's magnum opus—constitutes a powerful contention in favor of "democratic and libertarian planning" as the only alternative in the face of the shortcomings manifested by the market mechanisms in the Europe of the 1930s. Mannheim later broadened these perspectives in his *Freedom, Power and Democratic Planning* (New York: Oxford University Press, 1950). Moreover, I should also mention the work of the Polish Marxist economist Michal Kalecki, who in the early 1940s sketched a theoretical model that can be regarded as the "left-wing" version of Keynesianism. See his *Theories in Economic Dynamics* (London: Unwin University Books, 1965) and his *Selected Essays on the Dynamics of the Capitalist Economy* (Cambridge: Cambridge University Press, 1971). An outstanding Marxist reading on the meaning of Keynes's work can be found in Mattick, Paul, *Marx and Keynes* (Boston: Porter Sergent, 1969). An account of the showdown is to be found in Skidelsky, Robert, ed., *The End of the Keynesian Era* (London: Macmillan, 1977).

51. Vobruba, George, "Keynesismo come principio politico. Per una teoría dell'immagine strumentale della societá," in Donolo, Carlo, and Franco Fichera, *Il governo debole* (Bari: De Donato, 1981), p. 166.

52. On this subject, see the fascinating account of the international difussion of Keynesianism provided in Hall, Peter A., ed., *The Political Power of Economic Ideas: Keynesianism Across Nations* (Princeton: Princeton University Press, 1989). See also, in a much more polemical vein, Krugman, Paul, *Peddling Prosperity: Economic Sense and Nonsense in the Age of Diminished Expectations* (New York and London: Norton and Co., 1994).

53. Barcellona, Pietro, *Oltre lo stato sociale* (Bari: De Donato, 1980), Ch. 3.

54. Cf. Offe, Claus, and Volker Ronge, "Tesi per una fondazione teorica della nozione di 'stato capitalistico' e per una metodología materialistica della politologia," in Basso, Lelio, ed., *Stato e crisi delle istituzioni* (Milan: Gabriele Mazzotta, 1978), pp. 35–51.

55. As proved by Claus Offe in his *Contradictions of the Welfare State* (Cambridge, MA: The MIT Press, 1985), Chs. 6–8.

56. Gough, Ian, *The Political Economy of the Welfare State* (London: Macmillan Press, 1979), Ch. 1.

57. Offe, C., and V. Ronge, "Tesi," pp. 35–51 and 79–81.

58. Cf. the veritable "neoconservative manifesto" published under the auspices of the Trilateral Commission by Crozier, Michael, Samuel P. Huntington, and Joji Watanuki, *The Crisis of Democracy.* See also, on this subject, Brittan, Samuel, "The economic contradictions of democracy," *British Journal of Political Science* 5 (April 1975), pp. 129–159, and his "Can democracy manage an economy?" in Robert Skidelsky, ed., *The End*, pp. 41–49.

59. Cf. Bowles, Samuel, and Herbert Gintis, *Democracy and Capitalism: Property, Community and the Contradictions of Modern Social Thought* (New York: Basic Books, 1986). See also, from the same authors, "The crisis of liberal democratic capitalism: The case of the United States," *Politics and Society* 2(1) (1982), pp. 51–95.

60. Friedman, Milton, and Rose Friedman, *Free to Choose,* pp. 264–282.

61. More, Thomas, *Utopia* (Harmondsworth: Penguin Books, 1965), p. 129.

3

Alexis de Tocqueville, Democracy, and the "Statism" of Bourgeois Society

An Intellectual Aristocrat
Between Democracy and Revolution

Little more than 160 years ago, Alexis de Tocqueville arrived in New York. He was a twenty-six-year-old Norman aristocrat who belonged to a family having long historical ties to the French monarchy. One of his grandfathers had been guillotined during the French Revolution, and his parents providentially escaped a similar fate thanks to the fall of Robespierre. His ancestors had served the Bourbon bureaucracy for centuries, and young Alexis did not even dream of discontinuing that tradition. Consequently, in 1827 he became magistrate at the court of Versailles of the restored Bourbon monarchy just when it was on the verge of its final collapse. In fact, the decrepit and reactionary projects of Charles X soon came to clash against the harsh reality of a fully bourgeois France.

The fall of the last Bourbon meant the rise of the "newcomer" Orleanist dynasty, embodied in the person of Louis Phillipe. But the advent of the July Monarchy—as Marx points out in his famous analysis of the 1848 revolution—meant something more: the rise of finance aristocracy as the hegemonic bourgeois fraction in France. This change considerably altered young Tocqueville's plans. He considered his oath of loyalty to the new reigning dynasty to be repugnant and aberrant to his soul because he was strongly attached to Bourbon legitimism by his enduring family tradition. To escape such an unfortunate contradiction he requested and obtained permission to study the functioning of the U.S. penal system. In this way he would accompany his beloved friend, Gustave de Beaumont, who would travel to the United States moved by similar purposes. Tocqueville's letters would later reveal that what he really wanted to examine was the structure and functioning of U.S. democracy, for which he had already prepared a detailed project that he was careful not to make known. The result of the trip, which lasted nine months, could not have been more productive. Aside from collaborating with Beaumont in writing the official report on the U.S. peniten-

tiary system and its application in France—which appeared in 1833—
Tocqueville published in 1835 (before he turned thirty-five) the first part of
an extraordinary book: *Democracy in America,* the complement of which
would appear in 1840.

The success of his work was tremendous, and the book was immediately translated into the main European languages. None other than John Stuart
Mill promoted its publication in England, and afterwards Tocqueville
became an assiduous collaborator for the prestigious *London and Westmin-
ster Review,* which had already become the theoretical organ of the most
sophisticated expressions of liberal thought. By 1836 the book had been
translated into English and Spanish; and in 1855 and 1864 there were versions of it printed in Mexico and Argentina. Therefore, its repercussions
were felt immediately and with great strength in all of Latin America, and
Tocqueville's work became the center of a lively debate in the young
republics. Latin American liberal intellectuals and publicists had traditionally looked to France and Great Britain in search of inspiration to defeat the
obscurantism and backwardness inherited from the decrepit postcolonial
order, and Tocqueville's book reinforced this pattern. In an enlightening
study, Argentine scholar Natalio Botana traces the influence of Tocqueville—and of the republican tradition in general—on that country's greatest
statesmen and political thinkers, especially Domingo F. Sarmiento (a very
good friend of U.S. educator Horace Mann) and Juan B. Alberdi, drafter of
the 1853 liberal constitution. Former Argentine president Bartolomé Mitre
declared in 1880 that *Democracy in America* had been the standard reference book of his generation. Botana also points to the essential role that
Tocqueville's formulation exerted on Sarmiento's tireless intellect: "Toward
him Sarmiento turned his eyes when writing his *Facundo* (secretly dream-
ing of emulating Tocqueville): 'We have badly needed a Tocqueville in
South America, and very especially in the Argentine Republic.' Sarmiento
never allowed anyone to dispute the privilege of having been the first to
introduce *Democracy in America* to Santiago."[1]

Upon his return to France, Tocqueville fully embarked on his political
career. In 1839 he was elected representative of his native district in
Normandy and held his post until the 1848 revolution. In 1849 he was
reelected to the Constituent Assembly of the Second Republic and to the
new Legislative Assembly, of which he would later became vice-president.
He was also minister of foreign affairs in Barrot's cabinet for a brief period
of time. It is amazing to realize that an outstanding talent like Tocqueville's
was insufficient to leave any significant imprint on French political history.
His exceptional analytical skills aided him very little in contending with the
turbulence of French politics during those dramatic years. Resolutely
opposed to Louis Bonaparte's coup d'état, he proposed a constitutional
indictment—as decorous as it was ineffective—against the future emperor
when it was already obvious that Bonaparte's ascension to the throne was

irresistible. That was the end of Tocqueville's brief political career. Defeated and humiliated, he retired to Normandy, where he remained until his rather premature death at age 54 in 1859. There he began to write what he mistakenly thought would be his magnum opus, a history of the French Revolution, of which he would publish only a small yet memorable initial study: *The Ancien Regime and The Revolution.* The rest of his notes on the history of the decadence of aristocratic France, unpublished for many years, were to be printed much later.[2]

The United States as a Test Case

Alexis de Tocqueville went to the United States to study the riddle that U.S. democracy posed to a conservative though enlightened French aristocrat. His purpose was not simply to satisfy a mere intellectual curiosity; furthermore, he was more interested in democracy than in the United States. His obsessive concern was to understand the functioning of a democratic regime and its possible implications for the preservation or destruction of freedom. In his words,

> So I did not study America just to satisfy curiosity, however legitimate; I sought there lessons from which we might profit. Anyone who supposes that I intend to write a panegyric is strangely mistaken. . . . Nor have I aimed to advocate such a form of government in general, for I am one of those who think that there is hardly ever absolute right in any laws; I have not even claimed to judge whether the progress of the social revolution, which I consider irresistible, is profitable or prejudicial for mankind. I accept that revolution as an accomplished fact, or a fact that soon will be accomplished, and I select of all the peoples experiencing it that nation in which it has come to the fullest and most peaceful completion, in order to see its natural consequences clearly, and if possible, to turn it to the profit of mankind. I admit that I saw in America more than America; it was the shape of democracy itself which I sought, its inclinations, character, prejudices, and passions; I wanted to understand it so as at least to know what we have to fear or hope therefrom.[3]

What could be expected, or feared, from democracy? This was a pertinent question for an intellect preoccupied with the decay of European aristocracies and the upsetting of European societies resulting from the French Revolution, which eliminated the old regime and inaugurated a revolutionary period that was still creating turbulence in the European scenario more than half a century later. Tocqueville's apprehensions were to be confirmed by the outburst of the 1848 revolutions. Both the images of threatening plebeian masses—who seized power for a few days—and the scenes of the shipwreck of the old monarchies condemned by the inexorable progress of democracy tormented his spirit profoundly. The old Europe was falling apart, and Tocqueville was perfectly aware that it was impossible to avert the collapse of an old order that the French Revolution had only dramatically accelerated. Only England remained standing. There the winds of revolution had not acquired the intensity found in the rest of the continent, partly because of the timely—though not less uncertain—agreement between an aristocratic nobility that had not forgotten the decapitation of uncompromising Charles I and a vigorous industrial bourgeoisie whose economic and political ascendancy was not impaired by the survival of innocuous aristocratic rituals and pageantry.

But it was the United States where the advance of the democratic revolution had reached its end, and it was necessary to cross the Atlantic to observe the nature of the new political and social processes that were shaking the foundations of the old world. It should be noted that, by doing so, Tocqueville proceeded with the same methodological criteria that Marx endorses in the preface to the first edition of *Capital:* it is necessary to study social phenomena "where they appear in their most typical form and most free from disturbing influence." And whereas Marx studied the capitalist mode of production by observing the trends that assert themselves with "iron-like necessity" in England, Tocqueville wisely decided to study "democratic revolution" in its classical locus: the United States.[4]

Tocqueville hoped that a close examination of U.S. democracy would provide him a comprehensive understanding of the immediate fate of France and Europe. It would also permit him to identify what could be expected or feared from the inevitable democratic revolution: would democracy open new horizons for freedom in modern societies, or would it push those societies into new and more refined forms of despotism? Tocqueville's attitude is correctly interpreted by Harold Laski, who compares the significance of the former's analysis of the United States with Lord Bryce's in *The American Commonwealth.* Whereas the English aristocrat was primarily interested in understanding the nature of the modern British "fragment" in the New World, Tocqueville was writing a book on French civilization, and the United States appears in its pages more as a source of inspiration than as a central theme. Actually, Laski adds, Tocqueville was more concerned with the possibility of discovering in the U.S. conditions the means for analyzing the future of France than in understanding the United States itself.[5]

Hence, Tocqueville's importance is that he was not only a historian or sociologist who studied and analyzed a concrete society, but also a theorist who transcended the immediacy of his object and posited a set of generic problems regarding the possibilities and limitations of democracy in bourgeois society. It is for this reason that, over time, his work became a classic in political theory. Therefore, two different levels of analysis can be discerned in Tocqueville's work: the historiographic level and the political science level.

This chapter is concerned not so much with the accuracy of

Tocqueville's historical observations as with Tocqueville as a political theo-rist. Historiographical criticism has made great strides in its research on the Jacksonian era in the United States, and nothing seems to have emerged as a rebuttal of any major Tocquevillian thesis. What have made Tocqueville a classic in political thought are his subtle reasonings on the democratic state and the future of freedom in capitalist society, not the exactness of his minute historical observations. It is in the field of political science that his fundamental legacy can be found—which amply compensates for the rela-tive imperfection and transience of his historical observations. It is here where one finds the relevance of his thoughts, of his "hopeful pessimism" regarding the future of democracy. His meditations could not be more time-ly these days, when the authoritarian involution of modern capitalism is a source of deep concern, thus placing Tocqueville's arguments at the center of today's debates. It is that permanence that makes him—together with Wilhelm Von Humboldt, Benjamin Constant, and John Stuart Mill—a lead-ing exponent of nineteenth-century liberalism.[6]

Democracy: Political Regime or Social Condition?

Tocqueville introduced a fundamental innovation into liberal thought, which took him far from his seventeenth- and eighteenth-century predecessors: he characterized democracy as a social condition in which the principle and practice of equality prevailed.[7] In his view, democracy and equality merge into a single sociological and political unit. And even though, for the most part, the two fundamental notions of his entire theoretical argument—democracy and freedom—are not specifically defined, it seems quite clear that Tocqueville departed from liberalism's classical tradition and produced a substantive (not merely formal) definition of democracy.[8] In fact, within the liberal theoretical tradition of the seventeenth and eighteenth centuries, citizens were considered in their juridical abstractness as atomized particles whose rights and guarantees were constituted independent of the concrete social conditions of individuals. In addition, these rights and guarantees were supposed to precede the birth of the state created by the individuals after signing a social compact. For these reasons, the impoverished pre-Tocquevillian liberal discourse on democracy inevitably tended toward for-malism: it dealt with possible forms of government—and the relations between the individual and the state—never on a historical condition of society. In Tocqueville's terms, however, democracy is defined with respect to civil society. Its true essence is social equality, whereas its opposite, aris-tocracy, is defined by a structural situation of institutionalized privilege and inequality. Democracy is thus a new type of society that replaces the archa-ic aristocratic social order, which is certain to disappear. Tocqueville posits this issue as follows:

> A great democratic revolution is taking place in our midst; everybody sees it, but by no means everybody judges it in the same way. . . . Running through the pages of our history, there is hardly an important event in the last seven hundred years which has not turned out to be advantageous for equality. . . . Everywhere the diverse happenings in the lives of peoples have turned to democracy's profit; all men's efforts have aided it, both those who intended this and those who had no such intention, those who fought for democracy and those who were the declared enemies thereof. . . . Therefore, the gradual progress of equality is something fated. The main features of this progress are the following: it is universal and permanent, it is daily passing beyond human control, and every event and every man helps it along. Is it wise to suppose that a movement which has been so long in train could be halted by one generation? Does anyone imagine that democracy, which has destroyed the feudal system and vanquished kings, will fall back before the middle classes and the rich? Will it stop now, when it has grown so strong and its adversaries so weak?[9]

Therefore, it is understandable that the young Tocqueville confesses having written his book under the impulse "of a kind of religious dread inspired by contemplation of this irresistible revolution advancing century by century over every obstacle, and even now going forward amid the ruins it has itself created."[10]

A revolution that provokes the intermingling of social classes and their subsequent confusion. A revolution in which the barriers that have for centuries segregated human beings into watertight compartments are broached in the face of the pulverizing power of civil society. It is a revolution in which "great estates were broken up, power shared, education spread, and intellectual capacities became more equal."[11] It is in this light that Tocqueville should be understood when he exhorts "to educate democracy; to put, if possible, new life into its beliefs; to purify its mores; to control its actions; gradually to substitute understanding of statecraft for present inexperience and knowledge of its true interests for blind instincts; to adapt government to the needs of time and place; and to modify it as men and circumstances require."[12]

Therefore, the point is not to try uselessly to reconstruct aristocratic society, because, as Tocqueville says, "I am convinced that in the age now opening before us those who try to base authority on privilege and aristocracy will fail. . . . There is therefore no question of reconstructing an aristocratic society, but the need is to make freedom spring from that democratic society in which God has placed us."[13]

According to Tocqueville, what is needed is to recover the libertarian heritage that he perceives pulsing within the creases of feudalism, a legacy that nevertheless could not rely on the same social classes, institutions, and practices of the old regime. The twilight of the age of the aristocracy had begun, and all attempts to recast a principle of inequality among individuals in the new society would be futile, especially if legally sanctioned. Tocqueville rejects any such attempts as anachronistic, thereby sharply distinguishing himself from the reactionary positions of Bonald and de Maistre and from the more realistic and sophisticated conservative argument of Edmund Burke.

In short, in Tocqueville there is a radical shift of the center of gravity of the democratic-liberal theoretical discourse, a movement that swings away from the state and attempts to find the roots of democracy in civil society. There is radical transition from juridical and formalistic politicism to a full-scale societalism. Whereas Hobbes defines citizens by their political obligation—which he understands to be an unconditional surrendering to the state—Tocqueville defines them in terms of their pertinence to a social formation historically characterized by the equality among its members.

To be sure, Tocqueville does not get to the bottom of the question. He ignores the anatomy of modern bourgeois society, for which he would have had to start a systematic critique of classical political economy in anticipation of the road to be taken by Marx a few years later. Yet, in his search for the social roots of democracy, and despite exaggerating the extent of egalitarianism in U.S. society, Tocqueville produced a true revolution within the liberal bourgeois paradigm. He was the first to consistently explore the relation between the substantive and formal aspects of democracy, that is, the dialectical nexus between concrete equality and formal freedom, which would later become the cornerstone of Marxist criticism of bourgeois politics and ideology. As a result of his study he arrives at two worrisome conclusions. First, he notes that democratic formalisms are irrelevant if they do not rest on a generalized condition of equality. Therefore, political freedom, tolerance, and pluralism are unlikely to root themselves in a ground that has not yet rid itself of aristocratic and hierarchical vestiges. Marx would later develop this same argument to its logical end by positing that the relations of production of bourgeois society constitute a structural limit to the various projects of capitalist democracy and bourgeois reform. Second, Tocqueville acknowledges that although equality favors the development of liberty, it can also generate a new form of despotism that could cancel out even the narrow freedoms compatible with the aristocratic order.

These two conclusions form the basis of Tocqueville's thoughts, and they inform and unify the whole of his intellectual production, including his analysis of the development of the French Revolution. His "sociologism" pushes him to decipher the significance of political institutions in terms of the nature of civil society, its structures, values, customs, mores, and ideologies. It is the social condition that determines—or at least decisively influences—political life; and in the United States that social condition is equality, the fundamental fact from which all the rest derive.[14] This solid anchoring of the political in civil society explains Tocqueville's skepticism toward a certain bourgeois reformism that he does not hesitate to qualify as naive given that institutional changes were unlikely to modify the structure and historical course of society. Accordingly, France could not hope to be free because it remained a divided and unequal society. Yet, anguished in the face of this dead end, Tocqueville stepped back, softened his radical sociologism, and recognized that the study of the United States could eventually provide France with better laws and political institutions, which could save French society from the horrors of despotism.[15] In this way Tocqueville's methodological observations conclude with a profound criticism against historical optimism and the "stadolatry" of bourgeois reformism, which trusted—since the age of the Physiocrats—its ability to reform society through the manipulation of political and state institutions (a thesis that has also had a profound influence in certain variants of socialist thought).

Nevertheless, Tocqueville's sociologism has other noteworthy implications. In fact, carried to its logical conclusion—something Tocqueville does not do—his totalizing observations wind up in a radical questioning of the liberal argument of negative freedom. According to this argument, the struggle for freedom basically involves restricting governmental actions and prerogatives, all of which are dogmatically considered contrary to individual freedoms.[16] To be sure, Tocqueville does not go that far, but he does open a path to be traveled later by Marxist political criticism. Like Rousseau, Tocqueville should be regarded in some specific themes as an admirably perceptive forerunner of socialist political thought. The point, then, is to make an effort to place the debate regarding freedoms on a coordinate where the state and civil society intersect. Confining the debate to just the state—understood, in the typical politicist reductionism of liberalism solely as a political association, as that mythical nightwatchman Gramsci speaks of—can do nothing but yield a deformed perspective of the issue of freedom. Therefore, in these neoconservative times, the importance of Tocqueville's work is undeniable, especially considering the wide diffusion reached by the orthodox theses of Milton Friedman and Friedrich Von Hayek, which one-sidedly reduce the problem of freedom to the thorough trimming of government powers and attributes.[17]

Furthermore, Tocqueville, in the last part of *Democracy in America,* expresses his disbelief regarding another of the great historical myths of liberalism: that of a self-regulated, free, and harmonious civil society permanently adjusted to changing levels of equilibrium. Tocqueville was too refined an intellectual to believe in the superstition of the invisible hand. In his work one finds the seeds of an enlightening criticism against certain deep-seated tendencies of bourgeois society. Yet such criticism could be fully developed only within the grand theoretical framework designed by Marx, which—by revealing the secret of surplus value—exposed the market mechanisms and the structural propensity of competition toward social inequality, concentration, and monopoly. Consequently, the liberal assumption that politics, like the economy, is ruled by the legality of a self-regulated market finds in Tocqueville a skeptic intelligence that points out its contradictions, in spite of the fact that his analysis fails to get to the bottom of the issue.[18]

The Divided Path: Two Possible Roads Toward Equality

Tocqueville's discourse opens the doors to a new conception of democracy, to a conceptualization that is political yet, above all, social. Democracy refers to a series of matters concerning both the nature of the political regime—representation, suffrage, organization and limits of political power, etc.—and, more important, the nature of civil society. In this regard the rule of equality constitutes the true distinctive landmark of democracy. The social foundations of democracy were not overlooked by Tocqueville, despite the limitations that his situation as an aristocratic intellectual placed on his theoretical perspective. It therefore seems appropriate to examine the reach of his outlook given that there are two different Tocquevilles. One is the Tocqueville revealed in U.S. mainstream political science, revered for his exemplary description and analysis of equality, democracy, and the perennial features of a new society that, according to its prophets, carries the burden of illuminating the march of modern civilization toward the heights of democracy—subtly confounded with "the American way of life." Then there is another Tocqueville who, as a political theorist, formulates critical observations in a manner that is hardly compatible with that of the panegyrists of U.S. democracy.[19] In other words, it is necessary to make the distinction between Tocqueville the historian, who provided so many inputs for the self-complacent and self-righteous discourse of the U.S. right, and Tocqueville the political theorist, who extracted from the U.S. scene the transcendent questions regarding the good society and the good political regime. On the basis of the doubts and tensions found throughout Tocqueville's fertile thought, what lessons can one learn from his observations?

As mentioned earlier, the focal point of Tocqueville's argument is that equality, which is the economic, social, cultural, and psychological foundation of democracy, is compatible not only with freedom, and hence with an egalitarian and democratic political regime in its formal aspects, but also with political despotism. However, freedom and tyranny are not mere "formal effects" of politics given that the forms of the organization of social power are always based on the structural characteristics of civil society. Furthermore, Tocqueville warns that tyranny can even be dressed up in democratic clothes. When confronted with his reasoning, the optimistic illusions of those who perceive politics in its reified isolation from the social totality, as well as the formalistic fetishism of those who contemplate only the norms and rites and disregard everything else, collapse. From this perspective, democracy—its construction and development—becomes a heroic endeavor, the most formidable of our era. It demands, as Machiavelli fore-saw, that rare amalgam of courage, strength, audacity, political skill, and civic spirit that he synthesized in the word *virtú*.

I will later discuss the rules of the virtuous political skills capable of preventing the realization of those somber tendencies that Tocqueville observed in anguish. I will start by identifying the contradictions he per-ceived in the democratic society, as well as the possible itinerary of a road from equality to despotism.

The democratic society is conceived as a completely atomized social formation, made up of free and independent individuals. It is, in brief, the civil society, as portrayed by Marx and Engels in *The German Ideology* and first theorized by Henderson, one of the intellectual giants of the Scottish enlightment.[20] This *burgerlichte Gessellschaft* arises from the remains of the decaying feudal regime in which the various forms of sociability were densely articulated through innumerable organic bonds, which made the very idea of the isolated individual unthinkable. The relatively recent appearance of individualism in the development of political theory, which can be traced no further back than Hobbes, is a clear indication of the strength of the communal bonds in precapitalist societies. Yet, with the destruction of the old community's ties, the downfall of feudalism, and the imposition of capitalist social relations, individuals were left independent and impotent. The multiplicity of links that bound individuals to feudal soci-ety—which also served the purpose of keeping that society strongly inte-grated—were dissolved in a more or less rapid fashion. However, that "lib-eration" of the individual from the controls, authorities, and prescriptions of the community ended up leaving the men and women more defenseless and unprotected than before.[21] The individual, for millennia hidden behind the Aristotelian dictum that defines man as a social animal, was suddenly placed at the center of the new economic and social scene. Renaissance humanism glorified this new social actor, the individual, in literature, painting, and sculpture. Not surprisingly, that significant epochal change was projected onto the most varied intellectual disciplines, among which political theory occupies quite a special place. Individualism asserted itself as the common sense of the new historical period that began with the dawn of capitalism, and for that very reason it became the indisputable starting point for all philosophical, economic, or political reflection: Luther, Calvin, and Hobbes cannot be understood independently of this fundamental fact.

But the consequences of this process of "individualization" made the Renaissance's optimism regarding men unwarranted. Tocqueville perceives quite clearly the unsettling long-run impact of the dissolution of the old order. Individualism cannot but promote the crudest materialism, that is, an exaggerated attachment to material goods and personal comfort. And a soci-ety in which its members are distraught by an exacerbated eagerness for pos-sessions and enjoyment of material wealth is condemned to political mediocrity. It would be difficult for society's best talents to find sufficient incentives to dedicate themselves to the public affairs, given that they would all be compulsively dedicated to ensuring the maximum possible enjoyment of material goods. Tocqueville believes that the materialism of bourgeois society conspired against the quality of its ruling class, thus revalidating an age-old concern that Plato had expressed regarding the oligarchic regimes of his times. Materialism is taken to extremes in capitalism because, according to Tocqueville, a democratic society—strongly egalitarian—is also extraordinarily mobile and insecure: nothing and nobody can guarantee the position of its members. Contrary to what occurred in the old aristocratic community, where the misfortune of the dispossessed was mitigated through the relative security offered by the organic character of feudal society, the individual in bourgeois society could lose everything without being able to rely on a social reassurance such as the one that consoled and protected the serf.[22] This explains the feverish pursuit of material well-being, the single true guarantee for equality pinpointedly recognized by Calvinism, which elevated the acquisitive passion to the category of a celestial message through which men would know whether or not they were predestined for salvation.[23]

In this way Tocqueville confirms that the political cost of materialist frenzy is onerous: conformism, apathy, and depolitization are features that characterize modern people, who are both independent and impotent. Citizens encapsule themselves in their private affairs and turn their backs on those of the community. Benjamin Constant, a fellow countryman of Tocqueville and famous political theorist as well, subtly perceives the scope of this phenomenon by comparing freedom in ancient and modern society:

> We can no longer enjoy the liberty of the ancients, which consisted in an active and constant participation in collective power. Our freedom must consist of peaceful enjoyment and private independence.... The aim of the ancients was the sharing of social power among the citizens of the same fatherland; this is what they called liberty. The aim of the moderns is the enjoyment of security in private pleasures; and they call liberty the guarantees accorded by institutions to these pleasures.[24]

One of the possible outcomes of this societal transformation—likely though not unavoidable—that so worries Tocqueville is modern despotism. He fears that the massive and irresistible tendency toward egalitarianism—which nonetheless is not enough to affect the foundations of capitalist society—brings with it a perverse counterpart having pernicious effects that must be neutralized: political and administrative centralization and bureaucratic expansion. A careful examination of Tocqueville's writings reveals that this issue is the common thread that runs through his various political analyses. It is the preoccupation that stirs in his two main works, *Democracy in America* and *The Ancien Regime and the French Revolution*. Whereas in the former the focus is placed in the United States, a country characterized by the weakness of the state vis-à-vis civil society, in the French case Tocqueville tries to examine an antithetical situation in which the state overwhelmingly imposes itself on civil society. Using the categories of Gramscian analysis, one could say that in the United States of the Jackson era, the relationship between the state and civil society was typical of what Gramsci called the "West," whereas absolutist France was a clear example of what he considered typical of Oriental societies. Tocqueville was interested in these two cases because, in this marked contrast between the United States and France, he thought he could find the answers to two questions: (1) which were the social processes that had led to freedom and despotism? and (2) why did society prevail and check the state in U.S. lands, whereas in the old France it was the state that completely overwhelmed a seemingly powerless community?

From this fruitful comparison—which young Tocqueville already had in mind when he set off to explore the roots of U.S. democracy—derives a diagnosis that foreshadows the one that would develop almost a century later another "hopeful pessimist": Max Weber. In fact, Weber would formulate an argument intended to reveal within the very rational nucleus of bourgeois society the profound and obscure tendencies that could deviate it toward a bureaucratic despotism. Nevertheless, as with Tocqueville, Weber's diagnosis—despite its greater complexity and comprehensiveness—fails to disclose the deep association between statism, bureaucratic hypertrophy, and the iron needs of capitalist accumulation. In order to do so, Weber would have had to adopt a theoretical perspective at variance with liberalism—a perspective that had as a starting point the criticism of capitalist society begun by Marx and Engels.

Tocqueville views the phenomenon of bureaucratic centralization as a process that fosters the elimination of the "intermediate powers" whose former strength and autonomy allowed them to play a mediating role that was absolutely essential to maintaining the balance of a feudal society. The aristocracy, the Church, the city, the guilds and corporations, and other privileged sectors constituted the natural counterweights of the power of the crown and retained—as Marx, Engels, Hintze, and Weber point out—the means and resources needed to ensure political domination and the administration of the community's affairs. In the countries where this social and political plurality consolidated itself, a gradually widening public space—in which the democratic practices of bourgeois societies would eventually take place—started to open: Western parliaments and cities. Yet the dissolution of feudal society, corroded by the destructive and creative force of capitalism, and the suppression of medieval particularisms led the centralized authority to progressively expropriate the old intermediate powers of their resources, prerogatives, and political and administrative functions.[25] In this way a national state was constituted, and it managed to monopolize—to varying degrees in the different countries—all political, administrative, and military functions, leaving room for the unbridled growth of an absolutist bureaucracy having ominous consequences that soon attracted Marx's attention. Tocqueville skillfully notices that beyond the dramatic changes experienced in late eighteenth-century France there was a fundamental continuity between the old regime and the postrevolutionary society: the process of growing political and administrative centralization was neither reversed nor interrupted by the 1789 revolution, but rather the old tendencies were exacerbated. Consequently, the inordinate growth of the bureaucracy was the sudden and violent achievement of six generations and not the surprising and unexpected outcome of the bourgeois revolution.[26]

How does Tocqueville explain this somber hyperbureaucratic result of the democratic revolution? He notes that the passion for equality favors political and administrative centralization. He also points to other causes, which he calls "accidental." The first such cause refers to the manner in which democracy emerges: gradually or through a revolutionary outburst. If democracy is the result of a slow process in a society that has already experienced the advantages of freedom—such as the case of the United States— political and administrative centralization, although not impossible, is a much less likely outcome. On the other hand, when societies lack any previous history of freedom and abruptly have access to equality, the outcome will almost certainly be bureaucratic centralization, as shown by the history of France and a great part of continental Europe. This bureaucratization is imposed beyond the will of the new ruling class and is due to the need to replace the disappeared intermediate powers of the old society that were swept away by the revolutionary storm.[27]

In his analysis Tocqueville mentions other causes that work in the same direction and are superposed on the manner of democracy's emergence. First, the defeated aristocracy—as with all ruling classes—prefers centralization over social disorder. When convinced that the changes brought about by the revolution are irreversible, aristocrats admit the facts and collaborate in the reconstruction of the bureaucracy required by the emerging regime. Moreover, Tocqueville notes that the wealthier the class, the greater the need for good administration of the public affairs. Second, if the masses are ignorant and uncultured there will soon arise an insurmountable gap between the intellectual capacity of the rulers and of the ruled, which tends to heighten the drive for centralization. Third, in situations of revolutionary crisis— which usually coincide with (or are the preamble of) an international conflict—the increase in military needs tends to centralize national energies and talents in the state bureaucracy to an extraordinary degree. Fourth, Tocqueville considers—erroneously, in my opinion—the most important accidental cause to be "the origins and inclinations of the ruler." Finally, the fifth accidental cause is related to the dissemination of the new form of industrial property, which requires large infrastructural functions to be developed and which can be carried out only by the state. Furthermore, to the extent that the state grows and its needs multiply, it becomes an ever larger consumer of the goods produced by industry. In this way industrialization favors bureaucratic centralization.

It is worth comparing the Marxist interpretation of bureaucratic hypertrophy with the one supplied by Tocqueville. Regarding France, Marx says,

> This executive power with its enormous bureaucratic and military organization, with its artificial state machinery embracing wide strata, with a host of officials numbering half a million, besides an army of another half million, this appalling parasitic growth, which enmeshes the body of French society like a net and chokes all its pores, sprang up in the days of the absolute monarchy. . . . The first French Revolution . . . was bound to develop what the absolute monarchy had begun—centralization, but at the same time the extent, the attributes and the agents of governmental authority. Napoleon perfected this state machinery. The Legitimist monarchy and the July monarchy added nothing but a greater division of labour. . . . The parliamentary republic, finally, in its struggle against the revolution, found itself compelled to strengthen, along with the repressive measures, the resources and centralization of governmental power. All the revolutions perfected this machine instead of smashing it. The parties that contended in turn for domination regarded the possession of this huge state edifice as the principal spoils of the victor.[28]

Continental Europe and the United States symbolized a historical contrast rich in interpretative suggestions for Marx. The absence of a feudal past and of the burdensome legacy of an absolutist state allowed the United States to elude the bureaucratic gigantism that crushed France. In European lands, on the other hand, bureaucratic concentration was the response to the particularism and the political fragmentation that were characteristic since medieval times. It was also the consequence of the weakness of the class alliance that, in the prolonged transition from feudalism to capitalism, controlled state life but was unable to overcome the prevailing antagonism within the heart of the state's own ruling classes. This hegemonic vacuum encouraged the unbridled expansion of a Caesarist bureaucracy, which began to develop a strategic political role when it found itself endowed with sufficient powers to assist in the arduous process of constructing a bourgeois hegemony. Marx also reveals that the concentration and centralization of capital that were slowly taking place in the market had to have repercussions in the state. Lenin describes the consequences of such repercussions in his analysis of the state in the imperialist stage.

In short, Marx posits that revolutions have so far done no more than perfect the state machinery. Obeying a sociological law, the state concentrates in its bureaucratic apparatus the fragmented power held by the classes, corporations, and institutions of the old regime, thereby creating the conditions required for the expanded reproduction of capitalist accumulation. In this way Marx highlights the connection between the rise of the bourgeoisie and the quantitative and qualitative expansion of the state, which would later be the object of many works inspired by the Bonapartist phenomenon. However, regarding these works it is interesting to observe how Max Weber, when speaking on the reasons bureaucracy is a virtually indestructible social organization, poses an argument that complements Marxist theses and should not be overlooked:

> When those subject to bureaucratic control seek to escape the influence of the existing bureaucratic apparatus, this is normally possible only by creating an organization of their own which is equally subject to the process of bureaucratization. Similarly, the existing bureaucratic apparatus is driven to continue functioning by the most powerful interests. . . . Without it, a society like our own . . . could no longer function.[29]

Thus, there are two powerful reasons to explain the paramount role of bureaucracy in modern societies. The implications of this phenomenon for the future of democracies can now be discussed.

The Leviathan and the Enslaved Individual

According to Tocqueville, political and administrative centralization, the unrestrained growth of state bureaucracy, and the consolidation of a new type of articulation between the state and civil society—in which the former establishes its supremacy over the latter—count among the most malignant threats to the future of democracies. Majority tyranny, that specter that has terrified liberal thought since its origins, is relegated to secondary importance in relation to a much more formidable threat: the suffocation of freedom in the hands of a new form of despotism.

With respect to this issue, the significant changes in Tocqueville's thought between 1835 and 1840 (the period between the publication of the first and second volumes of *Democracy in America*) should be highlighted. In the first part of his work, the threat to freedom comes from the disorders and distabilizing impacts caused by a mobilized and tumultuous civil society that needs to be controlled through efficient socializing and mediating agencies. This notion influences his appraisal of the role played by local governments, religious morality, and a compact network of voluntary associations, among others. Tocqueville's fears are the same that besieged mainstream liberal theorists: the unruliness of the masses and the tyranny of the majority. However, the image of the citizen and of civil society shown in Tocqueville's second volume is completely different: the danger of democracy is no longer attributed to the overflowing mobilization of civil society, because citizens no longer act or think. Majority tyranny is impossible, Tocqueville asserts, because the citizenry has been degraded to the extreme of an inert mass, and its most prominent characteristic is its generalized apathy. In this way there is a re-creation of the apocalyptic image, which recalls Hobbes's gloomy thoughts. However, Tocqueville's portrait is even more desolate because in the Hobbesian representation of the natural state, passion and interests were prevalent. To Hobbes, society was pushed over the edge of the abyss because it was alive and there was a struggle; politics was, in Weber's words, the "war of counterposed Gods." On the contrary, in Tocqueville's view, society appears as an elemental and inactive conglomeration; it lacks any projects or will and consequently is an unlikely depository of libertarian aspirations.[30]

How did this radical degradation of civil society occur? A basic explanation offered by Tocqueville can be summarized as follows: the disappearance (or gradual decadence) of the old classes, estatements, and institutions that mediated relations between individuals and the state left the former in an isolated and powerless situation that was not compensated for by their newly attained juridical and economic independence. Coincident with the disintegration of the old aristocratic society, there was a consolidation of dispersed powers in a single bureaucratic organization: the modern state. Consequently, the state's strengthening is just one aspect of the full imposition of capitalism; the other side is the pulverization and atomization of civil society.

However, to further explore Tocqueville's diagnosis, one should of course examine the phenomena of individualism and materialism characteristic of modern times. According to Tocqueville, they are where the seeds of modern despotism are sown. Why?

> I think democratic peoples have a natural taste for liberty; left to themselves, they will seek it, cherish it, and be sad if it is taken from them. But their passion for equality is ardent, insatiable, eternal, and invincible. They want equality in freedom, and if they cannot have that, they still want equality in slavery. They will put up with poverty, servitude, and barbarism, but they will not endure aristocracy. . . . This is true at all times, but especially in our own. All men and all powers who try to stand up against this irresistible passion will be overthrown and destroyed by it. In our day freedom cannot be established without it, and despotism itself cannot reign without its support.[31]

In other words, in the democratic age, individuals are moved by two passions. Yet one is stronger and more fervid than the other, and that is why most of them are willing to sacrifice political democracy in exchange for social democracy, that is, freedom for equality, be it real or illusory. The revolt against privilege makes any form of inequality intolerable, and the joint pressures of individualism and materialism push atomized citizens to resort to the state in order to fulfill their increased demands. Thus, the state appears as the agent par excellence of social leveling, and the very complexity and fragmentation of civil society fuel the state's tendency toward centralization. In the retreat toward their private affairs, citizens disown politics and distrust the state. Nevertheless, everyone believes that their private interests constitute something exceptional and therefore deserving of the government's preferential attention. The result of the inexhaustible demands and exasperated pluralism of bourgeois society is the expansion and consolidation of state power. This is why Tocqueville arrives at a disheartening conclusion: "In this way the simple fact of its continuing existence increases the attributes of power of a democratic government. Time works on its side, and every accident is to its profit; the passions of individuals, in spite of themselves, promote it; and one can say that the older a democratic society, the more centralized will its government be."[32]

In the final pages of his work Tocqueville no longer speaks of one revolution but of two. In open contrast with his 1835 introduction, he assigns state bureaucratization the same rank as the advent of egalitarian society. This new phenomenon not only has a strong authoritarian potential, but also represents in itself the triumph of the state over civil society, of governmental bureaucracy over social forces, and of authority over community's self-government.

Tocqueville's previsions, which inevitably emphasize the state's most negative overtones, anticipate the criticism of the welfare state that liberal theorists like von Hayek and Friedman would develop more than a century later. Two roads start from equality, Tocqueville asserts: one that leads to independence but in a crisis could end in anarchy; the other, "by a more roundabout and secret but also more certain road, leads them to servitude."[33]

The servitude Tocqueville refers to is completely unlike any other that has previously existed and is of a type that "such old words as 'despotism' and 'tyranny' do not fit."[34] Accordingly, Tocqueville notes that it would not be an updated version of the old despotism, with its tyranny over the bodies—jailed, tortured, executed—and its suffocation of society, making the need to limit the power of the sovereign the rallying call in struggles for freedom. The new despotic form is aimed not at bodies but at souls; "it would be more widespread and milder; it would degrade men rather than torment them."[35] How could this be possible? Tocqueville gives some clues when he examines, in the first part of his book, the dangers posed by an eventual majority tyranny in the United States:

> Formerly tyranny used the clumsy weapons of chains and hangmen; nowadays even despotism, though it seemed to have nothing more to learn, has been perfected by civilization. . . . Princes made violence a physical thing, but our contemporary democratic republics have turned it into something as intellectual as the human will it is intended to constrain. Under the absolute government of a single man, despotism, to reach the soul, clumsily struck at the body, and the soul, escaping from such blows, rose gloriously above it; but in democratic republics that is not at all how tyranny behaves; it leaves the body alone and goes straight for the soul.[36]

Four things guarantee the efficacy of modern despotism, which does away with the body and concerns itself only with the soul: materialism, conformism, depolitization, and apathy. These fatal by-products of modern bourgeois society ensure that immense spiritual power of contemporary despotism. In a passage that strikingly prefigures Foucault's vision of the subtle labyrinths that communicate physical punishment with political power, Tocqueville asserts that on these helpless and inert social atoms

> stands an immense, protective power which is alone responsible for securing their enjoyment and watching over their fate. That power is absolute, thoughtful of detail, orderly, provident, and gentle. It would resemble parental authority if, fatherlike, it tried to prepare its charges for a man's life, but on the contrary it only tries to keep them in perpetual childhood. . . . It gladly works for their happiness but wants to be sole agent and judge of it. It provides for their security, foresees and supplies their necessities, facilitates their pleasures, manages their principal concerns, directs their industry, makes rules for their testaments, and divides their inheritances. Why should it not entirely relieve them from the trouble of thinking and all the cares of living?[37]

The conclusion Tocqueville reaches anticipates more than a century in advance the vision of the totalitarian state that George Orwell emphatically portrays in his *1984:*

> Having thus taken each citizen in turn in its powerful grasp and shaped him to its will, government then extends its embrace to include the whole of society. It covers the whole of social life with a network of petty, complicated rules that are both minute and uniform, through which even men of the greatest originality and the most vigorous temperament cannot force their heads above the crowd. . . . It does not break men's will, but softens, bends, and guides it; it seldom enjoins, but often inhibits, action; it does not destroy anything, but prevents much being born; it is not at all tyrannical, but it hinders, restrains, enervates, stifles, and stultifies so much that in the end each nation is no more than a flock of timid and hardworking animals with the government as its shepherd.[38]

Tocqueville Today

After this brief examination of some of Tocqueville's central ideas, it is evident that the great issues of late nineteenth-century philosophical and political debate were anticipated in his work. Consequently, a review of his contributions can enrich this chapter's discussions of the contemporary state and the uncertain prospects of democracy. It would be presumptuous to expect the remaining pages of this chapter to delve into the rough and pathless recesses of a debate with tremendous reaches and ramifications. Nevertheless, the goal here is more modest: to point out some illuminating contributions that a careful reading of Tocqueville's ideas could offer for examining some crucial themes of our time.

One issue has to do with Tocqueville's argument that capitalist society "naturally" creates the conditions required for the appearance of statism. This is of utmost importance because the liberal tradition has always asserted—as Milton Friedman and the liberal economists still argue in our days—the existence of a radical incompatibility between the primacy of the individual, which is a true dogma of the liberal tradition, and the hypertrophy of the bourgeois state, viewed as a pathology foreign to the spirit and practice of capitalism and in conflict with the free play of the market forces. Tocqueville's indisputable merit stems from having questioned the validity of this reasoning: his loyalty to the liberal tradition did not prevent him from recognizing that the structure and contradictions of bourgeois society inevitably led to the creation of a burdensome and oppressive state bureaucracy. Nonetheless, this substantiation was not duly acknowledged by liberal thought after Tocqueville (except in the case of Weber). Proof of this omission is that the most insightful minds of contemporary liberalism—von Hayek, von Mises, or, with reservations, Friedman himself—insist on ignoring the genuine and profoundly capitalist roots of the bourgeois leviathan.

It is ironic that precisely within the heart of Marxist tradition are Tocqueville's poignant observations taken up and redeveloped, at least in part. Tocqueville's observation converges with that Copernican revolution in the social sciences that is synthesized in Marx's work and that allows one to understand statism as the final product of a long causal chain originating with the harsh needs of capitalist accumulation and reproduction. These needs are not transmitted mechanically but rather are expressed and mediated in a complex dialectical sequence of causations influenced by a wide range of powerful social, political, ideological, cultural, and economic factors. Tocqueville helps us to better perceive some of these mediations and thus to understand more fully the complexity of the links between bourgeois society and the capitalist state. Many other links and relations remain hidden, eclipsed by the liberal theoretical perspective and its age-old disdain for structural questions. It is in the totalizing and dialectical perspective of Marxism—that famous "viewpoint of totality" that Lukács speaks of—that the elements for a more comprehensive explanation of the deformation of the state that oppresses modern society can be found.

It also seems that Tocqueville's anticipation of the dynamics of the welfare state detects with extraordinary keenness some of the problems that would dramatically appear more than a century later. As a matter of fact, Tocqueville predicts with amazing accuracy certain features and political patterns characteristic of the mature phase of the Keynesian capitalist restructuring, especially in the United States. The tendencies toward civic apathy, conformism, quietism, and depolitization that—with the exception of the outbursts of political and social participation in the 1960s—have been the prevailing features of U.S. politics since the end of World War II. They constitute unequivocal symptoms of the reflux of class struggle and of the integration of the working class into the capitalist state. The consequences of these symptoms—which to a greater or lesser degree affect all modern societies, be they central or peripheral—are apparent in the degradation of politics to the condition of a mass spectacle mediated by television. This degradation becomes evident when one observes the decay of public institutions, the deterioration of the content and form of political struggles, and the alarming mediocrity of leadership circles.[39]

It is evident that Tocqueville could not grasp the reasons the bourgeoisie needs an increasingly interventionist state in order to carry on capitalist accumulation. For this he would have needed a general theory on the capitalist mode of production, which was unavailable at the time he was writing. Nonetheless, he was able to predict the debasement of politics in bourgeois society as a consequence of the unquestioned primacy of that "sordid materialism" of civil society that Marx speaks of. The history of this decadence is amply illustrated by the dismaying abyss that separates a Disraeli or a Gladstone from Thatcher; or Jefferson, Madison, and Lincoln from Nixon, Ford, and Reagan; or by the radical differences between the New England town meetings and contemporary electoral struggles inspired by market sales strategies. Having said this, I should add that Tocqueville's analyses are at fault for their bias when they consider unbridled individualism—as opposed to the sobriety of the aristocracy?—as the cause of the ills of modern society. Tocqueville fails to realize that these ills have much deeper roots and that they originate in the same structural matrix of capitalism, in its inherent alienation and fetishism.

If the bourgeoisie cannot survive without the aid of the overgrown state—as shown by the actual functioning of mature capitalism, despite its ultraliberal prophets—neither is the working class inclined to reverse the social advances conquered in its secular struggle against the bourgeoisie, which are today crystallized in the welfare state. At least partly, the welfare state is also a product of the struggle of the subordinate classes, and to understand the Keynesian state as the work of the conservative designs of an omniscient bourgeoisie is an unforgivable mistake. How, then, can the debasing effects of state hypertrophy, predicted by Tocqueville and ratified a century later by Gramsci, be avoided? In fact, Gramsci pays much attention to the significance of Taylorism and its political and statist correlates. Gramsci's notion of the "trained gorilla" as the prototype of the new worker and his contention that Americanism has been "the biggest collective effort to date to create, with unprecedented speed, and with a consciousness of purpose unmatched in history, a new type of worker and of man" also point in that direction.[40] It is unquestionable that the expansion of the welfare state has not only modified the modality and intensity of capitalist exploitation but also altered the forms of workers' consciousness and of class struggle.

Another subject on which Tocqueville's observations seem enriching regards the double character of democracy: social substance and political form. This dialectical unity of substance and form has received full recognition only within Marxism. It was young Marx who, from his criticism of Hegel and of the alienated and "inverted" character of politics and the bourgeois state, laid the basis for an integral theory of democracy, starting with the concrete man, that is, with the individual situated in a historically determined mode of production. This reasoning, as is well known, has consistently been rejected by liberal theorists, who have debased the very notion of democracy by making it equivalent to a mere method for the constitution of public authority. Tocqueville's sociologism prevents him from falling completely into the formalistic trap and conceptualizing democracy as a mere procedural formula. Notwithstanding, the substance on which he bases his reasoning is not strong enough to sustain it. In fact, he exaggerates the actual degree of equality that existed in the United States. Furthermore, in his eagerness to prove the reaches of the process of atomization that prevailed in bourgeois society, he glimpses the possibility of a spontaneous disappearance of social classes. It is a fact that U.S. capitalism did not do away with its classes, nor did universal suffrage transfer power to a political coalition that would effect a radical redistribution of wealth or promote growing levels of social equality. The histories of U.S. capitalism and other social formations show the objective limitations against which egalitarianism has stumbled as an ideology, as well as the expectation of a continuous upward social mobility that many hoped would imperceptibly transform class society into a community of equals. The "egalitarian revolution," which according to Tocqueville had been advancing since the eleventh century and would sweep away anything that came across it, stopped with unequivocal signs of respect and veneration at the doors of bourgeois property. Its past accomplishments are undeniable. However, it is no less true that Tocqueville projects its advance mechanically and underestimates the objective obstacles that would redefine the egalitarian flood and deviate it when it confronted the much more solid fabric of capitalist society.

Nonetheless, this mistake should not make one lose sight of the fact that social democracy and political democracy are inseparable. The latter cannot be sustained without reaching a minimum threshold—which is historically variable, of course—of the former. Tocqueville's perplexity in the face of the sociological fragility of democracies and the advance of bureaucratization is largely explained by the fact that in his theoretical model there are few elements to decipher the enigma posed by social revolutions. More important, it is explained by the fact that his discourse fails to understand that the full realization of freedom—that is, of political democracy—is possible only in a social formation in which the social relations of exploitation among individuals have been abolished. Tocqueville does not go that far. Marx's rare insightfulness allows one to pass through, unscathed, those labyrinths of appearances that have trapped so many others. Marx's criticism of capitalist exploitation, fetishism, and alienation allows for the conception of a democratic project—some would say a utopia, but it does not matter: history is also moved by utopias—that is liberating and rehumanizing in all aspects of social life. Social democracy and political democracy, social revolution and political revolution, and social emancipation and political emancipation are dichotomies that recover their true unity only within Marxist tradition. Liberalism's insistence on maintaining these dichotomies is as spurious as it is self-destructive.

This means that a socialist theory of democracy must integrate these polarities. And in order to do so it must overcome old obsessions that, because of a defensive ideological stance, led it to correctly identify the main vices of bourgeois democracy in its formality and lack of content while still giving in—intentionally or not—to a suicidal attitude of disdain for the so-called formal freedoms and merely political superstructural safeguards that were the main theme within the liberal tradition. Rosa Luxemburg warned against the tragic consequences of this attitude, as can be seen in Chapter 7.

Some aspects of Tocqueville's thought are surprisingly similar to Max Weber's. The long-term historical perspectives are the same, and their conclusions—pessimistic, without a doubt—are also quite alike. Despite the restrictions imposed by liberal thought on their theoretical perspectives, they are both able to rid themselves of the evolutionist optimism so characteristic of that strand of thought. The result is a special sensitivity for understanding history's contradictions: Tocqueville holds that egalitarianism could lead either to freedom or to modern despotism; whereas secularism and rationalization, according to Weber, could make people freer or imprison them in an iron cage. Therefore, history is dialectic, and its tragedy lies in that it can advance either through its "wrong side" or through its "right side." Freedom liberates and enchains; individualism emancipates and alienates; democracy destroys aristocracies and can create a leviathan; rationalization illuminates the mind but weakens the will. Tocqueville sees in democracy, as Weber does in socialism, the origins of despotism. Nevertheless, neither of them want—and this is important to highlight—a return to the past.

To what extent is this sober and responsible attitude shared by the neoconservative theorists who examine the "crisis of democracy" and recommend that we moderate our democratic "excesses"? Although it is difficult to ascertain, it seems reasonable to hypothesize that these theorists dream about a restorative project of capitalist "order and discipline" that is incompatible with the current levels of political mobilization and organization of the subordinate classes. In this way, in the "realist" neoconservative discourse, democracy is emptied of all of its contents and reduced to its formal aspects, which do not exhaust the whole meaning of democracy. Once this process is consummated, democracy becomes a mere legitimizing formula of state despotism to which bourgeois hegemony seems to be ever more addicted. The decadence of the institutions of representative democracy and of the fragile agreed-upon mechanisms of direct political participation leads to the reinforcement of bureaucratic centralism and of the state spheres and institutions in which the dominant classes impose themselves, ignoring the transparency and publicity demanded by democracy. It is the paradise of lobbies, pressure groups, and representatives of big capital, intimately articulated to the political class that in capital's name—and for capital's benefit—manages the crisis and "administers" democracy. The other side of this process is the decadence of parliaments, the demobilization of political parties and unions, the manipulation of public opinion, and the immobility and apathy of the citizenry—that is, the death of civil society.

A bad joke is what history played on Tocqueville: from a model to find a remedy for the maladies of French anarchy, the United States seems to have become the prototype of authoritarian involution in mature capitalism. Here too, history marched on the "wrong side" despite the wealth and vitality that the political institutions of Jackson's United States possessed to neutralize the threat of bureaucratic despotism. Political parties, local governments, division of powers, public freedoms, and the whole set of social and juridical safeguards were swallowed up and transformed by the advances made by the concentration and centralization of capital. But U.S. monopoly capitalism did not do away with those respectable political institutions inherited from the heroic colonial times: it simply transformed and converted them to best serve the logic of its own enlarged and ceaseless reproduction. When transforming the whole of civil society in its own image, it could not respect the institutions of political democracy. The society of equals contemplated by Tocqueville was reduced to a demobilizing illusion, the always more distant "American dream." Universal suffrage became an indifferent grimace made with resignation by less than half of the population every two years. And of local powers it is better not to speak. A century and a half after Tocqueville's visit, the United States has once more become a model. Yet now, if one is to believe neoconservatives, it is a model of the crisis of democracy, the ingovernability of civil society, and the imperative need to trim the democratic achievements and hopes of past generations and to impose a political order that disregards mass legitimacy.

Tocqueville's formula has fallen out of favor with ideologues of capitalism because it is fundamentally similar to the one proposed by Weber to escape the iron laws of bureacratization: a full recovering of politics, the reactivation of the citizenry, and the reanimation of public life. In this proposal Tocqueville expressed his trust in civil society: its vitality—to be sure, related to Machiavelli's *virtú*—would allow it to overcome the obstacles and traps that led it to bureaucratic despotism. Holding fast to this hope, he believed that democracy was still possible. "Only history decides," Weber would say later. For the theorists of the crisis of democracy, however, the issue is about something else: given the crossroads at which capitalist societies find themselves, the neoconservative diagnoses and recommendations are ostensibly antidemocratic because they welcome the paralyzation of the movements and impulses born in civil society as well as the freezing of the expressions of class struggle that constitute the very essence of democracy.

In order to save capitalism, these theorists are ready to sacrifice democracy. Neoconservatives consecrate as virtuous the degradation of politics and the overwhelming of classes and groups of civil society by a bureaucratized state—which enslaves souls without tormenting bodies, as Tocqueville said—subtly but firmly ensuring the stability of bourgeois domination. Instead of deepening political democracy, the neoconservative formula intends to mutilate it because, in the long term, monopoly capitalism creates a profoundly divided society, a true classist apartheid that is structurally incompatible with democracy. A civil society of that type, asleep and drugged with the opium of the misnamed "mass culture" and mass media, and a trimmed and a manacled political democracy constitute the desiderata of this new group of bourgeois ideologues. The history of the democratic restoration in Latin America in the 1980s is a good example of this deplorable neoconservative deviation: the endless succession of structural adjustments demanded by the implementation of orthodox monetarist programs have broken down the expectations of justice that large sectors of Latin American societies had deposited in democratic restoration. The de facto predominance of the interests of the dominant classes—defeated in the electoral arena yet retaining the upper hand of the state apparatus, where key societal decisions are made—produced an unfortunate emptying of the democratic formula. It is my belief that the ominous repercussions of that predominance will be felt before long.

Notes

1. Botana, Natalio, *La tradición republicana* (Buenos Aires: Sudamericana, 1984), pp. 11 and 270. See also Morse, Richard, *El espejo de Próspero* (Mexico: Siglo XXI Editores, 1982), pp. 97–111; Romero, José Luis, *A History of Argentine Political Thought* (Stanford: Stanford University Press, 1963), Ch. 5; and Germani, Gino, *Política y sociedad en una epoca de transición* (Buenos Aires: Paidós, 1962), Chs. 7–9.

2. For more information on Tocqueville's social and political background, as well as on his political career, see Lively, Jack, *The Social and Political Thought of Alexis de Tocqueville* (Oxford: Clarendon Press, 1962); Mayer, J. P., *Prophet of a Mass Age* (London: n.p., 1939); Pierson, G. W., *Tocqueville and Beaumont in America* (New York: n.p., 1938); Brogan, Hugh, *Tocqueville* (London: Collins/Fontana, 1973); Jardin, André, *Alexis de Tocqueville, 1805–1859* (Mexico: Fondo de Cultura Económica, 1990).

3. Tocqueville, Alexis de, *Democracy in America* (Garden City, NY: Doubleday & Co., 1969), pp. 18–19.

4. Marx, Karl, *Capital* (New York: International Publishers, 1967), Vol. 1, p. 8.

5. Laski, Harold, *The American Democracy* (London: Allen and Unwin, 1949), pp. 16–17 and 722.

6. On this subject see Lively, *The Social and Political Thought,* p. 8.

7. For a broader discussion of this issue, see Chapter 1 of this book.

8. Lively, *The Social and Political Thought,* p. 49; Aron, Raymond, *Ensayos sobre las libertades* (Madrid: Alianza, 1966), p. 22; Drescher, Seymour, *Dilemmas of Democracy: Tocqueville and Modernization* (Pittsburgh: University of Pittsburgh Press, 1968), p. 20.

9. Tocqueville, Alexis de, *Democracy,* pp. 9, 11, and 12.

10. Ibid., p. 12.

11. Ibid., p. 14.

12. Ibid., p. 12.

13. Ibid., p. 695.

14. Zetterbaum, Marvin, "Alexis de Tocqueville," in Strauss, Leo, and Joseph Cropsey, *History of Political Philosophy* (Chicago: The University of Chicago Press, 1972), pp. 715–718.

15. On this subject see Horwitz, Morton J., "Tocqueville and the Tyranny of the Majority," in *The Review of Politics* vol. 28, no. 4 (July 1966), pp. 296–298.

16. In this regard see Chapter 2 for a full development of the argument.

17. In addition to Friedman's classic theses see also von Hayek, Friedrich, *The Constitution of Liberty* (Chicago: University of Chicago Press, 1960) and his *The Road to Serfdom* (Chicago: The University of Chicago Press, 1944).

18. See Pipitone Allione, Ugo, *Desarrollo contra equilibrio* (Mexico: UNAM, 1978).

19. On this issue see Thomas Molnar's book entitled *El modelo desfigurado* (Mexico: Fondo de Cultura Económica, 1980).

20. Ferguson, Adam, "An essay on the history of civil society" (Edinburgh: Edinburgh University Press, 1966) (originally published in 1767).

21. This subject was studied by a few conservative scholars interested in the analysis of mass societies and totalitarianism. See, among others, Kornhauser, William, *The Politics of Mass-Society* (London: Routledge & Kegan Paul, 1960), and Nisbet, Robert A., *The Quest of Community* (New York: Oxford University Press, 1953) and also his *Twilight of Authority* (New York: Oxford University Press, 1975).

22. Further elaboration on this topic can be found in Bendix, Reinhard, *Nation-Building and Citizenship: Studies of Our Changing Social Order* (John Wiley & Sons, New York, 1964), pp. 33–54.

23. The standard literature on this subject matter includes the classic books by Max Weber, Werner Sombart, R. H. Tawney, and E. Troeltsch.

24. Constant, Benjamin, "The liberty of the ancients compared with that of the moderns," *Political Writings* (Cambridge: Cambridge University Press, 1988), pp. 316–317.

25. Cf. Anderson, Perry, *Lineages of the Absolutist State* (Londres: New Left Books, 1974), pp. 15–59 and 85–112.

26. Lively, *The Social and Political Thought,* p. 154.

27. Incidentally, to what extent did aristocratic France really enjoy the benefits of freedom? It seems that Tocqueville's vision on this issue is an extremely idealized reconstruction of much more unpleasant social realities. Cf. *Democracy,* pp. 616–689.

28. Marx, Karl, *The Eighteenth Brumaire of Louis Bonaparte,* in Marx, Karl,

and Friedrich Engels, *The Marx-Engels Reader* (edited by Robert C. Tucker) (New York: Norton & Co., 1972), p. 514.

29. Weber, Max, *The Theory of Social and Economic Organization* (edited by Talcott Parsons) (New York: The Free Press, 1964), p. 338.

30. Cf. Drescher, S., "Tocqueville's Two Democracies," *Journal of the History of the Ideas* 2 (1964), pp. 201–205, and in his *Dilemmas,* p. 42.

31. Tocqueville, *Democracy,* p. 506.

32. Ibid., p. 672.

33. Ibid., p. 667.

34. Ibid., p. 691.

35. Ibid., p. 691.

36. Ibid., p. 255.

37. Ibid., p. 692.

38. Ibid., p. 692.

39. The decay of political life in advanced societies has been noticed by a host of scholars. See Chapter 8 for a brief discussion on this issue. One aspect of this regrettable involution is examined in Edelman, Murray, *Constructing the Political Spectacle* (Chicago: University of Chicago Press, 1988).

40. Cf. Gramsci, Antonio, "Americanismo and Fordism," in *Selections from the Prison Notebooks* (New York: International Publishers, 1971), p. 302.

4

"Stadolatry" and the "State-Centered" Approach: The Relative Autonomy of the Capitalist State

The concept of the state has become one of the very few in contemporary social sciences that is able to foster a rich theoretical and methodological debate, not to mention the inflamed political controversy raised by its practical existence. This level of debate is surprising because, for some time before this impressive comeback, the concept of the state was excommunicated from academia, its theoretical value condemned as a result of its allegedly inherent vagueness and formalistic bias as well as its equally reproved heuristic worth. It was in 1953, the period of miraculous capitalist recovery after the war and of the institutionalization of the class struggle, when David Easton eloquently voiced the prevailing consensus among the social scientists, saying that "neither the state nor power is a concept that serves to bring together political research."[1] However, in less than three decades the movement of history made him an astonished witness of the resurrection of the concept, "now risen from the grave to haunt us once again."[2]

The perfunctory dismissal of a concept that had played a crucial role in the development of Western political thought thus received a practical rebuttal. The theoretical funerals of the state proved to be premature, and the pompous burial rites given by the mainstream political scientists now appear like the magic ceremonies of rather primitive peoples, anxious to control the riddles posed by the real world with the efficacy of cabalistic formulae.

However, because reality exists independently of our intellectual abilities to create adequate concepts to understand it, it is hardly a surprise to learn that "the state has now laid siege to the political system."[3] The reasons for this conceptual revival, which marks a significant change in the intellectual climate of Western social sciences, are multiple. Easton specifies four causes as the most important ones: the cyclical revival of Marxism in the United States; the conservative longing for strong traditional authority; economic liberalism's need to find an easy source of blame for the fiscal chaos of the early 1970s; and the recent trends in policy analysis research.[4] To these should be added three other causes (though their exploration is beyond the scope of this chapter): the undeniable "statification" of capitalist accumulation and of everyday life in bourgeois societies; the enduring and pervasive character of political crisis in contemporary states; and the intellectual poverty of conventional Western political science.

J. P. Nettl was the first to express a solitary criticism, and sensible methodological advice, against the prevailing orthodoxy of the 1950s and 1960s. In the opening statement of his famous article, "The State as a Conceptual Variable," he writes, "The concept of state is not much in vogue in the social sciences right now. Yet it retains a skeletal, ghostly existence largely because, for all the changes in emphasis and interest of research, the thing exists and no amount of conceptual restructuring can dissolve it."[5]

Not only did the state exist, but all the empirical indicators consistently revealed that state intervention in a variety of areas experienced a dramatic increase after World War II. This process has been so widespread and profound that, in recent years, it has begun to cast serious doubts about the future of democracy in a world system increasingly dominated by almost omnipotent and tendentially authoritarian national states.

How can we account for this paradoxical fact? On the one hand, the unprecedented increase in the practical importance of the state in capitalist societies and, on the other hand, the disappearance of the theoretical concept of the state from the conventional lexicon of the social sciences. It is essential to examine the dialectical relationship between historical praxis and theoretical production in order to understand the conformation and crisis of the successive hegemonic paradigms in the social sciences. This is one reason Nettl rightly establishes the links between different theoretical models of politics and the nature of the state structures in the countries in which these conceptual developments took place. However, these theoretical models are also partly explained by the differences in the processes of national unification and capitalist development, not only by the formation of the state structures. In continental Europe, for instance, political unification and the development of commerce and industry were primarily achieved under the direction of an active national state that protected the bourgeoisie from the internal enemies—the proletariat and recalcitrant feudal lords—and from the external contenders, the other bourgeoisies that were fighting to secure a safe place in the international market. The cases of Italy and Germany, despite their differences, are clear examples of this pattern. On the other hand, the Anglo-Saxon experience was quite different: there, the bourgeoisie assumed a leading role and the state then appeared just as a *veilleur de nuit*.

Thus, in some countries of continental Europe the relative delay in the development of capitalism, the harsh and prolonged processes of political unification and state formation, and the discontinuities and frequent crises in the democratization of the political institutions gave the state a leading political and economic role; the result was Hegel and stadolatry, the exaltation of the state as the sphere of the rational and universal. In England and the United States, on the other hand, the completion of the bourgeois revolution left to the state a much less important place in these social formations, and consequently, its visibility and relevance as a social institution were pretty low; the result was Adam Smith and the myth of the invisible hand.[6]

The Theoretical Withering Away of the State

As a result, the historical tradition of Anglo-Saxon social and political thought tended to neglect or at least considerably underestimate the role of the state in society: thus, the state as a social institution "withered away" as a relevant issue in the social and political theories elaborated in those societies, and the "stateless" bias was unfortunately left as a bequest to the modern social sciences. But that bias does not mean that the state as an institution is completely ignored. What accounts for the comparative neglect of the state as a focus of political analysis is the fact that the Anglo-Saxon liberal tradition, as well as the social sciences that evolved within that intellectual universe, as Miliband rightly observes, "takes as resolved some of the largest questions which have traditionally been asked about the state, and makes unnecessary, indeed almost precludes, any special concern with its nature and role in Western-type societies."[7]

Miliband summarizes very well those questions that are taken as resolved:

> A theory of the state is also a theory of society and of the distribution of power in that society. But most Western "students of politics" tend to start, judging from their work, with the assumption that power, in Western societies, is competitive, fragmented and diffused: everybody, directly or through organized groups, has some power and nobody has or can have too much of it. In these societies, citizens enjoy universal suffrage, free and regular elections, representative institutions, effective citizenship rights . . . and both individuals and groups take ample advantage of these rights, under the protection of the law, an independent judiciary and a free political culture.[8]

One of the consequences of the conscious or unconscious adoption of such assumptions concerning the distribution of power in Western societies is to exclude ex ante the mere possibility that the state might be a rather special institution for which the main—but not only—purpose is to uphold the preeminence in society of a particular type of social relations of production and of a corresponding "pact of domination." Once the theoretical assumption is accepted, the intellectual debate is over. The state is downgraded to the level of a neutral and impassable marketplace, to the mere political reflection of the economic market, with its typical impersonal, competitive, and free exchanges. The state thus becomes simply an arena in which political parties and other collective actors compete according to a given set of rules of the game, sanctioned and guaranteed by the state itself. Both the fact of the public competition of a plurality of social groups and the nature of the rules of the game guarantee that nobody will accumulate too much power, thus preserving the general equilibrium of the system. There are elites, of course, but they lack the required consciousness and cohesion to transform themselves into a ruling class. The state, above and beyond the ceaseless struggle of interests, remains aloof and unbiased, preventing the concentration of power and helping to accommodate and reconcile conflicting aspirations; the state becomes the impartial arbiter of social competition, "the mirror which society holds up to itself."[9]

Therefore, this approach solves the problem of the state by assuming its class neutrality and that power is distributed throughout the society and not concentrated in any privileged group. However, Miliband's classic study of the state in advanced capitalist societies adds more evidence in favor of those who maintain that "the pluralist-democratic view of society, of politics and of the state in regard to the countries of advanced capitalism, *is in all essentials wrong*—that this view, far from providing a guide to reality, constitutes a profound obfuscation of it."[10]

This interpretation of the state as the "mirror of society," as the expression of the consensual social order, representative of the totality of the nation, and as the neutral market in which the citizens—individually or in groups—exchange political power is intimately associated with the liberal tradition and in its earlier formulation had been radically criticized by the young Marx, who argued that the state is the mediated expression of political domination in class-divided societies. Consequently, the state can be anything but neutral with respect to the class struggle; like the market, the state is where formally equal subjects but substantially unequal individuals establish asymmetrical political relations. This inequality is rooted in the differential positions and functions in the productive process, which allow the dominant classes to express their economic predominance, always through a diversity of means and in a rather mediated form, as political direction and authority.

But Marxist theory has not been immune to ideological deformations, to the extreme that in its instrumentalist versions the state and all that is commonly included in the "superstructure" are reduced to the condition of a simple instrument in the hands of the dominant class. Thus, a vulgar economicism replaced the analytical wealth of Marxist theory, the net result of which is convergent with the implications of the pluralist-democratic interpretation: the state and the political order lose their specificity and relative autonomy from the civil society. The mirror now projects another distorted picture: that of the state as the immediate and mechanical reflection of a monolithic dominant class.

The Relationship Between State and Civil Society

Among the consequences derived from these unhappy coincidences are the impossibility of theoretically considering the relations between state and civil society and, even more significant, the problem of the relative autonomy of the state. In mainstream political science the links between state and society have been dissolved, creating instead the fiction of the independent and isolated citizen who joins different, and hopefully cross-cutting, interest groups that play politics in a neutral market-like site called the political arena. Political power is supposed to be dispersed in a plurality of groups, associations, and institutions engaged in a never-ending public competition for the appropriation of particular parcels of a rather phantasmagoric state. The state is reduced to the government, and the latter is downgraded to a congeries of agencies and offices lacking any degree of coherence and unity, perpetually responsive to the changing correlation of forces produced by the feverish initiatives and reactions of the myriad of interest groups of the civil society. It is through this route that liberal thought flows into a coarse societalism, where the anarchy and/or poliarchy of the market is linearly translated into the political sphere. The result of all this is to shut the doors that may have allowed one to theoretically formulate the specificity and variable degree of relative autonomy of the state and political process vis-à-vis the dynamism of civil society.

In the instrumentalist version of Marxism the result is the same: the state and political life, like the ideology and all the juridical and political superstructure, is conceived as a simple reflection of the development of the productive forces, foreclosing the possibility of thinking in terms of a complex and dialectical relation between economy and politics. The difference between liberal theories and vulgar Marxism is that in the former the civil society is not supposed to be structurally divided along class lines, whereas for the latter the class cleavage is dogmatically and vaguely asserted. But the strong societalism of these two approaches leads to the nullification of the state, deprived of any possible margin of autonomy in its actions. Posed as a simple "parallelogram of forces" of citizens and competing interest groups in the case of the liberal discourse, or as a docile instrument for the direct class rule in the case of vulgar Marxism, the problem of the relative autonomy cannot even be posed unless one breaks with those theorists' shared assumptions.[11]

It is clear that these two polar alternatives do not offer any good prospects for the student of politics: rather, they are serious obstacles for the development of historical research. The problem, then, is to overcome the theoretical impasse surrounding the question of the state. The difficulties in such a task are great: the liberal tradition has very little to offer because it has not devoted much time and energy to what appears to be a nonproblem within its own theoretical paradigm. Not only can the problem not be solved within liberal theory, it cannot even be adequately posed. On the other hand, in the Marxist tradition the discussion of the state made little progress after Lenin's contributions on the eve of the socialist revolution in Russia. There is an outstanding exception, though: the contribution made by Antonio Gramsci in his remarkable theoretical and historical analysis of the capitalist state. But, as Perry Anderson conclusively shows, the Gramscian legacy is far from being free of ambiguities and contradictions, despite its invaluable theoretical wealth, and the slow and laborious struggle to fully recover and develop his rich heritage is just in its beginnings.[12] However, this situation should not obviate two important facts. First, that contrary to what happens in the liberal tradition, Marxist theory at least offers the possibility of a theoretical understanding of the state. Though the theory has not yet developed, the promise is there, and it is possible. Second, the theoretical underdevelopment of the Marxist theory of the state largely reflects the destructive role of dogmatism. This accounts for the fact that, until recently, the bulk of the so-called Marxist interpretations had been repetitious and mechanical "deductive inferences" derived from the primitive theoretical statements linking, at the most abstract level, state and civil society. As in the case of other central categories of Marxist thought (e.g., imperialism, class), the concept of the state has also reached the status of a universal *explanans:* people attribute to it magical characteristics by which the theoretical category in itself becomes a generic pseudoexplanation of particular historical configurations. No concrete analysis is necessary, and as Fernando H. Cardoso writes regarding the concept of dependence, "the charm of the word effectively conceals the indolence of the spirit."[13]

The Copernican revolution in the social sciences produced by the work of Karl Marx has its heavy toll: legions of intellectuals and politicians enthusiastically adhered to the new theory, but only a few of them considered the Marxist synthesis as a scientific starting point rather than as the "doctrinal revelation" or the final station on the long road of human knowledge. The consequences of all this, undoubtedly explainable by the fact that Marxism as a revolutionary ideology played a crucial role in the major political and economic events of the twentieth century, were the theoretical deformation and stagnation of the Marxist theory. This process of "vulgarization" was obviously pushed by the dogmatism prevailing in the Second and Third International and by the defeat of the proletarian revolution in the West. But, much earlier, both Marx and Engels lived long enough to be alarmed by the widespread use of their formulations and by the fact that Marxism had become "an excuse for not studying history."[14]

Fundamentals of the Marxist
Theory of the Capitalist State

To summarily put together the fundamentals of the Marxist theory of the capitalist state, it is first necessary to draw an analytical distinction between state and society in the capitalist mode of production. I will not deal with the scope and limits of such a distinction in feudal or communist societies, because these two cases deal with quite different problems. Rather, I will concentrate on the analysis of the bourgeois state, particularly in its democratic representative form, thus excluding the so-called exceptional forms, a theme to which I will come back later.

How, then, is the relationship between state and society in capitalism to be characterized?

The bourgeois state, in the first place, is the juridical, political, and ideological consecration of the formal separation between a class-divided civil society and the political society, between the bourgeois and the citizen, and between the realm of the private as opposed to that of public life. The state claims to be the official representative of the nation as a whole, without exclusions: consequently, it rests on the popular legitimacy, superseding the ancient metasocial and religious foundations of the precapitalist rule. In other words, the bourgeois democratic state is founded on popular sovereignty, expressed either through the active consensus of the people, as demanded by Jean J. Rousseau, or simply in its passive acquiescence, as posed by Immanuel Kant. Thus, the bourgeoisie rules no longer "by the grace of God," as did the former aristocracies, but by the general will of the nation. Here lies the historical origin of the problem of the hegemony because, as Gramsci notes, "the bourgeois class poses itself as an organism in continuous movement, capable of absorbing the entire society, assimilating it to its own cultural and economic level."[15]

Second, "the people" is a collective juridical fiction made up of individual citizens regardless of their position in the productive process. The citizen is an abstraction, not conditioned by the place he or she occupies in the society: citizens are supposed to be free, equal, independent. Together, and through the mediation of the representative political institutions of the bourgeois state, the individual citizens enable self government and the political organization of the society to materialize.

Third, the liberal state appears as the living embodiment of the general will expressed through universal suffrage. Contrary to what had been the case in precapitalist social formations, both in the ancient world and in the Middle Ages, the domination of the bourgeoisie is not apparent: the political and juridical institutions of the state are founded on the principles of freedom and equality, as well as on the explicit separation and insulation of the public sphere from the realm of private matters. The laws and the egalitarian ideology that permeate this type of state; the parliamentary representation; the universal suffrage; and the nature of the "political class," the party system, and the democratic freedoms consecrate the formally effective separation between state and civil society, thus concealing the class nature of the bourgeois state.

The political superstructure of capitalism therefore had a structural and effective degree of relative autonomy from civil society. If the bourgeoisie is the ruling class of this capitalist state, its rule is not put into effect without mediations. The political institutions and the ideological apparatuses of the liberal state structurally required a margin of autonomy from the dominant classes, but this autonomy, as will be shown later, cannot be absolute. The bourgeois state is not just an instrument of class rule; it is something much more complex than that. In order to be the social institution through which the dominant classes assert their supremacy over the rest of the society and ensure the general conditions for the reproduction of the bourgeois relations of production, the state has to be able to represent the people; it has to be able to express, up to a certain degree, the totality of the nation. This dual character of the state (1) as the expression of a pact of domination agreed upon by capital-owners and allied classes, and (2) as the embodiment of popular sovereignty summarizes the contradictory unity and the inherent complexity of the capitalist state. Simplistic and mechanical interpretations of the state, either as a pure class instrument performing the function of political domination (vulgar Marxism) or as the impartial representative of the nation (liberal theories), fail to capture this dialectical contradiction that constitutes the inner core of the capitalist state.

This dialectrical contradiction is pointed out by Marx when he describes the capitalist state as the "official *résumé* of the society."[16] In a society structurally divided by the class cleavage, it is impossible for the state to escape the fundamental determinations arising from the very nucleus of the mode of production. Therefore, as a capitalist institution it must express the variable predominance of these class interests, which are variable because of the changing outcomes of the class struggles and are organized in a specific and historically mutable pact of domination. These interests find objective existence in the state policies and in the political and administrative organization of the state apparatuses. On the other hand, the peculiarities of bourgeois rule, derived from the nature of the articulation between economy and politics in capitalist societies, make the state the institution in charge of protecting the "universal interests" of the society and, at the same time, transform the state's institutional system into a strategic arena for the class struggles, where the subordinated classes can overcome the atomization and dispersion of the market and reach an organic unity. These two elements—(1) the necessity of looking after the universal interests and the collective goods of the society, called forth by the self-destructive tendencies of capitalist production and by the insertion of these social formations in a world market and in a competitive state system, and (2) the fact that the political institutions of the state become the crucial arenas of the social antagonisms—contribute to the formation of a state bureaucracy that, under given circumstances, can become an outstanding political actor, able to take important policy initiatives and to shape the course of the class struggles and even some structural features of the social formation.[17]

Thus, it is clear why the Marxist analysis of the capitalist state rejects the claims that liberal theorists have made concerning the neutral character of the state, which only by an illusion can be conceived of as an independent representative of the civil society. As Marx writes in his *Critique of Political Economy:*

> My inquiry led to the conclusion that legal relations and also forms of the state are to be explained neither by themselves nor by the so-called universal development of the human mind, but on the contrary have their roots in the material conditions of life, which Hegel, following the precedent set by the English and French of the eighteenth century, sums up in their entirety under the name of "civil society" and that the anatomy of civil society has to be studied in political economy.[18]

If the state is so related to the civil society, the question of its representative character and neutrality has to be examined from the viewpoint of the anatomy of civil society. Such analysis reveals that in capitalist societies the people are fragmented and organized in social classes, the structural bases of which are anchored in the productive process. In the capitalist mode of production there are two classes, bourgeoisie and proletariat. But the modes of production are not likely to exist in their purest form. They will be always found dissolved and combined; this particular combination and amalgam of several modes of production, coexisting at a single point in time, is called in Marxist theory a social formation, and as a result the anatomy of the civil society becomes extraordinarily complicated. In practical terms this implies that one of the modes is predominant and will set the tone of the entire social formation, but the other modes of production, with their characteristic social classes, will coexist in a subordinated manner with the former. There are classic studies in Marxist theory that exemplify this point, such as Lenin's *Development of Capitalism in Russia,* in which Lenin finds several modes of production (patriarchal peasant economy, petty commodity production) subordinated to the capitalist mode of production; or Marx's *Eighteenth Brumaire,* in which Marx analyzes the political implications of the coexistence of the peasant production with mercantile petty commodity production and with the modern capitalist mode of production in nineteenth-century France.[19]

All of this means that in every concrete, historically identifiable society, one will find a peculiar, and sometimes unique, amalgam of different modes of production. Therefore, in addition to the classes typical of capitalism, bourgeoisie and proletariat, one also finds a whole range of social groups and institutional actors, such as the bureaucracy, the army, and the church, in addition to classes belonging to the other economic regimes: landlords, peasants, and the petty bourgeoisie. These classes, as those proper of capitalist societies, are determined by the position they occupy in a given system of social production, by their relation with the means of production, by the roles they play in the social division of labor, by the ways they acquire their share of the social wealth, and by the magnitude of the share they are able to get.[20]

Now one can ask: how is the relationship among the civil society, this complex articulation of several modes of production, and the state to be characterized? Contrary to what many pseudo-Marxists have assumed, the "identification of the predominant type of exploitation is necessary, but by no means sufficient, for analyzing the political structure" of a specific social formation.[21] Marx himself warns against this oversimplification: the relationships between owners of the means of production and the direct producers will certainly reveal the "hidden basis of the entire social structure" and "the corresponding specific form of the state." However, Marx continues, "this does not prevent the same economic basis—the same from the standpoint of its main conditions—due to innumerable different empirical circumstances, natural environment, racial relations, external historical influences, etc., from showing infinite variations and gradations in appearance, which can be ascertained only by analysis of the empirically given circumstances."[22]

In other words, the specific forms of the state cannot be "deduced" from the observation of the economic basis. This means that Marx's societalism does not imply a monistic and unilateral socioeconomic causation or a denial of the practical efficacy of the political structures in the unfolding of social history. For instance, the development of capitalism was not accompanied by the same state forms in England and in Germany; and in the periphery of the capitalist system, the dependent development of Argentina, Brazil, and Chile witnessed the constitution of different types of state formations. For the student of the state it is not enough, then, to identify some crucial historical actors like bourgeoisie, landed nobility, and so on. If some real knowledge is to be acquired, it is necessary to analyze those innumerable "empirical circumstances" mentioned by Marx and to carry out concrete studies of the societies and states in question. Historical materialism is not to be regarded as a "general historico-philosophical" theory, the supreme virtue of which consists in being "super-historical."[23]

The Class Character of the State

The foregoing indications suffice to outline the basic elements of the Marxist theory of the state and the structural foundations of its relative autonomy. It seems to be fairly obvious that such a matter implies, as a necessary condition for its correct theoretical formulation, the rejection of both the instrumentalist thesis, closely associated with the Marxisms of the Second and Third International, as well as a whole variety of political theories inspired in the liberal tradition.

In the most extreme and less sophisticated versions, the Marxist theory ends in a monistic and economicist "philosophy of history," in which all the superstructural phenomena are downgraded to a mere reflection of the movement of the productive forces, whose final and inexorable stop is socialism, and the state becomes the ductile tool used by an omniscient and cohesive ruling class. The strong economicism of the Second International, as voiced by its foremost theoreticians like Karl Kautsky and Edward Bernstein, "derived" the final triumph of socialism from the ceaseless unfolding of the productive forces under capitalism. This economicism wraps up in a lukewarm reformist optimism, sharply counterposed to the revolutionary legacy of Marx and Engels: not only would socialism come "naturally," but it would no longer be necessary to smash the state machinery because once the working class takes over the state—which is thus considered a simple physical tool!—through parliamentary and electoral tactics, then the state could be used for a new and higher ethical purpose: the building of socialism. The simplicity of this argument clearly shows the gulf that separates it from the classic analysis by Marx and Engels of nineteenth-century European politics. It was V. I. Lenin who reversed this trend in social democracy by means of a drastic revalorization of politics and of the organizational aspects of the class struggles. Hence, his early formulation of the theory of the political party was conceived as a critique of the economicist trends prevailing in the labor movement.[24]

On the other hand, the Third International remained trapped within the ideological framework of the economicist tradition, but that framework was expressed in another version: fatal catastrophism. The Stalinist interpretation also considers the capitalist state as an instrument that the bourgeoisie wields for the political subjugation of the proletariat and the popular masses. This "state-instrument" evolves according to a definite and rigid pattern marked by the orderly succession of modes of production that, at a given time, would be objectively ripe for the revolutionary assault of the masses. All the popular classes are by definition outside the state, and the strategy simply consists of a patient accumulation of forces up to the decisive day when the economic catastrophe would produce the collapse of the entire structure of the bourgeois state. The proletariat would then replace the old dominant class, taking over the state apparatus and starting the construction of socialism.[25]

These instrumentalist theses, which foreclose the study of the state's relative autonomy, have been practically disproved and theoretically refuted so many times that it would be superfluous to engage here in another round of refutations. It is more interesting to analyze the liberal theories that have raised the issue of the autonomy of the democratic state. Thus far, the most articulated and complete argument on this regard has been forwarded in a book by Eric Nordlinger that, according to its author, "has directly challenged the fundamental empirical premise of liberal democratic theory—the state's consistent constraint by civil society, its barely wavering responsiveness to the demands of the politically best endowed private actors."[26]

Upon reading this statement, one cannot help but question, on the one hand, the extent to which the key words—state, autonomy, civil society—refer to the same concepts that are used in the Marxist tradition and, on the other hand, how it could be possible to formulate the problem of the relative autonomy of the state within a liberal theoretical framework. After all, in the latter intellectual tradition the state is reduced first to the government, and the government to the simple summation of its officers; the autonomy of the political sphere is then tendentially absolute, and civil society is not supposed to have the crucial discontinuities and cleavages introduced by social classes. Therefore, civil society places no constraints on the state as such; instead of constraints the liberal formulation has the concept of representation, which has little to do with the Marxist notion of class domination. The government, in the liberal tradition, expresses the electoral alignments existing in society on the basis of the principle of majority rule, representing the plurality of issue-centered majorities that have expressed preferences concerning given issues. Thus, the comparability of the statements regarding the state's autonomy in Marxism and in liberal theory is purely nominal, and the whole meaning of the problem is altogether different.

Additionally, because in liberal political theory social life is made up of a collection of independent spheres or orders not linked by structural relations of causality, and because the state is conceived as being just a technical and administrative institution in charge of the general affairs of the community, the state's eventual autonomy is a sign of distress; it means that the state is becoming irresponsive to—and independent of—the citizen body. In strict terms this is equivalent to dictatorship, or to a political pathology. Governments are not supposed to be autonomous and strong, but rather dependent on the ever-changing preferences of the electorate (not individual classes or elites) and comparatively weak vis-à-vis the actors in civil society. The autonomous state then poses serious questions regarding bourgeois democracy, but these issues are perfunctorily examined in the last few pages of Nordlinger's book. For instance, how is it possible to reconcile a plea for an autonomous government with the classic liberal theory of "representative government"? What about the "checks and balances" so dear to liberalism? It seems that some of the best legacies of the liberal tradition (for instance, the distrust of the state—something that was buried under the "stadolatry" of the Soviet model and that the more enlightened Marxist theorists are trying to recover) are sacrificed to the political and administrative efficacy of the state, thus giving impetus to an unjustifiable "statism" that throws away some of the most valuable assets of classical liberal political theory. This situation is more paradoxical if one considers the contrary movement taking place in the Marxist field: the revalorization of civil society and a growing diffidence regarding the state, an attitude that can be found in any major Marxist writer from Marx to Gramsci.[27]

The Multidimensionality of the State in Marxist Theory

In the Marxist tradition the whole problem of state autonomy is posed in entirely different terms. The state is always the expression of class domination, an assertion fully incompatible with the theorizing based in the liberal tradition. Moreover, in the case of Nordlinger this incompatibility is even more pronounced because in his conceptualization the state melts into the collection of bureaucrats who occupy its formal apparatuses and carry out its main tasks. In a typical liberal twist the state is reduced to the government, which is "made up of and limited to those individuals who are endowed with society-wide decision-making authority."[28]

On the contrary, in Marxist theory the state is an extremely complex social and political institution, and although civil society has a major role in shaping the state structures and processes, the state is not regarded as an inert or ineffectual apparatus incapable of taking initiatives bound to produce significant modifications to civil society. This approach means that the state has to be simultaneously regarded as: (1) a "pact of domination," through which an underlying alliance of classes and social forces tries to build a hegemonic system and to establish an entire historical bloc; (2) the different levels of the government and an imposing set of "public" apparatuses and agencies that may, under given circumstances, become "corporatist" actors endowed with strong power resources; (3) a privileged arena of the class and social struggles, in which many kinds of societal conflict take place and are provisorily "solved"; and (4) the official representative of the "universal interests" of the society and, as such, the expression of the national community in the interstate system.

It is impossible, therefore, to fully recover the deep meaning of the state phenomenon if these four dimensions are not simultaneously reckoned. Thinking of the state exclusively as a mere pact of domination, as the vulgar Marxists do; or as a bureaucratic and corporative actor, as some advocates of the "state-centered" approach do; or as a neutral arena for groups pursuing contradictory goals, as claimed by the liberal-pluralist tradition; or as the unbound representative of the national will, as argued by the distant disciples of Hegel, leads to one-sided and misleading interpretations of the subject and is capable of rendering only a caricature of the state. The theoretical superiority of Marxist theory of the state rests precisely in its ability to conceive of the state in the wealth and multiplicity of its determinants, none of which by themselves can fully explain the phenomenon in its entirety.[29]

Thus, the problem of state autonomy cannot even be considered within the liberal framework because of the absence of any fundamental premise that could establish some kind of structural relationship between economy and politics. In other words, to speak of autonomy (or relative autonomy) logically implies a prior assumption about the system of social relations that bind in an organic and significant totality the different aspects of social life. Historical materialism argues that the law of motion of a mode of production is to be found in the structural contradiction between the productive forces and the social relations of production. Within this formulation it is meaningful to question what the limits are of this structural determination—given that it is not absolute—exerted by the material foundations of social life.

But in liberal thought (and even Max Weber did not escape this), society is conceived of as being formed by a set of different parts or "institutional orders" of "factors" that, in their concrete historical existence, are likely to be combined in multiple forms, without recognition at even the most abstract level of any fixed causal ordering of the hierarchy of determinations. According to Max Weber, classes are economic phenomena, status groups are social creatures, and parties are political structures. In addition, there can be an infinite number of possible empirical combinations, as observed in concrete history; this feature invalidates any attempt to build an abstract and comprehensive general theory. Social theory thus downgrades to an ingenuous but rather sterile combination of formal taxonomy and historicism, as shown in some parts of the work of Max Weber.[30]

However, the truth is that societies are not collections of disparate parts and factors randomly organized by mysterious and unknown forces. An epistemological debate on the impact of fetishism in bourgeois social thought is beyond the scope of this chapter.[31] It is enough to recall that George Lukács persuasively criticizes this bourgeois tendency toward the fragmentation and reification of social relations in his renowned *History and Class Consciousness,* in which he argues that "dialectics insists on the concrete unity of the whole," a unity that "does not reduce its various elements to an undifferentiated uniformity, to identity."[32] This idea, of course, is one of the cornerstones of Marxist methodology, as outlined by Marx in the 1857 introduction to *Grundrisse;* there Marx establishes that "the concrete is concrete because it is the synthesis of many determinations, hence unity of the diverse."[33] The social determination and the number of factors in operation in any concrete social formation are many, but the dialectical method, according to Lukács, shows that "the apparent independence and autonomy which they possess in the capitalist system of production is an illusion only in so far as they are involved in a dynamic dialectical relationship with one another and can be thought of as the dynamic dialectical aspects of an equally dynamic dialectical whole."[34]

Thus, the problem of state autonomy can make sense only within an analytical scheme that assumes the unitary and contradictory character of a dialectical reality. And this implies the adoption of a methodology that enables the analyst to produce a theoretical reconstruction of the sociohistorical totality. This method, however, has nothing to do with some economic monism or determinism:

> It is not the primacy of economic motives in historical explanation that constitutes the decisive difference between Marxism and bourgeois thought, *but the point of view of totality*. . . . The capitalist separation of the producer from the total process of production, the division of the process of labour into parts at the cost of the individual humanity of the worker, the atomisation of society into individuals who simply go on producing without rhyme or reason, must all have a profound influence on the thought, the science and the philosophy of capitalism.[35]

It is therefore reasonable to conclude that posing the issue of state autonomy means, tacitly or explicitly, asserting that the state is somehow structurally articulated with the relations of production: only then is it a class state.

However, to assert that a state is a capitalist state means that there are observable indicators that would show, in an equivocal and concrete manner, the ways in which the state is organically linked to the reproduction of capital. The instrumentalist theories have already been rejected; they pose a relation of externality between the state and the dominant classes, the former being just a "thing" that today is in the hands of the bourgeoisie but tomorrow can be taken over by the proletariat. It is thus necessary to resort to other types of arguments. These other arguments must make it possible to differentiate a bourgeois state from a state taken over by the bourgeoisie, the class character of which would disappear as soon as its political representatives were removed from the upper ranks of the state apparatus. It is clear that such a "class state" would be extremely weak and unreliable. Then, in a stricter sense, speaking of a class state means that "one can speak of a 'capitalist state' or an 'ideal collective capitalist' only when it has been successfully proved that the system of political institutions displays its own class-specific selectivity corresponding to the interests of the accumulation of capital."[36]

Thus, the class character of the state does not reside in the social origins of the policymakers, the state managers, or the "reigning class," but in the internal structure of the state apparatus itself, which puts into effect the necessary selectivity of the public policies sponsored or neglected by the state. In other words, the class character of the state is not a function of the nature of the ruling circles that have succeeded in capturing it, nor of its ideology, party system, or any other given characteristic. According to Claus Offe, the concrete articulation of the state with capitalist reproduction rests on some selectivity mechanisms that are "built into the system of political institutions."[37] These arrangements are of two sorts: the first allows the state to distill a "class-interest out of narrow, short-term, conflicting, incompletely formulated interests" of the competing units of capital, in order to uphold and protect the collective long-run interests of the capitalist class; the second selectivity mechanism enables the bourgeois state to exert a "complementary selectiveness which consists in protecting collective capital against anti-capitalist interests and conflicts."[38]

Accordingly, Claus Offe and Volker Ronge argue that the capitalist character of the state is confirmed because it unmistakably upholds a set of rules and social relations that are at the very foundations of class rule, such as the perpetuation of the commodity character of the labor force in the capitalist mode of production. In addition, some institutional and decisionmaking features of the capitalist state further reinforce its dependency on the dominant classes: (1) production cannot be organized following political rules because production goals and strategies are set as a result of the initiatives and calculations of private individuals; (2) political power indirectly depends upon private accumulation, via taxation and capital markets; (3) the institutional self-interest of the state, unable to control production and the flow of resources needed to mobilize and finance the state apparatus, leads the state to promote capitalist accumulation; and (4) in democratic political regimes the electoral procedures conceal the fact that the material resources of the state and its use depend on the accumulation process. To sum up: if the institutional form of the capitalist state is determined by the rules of representative democracy, its material content is determined by the general course of the accumulation process.[39]

Similar arguments have been advanced by Goran Therborn: the class character of the state has nothing to do with the interpersonal relations that the members of the several economic and social elites establish with the political personnel occupying the upper levels of the state apparatus. One can determine the fundamental nature of the class character of the state by looking at "the effects of the state upon the production and reproduction of given modes of production."[40] Therborn strongly suggests that in order to understand the influence of the state on the overall process of social reproduction and transformation, it is necessary to consider two sources of determinations. The first source originates in the state power itself, that is, in the specific historical crystallization of relations of forces condensed in a pact of domination that controls the state and puts forward a set of policies concerning the productive process. On the other hand, the second source of determinations includes the structure of the state apparatus and the class bias of its organizational forms. Thus, in order to ascertain the class character of the capitalist state, the key issues are what the state does and how it does it, or, in other words, the class-laden policies favored by the state and the bureaucratic structures and procedural styles that implement them. Therborn concludes his analysis asserting that "the class character of the state power is thus defined by the effects of state measures on class positions" with respect to relations of production, the state apparatus, and the ideological system.[41]

Two articles by Fred Block also fit within this broadly defined range of structural explanations of the class character of the state, although the specifics of his arguments differ from both Offe's and Therborn's. Block starts his analysis with a radical criticism of the notion of "relative autonomy," especially in the Poulantzas formulation. He rightly contends that Poulantzas's contributions are just a "slightly more sophisticated version of instrumentalism" and that instrumentalist theories of the state require strong assumptions regarding the ruling class as a conscious, cohesive, and organized political actor. Empirical research has shown that dominant classes seldom meet these standards; on the other hand, serious theoretical reflection by many scholars—Block, Skocpol, Trimberger, Cardoso, Stepan, and O'Donnell, to mention just a few—has persuasively proved that the state is hardly a docile instrument in the hands of a pact of domination, but rather a much more complex and powerful political actor endowed with an enormous capacity to intervene in social life. However, once the nature and potentialities of the capitalist state are established, the burning issue of the limits of its autonomous initiatives still has to be tackled. As discussed previously, those limits are structurally fixed by the need to reproduce and reinforce the social relations proper of bourgeois society. It is for this reason that one cannot agree with Block's assertion that the key problem of the relative autonomy formulation is its conceptualization of the dominant class as a class-conscious political actor. This problem is certainly a serious one, and Block is on the right track when he calls attention to the issue, but the issue is not the crucial one.[42]

Moreover, the flaws and defects of instrumentalism should not be extended to all Marxist theory. If the ongoing relations of production are structurally enhanced and upheld by the state, then the question of how important the dominant classes' consciousness and organization are is far from being the key issue. The real problem consists in ascertaining the structural limits, always variable but omnipresent, of the state autonomy. The lack of awareness of the subtle equilibrium coexisting in the state between its structural determinants and its capacities for autonomous intervention may lead the observer to two symmetrical, equally censurable mistakes. On the one hand is the swift re-creation of the Hegelian myth by which the state, being endowed with total and boundless autonomy, becomes the effective demiurge of history. On the other hand, as in some "left-wing functionalism," is a reciprocal fable by which all state interventions—no matter when, how, and why—are always conducive to the perpetual reproduction and consolidation of capitalist domination. This fable is easily perceived in Poulantzas's work, in which the state's relative autonomy is nothing more than the means by which the state adjusts more efficiently to the desires of the dominant classes, thus excluding a priori any possibility of contradictions, even transient ones, between the dominant classes and the state.[43]

In order to overcome these difficulties, Block proposes a new conceptualization of the relationships between the state and dominant classes that hinges on the division of labor between a capitalist class—interested in accumulation but ignorant regarding how to preserve the social order and/or ensure political domination—and the state managers, whose tasks and skills deal precisely with these matters. However, Block argues that in order to have a persuasive argument, it is necessary to specify the structural mechanisms "that make the state serve the capitalist ends regardless of whether capitalists intervene directly and consciously."[44] To this end there are two major structural mechanisms: one that reduces the possibilities that the state managers will act against the general interests of the capitalists, and another that compels the state managers to pursue policies that are in the general interests of capital.[45] State managers therefore contribute, by their policies, to the reproduction of capitalism as a result of both the intensity of the class struggle—which forces them, in the long run, to intervene in order to "rationalize" the capitalist exploitation—and the necessity to maintain at all cost minimum levels of "business confidence" and economic activity, which are preconditions of the political and financial stability of the state and which prevent the state managers from assailing the capitalist class. The managers know that without the "benevolence" of capital there is no political stability.

In later works Block changes his mind and acknowledges that the central problem of the state's relative autonomy lies in the difficulty of specifying its limits.[46] Yet, those limits can be accurately established only as a result of historical observations. From a theoretical viewpoint it is possible to sketch only the general conditions that set the boundaries of state action. But these conditions provide barely the starting points for the analysis; the specific conclusions regarding a concrete historical formation can be the outcome only of empirical research. The state's relative autonomy in France and Argentina, for instance, cannot be inferred from the general laws of capitalist accumulation. Determining the degree of state autonomy calls for "a concrete analysis of the concrete situation," and one cannot do this simply by deducing syllogistically the margins of state autonomy from the major theoretical premises.

This rapid review suffices to sustain the general thesis that the class character of the state is rooted in deep-seated structural mechanisms that articulate, in an always uneasy compromise and through a complex series of processes, the necessities of the capitalist accumulation with the imperatives arising from the "general and universal" interests of the society as a whole. But having asserted the class character of the state, or more specifically, having shown that a given state is capitalist (which implies much more than a state simply being "used" by a bourgeoisie), one must ask: what place, if any, is left for the relative autonomy of the state?

Structural Foundations of the
Relative Autonomy of the Bourgeois State

The straightforward answer is quite clear: the capitalist state is structurally endowed with a variable degree of independence with respect to the dominant classes. Louis Althusser rightly summarizes this view when, referring to the specific relationships between structure and superstructure, he notes that "Marx has at least given us the 'two ends of the chain', and has told us to find out what goes on between them: on the one hand, determination in the last instance by the (economic) mode of production; on the other, the relative autonomy of the superstructures and their specific effectivity."[47]

In what perhaps is one of his most remarkable theoretical achievements, "Contradiction and Overdetermination," Althusser rigorously proves that in Marx's thought the autonomy of the superstructural sphere in capitalist societies is explicitly asserted, despite the fact that this autonomy, being considerably large, falls short of being absolute.

The Marxist theoretical corpus supplies some guidelines for searching the concrete mediations that connect the two extremes of the chain. Block himself points out that social antagonisms and the character of social classes are the more important domestic factors limiting state autonomy, whereas the world markets and the competitive system of nation-states are some of the international aspects more relevant to the issue. Given these considerations Block concludes, "When these contextual elements are taken together, one can see how the exercise of state power has generally served the needs of the capitalist accumulation process. On the one hand, state managers are reluctant to disrupt the accumulation process, but on the other hand, they face pressures to intervene to ameliorate the economic and social strains that capitalism produces."[48]

Even in exceptional periods: wars, depressions, and reconstructions, in which the state gains wide margins of autonomy—which would potentially allow for the introduction of major structural reforms in critical areas of the economy—the state managers preserve a keen awareness of their dependency on the capacity of the capitalists to generate a sizable economic surplus. Adam Przeworski emphasizes this issue when asserting that the capitalists appear as the bearers of the universal interests of the society and that, for that very reason, enjoy a unique position within the system: "Capitalists are thus in a unique position in a capitalist system; they represent future universal interests while interests of all other social groups appear as particularistic and hence inimical to future developments. The entire society is structurally dependent upon actions of capitalists."[49]

Without the surplus generated by the capitalist economy, the state becomes a nonviable enterprise. Bureaucrats and state managers know too well that exceptional situations such as economic downturns, wars, major crises, or periods of national reconstruction are short-lived, and that although under those circumstances the degree of freedom in their decisions may significantly increase, they will eventually have to normalize their relations with the bourgeoisie and once again depend on its cooperation. Besides, the bureaucrats and the political class also know that the capitalists have a disproportionate amount of influence over other crucial instruments of social and political control, like the mass media and the political parties, that may effectively curtail the former's autonomous pretensions.[50]

Thus, there are many factors and circumstances that influence—in terms of both expanding and contracting—the concrete degrees of autonomy enjoyed by state managers. But, as mentioned previously, these factors cannot be deduced from Marxist theory, in a futile exercise of "pedantic doctrinarism" as Gramsci calls it, but rather have to be ascertained through empirical research.

The foundations of this unprecedented autonomy of the state lie in the specific form of articulation between economy and politics proper of capitalist societies, and even more so in the whole articulation of the social totality. This complex and flexible pattern of societal integration constitutively allows for an ample degree of independence (notwithstanding its definite limits) among the different instances and levels of the social formation unknown in precapitalist modes of production. In the ancient world and in the Middle Ages, property and authority were intimately bound together, whereas given the expropriation of the direct producers in capitalist societies, the reproduction of bourgeois social relations is essentially an economic process of an almost automatic character. This structural differentiation allows for a relative separateness between property and authority and, consequently, between production and politics. Marx refers to this problem in *Capital:*

> It is furthermore evident that in all forms in which the direct labourer remains the "possessor" of the means of production and labour conditions necessary for the production of his own means of subsistence, the property relationship must simultaneously appear as a direct relation of lordship and servitude, so that the direct producer is not free; a lack of freedom which may be reduced from serfdom with enforced labour to a mere tributary relationship. . . . Under such conditions the surplus-labor for the nominal owner of the land can only be extorted from them by other than economic pressure, whatever the form assumed may be.[51]

The indistinction between economy and politics in precapitalist social formations had attracted Marx's attention since his youth, when he was still under the influence of Hegel's imposing philosophical system. Following Hegel's steps, the young Marx made the dichotomy between private and public one of the cornerstones of his earlier analysis of bourgeois society, radically transforming the traditional Hegelian formulation. The sphere of the particular acquired in his new theory a definite economic content, referring back to the material interests of the private individuals, while the sphere of the universal become the expression of the public and general interests of the society. Consequently, the Hegelian relationship between particular and universal became, in Marx's analysis, a novel formulation of the connection between economy and politics.[52]

Thus, extraeconomic coercion was a crucial component in the reproduction of social relations in precapitalist economic regimes. This coactive mechanism purported a much more rigid and fixed articulation between economy and politics, such that the degrees of autonomy of the latter were by necessity almost nonexistent. In the ancient world, as in feudalism, the productive process required the political subjugation of direct producers, and economic exploitation appeared immediately visible as political domination, with public authority simply being the other side of property. An ancient French saying captures quite well this reality: *Nulle terre sans maitre!*[53]

In the capitalist mode of production, however, the situation is completely different, because exploitation does not need to rest on the disciplinary virtues of the extraeconomic coercion. Rather, it is concealed under the guise of the "exchange of equivalents" traded in the marketplace, in which wage earners freely sell their labor force to the capitalists and nobody is forced to work or to give away a part of what his or her labor power has produced to the property owners. Contrary to all previous forms of economic exploitation, capitalist exploitation is opaque, veiled by the fetishism that envelops social relations in bourgeois society. In the ancient world as well as in feudalism, slaves and servants had a keen awareness of the oppressive nature of the ongoing economic system: the signs and marks of economic exploitation were readily visible to everyone, and the subordinate classes did not need to exert themselves intellectually to become aware of it. The fetishism of capitalist society placed a thick curtain before the eyes of the society, thus preventing men and women from becoming aware of class exploitation. Furthermore, because in democratic capitalisms the constitution of political authority takes place by means of an egalitarian electoral mechanism (universal suffrage), and in a particular domain (the state, which does not appear to intersect with the productive process), the contours of class exploitation became even more blurred.

In sum, the reproduction of capitalist relations is overwhelmingly ensured through the workings of the markets, leaving a subsidiary role to other noneconomic factors such as the state. In the words of Marx,

> Capitalist production, therefore, of itself reproduces the separation between labour-power and the means of labour. It thereby reproduces and perpetuates the condition for exploiting the labourer. It incessantly forces him to sell his labour-power in order to live, and enables the capitalist to purchase labour-power in order that he may enrich himself. . . . In reality, the labourer belongs to capital before he has sold himself to capital. His economic bondage is both brought about and concealed by the periodic

sale of himself, by his change of masters, and by the oscillations in the
market-price of labour-power. . . . Capitalist production . . . produces not
only commodities, not only surplus-value, but it also produces and reproduces the capitalist relation; on the one side the capitalist, on the other the
wage-labourer.[54]

This mode of production, resulting from the dissolution of the old forms
of communal integration that prevailed up to the Middle Ages, gave rise to
the atomism, fragmentation, and individualism characteristic of civil society, features that call for a largely expanded autonomy of the political
sphere. If one adds that the exploitation of a mass of dispossessed free laborers occurs, as in democratic capitalisms, while full citizenship rights are
simultaneously extended to all sectors of the population, it is then understandable that the relative autonomy of the capitalist state is built into that
state's very structure.

Furthermore, with the rise of bourgeois society and the property relations proper of this kind of society, a clear demarcation between the spheres
of the public and private was drawn. Thus, in the new mode of production
the political superstructure has, from its very foundations, a degree of independence that is structurally granted by the particular form of articulation
between economy and politics typical of capitalist society. For the first time
in history, relations of production reproduce themselves in an ever expanded fashion, without the extraeconomic coaction previously required to
extract the surplus labor from the direct producers.

Some reflections made by Engels are also pertinent to underline these
considerations anchored in certain passages of *Capital.* The concerns that
the popularization of Marxism aroused in Engels's mind were expressed in
several letters addressed to intellectual leaders affiliated with the growing
social democratic movement. The message of these letters is clear enough:
the historical process has a dialectical nature irreducible to simplifying
monisms of any sort. In his letter to J. Bloch, Engels asserts, "According to
the materialist conception of history the determining element in history is
ultimately the production and reproduction in real life. . . . If therefore some-
body twists this into the statement that the economic element is the only
determining one, he transforms it into a meaningless, abstract and absurd
phrase."[55]

In other words, Engels reasserts the determining role of the economic
element but in the last instance and within a dialectical complex of interact-
ing factors. In the same letter he poses the example of Prussia and observes
that

the Prussian state arose and developed from historical, ultimately economic causes. But it could scarcely be maintained without pedantry that among
the many small states of North Germany, Brandenburg was specifically
determined by economic necessity to become the great power. . . . Without
making oneself ridiculous it would be a difficult thing to explain in terms
of economics the existence of every small state in Germany.[56]

It is quite clear then that in Engels's formulation, the formation of the national state cannot be conceived of as if it were a simple emanation of the economic base or of the market exchanges. Many things intervene, and among them should be stressed the position of every single state in the international system of competing national states, as exemplified by the critical cases of Prussia and Austria. These particulars are theoretically elaborated upon by Engels in a letter to K. Schmidt:

> Society gives rise to certain common functions which it cannot dispense with. The persons appointed for this purpose form a new branch of the division of labor within society. This gives them particular interests, distinct, too, from the interests of those who empowered them, they make themselves independent of the latter and the state is in being. . . . And now the new independent power, while having in the main to follow the movement of production, reacts, by virtue of its inherent relative independence, that is, the relative independence once transferred to it and gradually further developed, in its turn upon the conditions and course of production.[57]

Engels concludes with a critical remark on those who, like Barth, supposed that he and Marx had denied the historical efficacy and initiative of the state: "What these gentlemen all lack is dialectics. They always see only here cause, there effect. That this is a hollow abstraction, that such metaphysical polar opposites exist in the real world only during crises, while the whole vast process goes on in the form of interaction—though of very unequal forces, the economic movement being by far the strongest, most primeval, most decisive—that here everything is relative and nothing absolute—this they never begin to see. Hegel has never existed for them."[58]

What emerges from these lengthy quotes is that even though the consideration of the structural and long-run trends in historical development is a necessary condition for the analysis of political processes, these factors alone are insufficient to provide an adequate explanation of the movements that take place in the political realm. It is therefore necessary to use a dialectical theoretical approach able to reconstruct the social totality—always inevitably composed of structural and superstructural factors—in order to (1) unravel complex sets of interactions and influences and (2) ascertain their own patterns of transformation and the relative autonomy of the political sphere with regard to the movements and modifications of the productive process.

These methodological guidelines are brilliantly summarized by Althusser in a passage referring to the "overdetermined" contradiction:

> This overdetermination is inevitable and thinkable as soon as the real existence of the forms of the superstructure and of the national and international conjuncture has been recognized—an existence largely specific and autonomous, and therefore irreducible to a pure phenomenon. We must carry this through to its conclusion and say that this overdetermination does not just refer to apparently unique and aberrant historical situations

(Germany, for example), but is universal; the economic dialectic is never active in the pure state; in History, these instances, the superstructures, etc. . . . are never seen to step respectfully aside when their work is done or, when the Time comes, as his pure phenomena, to scatter before His Majesty the Economy as he strides along the royal road of the Dialectic. From the first moment to the last, the lonely hour of the "last instance" never comes.[59]

Conjunctural Reinforcements
of the Capitalist State's Relative Autonomy

The observations made so far regarding the state's relative autonomy deal with one of its major determinants, the structural one: the articulation between economy and politics in the capitalist mode of production. As a result, the state detaches itself from the anarchy of the competing interests of the individual units of capital. According to this structural meaning, the relative autonomy of the capitalist state implies that this type of state by its very nature will pursue a series of policies aimed at ensuring the protection and promotion of the general and political interests of capital as a whole, reinforcing its natural tendency toward expanded reproduction. The outcome of this process is nicely expressed in a brilliant essay by Ellen Meiksins Wood, precisely dealing with the separation of economy and politics in capitalist societies:

> This is the significance of the division of labour in which the two moments of capitalist exploitation—appropriation and coercion—are allocated separately to a "private" appropriating class and a specialized "public" coercive institution, the state: on the one hand, the "relative autonomous" state has a monopoly of coercive force; on the other hand, that force sustains a private "economic" power which invests capitalist property with an authority to organize production itself—an authority probably unprecedented in its degree of control over productive activity and the human beings who engage in it.[60]

This structurally based division of labor between the two moments of capitalist exploitation, traditionally fused into one moment in previous economic regimes, explains the autonomy of the political domain characteristic of modern bourgeois societies. However, there exists in the Marxist tradition a second source of autonomy of the capitalist states, resulting from temporary and exceptional equilibria reached in particular junctures of the class struggle. Because of the dangers involved in these "catastrophic" equilibria, the state is pushed by the dynamic of social antagonisms to increase the range, scope, and quality of its regulatory interventions, thus increasing its autonomy from the dominant classes in order to safeguard the viability and stability of the status quo. This situation was widely acknowledged after publication of Marx's classic studies on Bonapartism in France and—to a lesser degree—Engels's analyses of state and politics in Bismarckian Germany and Gramsci's notes on this issue. This second determination of the capitalist state's autonomy has been far more universally recognized among both Marxist and non-Marxist writers. In contraposition to the first structural determinant (which is the more crucial one in this chapter), this second source of state autonomy may be called conjunctural because its origins lie in a particular and transient crystallization of the correlation of forces in the class struggle.

This conjunctural autonomy of the capitalist state, besieged by the intensification of the class struggles, has been presented many times as evidence of the noninstrumentalist character of the state in Marxist theory. However, this theoretical defense is weak and misses the substantive point: that in capitalist societies the relative autonomy of the state has structural foundations.

In this sense it is quite illustrative to consider the treatment that Nicos Poulantzas gives this issue in his *Political Power and Social Classes,* perhaps the most ambitious theoretical attempt aimed at founding a systematic Marxist theory of the capitalist state. All through the lengthy fourth part of his book, the relative autonomy of the state appears almost entirely assimilated into the phenomena of Bonapartism and the ephemeral *décalage* between the represented and the representatives in the political scene; that autonomy's structural determinants are never brought to the fore. This is a serious mistake that purports the idea that, in Marxist theory, state autonomy is possible only under exceptional circumstances of the class struggle. If this were the case, then the relative independence of the political superstructure would be a short-lived countertrend unable to modify or reshape, not to mention neutralize, the iron laws that link the state with the dominant classes. An argument of this sort does in fact uphold, in subtler ways, the instrumentalist thesis: the capitalist state is just the political instrument of the bourgeois hegemonic fraction, deprived of all possible autonomy and practical efficacy. This omission in the consideration of the structural determinants of state autonomy can have only devastating impact on Marxist political theory, impoverishing its analytical capacities and depriving it of its ability to explain most of the crucial political problems of our time.

Typical examples of this conjunctural relative autonomy are the many instances and variants of Bonapartism. A much quoted passage of Engels's *Origin* poses the problem in the following terms: "By way of exception, however, periods occur in which the warring classes balance each other so nearly that the state power, as ostensible mediator, acquires, for the moment, a certain degree of independence of both."[61]

The historical illustrations used by Engels—Bonapartism, the Absolutist states, and Bismarck's rule—are far from being strictly comparable. Neither are they good examples of a situation of equilibrium in the correlation of social forces. However, I am not concerned here with historiographical discussions but with the theoretical contents of the Engelsian formulation that establishes a causal link between situations of catastrophic equilibrium and the growing independence and autonomy of the capitalist state. The Gramscian reflections on the concept of "organic crisis" of course have their starting point in this Engelsian codification.

In this connection it is worthwhile to realize that, although in the Marxist tradition the Bonapartist regimes have been considered as "exceptional and short-lived" interludes in the history of social conflict, the fact is that they have shown a permanence and stability that far exceeds what was originally expected. This was the case with the protracted phase of Absolutist rule in Western Europe, with the history of the two Bonapartes in France, and with Bismarck in Germany.[62] And this also has been the case in peripheral and dependent capitalisms, where these "exceptional" situations seem to have constituted more the rule more than the exception.

Thus, it is important to call attention to the fact that the Bonapartist regimes can give rise to enduring forms of state power, the importance of which goes far beyond their ability to disentangle a critical conjuncture of the class struggle. In this regard the classic example of Louis Bonaparte, whose rule extended over two decades and whose fall was, to a large extent, a product of the defeat by the armies of Bismarck, speaks for itself. This long period of political stability—an achievement that caught Marx by surprise—took place after the Parisian proletariat had been swept off the political scene and completely defeated after the failure of the June insurrection and the inauguration of the Cavaignac dictatorship. It is therefore impossible to speak of an "equilibrium" among warring classes, because by the time the Bonapartist regime was set up the defeat of the proletariat was already a fait accompli. This proves that the Bonapartist regime, as an extreme case of a state's relative autonomy, can go beyond its premises and become an enduring form of bourgeois rule even after the critical conditions of the class struggle present at the regime's origins have entirely disappeared.[63]

Gramsci's elaboration on this matter reaches the same conclusion: for him the constitution of a situation of organic crisis is a precondition of Bonapartism. In the sections of the *Quaderni del Cárcere* devoted to the analysis of Caesarism, Gramsci argues that an organic crisis breaks out when the dominant classes have lost their capacity of hegemonic direction, an event that

> occurs either because the ruling class has failed in some major political undertaking for which it has requested, or forcibly extracted, the consent of the broad masses (war, for example), or because huge masses (especially of peasants and intellectual petit-bourgeoisie) have passed suddenly from a state of political passivity to a certain activity, and put forward demands which taken together, albeit not organically formulated, add up to a revolution.[64]

In a situation of hegemonic crisis, therefore, the link between representatives and represented is broken. The traditional institutions in charge of processing the political representation of classes and social groups—the party system, the parliamentary and electoral arenas, etc.—fall in disarray, severely impairing their effectiveness and losing almost all relevance. One of the outcomes of this disarticulation of the structure of interest representation is the reinforcement of the political autonomy of the state bureaucracy—civil and military—and of all the bodies and agencies in the state apparatuses that are relatively isolated from the impacts derived from the changes in the political arena. Confronted by this situation, the conservative groups, if they have the organizational and ideological resources needed for a rapid reconstruction of their political apparatuses— changing cadres and programs and making some corporative sacrifices— could eventually find an organic solution to the crisis and regain control over the situation. But when these regressive forces are unable to reach this kind of solution and the progressive classes are not yet mature enough to defeat the established powers, then "no group, neither the conservatives nor the progressives, has the strength for victory, and . . . even the conservative group needs a master."[65] The situation is then ripe for the Bonapartist experiment.

Gramsci was the first in the Marxist tradition to acquire a keen consciousness of the diversity of historical meanings likely to be expressed in a Bonapartist "solution." Hence arises his distinction between "progressive" and "regressive" Caesarism. Whereas in the former the revolutionary thrust predominates, in the latter the strength of the restorative impulse prevails. The concrete political compromise crystallized in the Bonapartist regime is therefore colored by these two major alternatives open by the historical dialectics.

However, Gramsci warns that two provisos have to be made regarding the likelihood of having these Caesarist "solutions" stabilized. On the one hand, it is necessary to consider the extent and intensity of the objective contradictions between the historical actors that are the concrete "bearers" of the progressive and regressive alternatives, or, to put it in Gramsci's words, the extent to which those actors are "absolutely incapable of arriving, after a molecular process, at a reciprocal fusion and assimilation."[66] On the other hand, Gramsci warns against "catastrophism," that deep-rooted and vicious propensity within the ranks of the left to consider every crisis in apocalyptical terms, regarding it as the "terminal" juncture leading to the downfall and crash of capitalist social formations. He emphasizes the need to ascertain whether the crisis was brought about by intractable and insurmountable problems or if it was caused by transient and circumstantial political disarrangements within the dominant classes and their hegemonic apparatuses. For Gramsci the latter was the case in France during the rule of Louis Bonaparte, because the political fragmentation of the French bourgeoisie into four divisions was far from being inevitable and was insufficient to produce the collapse of the capitalist social and economic order. In light of these qualifications, Gramsci concludes

> In the modern world, the equilibrium with catastrophic prospects occurs not between forces which could in the late analysis fuse and unite—albeit after a wearying and bloody process—but between forces whose opposition is historically incurable and indeed becomes especially acute with the advent of Caesarist forms. However, in the modern world Caesarism also has a certain margin—larger or smaller depending on the country and its relative weight in the global context.[67]

It should be interesting to explore the extent to which some formerly ephemeral political difficulties have become endemic in capitalist societies. Thus, the growing troubles impairing the constitution and maintenance of bourgeois hegemony in modern capitalism cast some doubts regarding the "exceptional" nature of the so-called Bonapartist interludes. Already in 1866 Engels envisaged this tendency when, in a letter to Marx, he wrote,

> Bonapartism is a true religion of modern bourgeoisie. It is becoming clearer and clearer to me that the bourgeoisie doesn't have the stuff to rule directly itself, and that therefore, where there is no oligarchy as there is here in England to take over, for good play, the managing of state and society in the interest of the bourgeoisie, a Bonapartist semidictatorship is the normal form; it carries out the big material interests of the bourgeoisie of any share in the ruling power itself.[68]

These observations by Engels and Gramsci seem to point to the same theme: the early realization of the enormous obstacles challenging bourgeois hegemony in modern capitalist societies. In light of this deficit in leadership the state assumes a role of ever-growing importance, largely increasing its relative independence and significantly diversifying the quality of its interventions. This is the basic meaning of the celebrated Gramscian equation of state = hegemony + dictatorship. If the bourgeois order cannot be reproduced and stabilized by the dominant classes—with the help of their organic intellectuals and political representatives—then the capitalist state steps in to perform the task. To this end the state bureaucrats recruit new cadres, develop fresh political apparatuses, articulate new ideological discourses, reorganize the economy and society, and, if successful, create a new and enduring social consensus. The state assumes the defense of the besieged bourgeois order, restoring the viability of the system as a whole threatened by the incompetence and contradictions of a fragmented capitalist class. The unprecedented intensification of class struggles and social—gender, ethnic, religious, etc.—conflicts of all sorts, the growing vulnerability of national economies to the unsettling influences of the capitalist international markets, and the growing difficulties obstructing the continuous expansion of the accumulation process in late capitalism seem to be some of the major factors that condemn the bourgeoisie to a purely economic role and to chronic political impotence.

It should be stressed that the state's relative autonomy is reinforced not only by the seemingly insurmountable political ineptitude of the bourgeoisie; the democratization of the bourgeois state also favors the trends toward greater state independence. Although the situations in advanced and peripheral capitalisms are not strictly comparable, among the latter the bourgeoisie has proved to be even less able to establish a solid and stable hegemonic system than its more developed counterparts. If this is correct, then the pessimistic interpretations of the transformations experienced by the bourgeois state seem to be backed by the facts. Even long-established capitalist democracies appear to have embarked on an ominous journey for which the destination seems to be what Nicos Poulantzas calls *étatisme autoritarie,* a state form characterized by the incurable weakness of the representative mechanisms and institutions and by the irresistible predominance of state bureaucrats.[69] The *étatisme autoritarie* can no longer be regarded as exceptional or transient; on the contrary, it should be regarded as the new normal form of the bourgeois democratic republic in the current phase of the world capitalist system.

There are many general factors that explain the erosion of bourgeois hegemony and the unprecedented increase in the importance of the state. To all these some "national peculiarities" must necessarily be added in order for one to fully understand this phenomenon in each particular historical circumstance. Although a thorough discussion of these factors exceeds the scope of this book, the concrete manifestations of this crisis seem to have been very much discussed in recent years: take, for instance, the cases of the "crisis of democracy," or the already mentioned theses of the "ungovernability of democracy," or the "crisis of the welfare state," etc.

Three main sets of factors seem to explain the pervasive problems besieging bourgeois hegemony in contemporary capitalism.

The first concerns the inner contradictions of the capitalist class, which, compared with all other ruling classes hitherto known, "is least well adapted, and tends to be most averse, to taking direct charge of the operation of the state apparatus."[70] The reasons for this ineptitude are of different types, but they revolve around the fact that capital does not exist in a unified form but instead is always fragmented and internally divided: industrial, finance, and commercial capital are in an incessant struggle for the appropriation of the surplus value proceeding from the capitalist exploitation. To this highly divisive condition other complicating factors are added, derived from the survival of propertied precapitalist classes, like the landowners, that would fight with no less determination for the defense of the ground rent; or the contradictions and divisions due to the intervention of imperialist bourgeois sectors; or the fight among different individual capitalists to preserve their market shares; and so on. As a result, the dominant classes in capitalist

social formations are so deeply divided and weakened by structural cleavages (Mao's famous "secondary contradictions") that for them to arrive at an
effective degree of "class unity" is a rather extraordinary accomplishment.
Thus, Hal Draper is right when he argues,

> No other ruling class is so profusely criss-crossed internally with compet-
> ing and conflicting interest-groups, each at the other's throat. . . .
> Competing national groups (countries) are split by regional group interests,
> different industrial interests, antagonisms within an industry, rivalry
> between producers of consumer's and producer's goods, light and heavy
> industry, and so on, aside from religious, political, and other ideological
> differences.[71]

A second factor that explains the political ineptitude of the bourgeoisie
and the growing autonomization of the state is the development of the class
struggles and other social antagonisms, as well as the enhanced organizational capabilities of the subordinated classes to resist the bourgeois rule.
Because the bourgeoisie is weakened by its extraordinary disharmony, inco-
herence, and internal conflicts, it faces great difficulty in organizing a united front and in deciding on a common strategy to fight against the demands
of the popular classes. Incidentally, this is one of the structural reasons for
the great importance achieved by the intellectuals in bourgeois society,
because those individuals are much required for the continuous and trouble-
some task of developing an operative consensus.

However, Gramsci points out that in critical conjunctures, when the
class struggle reaches the peak of its intensity and the stability of capitalist
society seems to be in jeopardy, the bourgeoisie is usually able to react in a
swift manner and to secure

> the passage of the troops of many different parties under the banner of a
> single party, which better represents and resumes the needs of the entire
> class. . . . [This is] an organic and normal phenomenon, even if its rhythm
> is very swift—indeed almost like lightning in comparison with periods of
> calm. It represents the fusion of an entire social class under a single lead-
> ership, which alone is held to be capable of solving an overriding problem
> of its existence and of fending off a mortal danger.[72]

This fusion of an entire class, like the French "extraparliamentary bourgeois mass," implies that the class rallies behind a Bonapartist messiah
pushed by the exacerbation of the class struggles. It is the mounting pressure
from below, posing unusual demands to the state and the dominant classes,
that prompts the vigorous expansion of the state apparatuses and activities
even before a situation of organic crisis is reached. The combination of an
incompetent bourgeoisie, unable to be not only dominant but also a true ruling class—in the sense of moral and intellectual direction and leadership—
with the threat of political mobilization of the subordinated classes, no mat-

ter how coordinated and well organized these impulses are, has almost invariably been followed by a significant increase in the state's relative autonomy. Not only can state managers mobilize material and symbolic (as well as personal) resources to repress and demobilize the popular sectors, but they can also apply some selective policies that, although adversely affecting the interests of one or more individual capitalists or bourgeois groups, could be successful in preventing a catastrophic outcome for the dominant classes.

Of course, this last situation is more likely to occur as a response to a severe domestic and/or international economic crisis, or in prerevolutionary junctures when the activation of the popular masses is perceived as capable of endangering the stability of the system. In these cases the price that capital has to pay in order to uphold its domination includes the sacrifice of some specific sectoral interests—or, in critical cases, of entire social classes, remnants of old forms of production—namely nationalizations, transfers of specific industries and services to state ownership, and "antifeudal" agrarian reforms. One could say that the price the European bourgeoisie paid to prevent the socialist revolution from occurring in the West—after the nightmare of the Russian Revolution, the working-class offensive in the aftermath of World War I, and the Great Depression—included the extension of full citizenship to the popular classes and the establishment of the welfare state, two broad sets of policies that modified, in a statist and at the same time democratic direction, the relationship between state and dominant classes in advanced capitalism.

Other factors accounting for the increased role of the state include the outcome of the very logic of the state activities. Theda Skocpol has very well summarized this point, supplying evidence resulting from several historicomparative researches conducted within the framework of the Weberian-Hintzean tradition. She points out three possible itineraries through which the state's own structure and policies are likely to increase its degrees of autonomy:

> The linkage of states into transnational structures and into international flows of communication may encourage leading state officials to pursue transformative strategies even in the face of indifference or resistance from politically weighty social forces. Similarly, the basic need of states to maintain control and order may spur state-initiated reforms (as well as simple repression). As for who, exactly, is more likely to act in such circumstances, it seems that organizationally coherent collectivities of career officials relatively insulated from ties to currently dominant socioeconomic interests, are likely to launch distinctive new state strategies in times of crisis.[73]

It seems clear that the organizational dynamics of the state apparatus involve a built-in trend toward the assertion of state managers' autonomy and capacity for policy initiative. This convincing argument has also been theoretically examined by Fred Block in an effort to overcome what he considers the flaws inherent in the orthodox formulations of the relative autonomy of the state.[74] On the other hand, one could add in support of Skocpol's argument that the state's logic pushing toward a greater institutional autonomy was also reinforced by the new tasks and functions in capitalist reproduction assumed by the state after the Keynesian recomposition of the 1930s and 1940s. The enhanced role of the state (in both qualitative and quantitative terms) in capitalist accumulation had direct implications in terms of the organizational and administrative apparatuses. As a result, the state bureaucracy became bigger and stronger, endowed with larger legal and technical capacities for policy definition and implementation and, therefore, potentially capable of autonomous intervention in social life.

In conclusion, then, the capitalist state's relative autonomy is not accidental or transient but structural. It is built into the very foundation of this mode of production, and the laws of motion of the latter cannot be fully understood unless one assumes the relative autonomy of the state and all the so-called political superstructure. This basic feature is further accentuated by a set of conjunctural factors, some of which may have acquired, in late and dependent capitalism, a permanence bound to have structural consequences (for instance, the weakness of the national bourgeoisie besieged by imperialist capital, feudal landlords, and mobilized classes). At any rate, if relative autonomy is a distinctive and necessary characteristic of the capitalist state, it is nonetheless true that it also has definite limits: it cannot be absolute, and the invariant parameters of these variable degrees of relative autonomy are essentially fixed by the necessity to uphold the prevailing relations of production. This does not imply, as Skocpol seems to suggest, that in the Marxist tradition state autonomy is absorbed and diluted into the dynamics of capitalist economies and their typical class struggles; rather, it implies that every concrete state, in a given historical moment, has some definite degrees of independence established at the intersection of the structural and conjunctural determinants.[75] The problem, then, is to establish autonomy from whom, to do what, when, and how. The answers, of course, cannot be purely theoretical but must be a matter of empirical research.

The State as the Demiurge of History?

As mentioned at the beginning of this chapter, the outstanding role played by state policies in the capitalist recomposition of the postwar era placed the state at the center of the theoretical debate of the social sciences. In the 1980s, when the attack on the state became part of the standard neoconservative rhetoric, a paradox arose: the radical revaluation of the state as a key explanatory variable of historical processes in "state-centered" approaches in political science coincided with the neoliberal fervor that tends to make the state the public enemy to be defeated.

The rise of the state as a crucial causal factor was spurred by, among other things, the examples of the so-called revolutions from above that took place in a host of Third World countries and that revealed the exceptional relevance of state structures, initiatives, and policies in the reshaping of the modern world. These cases were regarded as outstanding instances of state autonomy, that is, as "historical situations in which strategic elites use military force to take control of an entire national state and then employ bureaucratic means to enforce reformist or revolutionary changes from above."[76]

The experiences of revolutions from above are well known in the historical experience of the West, even though in the metropolitan countries they fell short of acquiring the intensity manifested in the peripheral nations. Bonapartism was "invented" in a country as central to the capitalist international structure as France. Variants of an authoritarian and/or conservative reformism were found in Prussia between 1806 and 1814 and much later with Otto von Bismarck in Wilhelminian Germany, as well as in backward Russia, with the abolition of serfdom and the Stolypin reforms. Contrary to what Samuel P. Huntington asserts, this conservative reformism was not infrequent or uncommon in the history of capitalism. If capitalism had not been a social and economic regime endowed with extraordinary capacities for self-rationalization and endogenous reform, it would surely have perished at the hands of its many enemies. It is precisely this unprecedented flexibility of capitalism's inner structure and its ability to adapt to rapidly changing domestic and international conditions that perplexed the adversary "collapse theorists" of the Second and Third International as much as they reinforced the faith of bourgeois ideologues in the eternal life of this mode of production.[77]

According to one of the leading students of this phenomenon, Ellen Kay Trimberger, the extreme character of the revolution from above is due to the fact that a bureaucratic elite—civilian or military—strongly rooted in the state apparatuses takes over the upper ranks of the state to "destroy the economic and political base of the aristocracy, or upper class."[78] But what is the meaning of this formula?

I will assert, from the start, that revolutions from above can be adequately interpreted only if placed over the background of heterogeneous social formations in which capitalist relations of production coexist in uneasy harmony with other ancient modes of production. That arrangement was clearly the case in the four countries examined in Trimberger's book: Japan, Turkey, Egypt, and Peru. In all of them the strength of precapitalist classes, institutions, and cultural patterns was perhaps the most typical feature of these societies, and the revolutions from above that broke out there were all of an antifeudal and capitalist nature. In fact, these revolutions took the routes toward modern capitalism followed by some nations that arrived late at industrialism and modernity. Barrington Moore, Jr., poses this argument with full force when asserting, "The second main route to the world of modern industry we have called the capitalist and reactionary one, exemplified most clearly by Germany and Japan. There capitalism took hold quite firmly in both agriculture and industry and turned them into industrial countries. But it did so without a popular revolutionary upheaval."[79]

The crucial absence of this Jacobin ingredient allows one to understand the true character of the revolution from above as a bourgeois revolution produced under the triple threat of imperialist domination, feudal reaction, and socialist revolution. As Moore rightly observes, such revolutions are "reactionary," and this is paradoxical only in appearance: even if the scope of the structural transformations—no matter how partial and incomplete—unleashed by these revolutions in archaic social formations cannot be underestimated, the fact is that these initiatives were never meant to overcome capitalism. In all the cases the goal of the revolutionary thrust was to establish bourgeois supremacy and destroy the reactionary and socialist enemies. The revolutionary project exhausted itself in the full imposition of capitalism in areas that hitherto were marginal parts of the international system, in which comparatively weak bourgeois groupings were besieged by the predominance of imperialist capital, the backwardness of reactionary landowners, and the dreadful presence of vast popular masses too unreliable for an attack against the pillars of the ancien régime aimed at imposing a liberal and democratic capitalism.

The limits of the revolution from above exemplify the boundaries within which the autonomy of the state as a political actor is effective. Contrary to what is argued by the advocates of "state-centered" approaches, there is no historical evidence to support the belief that the autonomous initiatives of the state could eventually supersede the boundaries of capitalism. Moreover, the triumphant anticapitalist revolutions—in Russia, China, Vietnam, and Cuba—were in all the cases revolutions from below. Thus, neither by the positive nor by the negative will it be possible to sustain that revolutions from above have the capacity to transcend capitalism. This result confirms an insightful interpretation by Rosa Luxemburg:

> Every legal constitution is the product of a revolution. . . . During every historic period, work for reforms is carried on only in the direction given to it by the impetus of the last revolution, and continues as long as the impulsion of the last revolution continues to make itself felt. Or, to put it more concretely, in each historic period work for reforms is carried on only in the framework of the social form created by the last revolution. Here is the kernel of the problem.[80]

To sum up: the history of state reformism, both in Latin America and abroad, clearly reveals the limits of the capitalist state's independence vis-à-vis the dominant classes. Neither the reformism of the developed countries nor the diversity of revolutions from above have been able to supersede cap italism.

In the case of revolutions from above, the state initiatives are considerably enhanced by the failure of, or the extreme dangers posed by, a popular uprising capable not only of dismantling the ancien régime but of subverting capitalist society as well. Following Engels's observations regarding the peculiarities of the bourgeois revolution in Germany, Lenin argues that in cases like this the journey toward modern capitalism progresses along a "reactionary road," also called the "Junker road." This route distinctly rests on the predominance of latifundia and a strong and active state apparatus that serves as the coercive custodian of capitalist accumulation. The Junker road sharply contrasts with the "farmer road" followed in the historical experience of the United States, where the establishment of capitalism came hand in hand with the development of a powerful class of small landowners, the farmers, and with comparatively little state intervention.[81] However, Lenin's polar types did not preclude the existence of infinitely diverse combinations of different types of social and economic evolution, as proved by the enormous variety of concrete historical experiences.[82]

Therefore, revolutions from above are not at all analogous to the Junker road; rather, they are located in a grayish area in which both the Prussian and the farmer routes of capitalist development overlap. The Gramscian concept of "passive revolution" points directly toward this notion: there are revolutionary processes in which the Jacobin component—which was outstanding in the very special case of the French Revolution—is missing and for which the final result is the constitution of a capitalist social formation, like that in Germany, suffused with authoritarian legacies. In cases like these, capitalism is established without mass mobilization and without the destruction of the pillars of the old order: the crown, the landed upper classes, the Church, the praetorian army, and the patrimonialist bureaucracy. This feature may well be the one that distinguishes revolutions from above, which effectively destroy the foundations of the old regime, from the typical transformations, à la Junker, where latifundia and other precapitalist institutions are slowly transformed and accommodated to the new requirements of capitalist accumulation. It may be superfluous to underline the fact that, in Latin America, the Junker road has been the prevailing route toward the constitution of a capitalist economy, the only exception being Mexico, where the popular armed struggles of 1910–1917 were instrumental in the complete destruction of the ancien régime. The predominance of some variation of the Prussian way of establishing and developing capitalism in Latin America is not alien to the structural problems that have prevented the constitution of a bourgeois hegemony and a democratic capitalism in the region.

This last observation leads one to examine not so much the differences between the concepts of passive revolution and revolution from above as one of their crucial similarities: in both cases capitalism is implemented without existing political institutions being democratized. Traditional polit-ical despotism is thus barely "modernized," reconverted into a conservative and authoritarian capitalism equally mistrustful of the masses. It could be argued, therefore, that the revolution from above bears a strong resemblance to what Gramsci calls "progressive Caesarism"; in both cases there is a rev-olutionary element expressed in the destruction of the old regime, although the typical examples of the Junker model, such as German conservative cap-italist modernization under Bismarck, would point toward what Gramsci calls "regressive Caesarism."

The "New Reductionism," or the Traps of the Faith

The economist reductionism that has plagued socialist thought since its beginnings has taken a heavy toll on Marxist theory. However, the ardent passion that not infrequently seized some of the standard bearers of this much needed critique gave rise to an injudicious consequence: the exagger-ation of the potential margins of autonomy of the capitalist state. Even more injudicious, in some cases the arguments seem to wind up in a fallacious and barren dilemma: societalism, with economism being one of its variants, or state-centrism. Nevertheless, both reductionisms are completely wrong and have little to offer in terms of developing social and political theory. Moreover, not only do they impoverish the theoretical work, making it more difficult for one to understand the world, but reductionisms of any sort are also formidable obstacles to the much more demanding task of trying to change the world.

In the conclusion of an otherwise penetrating essay, Theda Skocpol invites her readers to return to the classic German conceptions of the state, to take inspiration in the plentiful and stimulating sources of the Weberian-Hintzean tradition, which is overwhelmingly superior to the conventional wisdom of mainstream political science. According to Skocpol, only after the full recovery of that rich theoretical legacy would it be possible to devel-op "middle range" theories concerning the role of the state in revolutionary processes and in social reforms, as well as in the promotion of welfare-ori-ented public policies, the creation of new political cultures, the institution-alization of social conflicts, and the setting of priorities in national agen-das.[83] However seductive this proposal may be, the fact is that unless it is accompanied by a similar emphasis placed on the side of civil society, the result will surely be the substitution of one (virtuous?) reductionism for another (evil?) one and the reification of the state as an independent entity transmuted, by the whim of the theory, into the veritable deus ex machina of history. Mutually exclusive polarities, like "state versus civil society," end up in a blind alley, promoting fruitless and byzantine debates whose theo-retical and practical significance is hard to understand. What is first, the state or the civil society? What is more important, the state or the civil society?

The return to Weber and Hintze and the revalorization of the German *staatslehre* tradition are fine, with two provisos. The first is that the recovery of Weberian-Hintzean perspective is not made on a reductionist key, replacing the decaying "economicism" now pervading the social sciences with the dubious fruitfulness of German "politicism." In order to prevent this from happening, recourse to the Marxist idea of totality is of the utmost importance. Second, the recuperation of the Weberian-Hintzean heritage cannot, and must not, be made uncritically, without rigorous scrutiny of its main definitions and theoretical arguments. Despite its immense wealth the German classical state tradition is far from being flawless, and some of its problems are serious ones. It would be deplorable to overlook those problems in the excitement of the moment.

Take, for instance, the muddled polemic of Weber with the coarsely "economicist," mummified Marxism of the Second International. It is surprising to discover Weber's ineptitude in distinguishing the politically provocative pamphlets of the German and European labor movement from the highly sophisticated scientific theorizing developed by Karl Marx during some twenty years in the reading room of the British Museum. I am not saying that Weber should have been a Marxist—if anything, that is a ridiculous pretense. But I do believe that Weber should have regarded Marxist theory much more seriously, studying it with the same care he took when examining other theories. It is certainly not an accident that two of Weber's most distinguished students, Ernst Bloch and George Lukács, embraced Marxism, disillusioned with the superficiality of Weberian criticism of the German philosopher and economist.[84]

Nevertheless, Weber's critique of the Second International Marxism buttressed a theoretical conception leading toward the reification of the state and strongly centered in the state's administrative and bureaucratic apparatuses, with total disregard for the movements and contradictions of the social formation on which the state rests. Moreover, this "apparatistic" bias goes hand in hand with the deliberate suppression of the issue of the pact of domination that invariably underlies the institutional materiality of the state. The state's government and the state's apparatuses, institutions, bureaucracies, agencies, and jurisdictions are simply indecipherable without due consideration to their relationship with the ruling classes whose political domination is ensured by the state.

In addition, given that one of the cornerstones of Weber's political theory is the rigid separation between economy and politics, it is not surprising to learn that in his analysis of the capitalist state he ends up totally disconnecting the administration of the res publica—embodied in the state's bureaucracy—from the overall class domination, the reality of which withers away in the conceptual labyrinths of Weber's ideal types. Weber certainly acknowledges that there is domination in the state, but he immediately adds that this is not class domination but rather rule by state managers. Although this theoretical perspective enhances the possibilities of studying the state as a collective actor, it certainly takes a heavy toll: the class basis of the state dissolves into thin air, and the links between state and civil society are severely undermined.

In this regard, the theoretical and methodological guidelines of Marxist theory seem, at least prima facie, more fruitful. Instead of regarding the state in its impossible isolation, as an autonomous "part" in the congeries of social fragments, it seems more enlightening to recover young Marx's suggestion and to examine the state as "the official *resumé* of the society," strongly arguing that "the state and the organization of the society, from a political standpoint, are not two different things. The state is the organization of society."[85]

State and society, in this heuristically richer proposal, cannot be regarded as isolated sectors. The former cannot be fully understood without its articulation with civil society, nor can the latter adequately be explained in itself without one resorting to the fiction of a "stateless" society, a proposal no less fantastic than the idea of a state apparatus floating above society and history. As mentioned previously, this kind of intellectual construction is exactly what Gramsci has in mind when he exposes the fallacies of free-market theories that assume the "artificial" and "intrusive" nature of state interventions.[86]

To sum up, the Weberian formulation not only results in a one-sided and incomplete idea of the state—downgraded to its apparatuses and bureaucracy—but also promotes a mistaken vision of political life. Weber regards politics as the pure realm of imposition and coercion, as the "war among opposing Gods." A political scientist rooted in the realist tradition of Machiavelli and Marx would hardly deny the role of force in history, but Weber's argument—echoed in the state theory of the Nazi constitutional scholar Karl Schmitt—overstretches the point to unacceptable limits because of its extreme one-sidedness. His argument completely disposes of the no less crucial consensual mechanisms—psychological, social, and cultural—through which class domination and economic exploitation are internalized and tolerated, and it seems to ignore that class rule is always a variable combination of force and consent, repression and persuasion, hegemony and domination. The eloquent Machiavellian metaphor that depicts the prince—that is, the state—as a centaur, half man and half beast, is completely alien to Weber's thought because in Weber's conceptual framework force prevails without ideological and/or psychological counterweights. The Gramscian concept of hegemony, of moral and intellectual leadership, has no room in the "iron cage" of Weberian theory, thus impoverishing one's understanding of the phenomenon of class rule in contemporary societies.

Given the foregoing comments it is quite clear that the reifying trends of the state-centered approach cannot be considered as safe roads for the progress of one's knowledge of "really existing capitalisms." There is a great danger of falling into a new brand of reductionism—perhaps more refined, documented, and sophisticated than the older brand but not much more fruitful for producing an adequate explanation of the social totality. The miseries of instrumentalism and economism will not be cured with a statist reductionism. "Stadolatry" is not a good medicine to remedy the ills of the more exacerbated versions of economism and societalism. What is required, on the contrary, is an integrated approach that takes into account the dialectical relationship between state and society, between economy and politics, able to discover the complex, nonlinear, nonmechanical, and non-deterministic links that fuse them in an organic totality.

Some of the tools for this job are to be found in the Marxist tradition, which has nothing to do with reductionisms of any sort. Yet, despite the fact that the fundamental premises of Marx's theoretical heritage seem to be a fertile ground for the development of a new theoretical synthesis, the pertinent warnings of Norberto Bobbio regarding the shortcomings of Marxist political theory must be fully acknowledged. However, Bobbio's reservations are not enough to discount the fact that Marx's theoretical perspectives on politics and the state are potentially more fruitful than those found in other theoretical traditions. The viewpoint of the totality, to use the felicitous phrase of Lukács, gives Marxist thought a decisive advantage precisely where other theoretical approaches succumb to the confusion of fragmentation and partiality. But this theoretical promise, in order to ensure its maturation, calls for both theoretical imagination and empirical research. It also requires one to understand that Marxism is not a collection of dogmatic beliefs officially interpreted by some infallible priest, and that the theoretical and practical success of its project of human and social liberation cannot be taken for granted.

Notes

1. Easton, David, *The Political System* (New York: Knopf, 1953), p. 106.

2. Cf. his "The political system besieged by the state," *Political Theory* 3 (August 1981), p. 303.

3. Ibid., p. 322.

4. Ibid., pp. 304–307.

5. Nettl, J. P., "The state as a conceptual variable," *World Politics* 20(4) (July 1968), p. 559.

6. Ibid., pp. 561–562 and 566–579 for some considerations regarding these relationships among capitalist development, formation of the national state, and intellectual tradition. However, this point is not sufficiently stressed by Nettl because the links he finds among economy, politics, and culture are rather tenuous and weak. On the other hand, it seems that his assertion that "England has been the stateless society *par excellence*," and in general his underestimation of the role of the state,

are highly questionable, as the analysis of Karl Polanyi, in his *The Great Transformation,* conclusively proves. Nettl's very notion of "Stateness" as a variable is strongly biased in the direction of a culturalist and ideological analysis, leaving aside the issues of the class basis of the state and its role as a historical actor.

7. Cf. Miliband, Ralph, *The State in Capitalist Society* (New York: Basic Books, 1969), p. 2.

8. Ibid., p. 2.

9. Ibid., pp. 3–4.

10. Ibid., p. 4 (emphasis in the original).

11. On this regard see Poulantzas, Nicos, *Poder político y clases sociales en el estado capitalista* (Mexico: Siglo XXI, 1969), pp. 346–350, and Cardoso, Fernando H., *Estado y sociedad en America Latina* (Buenos Aires: Nueva visión, 1972), pp. 229–247.

12. Cf. Anderson, Perry, "The antinomies of Antonio Gramsci," *New Left Review* 100 (November 1976–January 1977), pp. 5–78.

13. Cardoso, Fernando H., *Ideologías de la burguesía industrial en sociedades dependientes: Argentina y Brasil* (Buenos Aires: Siglo XXI, 1971), p. 60.

14. Engels, Friedrich, "Letter to Conrad Schmidt (1890)," in Selsam, Howard, David Goldway, and Harry Martel (eds.), *Dynamics of Social Change: A Reader in Marxist Social Science* (New York: International Publishers, 1970), p. 71 (emphasis in the original).

15. Gramsci, Antonio, *Selections from the Prison Notebooks* (New York: International Publishers, 1971), p. 260. See also Cerroni, Umberto, *La libertad de los modernos* (Barcelona: Martínez Roca, 1972), pp. 182–236; and Córdova, Arnaldo, *Sociedad y estado en el mundo moderno* (Mexico: Grijalbo, 1976), p. 59.

16. Marx, Karl, *The Poverty of Philosophy* (Moscow: n.d.), p. 202.

17. Cf. Block, Fred, "Beyond relative autonomy: State managers as historical subjects," in *Revising State Theory, Essays in Politics and Postindustrialism* (Philadelphia: Temple University, 1987), pp. 84–87; p. 36; Skocpol, Theda, "Bringing the state back in: Strategies of analysis in current research," in Evans, Peter, Dietrich Rueschemeyer, and Theda Skocpol, *Bringing the State Back In* (Cambridge: Cambridge University Press, 1985).

18. Marx, Karl, Prologue to *Critique of Political Economy,* in Marx, Karl, and Friedrich Engels, *Obras Escogidas en Dos Tomos* (Moscow: Progreso, 1966), Vol. 1, p. 347.

19. On this, see Sereni, Emilio, "Da Marx a Lenin: la categoria di 'formazione economico sociale,'" *Critica Marxista* 4 (1970); Luporini, Cesare, "Marx secondo Marx," *Critica Marxista* 2–3 (March–June 1972) and the special issue "Mode de production et formation economique et sociales," published by *La Pensée* 159 (October 1971).

20. See Lenin, V. I., "A great beginning," in *On Utopian and Scientific Socialism* (Moscow: Progress Publishers, 1970), p. 157.

21. Moore, Stanley W., *The Critique of Capitalist Democracy* (New York: Augustus M. Kelley Publishers, 1969), p. 26.

22. Marx, Karl, *Capital,* (New York: International Publishsers, 1974), Vol. 3, pp. 791–792.

23. Marx, Karl, "Letter to the editor of Otyecestvenniye Zapisky," in Selsam, Goldway, and Martel, *Dynamics,* p. 71.

24. Cf. Cerroni, Umberto, *Teoría política y socialismo* (Mexico: ERA, 1976), pp. 46–89; Lenin, V. I., *What Is to Be Done?* (New York: International Publishers, 1969).

25. For an analysis of the Stalinist conception see Claudín, Fernando, *La crisis del Movimiento Comunista* (Paris: Ruedo Ibérico, 1970), pp. 3–94.

26. Nordlinger, Eric A., *On the Autonomy of the Democratic State* (Cambridge, MA: Harvard University Press, 1981) p. 207.

27. Ibid., pp. 212–219. On the Marxist attitude concerning the state see Bobbio, Norberto, et al., *Il Marxismo e lo stato* (Rome: Mondoperaio, 1976).

28. Nordlinger, *On the Autonomy*, p. 11.

29. Cf. Cardoso, Fernando H., "On the characterization of authoritarian regimes in Latin America," in Collier, David, *The New Authoritarianism in Latin America* (Princeton: Princeton University Press, 1979), pp. 33–57; O'Donnell, Guillermo, "Tensions in the bureaucratic-authoritarian state and the question of eemocracy," in ibid., pp. 285–318; Rueschemeyer, Dietrich, and Peter B. Evans, "The state and economic transformation: Towards an analysis of the conditions underlying effective intervention," in Evans, Peter B., Dietrich Rueschemeyer, and Theda Skocpol, *Bringing the State Back In* (Cambridge: Cambridge University Press, 1985), pp. 44–77.

30. Weber, Max, *Economía y sociedad* (Mexico: Fondo de Cultura Económica, 1964), pp. 692–694.

31. See, on this regard, Kosik, Karel, *Dialéctica de lo concreto* (Mexico: Grijalbo, 1967); and Cohen, G. A., *Karl Marx's Theory of History: A Defence* (Oxford: Clarendon Press. 1978), pp. 115–133 and 326–344.

32. Lukács, George, *History and Class Conciousness* (Cambridge, MA: MIT Press, 1971), pp. 6–12.

33. Marx, Karl, *Grundrisse* (New York: Vintage Books, 1973), p. 101.

34. Lukács, *History*, pp. 12–13.

35. Ibid., p. 27 (emphasis mine).

36. Offe, Claus, "Structural problems of the capitalist state," in von Beyme, Klaus, ed., *German Political Studies.*

37. Ibid., p. 37.

38. Ibid., p. 38.

39. Offe, Claus, and Volker Ronge, "Tesi per ina fondazione teorica della nozione di 'stato capitalistico' e per una metodologia materialistica della politologia," in Basso, Lelio, ed., *Stato e crisi delle instituzioni* (Milan: Gabriele Mazzota editore, 1978), pp. 36–38.

40. Therborn, Göran, *What Does the Ruling Class Do When It Rules?* (London: New Left Books, 1978), p. 144.

41. Ibid., p. 161.

42. Block, Fred, "The ruling class does not rule: Notes on the Marxist theory of the state," in *Revising State Theory*, pp. 53–54.

43. Poulantzas, Nicos, *Clases sociales y poder político en el estado capitalista* (Mexico: Siglo XXI, 1969), pp. 331–402.

44. Block, *Revising State Theory*, p. 56.

45. Ibid., p. 58.

46. Ibid., p. 83.

47. "Contradiction and overdetermination," in Althusser, Louis, *For Marx* (New York: Pantheon Books, 1969), p. 111.

48. Cf. Block, Fred, *Revising State Theory*, p. 86.

49. Cf. *Capitalism and Social Democracy* (Cambridge: Cambridge University Press, 1985), p. 139.

50. Block, *Revising State Theory*, p. 88.

51. Marx, *Capital*, Vol. 3, pp. 790–791.

52. On this, see Draper, Hal, *Karl Marx's Theory of Revolution* (New York:

Monthly Review Press, 1977), Vol. 3, pp. 468–469; see also Lucio Colletti's brilliant "Introduction" to *Karl Marx: Early Writings* (London: New Left Review Editions, 1974), and the prologue by Adolfo Sánchez Vázquez to the Spanish version of Marx's *Critique of Hegel's Philosophy of Right* (Mexico: Grijalbo, 1968).

53. Ibid., p. 468.

54. Marx, *Capital,* Vol. 1, pp. 577–578.

55. Reproduced in Selsam, Goldway, and Martel, *Dynamics,* p. 76.

56. Ibid., p. 77.

57. In Tucker, Robert C., ed., *The Marx-Engels Reader* (New York: W. W. Norton, 1972), p. 644.

58. Ibid., p. 647.

59. Althusser, *For Marx,* op. cit., p. 113.

60. Wood, Ellen Meiksins, "The separation of the economic and political in capitalism," *New Left Review* 127 (May–June 1981), pp. 81–82. See also Luporini, Cesare, "Critica della politica e critica della economia politica in Marx," *Critica Marxista* 16(1) (January–February 1978), pp. 17–50.

61. Tucker, *The Marx-Engels Reader,* pp. 653–654.

62. On this, see Draper, *Karl Marx's Theory,* Vol. 1, pp. 385 passim. For the special case of Absolutism, see Anderson, Perry, *Lineages of the Absolutist State* (London: New Left Review Editions, 1974).

63. On this regard it is interesting to compare the concluding statements of Marx's *Eighteenth Brumaire,* written in 1852, with the self-critical assessment of his own predictions made in 1871 in *The Civil War in France.*

64. Gramsci, *Selections,* p. 210.

65. Ibid., p. 210.

66. Ibid., p. 221.

67. Ibid., p. 222.

68. Reproduced in Draper, *Karl Marx's Theory,* Vol. 1, p. 336.

69. Poulantzas, Nicos, *Estado, poder y socialismo* (Madrid: Siglo XXI, 1979), p. 254.

70. Draper, *Karl Marx's Theory,* Vol. 1, p. 321.

71. Ibid., p. 323. See also Evans, Peter, and Dietrich Rueschemeyer, "The state and economic transformation: Toward an analysis of the conditions underlying effective intervention," in Evans, Peter, Dietrich Rueschemeyer, and Theda Skocpol, eds., *Bringing the State Back In,* pp. 60–68.

72. Gramsci, *Selections,* p. 211

73. Skocpol, Theda, "Bringing the state back in: Strategies of analysis in current research," in Evans, Peter, Dietrich Rueschemeyer, and Theda Skocpol, eds., *Bringing the State Back In,* p. 9.

74. See his "Beyond relative autonomy" and "The ruling class," in *Revising State Theory.*

75. Skocpol, "Bringing," p. 5.

76. Cf. Skocpol, Theda, "Bringing," p. 9.

77. Cf. Huntington, Samuel P., *Political Order in Changing Societies* (New Haven: Yale University Press, 1968), pp. 344–345. On capitalist "revolutions from above," see Moore, Barrington, Jr., *Social Origins of Dictatorship and Democracy* (Boston: Beacon Press, 1966), especially pp. 440–442. The perplexity of the main theorists of the European labor movement in light of the resiliency and durability shown by capitalist structures is superbly portrayed in Claudín, Fernando, *La crisis del movimiento comunista* (Paris: Ruedo Ibérico, 1970), pp. 25–73.

78. Cf. Trimberger, Ellen Kay, *Revolution from Above* (New Brunswick: Transaction Books, 1978), p. 3.

79. Moore, *Social Origins,* p. 433.

80. Luxemburg, Rosa, "Reform or revolution?" in *Rosa Luxemburg Speaks* (New York: Pathfinder Press, 1970), p. 77.

81. A proviso must be made, of course, in order to account for the existence of the slave-owner economy in the U.S. South, a fact that more often than not is overlooked in many discussions on this issue.

82. Lenin, V. I., *The Development of Capitalism in Russia* (Moscow: Progress Publishers, 1967), pp. 31–34.

83. Cf. Skocpol, Theda, "Bringing," pp. 7–11.

84. Consider, for instance, that the sparse but highly derogatory critical notes that Weber addresses to Marxist theory deal with some of the most popular metaphors used by Marx and Engels in the Communist Manifesto. Did Max Weber ever read *Capital* or *The Eighteenth Brumaire of Louis Bonaparte*? One may only guess.

85. Marx, Karl, "Critical marginal notes on the article 'The king of Prussia and social reform: By a Prussian,'" in Padover, Saul K., ed., *Karl Marx On Revolution* (New York: McGraw-Hill Co., 1971), p. 14.

86. See discussion in Chapter 2 of this book.

5

Democracy and Social Reform in Latin America: Reflections on the European Experience

The situation of Latin America in the mid-1980s, when practically all the countries were embarked on a democratic transition, rekindled an old discussion regarding the limits and possibilities of both social reform and a democratic capitalism. As is widely known, this debate was a landmark for one of the most enlightened periods in the history of the Second International, when the brightest minds of the socialist movement made contributions of unique significance to socialist theory.[1] Roused at the end of the past century, when the prospects of socialist revolution had faded away, the controversy gained strength during World War I and the Russian Revolution. The heated discussion regrettably ended in a double divorce, both in terms of theory as well as in the political practice of the left: socialism disassociated from democracy, and social reform disassociated from revolution.

It could not have been a more unfortunate result: social democrats gave up their claims for change and their project for the construction of a socialist society—freed from the capitalist plagues that they had denounced during almost half a century—and contented themselves with the achievement of much more modest goals, such as attempting to insufflate some sense of social solidarity into monopoly capitalism. On the other hand, the communist revolutionaries ended up creating what would later be known as "really existing socialism," which sank in the stormy waters of a bureaucratic despotism that condemned the regimes to be politically authoritarian, morally unacceptable, and grossly inefficient in the administration of the economy.[2]

Almost a century after the climax of that controversy, the history of capitalism—both in the center and in the periphery—and the failure of socialism in the former Soviet Union and Eastern Europe make unavoidable a thorough reexamination of this dense and complex issue. In fact, one cannot seriously speak of democracy without also discussing socialism; neither can one think about socialism while ignoring the centrality of the democratic question. On the other hand, history's unappealable verdict shows—and

Latin America offers definitive evidence in this respect—that social revolutions were necessary to carry out transcendent reforms in the basic structures of society, and that the reformist impulse devoid of a clear vision of a political utopia—"construction of impossible worlds which give birth to the formation of possible worlds"—culminates in the disappointing administration of daily routines.[3]

The goal of this chapter will be to establish, in light of the concrete historical experiences of advanced capitalist democracies, the basis of the need for social reform at a time when Latin America is undergoing the most serious economic and social crisis of this century and when policies of structural adjustment heightening the region's societies' most backward and aberrant features are being put into practice.

It is important to prevent the arguments used in this chapter from becoming a sterile, fatally pessimistic vision of the present juncture. Such a vision can be the result of unilaterally insisting on destructive aspects and losing sight of what Massimo Cacciari accurately calls "the productivity of crisis," that is, the capacity of reasoning to open new paths that were closed until yesterday and to widen the horizon of visibility of social subjects.[4] Yet the perspective that argues the unlikelihood—or even worse, the futility—of reform in capitalist societies has a direct counterpart that is no less mistaken: the one defiantly expressed by Ludolfo Paramio, a Spanish theorist and a major advisor of Felipe González:

> Reformism is the superior form of labor movement consciousness, and the reforms that the labor movement has imposed on capitalist society do not amount to its improvement but are stages in its transformation into a socialist system. In order to accept this second assertion it is necessary to admit that we are witnessing a change in the relation of forces among classes, change that, despite its century-long duration, would clearly point toward the ascent of the proletariat as the new dominant class.[5]

This quote is significant because it summarizes a widespread, profoundly inaccurate conception among reformists; it mistakes the actors' intentions for actual social processes. The aim here is not to judge such intentions, which due to a sound methodological principle may be assumed to be noble and altruistic. Nonetheless, it is important to recall what history teaches regarding the gap between the concrete results of the actions of the most inspired individuals and their original intentions. Rosa Luxemburg has some thoughts that are fully pertinent to this matter:

> It is contrary to history to represent work for reforms as a long-drawn-out revolution, and revolution as a condensed series of reforms. A social transformation and a legislative reform do not differ according to their duration but according to their content. . . . That is why people who pronounce themselves in favor of the method of legislative reform *in place of and in contradistinction to* the conquest of political power and social revolution,

do not really choose a more tranquil, calmer and slower road to the *same* goal, but a *different* goal. Instead of taking a stand for the establishment of a new society they take a stand for surface modification of the old society.[6]

Not too many arguments are needed to demonstrate that the facts serve to prove Rosa Luxemburg's thesis: no matter how genuine and energetic, social reforms do not change the nature of the preexisting society. They can change many important features of social life, but not the fundamental structure on which society rests. Reforms are not a protracted revolution that unfolds by stages until they arrive at a new society with the imperceptibility of the traveler who crosses the Equatorial line—to use Edward Bernstein's famous metaphor. The construction of "possible worlds" does not work this way. Almost a century of reformism in the West was not enough to supersede capitalism. Contrary to Paramio's assertion, the system has not been transformed in the direction toward socialism but rather has consolidated itself as an increasingly segmented and exclusivist (though more flexible) capitalism, now endowed with a greater capacity to adapt and control its own crises, as well as strengthened by a democratic legitimacy unthinkable in more primitive phases of its development. And if one speaks of a correlation of forces, Paramio's diagnosis is even more reckless given that one must surely possess a keen vision in order to perceive those secular tendencies that would unequivocally demonstrate the rise of the proletariat as a new dominant class in the panorama of developed capitalist societies—not to mention the periphery. Rather, what most people distinguish are quite less exciting and promising phenomena, such as the reactionary neoconservative wave in Northern Europe or in the United States; or the capitulation of "Mediterranean socialisms" in Southern Europe, suddenly transformed into agents and administrators of capitalist adjustment. In a notable and controversial study, Adam Przeworski summarizes the experience of a century of reformism with the following words: "Reforms would lead to socialism if and only if they were (1) irreversible; (2) cumulative in effects; (3) conducive to new reforms, and (4) directed towards socialism. As we have seen, reformist socialists since the 1890's thought that reforms would indeed satisfy all these conditions and thus gradually cumulate in socialism. So far at least they have not."[7]

In short, social reforms have decisively contributed to making possible certain welcome changes *within* capitalist society. However, history has yet to register a single case in which reforms have managed to transcend capitalism and implement a superior form of economic and social organization. Accordingly, Latin America should enter the path of social reforms but should not forget the lessons of the past that show that reforms will not erase the basic character of real-world capitalist formations. Like the legend that Dante imagines at the gate of Hell, at the entrance of this path one can also read *Lasciate ogni speranza voi che entrate*. However, in the present national and international juncture, reforms are Latin America's only opportunity to advance socially, and the region will have to wait until objective and subjective conditions change before it can get a glimpse of more promising alternatives. The mistake of many reformists has been to confuse necessity with virtue: although under the present circumstances a reformist policy is the only feasible option, that does not make it an appropriate instrument for the historical supersession of capitalism. Reforms are necessary and perhaps are possible, but this fact does not make reforms ideal if one's eyes are fixed on the horizon of the socialist utopia. One may aspire to more while living in a time of a neoconservative reflux that forces people to be content with less. Edelberto Torres Rivas insightfully captures this paradox when he asserts that "in the 1990s we live in a stage in which revolution as a proposal for a better society is more necessary than ever, but at the same time revolution has become impossible in the current regional and international circumstances."[8]

In similar times, toward the end of his life a century ago, Engels wisely warned that one should not allow impatience to become a theoretical argument because by doing so one could make the mistake of misconstruing reforms and transforming them, with the heat of one's disappointments, into a revolution by stages. If many political forces are energetically and convincingly promoting the need to introduce thorough reforms in capitalism, it is because the progressive forces cannot remain passive until the uncertain "decisive day" of social revolution arrives. The pathetic situation in which great sectors of Latin American societies find themselves demands immediate corrections that the bourgeoisie will accept only if faced by overwhelmingly unfavorable forces. As history and society move dialectically, the result of these innovations will be a temporary strengthening of capitalist society. Correspondingly, once mature, these transformations will enable the transition toward socialism in accordance with Marx's theoretical stipulations. Those who—wearied by the triumph of capitalism—reproach this stance for its mixture of optimism and volunteerism should recall Rousseau's words: "If Rome and Sparta perished, what state can hope to last for ever?"[9] Or has capitalism become immortal?

Hence, a question arises: what are the actual possibilities that Latin America has for consolidating a democratic order, given the prevailing national and international conditions, and what is the role to be played by a reformist policy in this process? The current juncture, characterized by a prolonged international economic recession, foreign indebtedness, and harsh policies of structural adjustment (with the subsequent mass unemployment, skyrocketing poverty, social disorganization, etc.); the collapse of authoritarian socialisms and the renewed disequilibria in the international system; the enduring legacies of authoritarian experiences; and the deepening cleavages and disintegration of fragile social and economic structures loudly demand the immediate implementation of resolute reformist policies.

Consequently, one of the central theses of this book is that Latin American democracies will be able to survive only if they possess the audacity and wisdom required to promote an ambitious program of social reforms aimed at substantially transforming these societies. If the new democratic regimes lack this profound reformist vocation, they will languish and finally succumb to the combined attacks of crisis and the intolerance of the most reactionary sectors of their societies. Only sincere and genuine reformism will allow Latin Americans to resolve the present crises positively and creatively, thereby ensuring the consolidation of democratic institutions and present-day democratic achievements and establishing the basis for further developments.

Democratic Reconstruction: Europe's Lessons

History does not usually repeat itself. In those rare instances when it does, what had previously been a tragedy reappears as a farce. In this sense, the rich and varied European experience may be used for a reflection on the likely future of Latin American democracies and not as its ex ante codification. The second European postwar period and, to a certain extent, the first one (think of the Weimar Republic and the advent of fascism in Italy) seem to be fertile grounds for comparative imagination.[10]

In fact, as World War II ended, Europe was overwhelmed by the trauma of the conflict, which burdened the souls of the winners as much as those of the defeated. Moreover, the ethical misery of fascism had poisoned the European cultural atmosphere and corroded basic social solidarities, magnifying the obstacles to national reconstruction. In addition, the continent was overwhelmed by the physical destruction of great parts of its territory and of its productive units at an unprecedented scale. In short, for its reconstruction, Europe needed a miracle. Many maintain that an "economic miracle" did occur, and they do not cease to praise the wisdom of the postwar elite that recast European capitalism. Nonetheless, what was truly miraculous was that Europe was able to emerge in democracy from the marasmus of the postwar period.[11]

However, postwar Europe is not a mirror in which Latin America can see its own future. There are a series of circumstances that prevent one from establishing a direct analogy between postwar Europe and the present crisis of Latin America.

First and foremost, the economic and political reconstruction of Western Europe was carried out amidst an extraordinary expansion of the international capitalist economy. In fact, the period between 1948 and 1973 is regarded as the golden age of capitalism, characterized by high growth rates and sustained increases in output, trade, employment, and real wages. Latin American democratic transition, on the other hand, takes place within a recessive environment, in a descendent or relatively stagnant cycle of the evolution of the world capitalist economy.

Second, the European reconstruction took place within a global economic and strategic framework that favored the massive transfer of U.S. capital toward Europe. The Marshall Plan was not the only channel through which great amounts of money reached the devastated European economies and notably contributed to their accelerated reactivation. In Latin America, though, just the opposite is occurring: the burden of foreign debt forces the region to export capital to the United States and—to a lesser degree—to the industrialized countries of the Paris Club. The amounts of this capital export are roughly equivalent to the cost of one Marshall Plan every two years and, in terms of gross national product (GNP), represent a proportion equal to twice what the Treaty of Versailles specified for the Weimar Republic to pay as war reparations.

Third, in Europe, the defeated countries not only saw their cities and factories destroyed: the allies had also swept away the classes, groups, and institutions traditionally known as the bulwarks of authoritarianism and reaction. Germany emerged from the war without its notorious Junkers, with its despotic state bureaucracy in complete disarray, and with its army—the secular pillar of the reaction—dispersed and destroyed. Something similar happened in Italy and in Japan. None of this has occurred in Latin America, where democratic transitions in general took place under much more unfavorable conditions characterized by, among other things, the continuous presence of the authoritarian actors, who—patiently waiting for better times—reluctantly accepted the democratic flood.

Fourth, the European reconstruction was carried out within a Keynesian economic and political environment, which stimulated the adoption of expansive economic policies for the purpose of ensuring economic growth, full employment, and a sustained rise of the standard of living of the national majorities. On the contrary, the present juncture of Latin America is distinguished by neoliberal predominance, which imposed monetarist and recessive fiscal and structural "adjustments" on the region's economies. This dogma is fervently supported by the most varied governments of the area, and its global effect is to consecrate "social Darwinism" of the market, with its scandalous consequences for justice and equality.

Finally, the ideological climate of postwar Europe was dominated by the exaltation of recently recovered freedom and democracy, as well as by a condemnation of Nazism and totalitarianism. The prevailing mood in Latin America is quite different and expresses above all a cautious skepticism regarding democracy, social entitlements, and corrective state interventions, as consistently expressed by neoconservative intellectuals and politicians. Paradoxically, whereas a great part of the so-called post-Marxist left seems to have arrived at the conclusion that capitalism and democracy are no longer opposed because their contradictions seem to have been solved, the

most lucid representatives of the right do not cease to express their pessimism regarding this surprising marriage. In the 1970s British economist
Samuel Brittan, for instance, wondered whether democracy could manage
the economy. His answer was carefully negative, although he formulated it
with the elegance and tactfulness required to avoid upsetting the democratic consciousness of the times. The same can be said of Samuel Huntington
and the rest of the theorists involved in preparing the Trilateral Commission's report on the governability of democracies, although in this case the
concerns regarding the dysfunctions of democracy for capitalist accumulation were revealed quite straightforwardly. It is interesting to highlight this
incongruity: whereas scholars originally linked to socialist thought seem to
have become strongly convinced of the reconciliation of the rather odd cou-
ple formed by capitalism and democracy, the intellectual representatives of
the right do not cease to voice their skepticism, urging more "moderation"
in the exercise of democratic rights and advocating the depolitization of
social life. Who is more likely to be right?

In sum: those highly favorable postwar conditions, as well as the
ripeness of European political forces, made possible the democratic reconstruction of that continent. Equally important was the fact that this entire
postwar era was dominated by the unquestionable supremacy of Keynes's
theories regarding the role of public spending and economic policies at
large. As discussed in previous chapters, Keynes revolutionized the conventional wisdom of the economists of his times as he gave shape to a conscious
strategy of state-centered capitalist regulation and organization that
implied—to the dismay of neoclassic priests—piously burying the old myth
of the self-regulated market. This sacrilege, more than a half a century later,
continues to haunt the dreams of nostalgic souls such as Milton Friedman
and Friedrich von Hayek. In fact, Keynes not only proclaimed the end of
laissez-faire but also devised an elaborate set of prescriptions that in practice assigned to the state the key role in the process of capitalist accumulation. With Keynes, "capital becomes Marxist" as it recognizes the structural character of its endemic contradictions and the anarchy of the productive
process, thus transferring the tasks of its own organization to the state—that
"ideal collective capitalist" of which Engels speaks. The market, which had
been incapable of rationally organizing capitalist exploitation, yielded its
place to the state.[12]

The Keynesian revolution implied a drastic modification of the preexisting articulation between the state and civil society. The progressive "centrality" of the state in the process of capitalist accumulation and the ensuing
expansion of the state apparatuses and jurisdictions were precociously
detected by Antonio Gramsci. The institutional form assumed by the
decantation of these new practices, discourses, and state capacities came to
be known as the welfare state. And as Buci-Glucksmann and Therborn suggest, its insertion in the social totality was effected through two main

avenues: (1) a model of accumulation and development, which expressed the complex relation between the state and capital, and (2) a model of hegemony-domination, centered in the equally complex relation between the state and the popular masses.[13]

This process of integration of the masses into the state qualitatively changed the character of politics in advanced capitalist formations: to the horror of old liberals, the state came to promote—or at least welcome—the development and organization of the corporative representative structures of the popular classes. To be sure, this process was far from being homogeneous in central capitalist countries. Its character depended on the specific historical conditions and the weight of political, organizational, and ideological traditions proper of the labor movement and the left in each nation. Nonetheless, beyond these national variations this new chapter in the history of the state was marked by the rise of complex structures of intermediation that were quite successful at controlling the initiatives originated at the base and at defusing the threat of a radical protest, thus guaranteeing an extended period of "social peace." Yet, at the same time, this new model of governance made the legitimacy of the rulers heavily dependent on the consensus of the subordinate classes. Consequently, the Keynesian state required two logics, which were very difficult to synchronize, to be made compatible: one of an economic character, aimed at reactivating and stabilizing capitalist accumulation, and another, of a political nature, that tended to establish social peace, institutionalize social antagonisms, and create a stable and legitimate bourgeois democracy.[14]

This class compromise proved satisfactory as long as the economy retained its capacity for growth. Inasmuch as the growth rate fell, the exchange of goods liable for trade in the competitive political market—material well-being, jobs, salary raises in exchange for political legitimacy—became cumbersome and consensus began to erode. However, it is true that for quite a long time the Keynesian state retained an extraordinary capacity to process the contradictions of the renewed bourgeois society. This was reflected in the expansion of the state's social expenditures, which eloquently mirrored the scope—and also the limits—of the reformist policies put into effect during the postwar period.[15] In other words, the very materiality of the *Sozialstaat* hinged on its undeniable capacity to legalize and administer social reform. Bourgeois democracy could not socialize political power and the means of production—this was and still is, its structural limit—yet it could carry out effective policies of income redistribution and social reform that endowed capitalist democracy with a profound and long-lasting legitimacy in the eyes of the European popular classes. What had formerly seemed a fraud or a sham revealed itself as a promising reality during the golden years of the postwar period.

A quick glance at some of the data on the expansion of social expenditures in European countries shows the close relationship between the political integration of the popular sectors and the sustained increase of state social spending. Examination of the available figures leads to three general conclusions.

1. A statistical study on the evolution of the welfare state in Western Europe made by Peter Flora and Jens Alber shows the significant relationship between the proportion of votes from the left and the adoption of four different social security policies.[16] Although the authors do not offer an estimate of regression and correlation coefficients, the estimated regression line shown in Figure 5.1 would prove the intensity of the correlation. The thesis that the welfare policies of the Keynesian state were the result of a bourgeois stratagem to dupe the masses collapses when confronted with these facts. The data prove that the expansion of social benefits was the result of the militancy of the popular classes and their collective organizations. Whenever the popular classes lacked the necessary political strength, the dominant class retained its traditional prerogatives and refrained from promoting social policies for the poor, the elderly, the sick, the disabled, and so on. When, on the contrary, the pressure from below was efficiently articulated, the bourgeoisie grudgingly admitted the new social conquests of the workers.

2. The values shown in Table 5.1 prove that the presence of the masses within the heart of capitalist states had lasting effects on the size and composition of state spending: social expenditures expanded as the reforms and programs established during the postwar period were consolidated. The available quantitative evidence shows that in the period that ended two years after the outburst of the 1973 crisis—that is, between 1960 and 1975—the social expenditures of the capitalist states in education, health, social security, and other income protection programs consistently outpaced, in real terms, the growth rates of the GNP in all Organization for Economic Cooperation and Development (OECD) countries: 8.4 percent versus 4.6 percent.[17] In sum, social spending grew between 1960 and 1981 in all OECD countries, in the seven economies that constitute the most advanced nucleus of international capitalism as well as in the other members of the organization. The average of social spending as a percentage of GNP for the "big seven" was 13.7 percent in 1960, and it grew to almost twice as much by 1981, reaching 24.8 percent; for the entire OECD the figures were 13.1 percent and 25.6 percent, respectively. Additionally, it is important to point out that such a tendency persisted—although somewhat weakened—even *after* the outburst of the crisis in 1975: social expenditures grew at a yearly rate of 4.8 percent between 1975 and 1981, though GNP grew, for all the OECD countries, only 2.6 percent per year. Despite the fact that the growth rate of social spending after 1973 showed some signs of slowing down, it continued to be greater than or equal to the rate of growth of the GNP (except in Canada, the Netherlands, and the Federal Republic of Germany).

Figure 5.1   Social Insurance Legislation and Levels of Political Mobilization in Western Europe, 1880–1970

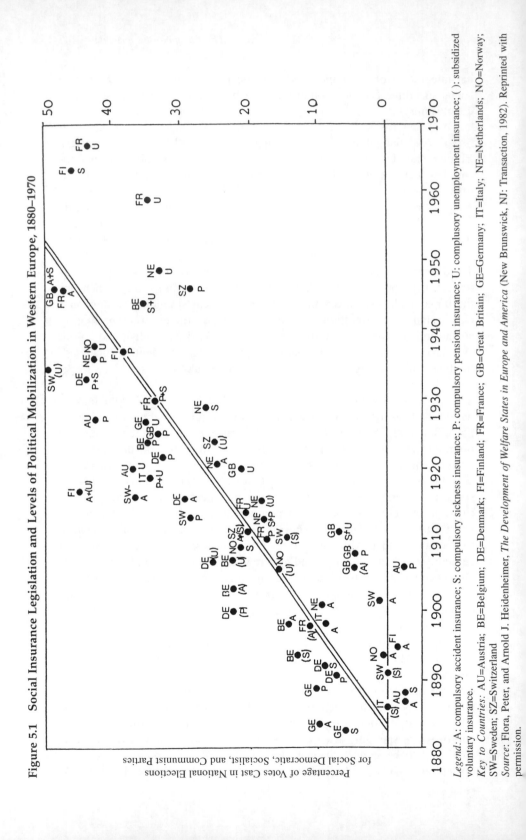

Legend: A: compulsory accident insurance; S: compulsory sickness insurance; U: compulsory unemployment insurance; P: compulsory pension insurance; (): subsidized voluntary insurance.

Key to Countries: AU=Austria; BE=Belgium; DE=Denmark; FI=Finland; FR=France; GB=Great Britain; GE=Germany; IT=Italy; NE=Netherlands; NO=Norway; SW=Sweden; SZ=Switzerland

Source: Flora, Peter, and Arnold J. Heidenheimer, *The Development of Welfare States in Europe and America* (New Brunswick, NJ: Transaction, 1982). Reprinted with permission.

This empirical evidence of developed capitalist countries allows one to reject the neoliberal thesis that economic "adjustments" are possible only if the social compromises made by the state are substantially cut. Except for a few cases, such a policy was not implemented by OECD countries.

Table 5.1   Social Spending in OECD Countries, 1960–1981[a]

	Social Expenditures as % of GNP		Yearly Growth Rate of GNP (%)		Yearly Growth Rate of Social Expenditures in Constant Values (%)	
	1960	1981	1960–1975	1975–1981	1960–1975	1975–1981
Canada	12.1	21.5	5.1	3.3	9.3	3.1
France	13.4[b]	29.5	5.0	2.8	7.3[b]	6.2
FRG	20.5	31.5	3.8	3.0	7.0	2.4
Italy	16.8	29.1	4.6	3.2	7.7	5.1
Japan	8.0	17.5	8.6	4.7	12.8	8.4
UK	13.9	23.7	2.6	1.0	5.9	1.8
USA	10.9	20.8	3.4	3.2	8.0	3.2
Average[e]	13.7	24.8	4.7	3.0	8.3	4.3
Australia	10.2	18.8	5.2	2.4	9.6	2.4
Austria	17.9	27.7	4.5	2.9	6.7	5.0
Belgium	17.4	37.6[c]	4.5	2.2[b]	9.3	7.9[c]
Denmark	—	33.3[d]	3.7	2.2	—	5.4[d]
Finland	15.4	25.9	4.5	2.9	7.5	4.8
Greece	8.5	13.4[c]	6.8	3.5	8.4	9.4[c]
Ireland	11.7	28.4	4.3	3.5	9.1	7.1
Netherlands	16.2	36.1	4.5	2.0	10.4	1.6
New Zealand	13.0	19.6	4.0	0.4	5.5	3.5
Norway	11.7	27.1	4.3	4.1	10.1	4.6
Sweden	15.4	33.4	4.0	1.0	7.9	4.7
Switzerland	7.7	14.9[d]	3.4	1.7	7.6	2.7[d]
Average OECD[e]	13.1	25.6	4.6	2.6	8.4	4.8

Source: OECD, *Social Expenditure 1960–1990. Problems of Growth and Control* (Paris: 1985), p. 28.
Notes: a. Or the last available year.
b. Excluding education.
c. Up to 1980.
d. Up to 1979.
e. Unweighted average.

3. It should be highlighted that the tendencies reflected in the data could wrongly be attributed to alleged "interventionist inclinations" of rulers intoxicated by social democratic statism, as some diehard conservatives are fond of saying. In fact, these trends remain evident regardless of the

different ideologies of the political party in office; they respond to more profound determinants than a simple change in the government's cast. All postwar capitalist governments have increased funding for ambitious social programs, including "center" or "right-of-center" governments, according to what can be gathered from an analysis of public policies in postwar Europe.[18]

A detailed examination of the various national experiences would allow one to obtain a more complete view of the complex but intimate relationship among the extension of citizenship, the shift in the center of gravity of the party system toward the left, the development of welfare legislation, and the expansion of state social expenditures. In brief, the history of the democratization of the capitalist state does not end with universal suffrage. As Figure 5.1 shows, it is also the chronicle of the birth of the state's social compromises, expressed in the launching of a set of public policies aimed at correcting the inequities and imbalances generated by the markets. In other words, the proposal of a capitalist democracy enjoyed a high degree of popular credibility and legitimacy because the reformist performance of the Keynesian state backed up—at least in part—the politicians' promises with effective initiatives. By virtue of the state's social policies, the abstract equality of the citizen acquired a material correlate that, although partial and insufficient, served to prove that democracy—that "government of the people, for the people, and by the people," in the felicitous formula coined by Abraham Lincoln—was not an illusion. Democratic performance corresponded to the democratic political format of the state.[19]

In a pioneering study British sociologist and political scientist T. H. Marshall considers it necessary to redefine the meaning of "citizenship" by dividing it into three distinct components: civil, political, and social. The civil element of citizenship is the one more closely bound to the liberal tradition. It includes all the rights required for the fulfillment of individual liberties: freedoms of speech and thought, the right to own property, to sign valid contracts, and to have a fair trial count among the most important. The institutional expressions of these rights are the independent courts of justice. The political aspect of citizenship, on the other hand, refers to the extension of suffrage and to the elimination of the obstacles that prevented certain social categories and groups from participating and having access to political power. This second set of rights is relatively alien to liberalism, its roots being found in the democratic and socialist traditions. Universal, secret, and equal suffrage; the parliaments; and the local assemblies and councils organically crystallize the existence of political rights. Finally, the social aspect of citizenship—also a postliberal contribution linked to the socialist and democratic heritage—includes the right to a minimum degree of economic well-being and security, the ability to fully share the benefits of the community's social and cultural heritage, and the right to enjoy a civilized life in accordance with the prevalent criteria and standards of the epoch. The institutional expressions of this modern aspect of citizenship—a typical product of the social progress in the twentieth century—are the educational and welfare systems, which supply the disadvantaged and the poor with the resources required for a dignified existence. Thus, the transition from the subject—the individual deprived of almost any rights and at the mercy of the powerful—to the citizen as the final sovereign in the democratic republic could not have been separated from the rise of a whole ensemble of entitlements and transfers, the "citizen wage."[20]

Some data from the British historical experience clearly illustrate this expansion of the social aspects of citizenship (see Table 5.2).

This new conception of citizenship was not the result of a theoretical or doctrinal development but rather the outcome of the twentieth-century democratic and social struggles, which superseded the framework of

Table 5.2   Historical Comparison of Social Policies of the Welfare State in Great Britain (circa 1860 and 1970)

	c. 1860	c. 1970
Income security	None, except for Poor Law provisions	Old age, disability, pensions, sickness, maternity, job hazards, unemployment. Family protection. National coverage.
Health	Asylums for mental patients, vaccination, and sewage system	Comprehensive and free health care for all.
Education	Some subsidies to religious congregations	Mandatory and free ten-year schooling. Widespread scholarships to secondary/ university students.
Housing	None	More than 25 percent of houses publicly allocated, with subsidized rents. Rent control in private sector.
Welfare expenses as percentage of GNP	1–1.5%	24%
Percentage of adults who can vote	8%	98%
Percentage of left-wing votes	—	48%

Sources: Policy information from Gough, Ian, *The Political Economy of the Welfare State* (London: The MacMillian Press Ltd., 1979), p. 2. Electoral data from Finer, Samuel, "Great Britain," in Macridis, Roy, and Rober E. Ward, *Modern Political Systems: Europe* (Englewood Cliffs, NJ: Prentice Hall, 1972).

nineteenth-century liberal democratic formalism. This veritable *aufhebung* of the concept of citizenship called for a state capable of carrying out a program of social reforms. Without overlooking the significant national differences that were observed in this endeavor, one should recognize that this objective was fulfilled to varying degrees in advanced capitalist countries. Furthermore, this endeavor proved that, within certain limits that were acceptable for the dominant classes and after fierce social struggles that mobilized millions of workers, wealth and incomes could be redistributed; homes, hospitals, and schools built; a more egalitarian society promoted; and an extraordinary range of public services for the betterment of the poor offered. More important, it was definitively proven that, with twenty years of social reforms, the democratic state was able to do much more for the collective well-being and dignity of the subordinate classes than the market had done throughout two centuries.[21]

The Conditions of Latin American Democratization and Reformist Policy

This brief summary of the most outstanding features of the social reconstruction of postwar Europe allows one to assess the substantial weight that the implementation of a reformist policy acquired in the European democratic consolidation. It also highlights the much more adverse conditions that surround the present struggle for democracy in Latin America: a long economic downturn, the systematic plundering of national savings through foreign indebtedness and capital flight, recessive policies intended to achieve the structural adjustment and the fiscal equilibrium of the economy, the survival of the social pillars of authoritarianism, and an ideological climate skeptical of the virtues of democracy. This set of circumstances can hardly be considered favorable for a successful democratic transition.[22]

As if this were not enough, one must add the role traditionally played in Latin America by the United States, which, as is well known, has largely contributed to aborting the few democratic experiences of the region. If the United States contributed to the collapse of fascism in Europe, conversely in its strategic "back yard" it has assiduously collaborated—more or less actively and outspokenly, depending on the case—in establishing all sorts of right-wing military dictatorships. From the tragedy of World War II, Western powers learned that the policy established in the Treaty of Versailles to ensure the forceful payment of German reparations was suicidal. Nevertheless, that lesson seems to be forgotten when newly born Latin American democracies are strangled by an absurd and immoral debt that everyone knows cannot be either paid or collected. In addition, Latin American countries have been attacked for decades with high interest rates—a product of the chronic U.S. fiscal deficit—and with a subtle protectionist scheme that has hampered Latin American exports to the industrialized nations.

The United States assisted the recovery of democracy in Europe, but in 1965 it invaded the Dominican Republic, and in the early 1970s the Central Intelligence Agency and the Pentagon destabilized Chilean and Uruguayan democracies. The United States traded with China and the former Soviet Union, whereas Cuba suffered from a criminal commercial embargo for decades, and Brazil's commercial policies are sharply antagonized. Franco's Spain was supported by U.S. diplomacy, yet Nicaraguan elections were not good enough when the Sandinistas triumphed, although they were fine when Chamorro was elected. Berlin was protected, yet Guatemala, the Dominican Republic, Grenada, and Panama were invaded. It would take too long to compile the inventory of U.S. interventions and policies actively opposed to democratization in Latin America. Although in recent years there seems to be a rectification of Washington's traditional policies regarding these issues, the role of the superpower as an unfriendly regional "police officer" remains an inescapable and threatening reality.[23]

Furthermore, Latin America has other disadvantages that make its path toward the consolidation of democracy even rougher.

First, there is the magnitude of the task to be carried out in the region, in light of the disasters provoked by the "wild capitalism" there. In addition to the secular problems that derive from backwardness and underdevelopment, one must consider the alarming deterioration of the health, education, and nutritional conditions of the popular classes and strata. More than a decade of "orthodox" neoliberal adjustments sponsored by the military has left behind massive societal dislocations that have seriously impaired the very fabric of Latin American societies. Unlike reformism in industrialized nations—with its emphasis on small, specific, and marginal improvements of a population whose basic needs are largely met—in Latin America a reformist project must provide such basic human needs to a large majority of the population. For this reason the issues that make up the Latin American agenda of social reform are much more fundamental and sensitive than those currently discussed in industrialized countries. Latin Americans belong to an era of wild and pre-Keynesian capitalism; they have to confront problems such as the elimination of extreme poverty, the decay of the inner cities, agrarian reform, illiteracy, infant mortality, and inadequate nutrition. In one way or another these problems have by and large been solved in mature capitalist countries, even though some growing sectors (for instance, the homeless in large U.S. cities) might show signs of acute scarcity as a result of neoliberal policies. Advanced societies deal with questions such as the rights of women and ethnic or cultural minorities to be recognized and have their autonomy and identity respected, or issues such as gender discrimination, the right to abortion, protection of individual rights, provision of collective goods, ecology, disarmament, and peace. Resolving such problems does not necessarily entail broad structural changes to society. However, Latin America shares these problems but has many more of its own, a fact that refers one back to structural and essential questions.

Second, it is important to notice the relative fragility and lack of experience of the leadership of the new democratic coalitions in Latin America. These are highly complex societies that have suffered profound and sometimes traumatic transformations in recent years. Given the brief, spasmodic, and nonaccumulative history of democracy in the area, it is not surprising to see social leaders, politicians, and state managers genuinely interested in a democratic order overwhelmed by events and reactions they had not anticipated and by the unforeseen difficulties of democratic governance in times of crisis. Neither is it surprising that democratic leaders become exhausted in endless disputes over the distribution of minuscule parcels of power while neglecting the seriousness of the threats that could end the democratic project sooner than expected. Additionally, the specter of ingovernability assiduously hovers above the new ruling alliances, stimulated by the unwanted consequences of the fierce electoral competition and the enormous difficulties in democratically ruling underdeveloped countries. Moreover, those countries that are in the middle of a profound economic crisis and are unaccustomed to democracy face authoritarian conspirators hoping to end the new experience. Finally, the democratic institutions are threatened by the lack of balance between a democratic electoral coalition and an alliance of conservative social forces. Whereas the former is inorganic, hard to mobilize, and vulnerable to demagogic manipulations from the right, a mighty political, economic, social, and ideological coalition of social classes and sectors—which grudgingly accepted democracy after the defeat of the military dictatorship—opposes the democratic performance of the state, vetoing the state policies from its privileged trenches in civil society. In fact, the control of the mass media by the dominant classes or the bourgeois skepticism regarding the new political rulers (thus making the bourgeoisie reluctant to invest) could have a much stronger impact on the social and political stability of a country than a general strike. Numerous historical instances indicate that this "bourgeois strike"—as Fred Block calls the withholding of investments and as Adam Przeworski ratifies—could become a lethal weapon against any reformist project in a democratic transition.[24]

The third additional disadvantage concerns the nature of the forces in the conjuncture of the democratic transition. Which forces are for the transition and which are against it? The question is of utmost importance given that, in Latin America, authoritarian actors have survived the transition and coexist with democratic forces. Because those in favor of despotism were not eliminated (for that a social revolution is required), the transition becomes extraordinarily complicated.

A broad social consensus in favor of democracy should not be confused with the relative defeat of authoritarianism by a democratizing alliance. In transitional junctures like those in Latin America, there are always two opposing projects, and where the democratic one is able to prevail, it almost always does so in a very fragile situation. In this sense it is appropriate to recall Gramsci's warnings regarding the different levels in which the problem of the correlation of social forces in changing historical junctures should be posed. The supremacy a given group commands in the electoral arena can never be mechanically transferred to the more global field of the state, conceived in its more integral, Gramscian sense. This field exceeds the consideration of its electoral and administrative apparatuses. And once this more global and complex aggregate level is reached, it becomes clear that building a democratic order requires those who wish to live in democracy to be capable of holding at bay those who, openly or covertly, do not. This is an elemental truth that has been repeatedly underlined by great minds of political thought, from Aristotle to Machiavelli to Gramsci.

A fourth factor points to the legacies of the lengthy authoritarian socialization experienced by most Latin American societies with respect to fundamental values, ideologies, and attitudes of the population. The frailty and brevity of Latin American democratic experiments increased the weight of agencies and institutions—such as the armed forces and the Church in the Argentine case—that exerted such profound and malevolent intellectual and moral influence on the society as a whole. This problem has manifested itself, with effects that are quite difficult to neutralize, in the conformation of a diluted and widespread authoritarian "political culture." This culture subconsciously affects, in an undesirable manner, even the actors and leaders who on a conscious level are sincerely identified with the democratic project. Hence, it is possible to detect the preliminary symptoms of either a subtle and subliminal disdain or an outright disillusionment and contempt toward democracy and electoral politics in certain strata of the population. These social sectors, burdened by the weight of the economic crisis or frightened by the ghost of ingovernability, could be pushed to embrace the return of the authoritarians under the novel forms of a fundamentalist neopopulism. The unusual support attained by the candidacy of General Hugo Banzer in Bolivia and the popularity of such rebellious leaders as former Lieutenant-Colonel Aldo Rico in Argentina are ominous reminders of the seriousness of the problem. The frustration of democratic expectations may open numerous opportunities to a new generation of authoritarian projects throughout Latin America.

Dilemmas of a Reformist Democracy

In any event, for the time being it seems true that the horrors of the authoritarian experiences of the 1970s and the fugacity of their alleged "achievements" rekindled a profound reevaluation of democracy among Latin

America's popular classes and strata. People have come to realize that even though democracy is not the magical panacea dreamt by many, at least it has the virtue of putting in the hands of the citizenry a few tools with which to defend itself from its oppressors.

As the following pages will show, democracy is afflicted by dilemmas threatening its very feasibility in the present Latin American circumstances. However, it is first necessary to introduce a few preliminary specifications. As is well known, there are several theories of democracy, and to evaluate and ponder their relative merits is beyond the scope of these pages.[25] Nevertheless, democracy may be understood as a synthesis of three great questions, each posed at a different moment in the long tradition of political theory:

1. Plato's and Aristotle's question in classic Greece: *Who governs?*
2. The central concern of liberal constitutionalism, from Locke to Montesquieu to the Federalists: *How to govern?*
3. Marx's perspective: *What does the government do?*

The *simultaneous* consideration of these three aspects of the problem of constructing a democratic order allows one to discard doctrinaire proposals or practical political projects that fail to address the complexities of the matter. A government supposedly of "the people," ruling through its party or corporative mediations, could satisfy the first criterion but not necessarily the other two. A populist democracy that neglects the institutional and constitutional components of democracy and that enshrines the virtues of the direct nexus between leader and masses could hardly be a valid and appealing political alternative. The same may be said of the self-complacent formalism of certain Latin American democracies of the 1950s and 1960s—with their elections, parties, parliaments, "free" press, etc.—for which a constant oligarchy, encased in a hollow institutional shell, remained in power and perpetuated the same policies.

The preceding considerations vividly illustrate the dangers of using one-dimensional criteria to characterize democratic states. It is not enough for Latin American democracy to place public authority in the hands of the people and to organize its political life within a constitutionalist framework ensuring division of powers, full respect for individual rights, public freedoms, and so on. Restored Latin American democracies must also promote a set of policies of social reform, without which the social basis that supports the regimes may sooner or later desert the democratic field. Those reforms are all the more necessary given that the market, left to its own forces, will never carry them out. So-called market failures are not corrected by market mechanisms but instead require the (hopefully enlightened and altruistic) intervention of the state. The neoconservative decade of the 1980s, especially the disastrous experiences of Ronald Reagan and Margaret Thatcher, have definitively proven that the "self-correcting" market mechanisms are no more than an illusion and that postneoliberal social reconstruction calls for a renewed role for the state.

The importance of democratic reform in Latin America is emphasized when one notes that the present criticism of democracy by supporters of authoritarianism is not what it was in the 1960s and 1970s. In those days, the discourse of the antidemocratic reaction likened democracy to anarchy and ungovernability, all of which served to justify aprioristically a military coup d'état. Contemporary right-wing criticism predominantly adopts a sort of populist stance and is directed against the paralysis, inefficiency, and incapacity of democratic governments to solve the problems that affect society. The traditional supporters of authoritarianism first ruin the countries and place them in debt, and then demand quick and painless solutions for the ensuing disasters. Democracy cannot be defended by simple appeals to its formal and institutional correctness; it also demands a much more profound practical justification. By reforming society, and making it better, more humane, and just, democratic governments not only strengthen the support of the masses for the democratic regime but also weaken their staunch adversaries. Both the logic of political competition and the strategy of institutional survival of the democratic state make reformism a top priority.[26]

It is no secret that one of the conditions of reform is the availability of resources to be redistributed through the democratic political process. The strong social and political consensus of the Keynesian state in Europe relied on that state's effective capacity to progressively redistribute an economic surplus that grew larger every year. This does not exclude tough bargaining and hard commitments—some of which may later be unfulfilled—given that the class compromise is normally reached on the basis of current tangible benefits and future expected improvements that may make present pains more palatable. But these kinds of political transactions need the presence of strong institutional guarantees to ensure that today's sacrifices will certainly be tomorrow's gains. In Europe the welfare state fulfilled that tutorial role, and in that way it greatly strengthened popular credibility in the emerging political democracies of the postwar period, especially in Germany and Italy and, much later, in Spain, Portugal, and Greece.

Unfortunately, Latin America is not in a similar situation: badly hit by the international recession, impaired by the resurgence of protectionist policies in the North, and strangled by external debt, its capacity to generate a surplus on which to base a reformist project is virtually nonexistent. That is one of the reasons payment of debts is hardly compatible with democratization: those funds that the region has transferred in exorbitant sums to the big banks throughout the decade are the ones that Latin America needs in order to finance the essential programs of social reform. If the more than $200 billion that the region exported to the centers during these years had been used for social programs and the promotion of economic development, the situation in Latin America would now be quite different; nobody would be talking of absolute poverty, of "informalized" popular sectors, of the increase of structural heterogeneity, of fractures and segregations that divide Latin American societies, and of the lack of prospects that burden youth and anguish the elderly.

The World Bank has estimated that in order to eradicate the extreme poverty generated in Latin America in the 1980s, it would be necessary to transfer only 0.7 percent of the region's GNP to the poor, a figure that is equivalent to a 2 percent tax on the incomes of the top 20 percent of the population. The estimates of the Economic Commission for Latin America and the Caribbean (CEPAL) are a little bit higher: 1 percent of the region's GNP to eradicate extreme poverty, and about 5 percent to eradicate all sorts of poverty in general.[27] In any case, both the World Bank and CEPAL agree that a reasonable program of income redistribution making use of some 1 percent of Latin America's GNP would produce a substantial improvement in the lot of the poor. However, nothing of this sort is being done, although 4 percent of Latin America's GNP is transferred yearly to the creditor banks abroad. If there is enough political will, a policy of income redistribution is financially feasible under current conditions. Such a policy would prevent the continuation of a process acutely portrayed by Agustín Cueva: "Latin American societies have become, from bottom up, societies marked by the images of the delinquent and the beggar, where people either deal with drugs or beg the charity of the North."[28] That is why policies of "wild adjustment"—usually referred to as "shock therapy"—and decisions to make payment of the foreign debt the top priority not only mean deepening the recession; they undermine the process of redemocratization as well. When the problem of the external debt is not confronted resolutely and rationally, when there is a refusal to do "what is obvious," as Guillermo O'Donnell has rightly argued,[29] the prevailing economic and social conditions in the region move ever closer to the model of the "zero-sum society," with the well-known intensification of the social and class conflicts and political polarization.[30]

Taking into account all of these matters, Latin American countries come against a series of dilemmas that must be confronted to ensure the long-term success of democratic reconstruction. In the first place, they must choose between the path of the reforms or the dead-end alley of conservative immobility. This is a crucial choice that is frequently made without the full awareness of leaders and protagonists involved in the decisionmaking process. As Machiavelli insightfully remarks, there are few things in politics that are more difficult than carrying out a reform. For one thing, rulers are seduced by the sirens' songs of "realism" or "possibilism," which lead most Latin American governments to abandon their reformist promises—artfully exacerbated by campaign rhetoric. Democratically elected governments thus become innocuous administrators of the status quo, ensuring with their impotence and intransigence the protection of the dominant classes. Speaking of the behavior of the prince in the new territories conquered through his *virtú,* Machiavelli remarks, "We ought to ponder the fact that there is nothing more difficult to manage, more dubious to accomplish, or more dangerous to execute than the introduction of new institutions; for the innovator makes enemies of everyone who is well off under the old order, and has unenthusiastic supporters among those who would be well off in the new order."[31]

The reasons for Machiavelli's cautious and "hopeful realism" are (1) the firmness and the activism of the antireformist camp, where all of those who benefited from the old order set aside old quarrels and gather together to join forces to resist innovation; and (2) the lukewarm response of the supposedly new beneficiaries of the reforms in their willingness to defend the innovators, a result of the fear inspired by the old order and the suspicion of common men and women regarding dreamlike projects unconfirmed by any concrete experience.

This appreciation of the difficulties of reform is also shared by modern theorist Samuel P. Huntington, who lists three issues for which the problems of the reformist-minded ruler are more serious than those that burden the revolutionary leader. In the first place, the reformist must simultaneously struggle on two fronts, against both the conservative and the revolutionary opposition. Second, given that his or her objective is to produce some type of change and not to completely subvert the old society, the reformist has to be a master of the strenuous and intricate art of controlling social change. The reformist must know how to lead and control the social forces that he or she unleashes and to guide them with a firm hand in the right direction. Finally, the reformist must choose from among a series of options and priorities and above all must achieve and maintain a highly delicate balance between socioeconomic reforms and the expansion of political mobilization and participation—a dilemma, of course, that no revolutionary leader is faced with.[32]

Under the present circumstances in Latin America—characterized by the reflux of revolutionary projects and the ideological ascendancy of neoliberalism—only a radical reformism can create the necessary conditions for consolidating the region's democratic advances. Obviously, this approach certainly transcends the timid attempts that the so-called social democratic parties have implemented in some countries of Latin America.[33] To ignore the need of profound and lasting reforms will serve only to heighten social conflicts, accelerate political decadence, and clear the ground for the return of despotism. Thus, social reforms are not only convenient but necessary, even though they are not aimed at "superseding" capitalism; they will at least allow for the modification of capitalism's functioning and the stabilization of a new correlation of forces more favorable for the popular classes. If the current processes of democratic transition and consolidation, overwhelmed by the pressures of bankers and the dominant circles of international capitalism, fail to launch resolutely a reformist project, the feasibility of those processes will certainly be threatened. It would not be much of an exaggeration to assert that the chances of their defeat might well be significantly enhanced, thus very likely opening the door to another dark cycle of political crisis and authoritarian restorations. This undesirable outcome could, in some cases, count on the broad support of popular masses disappointed by the ineffectiveness of democratic governments.[34]

If the "immobilist" path is mined by turbulent conflicts and protracted social decay, the reformist road brings about no less a deepening of societal antagonisms. This attitude, which provokes the hesitation of many democratic leaders—who, unlike Weber, do not believe that "politics is the war of opposing Gods"—is far from being aberrant, given that the very democratic dynamics intensify social conflicts, regardless of the moderation of the leaders, parties, and factions involved in the struggle for power. The objective conditions proper of democratic politics exacerbate social contradictions, and the inertia of a conservative "nonreformist" strategy, far from mitigating them, will only manage to make sure that they reach ever more dangerous levels. Only a reformist democracy can aspire to have some degree of control over a situation as delicate as the one that today characterizes Latin America. One cannot expect to reach genuine political stability—a condition quite different from the apathy and resignation prompted by hopelessness and repeated frustrations—when the region's governments refuse to face reality and avoid seeing the deplorable situation of their societies.

Consequently, although it is true that reforms will initially exasperate the contradictions of civil society, it is also true that if reformist policies are effective at resolving old social vindications, the pressure of the political "steam boiler" will reduce until it reaches manageable levels. Therefore, in the medium term the only realistic strategy for conflict resolution and the construction of a new and deep-seated democratic legitimacy is social reform, despite the fact that in the first stage it will agitate social tensions as it mobilizes the activist opposition of those sectors bound to the defense of the status quo. The price of social peace is a variable degree of political instability in the initial phases of the process. The circumstances that prevailed in Western Europe or in the United States were similar when the innovations that resulted in what today is called the welfare state were introduced. To pretend that these problems will not occur in Latin America, where timid reformist attempts were often met by bloody counterrevolutions, is a dangerous illusion.[35]

Once the path of reforms is chosen, new dilemmas appear for the ruling groups. What is the best strategy to ensure the success of the reform? It is frequently believed that slow and gradual reforms minimize social antagonisms and discourage the inflamed resistance of the staunch supporters of the old order. In the circumstances found in Latin America, nothing could be further from the truth: gradual reforms provoke greater resistance, prolong the agony of what has to be superseded, and deteriorate the global functioning of society. In order for reforms to be effective, they must be specific and fulminating; they must liquidate the issue and dissolve the social cleavages and conflicts that were structured around it. Machiavelli fully demonstrates the perverse and self-defeating effects of gradualism on the policy of reforms, and from a completely different theoretical perspective, Samuel P. Huntington reaches the same conclusions.[36] Once a revolution is consummated, it can afford to work slowly; yet no reform can proceed that way. Its very character of partial modification of what exists makes haste and surgical precision inseparable attributes for success. A reform that goes slowly summons against itself the worst of both worlds: it irritates and mobilizes its slanderers while discouraging its impatient supporters. In order to succeed it must be sudden as lightning.

The Latin American right has resisted modest proposals for reforms with the tenacity with which true social revolutions are fought. Not even the United States—during the Kennedy years—was able to impose, in the 1960s, a true agrarian reform in Latin America. Some laws were sanctioned; however, although they dealt with the matter, in practice they barely served to perform cosmetic touches on the region's decrepit agrarian structure. In a region where still today—although not equally in all countries—Thomas Jefferson's ideas would be regarded as "subversive," it is not surprising to find that social reforms have been satanized as social revolutions in disguise. The democratic reformism of Salvador Allende in Chile was removed by one of the bloodiest counterrevolutions of modern history, actively organized from its very beginnings by President Nixon and his eventual secretary of state, Henry Kissinger. The same occurred in 1954, when the reform-minded governments of Arévalo and Arbenz in poverty-stricken Guatemala were fiercely harassed from Washington, and in the Dominican Republic in 1965, where Juan Bosch's reformism proved to be too hot for the sensitive tastes of the traditional oligarchy and its U.S. friends. Since 1979 a counterrevolution has been organized and financed to defeat Sandinism militarily or to asphyxiate it from the economy, making it lose its prestige in the face of its people and precipitating its electoral defeat. In Grenada, on the other hand, Reagan resorted to the traditional methods of gunboat diplomacy and invaded the tiny island, killing the reform-minded Maurice Bishop.

In short, in Latin America, reforms are fiercely struggled against by the dominant classes and imperialist capital, which, perceiving such reforms as sure catalysts of the revolution, do not hesitate to launch bloody counterrevolutions to suffocate them. If economic pressures, financial asphyxiation, fraud, corruption, or other types of pressures succeed at aborting reformist processes and taming their leaders, then a counterrevolutionary bloodbath becomes unnecessary. However, it is also important to underscore the objectively reactionary role often played by self-proclaimed revolutionary "vanguards," instransigent opponents of all reforms as sham substitutes for the revolution. If the right blasts reforms as the catalysts of revolution, left-wing infantilism fights reforms because they allegedly prevent revolution from occurring. Simultaneous consideration of this constellation of factors—counterrevolution, "domestication," left-wing dogmatism—partially explains the low level of success of reforms in Latin America.

With or without reforms, the ruling coalition in democratizing polities will have to face the harsh reality of growing social antagonism. The latter will not disappear by magic if the reformist banners are put down. On the contrary, without the rational intervention of the public authorities, the irrationality of the market would be left in charge of distributing the burden of the crisis in an increasingly zero-sum society. Without much effort, one can predict the final result of an immobilist solution. The social conflict will be heightened to its extreme because the Darwinist logic of the market magnifies existing inequalities. Thus, the frustration of social reform will serve only to make things worse: it will not appease the discontents, nor will it moderate the posture of its recalcitrant opponents.

Civil Society, State, and Reformism

These observations have focused on the sphere of state initiatives. However, it is also relevant to refer to the active participation of the social actors involved in the democratic transition. The centrality of the state in that process hardly needs any justification. The recovery of the active participation of social forces, however, is something that is usually not taken into account. There is an elitist bias—as strong as it is unwarranted—in most of the mainstream literature on democratic transitions and consolidation. By considering democratization to be an "elite affair," one loses the benefits of a more integral view of society.

The great emphasis on the question of the state is a result of the structural centrality the state has acquired since the capitalist recomposition of the 1930s. So great is the state's importance for the feasibility of the process of accumulation (despite abundant antistate rhetoric propounded by the conservative right) that the monetarist counterrevolution has been unable to significantly alter the bureaucratic Moloch, the functionality of which for the reproduction of capital is beyond all doubt. The perverse ultra-Keynesianism of the Reagan administration—which replaced the welfare state with the warfare state—and the failure of the projects to "trim the state," especially at the center, are full proof of capitalism's dependence on the state. A book by Milton and Rose Friedman, in which they express their disappointment regarding the persistence of big government, eloquently demonstrates this idea.[37]

The present situation in Latin America does not escape capitalism's general tendencies. The experiences of monetarist authoritarianism ended up strengthening the state, and the heavy legacy of the foreign debt—which, as in the case of Argentina, resulted in at least a partial "socialization" of the private debt—has done so as well. After pointing out some of the macropolitical consequences of the financial crisis of the 1980s, one would not hesitate to underline the growth of the state's role, given that the state was forced to assume responsibility for the debts of private firms—hypocritical lovers of the free market—with foreign lenders. Moreover, the state's responsibility as a co-lateral in fulfilling the global obligations of the debt objectively reinforces its institutional significance and increases its extractive capabilities. In fact, Latin American states have redoubled and intensified their intervention in the markets in order to ensure—via investments, regulations, and an endless number of macroeconomic instruments—that the debt will be paid. Thus, the states encourage exports and promote a model of growth based on fiscal equilibrium and austerity, and increase of its tax revenues. These policies have heightened the poverty and marginalization of large sections of society, condemned to being the losers in this new capitalist plunder. In short, the recent economic experience has shown that despite their rhetorical overtones, the "market forces" have required the continued assistance of the state (although in changed forms). Even if a privatization process is resolutely launched and executed, the role of the state is very unlikely to be diminished. Market forces and the capitalist state are allies, not adversaries. As shown in previous chapters, the hostility of those who defend the market is not against the state but rather against the democratic components and potentialities of the modern state.

On the other hand, the social forces—as opposed to the market forces—cannot aspire to "democratize" the market. That would be simple nonsense. In that privileged reign of private interests and egotistic sovereignty, there is no room for arguments on distributive justice. These arguments have constituted, from the first chapter of Plato's *Republic* on, the heart of political philosophy and the most fundamental issue in the life of the polis. They are where the crucial issue of justice is resolved, and this explains why the polis, and not the market, is where the struggles for social reform take place. The market's inability to create a more just society has been fully shown by history: the solidarity logic of social reform is incompatible with the reign of the egotistical interests that constitute the raison d'être of the market.

For this reason, achieving the social reforms immediately demanded by the present situation requires choosing the path of politics and not of markets. From there, the desired transformations can be produced, even those that are needed to control the state. It is not the market that can undertake these tasks, but rather a democratically organized society. The control of statism can be guaranteed only by the social expansion of democracy—by the empowerment of the activism and initiative of civil society; its classes, groups, and institutions; and its parties, unions, and social movements. In other words, what is required is an immense progressive social activism that (1) will push forward the reforms that the state must institutionalize and legalize and (2) will simultaneously control the bureaucratic and antidemocratic deformations of the state. Hence arises the importance of deprivatizing the state. By so doing Latin Americans will be able to place the state more and more under the control of civil society. There must be an end to the veritable "colonization" of the state that is practiced with so much dedication—and with such collectively disastrous results—by the bourgeoisie and the classes and social groups allied with its hegemony. It is necessary to reconvert the state into a true public sphere, guaranteeing transparent functioning and the democratic character of its procedures.

It has already been shown how the market was incapable of preventing the bureaucratization and growing statism of modern societies. Only a militant democracy could prevent the sterile and nonsensical triumph of "the bureaucratic iron cage," as Max Weber calls statism. To begin to tread the path of social reforms is the only creative alternative open at today's juncture. If this enterprise is successful, it could neutralize the dislocating effects of the market and consolidate popular control of the state. This would open a path leading toward a better society, where justice, popular sovereignty, and public freedoms prevail.

The beginning of this chapter by necessity spoke of utopia, and this topic must be considered again here. We live in a very special age, and in the neoconservative West, politicians and state officials have embraced the cause of "pragmatism" with a fervor that borders on the irrational. A proposal that endorses a policy of profound reforms will surely be condemned by "realists" and "possibilitists" who will discard it a priori for its utopianism. It is not worthwhile to spend much time on such banal arguments: Keynes scorned the little practical men as poor slaves of some defunct economist.

The "realist" discourse ends in disillusionment and rage, thereby glorifying what exists and coldly emasculating, with the mere excuse of "technical knowledge," the creativity of human praxis. Hence, even an author as little given to lyricism as Max Weber asserts that "politics consists of a tough and protracted penetration through tenacious resistance which calls for both passion and moderation. It is absolutely true, as history confirms it, that what is possible in this world is never achieved if what is impossible is not tried time and again."[38] Weber ends by saying that for the possible to be achieved, it is necessary that individuals arm themselves "from now on with the kind of toughened spirit that allows to endure the destruction of all hopes, if men want to avoid being unable to achieve even what today is possible."[39]

Two lessons can be learned from these words. The first is the need to break that vulgar trap of neoconservative pragmatism, which raises a formidable barrier between what is possible and what the most complacent souls regard as impossible or utopian. Weber points out that the reign of the possible is the result of a struggle for what is impossible. To renounce that wisdom is to "make eternal the Gods of dusk," in the words of poet Silvio Rodríguez, and to reduce men and women to a sad and sterile role as dedicated officials of a prewritten history. The second lesson is that even that which is possible requires the passion aroused by utopia to be attained; the possible is a social construction of men and women in tension in pursuit of an ideal. Only the most radical reformism can be "realistic" in contemporary Latin America.

Notes

1. A discussion of reformism and the strategy of the labor movement—the famous Bernstein-Debatte—can be found in the classical works of Bernstein, Edward, *Evolutionary Socialism* (New York: Schocken Books, 1961); Kautsky, Karl, *Bernstein und das sozialdemocratische programm: Eine antikritik* (Stuttgart: Dietz, 1899), and, by the same author, *The Social Revolution* (Chicago: Charles J. Kerr, 1916) and *The Road to Power* (Chicago: S. A. Bloch, 1909). See also Rosa Luxemburg's "Reform or revolution?" and "The mass strike, the political party and the trade unions," in *Rosa Luxemburg Speaks* (New York: Pathfinder Press, 1970), pp. 33–90 and 153–218, respectively; Lenin, V. I., *What Is to Be Done?* (New York: International Publishers, 1969), and his *Two Tactics of the Social-Democracy in the Democratic Revolution* (Beijing: Foreign Languages Press, 1970); Trotsky, Leon, "Results and prospects," in *The Permanent Revolution & Results and Prospects* (New York: Pathfinder Press, 1970); Colletti, Lucio, "Bernstein and the Marxism of the Second International," in his *From Rousseau to Lenin* (London: New Left Books, 1972), pp. 71–159; Gustafsson, Bo, *Marxismo y revisionismo* (Barcelona: Grijalbo, 1975); Miliband, Ralph, *Marxism and Politics* (Oxford: Oxford University Press, 1977), pp. 154–190; and Quazza, Guido, ed., *Riforma e rivoluzione nella storia contemporanea* (Turin: Einaudi, 1977).

2. On the issue of economic inefficiency it is appropriate to examine the record very carefully. G. Therborn has shown that the overall economic performance of "real existing socialisms" was, for many years, far superior to that of many of the most advanced capitalist nations. See *Peripecias de la modernidad* (Buenos Aires: El Cielo por Asalto, 1992).

3. On this issue see Hinkelammert, Franz J., *Crítica a la razón utópica* (San José, Costa Rica: Departamento Ecuménico de Investigaciones, 1984), p. 28.

4. See Cacciari, Massimo, "Transformación del estado y proyecto político," *Cuadernos Políticos* 25 (Mexico: July–September, 1980), pp. 7–28.

5. Paramio, Ludolfo, *Tras el diluvio: La izquierda ante el fin de siglo* (Madrid: Siglo XXI, 1988), pp. 79–80.

6. Luxemburg, Rosa, "Reform or revolution?" pp. 77–78. See also my comments on Luxemburg's theory in Chapter 4.

7. Przeworski, Adam, *Capitalism and Social Democracy,* (Cambridge: Cambridge University Press, 1985), p. 241.

8. See his "La democracia electoral y sus dificultades en América Latina,"

paper submitted to the Encuentro Internacional de Latinoamericanistas organized by the Centro de Estudios Latinoamericanos de la Facultad de Ciencias Políticas y Sociales de la UNAM (Mexico: September 5–7, 1990), p. 2.

9. Rousseau, Jean Jacques, "The social contract," in Barker, Sir Ernest, ed., *Social Contract* (New York: Oxford University Press, 1962), p. 254.

10. A discussion of the recent processes of democratization is found in Huntington, Samuel P., *The Third Wave* (Norman and London: The University of Oklahoma Press, 1991), and in Rueschemeyer, Dietrich, Evelyne Huber Stephens, and John D. Stephens, *Capitalist Development and Democracy* (Cambridge: Polity Press, 1992).

11. On these issues see Shonfield, Andrew, *Modern Capitalism* (Oxford: Oxford University Press, 1965); Graubard, Stephen R., ed., *A New Europe?* (Boston: Beacon Press, 1963); and Maier, Charles S., "The two postwar eras and the conditions for stability in twentieth century Western Europe," *The American Historical Review* 86(2) (April 1981).

12. See Chapter 2 in this book.

13. Buci-Glucksmann, Christinne, and Göran Therborn, *Le défi social-démocrate* (Paris: Dialectiques, 1981), pp. 115–137.

14. See Agnoli, Johannes, *Lo stato del capitale* (Milan: Feltrinelli, 1978); Wolfe, Alan, *Los límites de la legitimidad* (Mexico: Siglo XXI, 1980). On intermediation mechanisms see Schmitter, Philippe C., "Modes of interest intermediation and models of societal change in Western Europe," *Comparative Political Studies* 10(1) (April 1977), pp. 7–38, and "Still the century of corporatism," *Review of Politics* 36 (January 1974), pp. 85–131. See also Przeworski, Adam, *Capitalism and Social Democracy* and his paper, with Michael Wallerstein, "The structure of class conflict in democratic capitalist societies," *American Political Science Review* 76, pp. 215–236, included in Chapter 5 of *Capitalism*. Finally see Poulantzas, Nicos, *State, Power, Socialism* (London: New Left Books, 1978).

15. See Gough, Ian, *The Political Economy of the Welfare State* (London: McMillan Press, 1979); O'Connor, James, *The Fiscal Crisis of the State* (New York: St. Martin's Press, 1973); Offe, Claus, *Contradictions of the Welfare State* (Cambridge, MA: The MIT Press, 1985), pp. 147–161, and his "Structural problems of the capitalist state," *German Political Studies* 1 (1974), pp. 31–57.

16. See Flora, Peter, and Jens Alber, "Modernization, democratization and the development of welfare states in Western Europe," in Flora, Peter, and Arnold J. Heidenheimer, eds., *The Development of Welfare States in Europa & America* (New Brunswick, NJ: Transaction Books, 1981), p. 62.

17. See Kohl, Jürgen, "Trends and problems in postwar public expenditure development in Western Europe and North America," in Flora, Peter, and Arnold J. Heidenheimer, *The Development*, pp. 310–318. Similar conclusions are found in a study carried out by the OECD, *The Welfare State in Crisis* (Paris: OECD, 1981).

18. Kohl, J., "Trends," pp. 323–326.

19. A few years after the publication of the original version of this article, there appeared an excellent work by José María Maravall in which he examines in more detail (looking at the figures of OECD countries, especially Spain) the relationship between the social performance of the welfare state and democratic legitimation. I fully agree with Maravall's conclusions on this issue, although not with his criticism of Claus Offe—who says that capitalist democracy has not been able to alter the logic of capital. As will be shown, the structure of the capitalist state was not changed by the advent (and crisis) of the welfare state. Contrary to what Maravall's interesting article suggests, the undeniable advance of democracy did not make capitalist societies "noncapitalist." See his "Las razones del reformismo: Democracia y política social," *Leviatán* 35 (Madrid: Spring 1989), pp. 27–50.

20. Marshall, T. H., *Class, Citizenship and Social Development* (New York: Anchor Books, 1965), pp. 78–79. On the "citizen wage" see Bowles, Samuel, and Herbert Gintis, "The crisis of liberal democratic capitalism: The case of the United States," *Politics and Society* 2(1) (1982), pp. 51–93. A more thorough treatment of this argument can be found in Bowles, Samuel, and Herbert Gintis, *Democracy and Capitalism: Property, Community, and the Contradictions of Modern Social Thought* (New York: Basic Books, 1986).

21. This does not mean that the performance of the Keynesian state was above criticism. There is overwhelming evidence that speaks of the structural processes of marginalization, exclusion, and superexploitation suffered by some significant sections of the populace amidst a general policy that undoubtedly was instrumental in improving the living conditions of the masses. Beyond this historical record, in addition, there are no guarantees regarding the continuity of this exceptional performance. On this first point see Miliband, Ralph, *The State in Capitalist Society* (New York: Basic Books, 1969); and Piven, Frances Fox, and Richard A. Cloward, *Regulating the Poor* (New York: Vintage, 1971). On the second point see Offe, Claus, *Contradictions of the Welfare State*.

22. One of the most serious issues on the agenda of Latin American transitions is, paradoxically, one of the least studied: the survival of jurisdictional corporatist prerogatives that the armed forces keep to themselves and that are irreconcilable with the functioning of a democratic order. An enlightening comparative discussion on this point can be found in Stepan, Alfred C., *Rethinking Military Politics: Brazil and the Southern Cone* (Princeton: Princeton University Press, 1988).

23. See Chapter 7 in this book.

24. Block, Fred, *Revising State Theory.* Przeworski, Adam, *Capitalism,* Chs. 4 and 5. There is more on this in Chapter 4.

25. On this issue see Macpherson, C. B., *The Life and Times of Liberal Democracy* (Oxford: Oxford University Press, 1977); and *The Real World of Democracy* (Oxford: Clarendon Press, 1966) by the same author. See also Zolo, Danilo, *Democracy and Complexity: A Realist Approach* (Cambridge: Polity Press, 1992); Rueschemeyer, Dietrich, Evelyne Huber Stephens, and John D. Stephens, *Capitalist Development and Democracy;* Held, David, *Models of Democracy* (Cambridge: Polity Press, 1987); Dahl, R., *Democracy and Its Critics* (New Haven and London: Yale University Press, 1989). See, in addition, Chapter 7 of this book.

26. This connection between political logic and social reform is explained in detail in Przeworski, Adam, *Capitalism,* Ch. 1. A fundamental precedent is found in Michels, Robert, *Political Parties: A Sociological Study of the Oligarchical Tendencies of Modern Democracy* (New York: The Free Press, 1966) (originally published in German in 1911).

27. Cf. Tokman, Víctor E., "Pobreza y homogeneización social: Tareas para los 90," *Pensamiento Iberoamericano* 19 (1991), pp. 84–86.

28. See his "América Latina ante el 'fin de la historia,'" paper presented at the Encuentro Internacional de Latinoamericanistas organized by the Centro de Estudios Latinoamericanos de la Facultad de Ciencias Políticas y Sociales de la UNAM, Mexico, September 5–7, 1990, p. 12.

29. "Deuda externa: ¿Por qué nuestros gobiernos no hacen lo obvio?" *Revista de la Cepal* 27 (Santiago: December 1985).

30. Thurow, Lester C., *The Zero-Sum Society* (New York: Basic Books, 1980).

31. Machiavelli, Niccoló, *The Prince* (Indianapolis: The Bobbs-Merrill Co., 1976), pp. 147–149.

32. Huntington, Samuel P., *Political Order in Changing Societies* (New Haven: Yale University Press, 1968), pp. 344–346. It should be noted, though, that these dilemmas were hardly absent in revolutionary situations. Lenin had to fight against

right-wing and left-wing opposition, too; and although a revolutionary leader is promoting sweeping changes, it is nonetheless true that a good deal of the old order always has to be saved. Finally, to what extent is it true that Lenin, Mao, or Castro were not crushed by the dilemma between socioeconomic reform and political activism and mobilization? Lenin's NEP, Mao's "cultural revolutions," and Castro's "zafra of the ten millions" seem to be expressions of this perennial political dilemma.

33. See Cueva, Agustín, "¿Hacia dónde va nuestra socialdemocracia?" *Estudios Latinoamericanos* 4(617), CELA, Facultad de Ciencias Políticas y Sociales, UNAM, January–December 1989, pp. 59–70. A critical analysis of the social democratic project in Mediterranean Europe can be found in Anderson, Perry, *Democracia y socialismo* (Buenos Aires: Tierra del Fuego, 1988), pp. 69–95.

34. The illusion of "democratic irreversibility" is quite widespread. A few comments on this issue can be found in Chapter 7 of this book. This danger is explicitly dealt with by Samuel P. Huntington in his *The Third Wave,* especially pp. 290–294.

35. On the impacts of social and economic reforms on democracy, see Bresser Pereira, Luis Carlos, José M. Maravall, and Adam Przeworski, "Economic reforms in new democracies: A social democratic proposal," in Smith, William C., Carlos H. Acuña, and Eduardo Gamarra, eds., *Latin American Political Economy in the Age of Neoliberal Reform: Theoretical and Comparative Perspectives for the 1990s* (New Brunswick, NJ: Transaction Publishers, 1994), pp. 181–212.

36. Machiavelli, Niccoló, *The Prince,* pp. 143–202 ; Huntington, Samuel P., *The Third Wave,* pp. 344–396.

37. Friedman, Milton, and Rose Friedman, *Tyranny of the Status Quo* (New York: Avon Books, 1984).

38. Weber, Max, "Politics as vocation," in *Escritos Políticos* (Mexico: Folios, 1982), Vol. 2, pp. 363–364.

39. Ibid., p. 364.

6

Neoliberalism's Strayed Reason: State and Capitalist Accumulation in Contemporary Societies

The State as Scapegoat

Discussions on the role of state expenditures and the need to reduce the size of the state have acquired exceptional significance and urgency given the current critical conditions in Latin America. There are several reasons for this urgency. There is the seriousness of the capitalist crisis, which began in the mid-1970s and still shows no signs of a genuine resolution. This crisis has stimulated a flood of criticism against the consequences of "excessive" state intervention in the functioning of markets. These charges have exhumed the classical arguments of liberal economic theory concerning the virtuous results of economic forces that are freed from noxious governmental interference. Latin American countries have been "disciplined" to unprecedented levels by the debt crisis, and the region's economic policies follow more closely than ever before the neoliberal blueprint established by the international financial community and its scholarly spokespersons. Thus, it is not at all surprising that antistate discourse of the centers has both assumed an extremely dogmatic and belligerent form and has spread rapidly throughout Latin America.

Furthermore, the condemnation of the state—the bête noire of neoliberal criticism—has appeared at a special moment. In fact, after a prolonged history of dictatorship and state-sponsored terrorism, most Latin American societies are attempting to consolidate their agonizing democratic achievements within the framework of an economic crisis even more serious than that of the 1930s. Therefore, these countries face a formidable twofold task: to overcome the crisis and to construct a democratic order. Thus, the question of the state must be subjected to a new examination because, beyond major ideological options, the political projects available to deal with the crisis and the challenges of democratic consolidation bring to debate certain "silent premises"—in this case those related to what to do with the state— that in times of change acquire surprising resonance.[1]

The right, loyal to its tradition, has chosen the easy path of slandering

the adversary, which in this case is the state. Just as they used to bluntly recommend the annihilation of their enemies without much ado, the conservative forces today, in accordance with their class interests, promote the swift
and thorough dismantling and privatization of the public sector and the
deregulation and liberalization of the markets.

The left, on the other hand, is on the defensive after the epoch-making
events epitomized by the fall of the Berlin Wall; in addition, it has inherited
a certain "stadolatry" alien to the Marxist tradition but nonetheless influential. Thus, the left has assumed a closed defense of the state. Although this
attitude is basically correct—especially because in capitalist societies more
than in any others, the Hegelian dictum according to which the state is the
superior sphere of ethics and justice is applicable—it has frequently prevented the left from identifying in a timely manner the state's problems, its
bureaucratic deformations, and its oppressive features. Dogmatism seems to
have prevented the left from seriously considering the necessity of state
reforms. Expectations of the revolution have caused the left not to propose
policies for the conjuncture: all the strategic effort went into planning the
glorious revolutionary journey. Confronted with a state that was grossly
oversized, chronically bankrupt, extremely inefficient, less than mediocre in
terms of educational and health services, and whose public enterprises could
not supply the goods and services expected by the population, the Latin
American left considered it a duty to doggedly defend the state. It refused to
open a serious discussion on the matter. Meanwhile, on the other end of the
political spectrum, the right made a skillful demagogic move and capitalized
on the discontent and the protests of the popular sectors in the face of a state
for which the effective performance in all of Latin America leaves much to
be desired.

Nonetheless, there is a second current that allows one to better understand the present significance of this doctrinarian antistate phobia: the boom
of neoconservative and neoliberal ideologies that since the advent of the
Reagan administration and Thatcher's government in Britain has exerted a
profound impact on the international system.[2] The ideological hegemony of
this political current has produced, among other things, a radical displace-
ment of the axis of social and political debate in Latin America. New issues,
priorities, and policies constitute the agenda of a neoliberalism possessed by
a religious fervor that calls for dismantling the state just when democratic
advances are being made, and to simultaneously exalt the market as the sole
underwriter of freedom and progress in Latin American societies.

In accordance with worldwide macroeconomic trends, the formula of
Latin American economic development after World War II assigned an
essential role to the state. What today is denounced by neoliberal advocates
as an aberrant Latin American "deviation" was in fact in line with the main
guidelines that presided over the phenomenal economic recovery of postwar
Europe, where nationalizations were widespread, global and sectoral planning become standard practices, governmental interventionism acquired an

ever-growing importance, and public budgets grew without pause. It was Raúl Prebisch who "reinvented" Keynes in Latin America—in a creative process having an influence that has been felt for almost half a century—and established the basic orientations for subsequent developmental efforts. However, the insistence of Prebisch's ideas on economic planning, the entrepreneurial role of the state, and the soundness of an economic policy that would regulate the functioning of the main variables of the system fell out of favor in light of the crisis of the second half of the 1970s, prompting what Prebisch appropriately calls "the return of orthodoxy."[3] The various neoliberal experiments implemented in the region were almost invariably started by military dictatorships—with little sympathy toward other components of liberalism, such as toleration, pluralism, public freedoms, and human rights—and were duly continued by successor democratic governments. The cases of Argentina and especially Chile count among the most outstanding in this regard, revealing the continuity of the basic policies despite the transition from a dictatorial regime to a new democratic government.

The theoretical and practical decomposition of Keynesianism was accelerated after the early 1970s in mature capitalist formations by the previously unheard of coexistence of inflation and recession. This "stagflation" laid bare the historical limits of Keynes's economic teachings.[4] The collapse of the "common sense" created by the long-lasting predominance of Keynesian premises left an enormous ideological and policy vacuum, now occupied by neoliberal proposals: free markets, unfettered private initiative, liberalization, privatization, deregulation, and so on.[5] In short, the deepness of the crisis, extraordinarily worsened in Latin America by the unprecedented economic bleeding caused by the foreign debt; the challenges of redemocratization; and the new global ideological climate, dominated by the neoconservative paradigm, hastened the search for solutions based on the alleged virtues of the market. The state, which since the 1930s had been an effective means to confront the crisis facing capitalism, was ideologically transformed into a scapegoat and depicted as the cause of the current economic difficulties. Previously, the state was part of the solution; now it has become—in the most screeching versions of neoliberalism—the totality of the problem.[6]

To this brief economic and ideological framework, it is important to add some background information regarding the political situation that has led to the virulent reemergence of liberalism in Latin America. The region is transiting the extremely rough initial phases of a new wave of redemocratization precipitated by the bankruptcy of military dictatorships. As Brazilian political scientist Ruy Mauro Marini rightly observes, these dictatorships were incapable of stabilizing a predictable and reliable model of domination in order to confront the crisis facing capitalism and to ensure the structural adjustment of the economy under new international conditions. Some dictatorships may have appeared successful because of their alleged economic achievements—for example, the cases of Chile and, to a lesser extent, Brazil—but they were regarded even by friendly bourgeois sectors as dismaying failures because of their inability to organize a stable system of political domination.[7] Under these circumstances, the fragile experiments of democratic transition had to address an impressive explosion of demands resulting from the deprivations suffered by large national majorities under military dictatorships or right-wing governments. These latter regimes were true forerunners in that their public policies were inspired by the canons of neoliberalism a few years before Thatcher or Reagan took office. As is well known, the results of these orthodox experiments were dreadful from the point of view of social justice and equity, and the young democracies could not—and should not—have turned their backs on the demands of the population.[8]

Given the complete inadequacy of the market's mechanisms to respond to the most basic needs of civil society, a broad and efficient state intervention is needed. There are at least two sound reasons for a democratic state to attempt to satisfy the demands of the citizenry. The first and foremost reason is that those demands are just, especially if the suffering caused by the rise of "wild capitalism" in the region is duly taken into account. There are no compelling market incentives to persuade entrepreneurs to invest in sewage and drinkable water systems for lower-class districts; or in health and educational services to be used by the poor; or in recreational activities for the elderly. These goods are either provided by the state or not provided at all. The second reason is that only the state can solve a problem crucial to all democratic transitions and consolidations: the construction of new democratic legitimacy, something unthinkable independent of governmental performance. For societies in which the poor have become as destitute as in Latin America, this goal inevitably requires maintaining a considerable level of public spending.

Consequently, the problem of the welfare state and the array of social services it is supposed to offer to the population have implications that greatly surpass the narrow debates of economic theory or mainstream political science. An analysis that attempts to estimate costs and benefits of different policies on the basis of a "rational choice" model is incapable of capturing the multiple aspects involved in state interventionism, for which the roots are much deeper, stronger, and complex than its bitter enemies suppose. There is no economic, political, or philosophical reason that one must accept neoliberalism's barbaric pretension of reducing the state to an enterprise, to be judged by the profits shown on the fiscal balance sheet. No one in his or her right mind would think that both the state and the firm fulfill the same tasks and should be appraised based on the same values. It is not a matter of neglecting the importance of fiscal equilibrium, but rather of assessing in proper terms the real nature of the state's tasks and purposes. In this sense it is useful to recall that neoliberalism's boom is not merely a technical response borne of the theoretical heritage of the Austrian school and of Adam Smith's thought. As shown in previous chapters, neoliberalism is above all a political program that contains, to different degrees of development, a political theory of the state, its nature, organization, and functions— including the crucial issues of interventionism and planning—as well as some key assumptions concerning the role that the citizenry, especially the popular classes, could play in the different structures of the modern state.

As a result, one should acknowledge that beyond its incurable theoretical limitations and its gross empirical inaccuracies, the neoconservative offensive has imposed the issue of the state as one of the most burning problems of Latin America, displacing from public consideration others such as mass poverty, the blatant unfairness of the tax system, industrial decay, ecological damage, and so on. Its faulty diagnosis and its self-serving proposals reign uncontested in the region. Its hegemony is overwhelming, having become a new common sense that permeates civil society, conquers political parties, and—thanks to its rather uncontested control over the mass media—pervades the entire culture with its "privatist" and "free-market" discourse. In their gross simplification, the prophets of the new creed carefully hide that what is in crisis is a *capitalist* state. Their program to downsize the state through privatizations, deregulations, and liberalization entails the wholesale dismantling of the state apparatuses and public enterprises and rests on a Manichean duality that does not withstand any rigorous analysis: a healthy capitalist economy supposedly oppressed and frustrated in its potential for development by a hypertrophied, deficient, and inefficient state. That simplification, which is at the base of the neoliberal doctrinarian project, is hopelessly wrong.

If there is a crisis of the state—which cannot be hidden either in the periphery or in the center—it is due to the fact that capitalism as a mode of production is in deep trouble. The grave problems that afflict it have made obsolete the state form that characterized it throughout the brightest quarter of a century of its history. It is true that capitalism is not faced with a terminal crisis, as has periodically been predicted by a host of left-wing thinkers. Yet, can anyone seriously underestimate the magnitude and the structural nature of the economic recomposition currently unfolding in the international capitalist system?

The point is not to predict a collapse when it is clear that there are still ways to overcome the pitfalls of the present juncture. However, how can one ignore the impact of ongoing transformations on the overall stability of the system? This impact is evident in the negative consequences derived from the hegemony of finance capital on a global scale and its inevitable counterpart, the "resurrection of the rentier," that historical actor Keynes recommends eliminating through economic "euthanasia" in order to purge the capitalist economy of its parasitical and speculative elements. One may also note the seriousness of the fact that the United States, thanks to the neoliberal policies pursued under the Reagan administration, went from being the world's largest creditor to being the world's largest debtor in only six years. One need not be a Nobel laureate in economics to infer that an international economic order for which the military and economic superpower exhibits such weaknesses can hardly restructure a new world order in place of the one created by Bretton Woods in the aftermath of World War II. It is obvious that the U.S. predicament is related to the fact that the great powers defeated by the United States on the battlefield—Germany and Japan—have become economic giants but continue to be dwarfs in military and strategic terms, all of which adds new imbalances to the system as a whole. And finally, one should consider the implications of a unified Europe and the growing obstacles international commerce comes against. One will then have a realistic view of the delicate nature of the present situation. In the face of these realities, it is in order to ask the following: what is in crisis, the state or capitalism?

The State and Economic Performance
in Latin American Capitalism in the 1980s

According to studies carried out by the Economic Commission for Latin America (CEPAL), as well by other international agencies such as the World Bank and the International Monetary Fund, the gross domestic product (GDP) in most countries of Latin America and the Caribbean fell rather precipitously in the early 1980s, especially after the outburst of the debt crisis in 1982.[9] If the 1980 figures are set equal to 100, the GDP per capita of the region had descended to 90.5 by 1983. In the following years there were slight increases, but the index failed to improve resolutely; by 1990 it barely reached 91.1. In short, after an entire decade, the so-called lost decade of Latin American development, the GDP per capita was still 9 percent lower than in 1980.[10]

The evolution of the annual rates of growth of the GDP is quite illustrative as well. During the three decades preceding the outbreak of the debt crisis in 1982, the Latin American economies grew at a remarkable 5.3 percent per year: 5.1 percent in the 1950s; 5.7 percent in the 1960s; and 5.5 percent in the 1970s, despite the problems created by the oil shock in the first half of the decade. In the 1980s the GDP grew at a rate of only 1.1 percent, only one-fifth of what had been the average postwar rate of economic growth, a poor performance comparable only to the Great Depression years back in the 1930s. As a result, in countries such as Argentina, Bolivia, Peru, and Venezuela the per capita income in 1990 was lower than in 1970, and in Brazil, Mexico, and Latin America as a region the per capita income of 1990 was lower than in 1980. Among the larger Latin American countries, only Chile and Colombia do not match this grim picture. In short, high rates of growth were a constant during the decades when, according to mainstream economics, the state was suffocating the dynamics of the market forces. However, once the state entered a crisis and neoliberal policies were carried out, the rate of growth of the GDP fell precipitously.[11]

The overall growth rate of all Latin America and the Caribbean witnessed a spectacular collapse in the 1980s. Given the regressive nature of these recessive trends, it is little wonder that the problems of mass poverty became critical in the region, reversing slight but positive tendencies shown since the 1950s toward a reduction of the number of people living in conditions of extreme poverty. Therefore, in the region as a whole, the number of poor increased from 135 million to 170 million, and the number of indigents grew from 62 million to 81 million. The total of both figures gives an overall increase of 54 million people, from 197 million up to 251 million, in the six years elapsed from 1980 to 1986. The poor and indigent represented, in 1986, 61.5 percent of the total population of Latin America and the Caribbean.[12] In Brazil, the largest country of the region, the percentage of the poor in 1989 went back to 1970 levels.[13] In Argentina only 3 percent of the households in 1974 were below the poverty line; by the end of the 1980s this proportion grew by a factor of ten, fanned by the 1989 hyperinflation and the tough stabilization program launched by President Menem.[14]

It is worth noting that in Latin America this socially regressive trend was not reverted but rather accentuated in the second half of the 1980s as a consequence of orthodox structural adjustment programs. Experts have shown that the future situation of the poor is still uncertain. If Latin America resumes its development, then by the year 2000 the region will benefit from a modest decrease in the proportion of the poor, down to some 56 percent, although the absolute number of the poor will by then reach 300 million, an increase of almost 50 million in comparison with the 1986 figures. This is the "optimistic" scenario. However, if Latin economies were to stagnate, then the total number of the poor would fluctuate around 312 million, or 60 percent of the total population. Finally, if Latin American economies were to fall deeper into recession, then the total numbers of poor and indigent would reach catastrophic, Calcutta-like dimensions.[15]

A look at the figures concerning consumption per capita provides another perspective on the social implications of economic stagnation and recessive restructuring in Latin American capitalism. In the 1980s consumption per capita declined by 29 percent in Argentina, 20 percent in Bolivia, 18 percent in Peru, 11 percent in Venezuela, 7 percent in Mexico, 6 percent in Brazil, and 2 percent in Chile. Of the large Latin American countries, in 1990 only Colombia had increased (by 11 percent) its level of per capita consumption relative to 1980.[16] Data concerning the evolution of real salaries are certainly worrisome, especially in light of the trends prevailing in the period before the debt crisis and the ensuing stabilization programs. A study by the International Labour Organisation reveals that the annual growth rates of real salaries in the 1970s, when Latin economies were still growing quite fast, were −1.8 percent for Bolivia, 2.2 percent for Mexico, −2.8 percent for Peru, −5.3 percent for Uruguay, and −0.5 percent for Venezuela.[17] This depressing performance significantly worsened in the following decade, when—because of the adjustment policies forcefully promoted by the creditor banks, the international financial organizations, and the governments of the OECD countries—most Latin American governments were busy freezing wages and salaries, dismissing public employees, and cutting "unnecessary" state expenses (almost invariably in health, education, and general welfare) while leaving military expenses practically untouched. Not surprisingly, urban minimum wages declined even more precipitously in the 1980s: 56 percent in Argentina, 45.4 percent in Brazil, 41.8 percent in Mexico, 29.6 percent in Venezuela, and 42.0 percent in Uruguay; in Chile urban minimum wages remained frozen between 1980 and 1992; in Colombia they grew 1.6 percent and in Costa Rica 23.3 percent.[18]

Available data regarding income distribution indicate that Brazil, one of the ten largest economies of the world, also has one of the world's most regressive income distribution structures. The Mexican case shows (although less sharply) the same tendencies as Brazil. When it comes to evaluating the success of a development model, it is significant that between 1960 and 1980 the poorest 50 percent of the Brazilian population reduced their share of the GDP from 17.4 percent to 12.6 percent during an era when propagandists, ideologues, and entrepreneurs constantly praised the "economic miracle" of the Brazilian military. The other side of this coin shows that the upper 10 percent of the population went from receiving 39.6 percent of the national income in 1960 to receiving 50.9 percent twenty years later. In those same years the richest 1 percent improved its relative situation from receiving 11.9 percent of the income to 16.9 percent, that is, almost a third more than the poorest 50 percent of the Brazilian population. With data indicating a situation that appears to be as scandalous as that of India, Brazil had the worst structure of income distribution among ten countries analyzed in 1988 by the World Bank.[19] Even in Argentina, a country with a strong tradition of social equality, a detailed study by Luis Beccaria arrives at conclusions fully congruent with those for Brazil: between 1974 and 1990 the poorest 30 percent of the households went from receiving 12.4 percent to 9.0 percent of the national income, while the upper 10 percent improved its share from 27 percent to 36.1 percent.[20] Therefore, it seems advisable for one to take into account all these data regarding wages, consumption, and income when assessing the congruence between the neoliberals' call for "giving free reign" to the market forces and the marked inequities brought about by a decade of neoliberal policymaking. A whole range of state interventions is needed to correct the inequity and unfairness of the neoliberal

model, which has seriously jeopardized the viability of democratic reconstruction in the area.

At this point it is important to consider the issue of the foreign debt. It
is beyond dispute that the foreign debt has played—and, through the Brady
Plan, still keeps playing—a role of unique importance for Latin America.
New democratic governments have lost substantial degrees of autonomy
because major policy decisions regarding the strategy of economic stabilization and development, as well as key decisions regarding investment and
expenses, have to be agreed upon by the creditor cartels and their supporting governments. On the other hand, the voluminous resources transferred
to the centers have contributed to a substantial reduction in the financial
strength of the national states and their capacity to design and implement
public policies. It impaired the overall performance of Latin American
economies in the 1980s.

The debt has become a sort of "imperial tribute," and its volume grew
out of control during the 1980s. In Argentina the foreign debt per capita
climbed from $981 in 1980 to $ 1,827 in 1987; from $454 to $876 in Brazil;
from $999 to $1,699 in Chile; from $719 to $1,317 in Mexico; from $742 to
$1,412 in Uruguay; and from $1,803 to $1,996 in Venezuela.[21] If one views
this issue from another perspective, the ratio of the total foreign debt to the
GNP, the facts are no less disquieting. Between 1970 and 1987 this ratio
jumped from 8.6 percent to 61.7 percent in Argentina; from 8.2 percent to
29.1 percent in Brazil; from 25.8 percent to 89.4 percent in Chile; from 8.7
percent to 59.5 percent in Mexico; from 11.3 percent to 42.2 percent in
Uruguay; and from 5.7 percent to 52.3 percent in Venezuela.[22] The ratio
between total foreign debt and exports followed a similar trajectory:
between 1980 and 1990 it went from 3.0 to 5.5 in Argentina, 3.2 to 3.7 in
Brazil, 2.5 to 3.0 in Chile, 2.5 to 3.5 in Mexico, and 1.5 to 2.7 in Venezuela.
For Latin America as a whole the ratio grew from 2.4 to 3.5.[23] In plain
words, the region's countries owe significant parts of all that they produce
and several times their total exports of goods and services. Despite the
Brady Plan and the policies of "debt capitalization," which in fact served to
sell out the public enterprises at prices far below their market value, the
World Bank points out that by 1990 the foreign debt/GNP ratio remained
stationary (at very high levels) in Argentina; declined to 25.1 percent in
Brazil, 73.5 percent in Chile, and 42.1 percent in Mexico; and increased to
46.9 percent in Uruguay and 71.0 percent in Venezuela. This is far from
being a peculiar phenomenon for a few Latin American nations. Between
1980 and 1990 the countries of sub-Saharan Africa saw the ratio between
foreign debt and GNP increase from 28.5 percent to 109.4 percent, whereas
in Latin America and the Caribbean as a whole the figures were 35.2 percent
and 41.6 percent, respectively.[24]

The preceding data show the vital character of the problem of Latin
America's foreign debt, which may be thought of as a tombstone for the

efforts of an entire generation. Looking at the ratio between the foreign debt and exports, one sees that despite the interruption of foreign loans since 1982, the severe fiscal adjustment programs, the large amounts paid to the creditors, and the enormous export effort carried out by several countries of the region, there is not a single country where the foreign debt has stopped growing faster than export expansion. Even Brazil, with its outstandingly aggressive export offensive, is no exception. In brief, Latin American countries owe almost as much as what they produce per year, and vast segments of Latin America—not only popular classes and the peasantry but also the old petty bourgeoisie and the previously blooming middle sectors of professionals and technicians—find themselves in a process of growing impoverishment. Extreme poverty, not just poverty, is the problem.

Latin America transferred $203 billion to the economic centers between 1982 and 1989. Despite that extraordinary effort—which, had it been applied to programs of social and economic development, would have substantially improved the region's present situation—Latin America is more indebted than before, and it faces a mortgage on its future with no means for a solution. As a matter of fact, between 1991 and 1994 the overall foreign debt of Latin America rose from $456 billion to $506 billion.[25]

The case of Argentina is particularly instructive on this matter because the democratic transition begun during the government of Raúl Alfonsín was progressively weakened by the economic drainage resulting from the foreign debt. Despite plans and projects that tend to reduce debt payments to limits compatible with national development, the truth is that during its first four years of democratic government, Argentina paid $10.453 billion, which represents nothing less than 97 percent of the commercial surplus of those years, 35 percent of all exports, and 3.5 percent of the GNP of the period.[26] On the other hand, the Menem government paid a grand total of $14.505 billion in less than three years, during which time the government was unable to guarantee minimum educational services, public hospitals went bankrupt, public investment plummeted, and wages and salaries were frozen. The recessive effects of this policy have been great. Still more serious—and with more delayed and persistent consequences—has been the loss of prestige that democracy has suffered in the eyes of the popular classes, who have witnessed how their demands have gone unheard under that regime. Meanwhile, a small section of the bourgeoisie notorious for its addiction to government contracts became immensely rich. Its privileged relation with the ruling circles allowed it to pocket—through subsidies, exemptions, reimbursements, and various types of incentives, tax breaks, and trade protection—a fluctuating amount of approximately $3 billion per year, a sum much greater than the combined deficit of all state enterprises![27]

A discussion of the crisis of the welfare state must take place within a framework that accounts for the effects on the poor. Otherwise the controversy raised by the neoliberal theses will be reduced to a mere abstract contraposition of doctrinarian preferences—neoliberals versus social democrats and neo Keynesians—that have little to do with the actual state of events. The neoliberal offensive ignores these data and seeks support from a profoundly unrealistic assumption about the ways capitalism functions, which underplays the central role of the state in the process of accumulation. Neoliberal antistate rhetoric does not line up with the strength and resilience of public expenditures and the subtle yet penetrating forms of state intervention that have always characterized the "really existing" capitalist formations.

The state in Latin America finds itself facing an iron dilemma. The dilapidation of the efforts and sacrifices carried out during the last thirty years in favor of development compels the state to either (1) augment its activism in order to stimulate investments and growth, thereby deepening its "interventionist" profile, and alleviate the situation of the swelled ranks of the poor; or (2) repress the protests from below, thereby seriously impairing the very feasibility of democratic reconstruction.

The state in Latin America has traditionally played an anticyclical role, correcting the direction of the economic cycle and contributing to the revitalization of the market through its interventions. Today it faces serious obstacles to fulfilling that role, and the consequences can easily be verified by an analysis of the investment patterns. It is a well-established fact that private investments are strongly encouraged by government initiatives that clear the ground for future private investments and ensure an attractive rate of benefit. Between 1980 and 1989 gross investments as a percentage of GNP fell for all countries in the region from 22.7 percent to 16.4 percent, thus reflecting a drop in the availability of national savings because of economic stagnation, the massive transfer of resources to creditor banks, and the exhaustion of foreign credit as a source of investments. As a result, Latin American economies have to face a reduction by one-third in investment rates relative to the period before the crisis, with the resulting adverse impact on the rate of growth.[28] In Argentina, the level of investment fell abruptly from 22.2 percent of the GNP in 1980 to 9.9 percent in 1989; in Mexico it fell from 24.8 percent to 17.8 percent; in Brazil from 22.9 percent to 17.7 percent; and in Venezuela from 25.2 percent to 14.5 percent. These cuts were even more significant in the public sector, where the Latin American governments were handcuffed by strict programs of stabilization and structural adjustment.[29] Despite these cuts, the fiscal deficit in most countries of the region continues to be quite high, nurturing neoliberal claims to trim state spending even further.[30] Neoliberal economists pretend to ignore the fact that the tax structures of the area continue to be scandalously regressive. Only in light of this information can one understand how, in the middle of this crisis, taxes on income, profits, and capital gains as a proportion of total state revenues fell between 1972 and 1989 in almost all of the region's countries: from 20 percent to 9.8 percent in Brazil and from 12.5 percent to 4.3 percent in Argentina.[31]

Destruction or Democratic Refoundation of the State?

At this point a few main conclusions may be summarized. The empirical data examined show that the neoliberal proposal for dismantling the "interventionist" state and strengthening the market forces has little application in the contemporary world. That proposal's blueprint was not put into practice either in the splendorous quarter of a century from 1948 to 1973 or in the recessive years that have followed. In addition, the neoliberal blueprint is completely alien to the booming capitalisms of Southeast Asia and Japan. Though it is not the goal here to overwhelm the reader with more figures and quotations, it is important to base this chapter's conclusions on empirical evidence. These data prove, despite neoliberal rhetoric to the contrary, the persistent importance of the state and of social expenditures in core capitalist countries.

The information in Table 5.1, regarding social expenditures in OECD countries between 1960 and 1981, summarized a global tendency that prevailed in all developed countries independent of their national idiosyncratic features or the ideology of their ruling political parties. This twenty-year trend seems to prove the solid nature of the welfare state, which despite finding itself pressed by an unprecedented fiscal crisis has not ceased to guarantee a wide array of social services that today are consubstantial with capitalist democracy and are almost irreversible altogether. The obstacles encountered by President Reagan and Prime Minister Thatcher to fully carrying out their plans aimed at dismantling the structures of the welfare state clearly indicate the enormous difficulties besieging any reactionary proposal. Thus, the state in advanced capitalist formations has remained loyal to its historical tendency, which explains why the rate of growth of social expenditures consistently remained above the rate of growth of the GNP both before and after the mid-1970s crisis.

To be more specific: neither Reagan nor Thatcher fulfilled their promises of carrying out a drastic trimming of state budgets. If something was proven with their respective governments, it was that not even the most fervid neoliberal discourse was able to bring back to life the dead ideas that were diligently buried by Keynes more than half a century ago. The ideologues and propagandists extolling the virtues of the market may talk, but their words vanished into thin air in the face of reality. If the state continues to weigh on the economy, it is because capitalist accumulation has become "statified" and requires ever more the support of public powers in order to survive. The history of the phenomenal deficit of the U.S. government is well known: in 1985 that deficit was 5.3 percent of the GNP, and that of the United Kingdom was 3.1 percent.[32] How can these chronic deficits,

Keynesian only in an aberrant sense, be reconciled with a dogmatically neoliberal discourse that extolls the virtues of least government, unfettered markets, fiscal equilibrium, and so on? Reconciliation is impossible: even under Reagan and Thatcher the size of U.S. and British state spending grew between 1975 and 1985. Despite this data, the political and intellectual spokespersons of neoliberalism in Latin America continue dauntlessly preaching their faith, thriving on the misinformation orchestrated by certain mass media and the enterprises interested in profiting from the triumph of those ideas.

In order to appreciate more clearly the concrete behavior of the governments during the years of the crisis, one may consider the figure in Table 6.1. An analysis of these figures—which refer not only to social spending but to overall public spending, including central government as well as regional and local authorities—confirms what has been said so far. Despite loud orthodox public speeches, the governments of core capitalist nations that increased their extremely harsh policies of fiscal adjustments—invariably proclaimed in all international economic forums—did not stop their expansion of public spending. Some countries managed to slow down their rate of growth, as in the United Kingdom or the United States, for instance, but this effort fell short of reversing the long-run tendency toward an increased weight of the state in the economy.

Table 6.1   Public Expenditures for Selected Countries, 1975–1985 (% of GNP)

Country	1975	1985	Average Yearly Growth Rate Between 1975 and 1985
Austria	40.3	50.7	2.32
Belgium	44.9	54.4	1.94
Canada	41.2	47.0	1.32
Denmark	47.5	59.5	2.28
Finland	37.2	41.5	1.10
France	42.4	52.4	2.14
FRG	45.6	47.2	0.34
Italy	43.1	58.4	3.08
Netherlands	54.3	60.2	1.04
Norway	46.5	48.1	0.34
Sweden	51.0	64.5	2.38
Switzerland	27.4	30.9	1.21
United Kingdom	46.1	47.8	0.36
United States	36.2	36.7	0.14

Source: Maravall, José María, "Las razones del reformismo: Democracia y política social," *Leviatán* 35 (Madrid: Spring 1989), p. 33.

It is also noteworthy to underscore the fact that seven of the fourteen countries included in the table—which, together with Japan and Spain, constitute the decisive nucleus of industrial production at an international scale—alloted more than 50 percent of their GNPs in 1985 to public expenditures. Consequently, the neoliberal sermons that the countries' rulers, ministers, and bankers used to utter in international fora, or in World Bank or International Monetary Fund meetings, are incongruent with the concrete practices they carry out in terms of economic policy. Latin American leaders should take note of this fact.

In addition, it seems appropriate to highlight the contrasts between the cases of Italy and the United Kingdom. Whereas between 1975 and 1985 the former had an outstanding performance in the constellation of industrialized countries, the latter has not yet found a successful strategy to regain its position in the highly competitive industrial markets. The Italian "miracle" took place in a progressive political framework marked by the steady presence of the left and by a pressure from below that increased public spending from 43.1 percent in 1975 to 58.4 percent in 1985.[33] This increase of more than fifteen percentage points reflects an outstanding economic performance that made the United Kingdom fall behind Italy in many key indicators of economic growth. In addition, given the rigid monetary discipline imposed by the conservative British government, the Italian case would appear rather irresponsible at first sight. Yet Italy's fiscal deficit—which has recently oscillated around 10 percent of the GNP—far from harming the dynamics of Italian capitalism, has considerably strengthened it. In short, the Italian experience serves as a sobering example to cool down the monetarist obsession with state downsizing, public spending cuts, fiscal equilibrium, and macroeconomic deregulation. The lessons of recent economic history beat a harsh reply to those arguments.

A quick look at some Latin American figures reveals that public expenditures were the main "adjusting" variable used to enable the massive transfer of resources required for payment of the foreign debt. Public expenditures were also the target of orthodox economic authorities tormented with the need to fight inflation. Once again, it is not a matter of neglecting the deleterious impact of inflation on the economy as a whole and on the standard of living of workers in particular. However, the pertinacious neoliberal belief that the only cause of inflation is the fiscal deficit is scientifically ungrounded and politically reactionary: there is not just a single cause of inflation, and the practical implications of that mistaken theory have irresponsibly worsened the lot of the poor even more.

In accordance with the prevailing orthodoxy, most Latin American countries have reduced public expenditures to the levels found at the end of the 1970s; the major cuts were made in social expenditures, causing considerable pain for the poor.[34] At the end of the 1980s public expenditures as a percentage of GNP were 32.8 percent in Argentina, 31.2 percent in Brazil,

36.4 percent in Chile, 31.1 percent in Mexico, and 27.0 percent in Venezuela. These figures disprove neoliberal theories about the "economic indiscipline" or "populist propensities" of Latin American economies: the size of the region's public sector is, in general terms, slightly over half the size of the state in most of the advanced countries. Given that these figures (with the exception of Chile) correspond to the period before the massive structural adjustment launched in the 1990s, it is quite likely that today's figures may be even smaller.

Comparative data gathered by the World Bank point to the same pattern: whereas in 1985 low-income countries had an average public expenditure equal to 23 percent of their GNP, the industrial market economies' public sectors were equal to 40 percent of their GNP.[35] The same trend is observed within Latin America: the public expenditures of poverty-stricken Guatemala, Peru, and Paraguay barely amount to 11.8 percent, 13.6 percent, and 14.6 percent of their respective GNPs. Reduced state expenditures are hardly a safe route toward economic development. These empirical findings, which the World Bank reproduces in its publications, are apparently unknown by the Bank's economists, who keep repeating that the key problem of Latin American capitalism is the overgrown size of its state.

A few final words should be said regarding tax policy. The most outspoken neoliberal critics of the welfare state—who seem quite determined to struggle against fiscal deficits, inflation, and excessive state activism—keep a telling silence with regard to tax policy. To put it bluntly, the Latin American situation is a veritable scandal: Latin bourgeoisies refuse being taxed, and so far they have managed quite successfully to prevent the organization of an efficient, fair, and progressive tax system. Once social security is excluded, total fiscal pressure in the OECD countries fluctuates around 30 percent of the GNP; with social security this figure rises considerably, reaching 56 percent in Sweden and 44 percent in France. However, in Latin America, at the end of the 1980s, when orthodox neoliberal programs were in full swing, the fiscal pressure excluding social security fluctuated around 17 percent for the countries of greater relative development; for Paraguay, Peru, and Guatemala the figure was 8 percent. But the most blatant example is provided by the data concerning direct taxes: whereas their average levels for the OECD countries fluctuated around 14 percent of the GNP, they were only 5 percent in Mexico; 4 percent in Brazil and Colombia; 3 percent in Argentina, Chile, Costa Rica, Uruguay, and Ecuador; 2 percent in Paraguay, Peru, and Guatemala; and 1 percent in Bolivia. These Latin capitalist states, which were strong enough to make massive cuts in fiscal budgets and social expenditures, proved to be astoundingly feeble in taxing the capitalists. This behavior sharply contrasts with that found in the newly industrializing countries of Southeast Asia and, of course, the OECD countries. The Latin American bourgeoisie wants to pay taxes as in Uganda and to consume as in Switzerland.[36]

In light of all this information, it is appropriate now to consider the central thesis of an article written by Ricardo Lagos, who maintains that "as a result of the twilight of neoliberal policies and of the crisis of the majority of Latin American economies, the economic role of the state will be strengthened."[37]

Many factors support this conclusion: the state will have to continue taking care of public needs that cannot be postponed; these needs will be greater in direct proportion to the deepening of the crisis that affects Latin American capitalist formations. In addition to the ordinary spending required for the state's functioning—to address the basic needs of health, education, housing, administration, and so on—there is also a need for government intervention to help create new jobs and solve the problem of the millions of unemployed; to promote the scientific and technological developments necessary to enable the region's countries to integrate themselves into the fast-changing international economy; to redress the barbarous inequalities of income and wealth inherited from the recent monetarist experiences; and to invest in productive activities that will encourage bourgeoisies, which are as averse to entrepreneurial risk as they are prone to financial speculation and the type of capitalism for which profits are a function of good relations with state officials and not the result of outstanding managerial performance.

In a country such as Argentina, where the housing deficit is over two million homes; where public hospitals lack the minimum equipment necessary to guarantee the health of the population; where there is a school dropout rate of 40 percent, as well as several million functionally illiterate people; where scientific investigation languishes, together with higher education, because of the state's fiscal bankruptcy; where 50 percent of the urban population lacks running water and sewage services; where public administration does not possess the most basic tools needed to carry out its task; where teachers, doctors, police—in addition to state employees—earn absolutely miserable salaries: what is the sense of shrinking the state, reducing fiscal deficits and social spending, and jettisoning the old social commitments the state acquired in more prosperous times?[38]

The market has proven to be completely incapable of solving these problems, not because Latin American markets have failed to work properly but because markets by nature are not concerned with justice and because their driving force is entrepreneurial profits. That is why private initiative has not created health programs aimed at supplying medical care for the elderly and the poor. Neither have private entrepreneurs done anything to ensure housing for low-income sectors, and their contribution to upgrading the technical skills of the work force has been insignificant. On the contrary, market dynamics sharpen social inequality by promoting extraordinary disparities in the distribution of income. As if all of this were not enough, private initiative has proven to be highly refractory regarding the progress of democracy in Latin American societies. In fact, it has proven much easier to democratize the state than certain supposedly pluralistic and open spheres of civil society. For all these reasons, the welfare state is badly needed: in light of the worsening social conditions in Latin America, not only may the welfare state guarantee the satisfaction of basic human needs—even if it does so partially and insufficiently—but it will also favor the strengthening of the region's fragile democratic transitions.

To be sure, this role does not do away with the need to promote a profound reform of the state. The neoliberal position, however, calls for the destruction of the state, a view that is as dogmatic and mistaken as the one held by some sectors on the left, which declare that there is little to object to in the functioning of Latin American states. An inefficient and bankrupt state can hardly benefit the popular classes: the services it provides are insufficient and socially expensive, the bureaucracy tends to behave oppressively vis-à-vis the population, and some of its leading ranks are corrupted in the process. Under such conditions this decaying state form serves only a small sector of Latin American societies. These sectors profit from the subsidies and concessions that complacent rulers hand over to their friends. In spite of all this, state reform cannot be equated with privatizations, which would simply transfer the social capital accumulated by the effort of many generations to private monopolies. Neither can state reform be identified with dismantling the regulatory legislation that states in advanced capitalist democracies use to organize, at least to a certain extent, the anarchy of the markets. Why not conceive of the reform of the state as a golden opportunity to allow the design of new democratic mechanisms and instruments aimed at improving and empowering popular control over the bureaucracy and the private actors that so successfully colonized the state apparatuses? It is of the utmost importance for progressive Latin American thought to confront the issue of state reform with seriousness and responsibility. This issue is too important to be handed over to the right or some short-sighted economist. Without such a reform, it is extremely unlikely that the new governments of the region will succeed at building a democracy that is both legitimate and effective, able to respond to the challenges imposed by the critical situation of Latin American countries.

Notes

1. Cf. Anderson, Perry, "Democracia y dictadura en América Latina en la década del setenta," in *Democracia y socialismo* (Buenos Aires: Tierra del Fuego, 1988), pp. 43–66.

2. A discussion of these issues, particularly the meanings of *neoconservativism* and *neoliberalism,* is found in my "La crisis norteamericana y la racionalidad neoconservadora," *Cuadernos Semestrales* 9, CIDE (Mexico: First Semester, 1981).

3. Cf. Prebisch, Raúl, "El retorno de la ortodoxia," in *Pensamiento Iberoamericano* 1 (Madrid: January–June 1982), pp. 73–78.

4. On this subject see Chapters 1 and 2 of this book.

5. See the special issue of *Pensamiento Iberoamericano* listed in note 3.

6. See, for example, the works of de Soto, Hernando, *El otro sendero: La revolución informal* (Lima: El Barranco, 1986); FIEL, *El fracaso del estatismo: Una propuesta para la reforma del sector público argentino* (Buenos Aires: Sudamericana Planeta, 1987); Sasso, Faustino Fernández, *El estado y yo, por Juan García (Taxista)* (Buenos Aires: Grupo Editor Latinoamericano, 1988).

7. Marini, Ruy Mauro, "La lucha por la democracia en América Latina," *Cuadernos Políticos* 44 (Mexico: July–September 1985), pp. 3–12.

8. See Ferrer, Aldo, "Monetarismo en el Cono Sur: El caso argentino"; Serra, José, "El debate sobre política económica en Brasil"; González, Norberto, "Ortodoxia y apertura en América Latina: Distintos casos y políticas"; Furtado, Celso, "Transnacionalização e monetarismo," all of which are in *Pensamiento Iberoamericano* 1 (Madrid: January–June 1982).

9. The following countries are included: Argentina, Bolivia, Brazil, Colombia, Costa Rica, Chile, Ecuador, El Salvador, Guatemala, Haiti, Honduras, Mexico, Nicaragua, Panama, Paraguay, Peru, the Dominican Republic, Uruguay, Venezuela, Barbados, Guyana, Jamaica, and Trinidad and Tobago.

10. CEPAL, *Anuario estadístico de América Latina y el Caribe* (Santiago: 1987), pp. 148–149. Figures for 1990 taken from CEPAL, *Equidad y transformación productiva: Un enfoque integrado* (Santiago: CEPAL, 1992).

11. CEPAL, *Equidad y transformación,* p. 36.

12. CEPAL, *Magnitud de la pobreza en América Latina en los años ochenta* (Santiago: 1991). See also Chapter 7 in this book.

13. Faria, Vilmar, "The current social situation in Brazil," mimeo (São Paulo: CEBRAP, 1992), p. 10. Faria argues that this figure may even underestimate the real impact of poverty and indigence on Brazilian society.

14. Cf. Beccaria, Luis A., "Distribución del ingreso en la Argentina: Explorando lo sucedido desde mediados de los setenta," *Desarrollo Económico* 123 (Buenos Aires: October–December 1991), p. 334.

15. United Nations Development Programme, *Desarrollo sin pobreza* (Santiago: CEPAL, 1990), p. 45.

16. Meller, Patricio, "Ajuste y reformas económicas en América Latina: Problemas y experiencias recientes," *Pensamiento Iberoamericano* 2(22–23) (Madrid: 1993), p. 49.

17. International Labour Organisation, *El trabajo en el mundo* (Geneva: 1984), Vol. 1, pp. 222–227.

18. CEPAL, *Panorama Social de América Latina, 1994* (Santiago: CEPAL, 1994), pp. 127–128.

19. Cardoso, Fernando H., *A democracia necessária,* (Campinas: Papirus, 1985), p. 90. Cited in Stepan, Alfred, *Rethinking Military Politics: Brazil and the Southern Cone* (Princeton: Princeton University Press, 1988), pp. 124–125.

20. Beccaria, Luis, "Distribución del ingreso," p. 333.

21. Population data for 1980 were obtained from the World Bank, *World Development Report, 1982* (New York: Oxford University Press, 1982), pp. 110–111. Data for 1987 were taken from the same source, 1989 edition; foreign debt data for 1987 were taken from the same source, pp. 228–229. Those for the year 1980 were extracted from *Integración Latinoamericana* 88 (Buenos Aires: March 1984), p. 90.

22. World Bank, *World Development Report, 1989,* pp. 234–235.

23. Meller, Patricio, "Ajuste y reformas," p. 17.

24. World Bank, *World Development Report, 1992: Development and the Environment* (Washington, DC: 1992), p. 261.

25. *Clarín* (Buenos Aires: June 6, 1994), pp. 18–19. During the 1980s the foreign debt of the region rose by $101 billion. This information can be found in a recent report of the Latin American Economic System (SELA) entitled "La deuda latinoamericana y el pago de nunca acabar," *Página/12* (Buenos Aires: February 20, 1990), p. 10.

26. See Pontoni, Alberto, "Deuda externa: Un nuevo rol para el FMI," *Página/12* (Buenos Aires: July 14, 1988), p. 9.

27. Canitrot, Adolfo, in EURAL, *Proyectos de cambio: La izquierda democrática en América Latina* (Caracas: Nueva Sociedad, 1988).

28. CEPAL, "Estadísticas sobre cuentas nacionales," mimeo (Santiago: CEPAL, 1989).

29. CEPAL, *Transformación productiva con equidad* (Santiago: CEPAL, 1990), p. 38.

30. BID, op. cit., pp. 228, 262, 290, 358, 392, 424, 432.

31. World Bank, *World Development Report, 1987* (Washington, DC: 1987), p. 275. Figures for 1989 were taken from the same source, 1991 edition.

32. World Bank, *World Development Report, 1987*, p. 273.

33. International Monetary Fund, *Government Finance Statistics Yearbook* (Washington, DC: 1987 and 1988).

34. CEPAL, *Equidad y transformación*, p. 95.

35. World Bank, *World Development Report, 1991: The Challenge of Development* (Oxford: Oxford University Press, 1991), p. 139.

36. CEPAL, *Equidad y transformación*, p. 92.

37. Lagos, Ricardo, "Crisis, ocaso neoliberal y el rol del estado," *Pensamiento Iberoamericano* 5a (Madrid: January–July 1984), p. 165.

38. See Alejandro Rofman's poignant article entitled "En defensa del estado, del gasto público y del déficit fiscal," *Nueva Sión* (Buenos Aires: August 6, 1988), p. 6.

7

Democracy in Latin America: Problems and Prospects

Approaches to the Democratic Question

The incomplete and relatively precarious democratization of political regimes in Latin America has fueled a heated debate on the meaning of democracy. A discussion of this sort is welcome in a continent, where (as a perceptive scholar, the late Agustín Cueva used to remark), in almost two centuries of independent political life, there has not yet occurred a single bourgeois revolution culminating in the implantation of a democratic regime. Bourgeois revolutions have been rare in Latin America, and the examples can be counted: Mexico between 1910 and 1917, Guatemala in 1944, and Bolivia in 1952.[1] Less exotic were the examples of conservative modernizations, in which right-wing or, in some cases, reactionary coalitions pushed forward major programs aimed at the destruction of archaic obstacles to capitalist development or oriented toward the swift restructuring of existing capitalist structures and institutions. In the past, Latin American history has seen many "enlightened" oligarchical alliances promoting major socioeconomic reforms: in this regard the cases of Argentina between 1880 and 1914, and of Uruguay at the turn of this century, stand out as shining examples of this type. However, in recent times the attempts at conservative modernization have become rarer: since the early 1960s, only two cases seem to have succeeded and are almost universally regarded as the most relevant ones: the military regimes of Brazil and Chile, which during their long tenure in power drastically transformed the foundations of their capitalist social and economic structures.[2]

However, none of these cases—not even the Jacobin ones, whose principal example is the Mexican Revolution—concluded their "pending questions" by establishing a democratic regime. Their overriding concerns seem to have been to uphold the functioning of the capitalist mode of production and, when deemed necessary, to carry out the reforms needed to that end; but none of these regimes had the least interest in introducing bourgeois democracy. The authoritarian imprint of Latin American capitalism has very deep roots, tracing back to both its colonial heritage and the dependent and reactionary modality of capitalist development by means of which these societies became integrated into the world markets. Many decades have passed, but the cumbersome legacies of the authoritarian political tradition are still at work.[3]

Despite the failures, reversals, and miseries of Latin American history, at the beginning of the 1980s the region seemed ripe to try democracy once again. This trend was reinforced by the fact that, beginning in the late 1960s, the democratic thrust started to gain momentum in an unprecedented manner in world history. At the beginning of the 1990s some 58 percent of the 187 countries of the world organized their political process according to democratic rules, and the number of democracies rose from forty-four in 1972 to 107 in 1994.[4] Impressed by these events, some theorists, such as Samuel P. Huntington, believe that we are facing a "third wave." Others, such as Francis Fukuyama, have seen in these developments the signs of a victorious capitalism that, hand in hand with a no less triumphant liberal democracy, are heralding the "end of history."[5] As a result of this democratic flood as well as of what Norberto Bobbio called "the harsh rebuttals of history" (which in this case includes the resounding failure of "really existing socialisms" and the inability of social democracy to transcend capitalism), a significant portion of Latin American social scientists as well as of the left has adhered to a naive conception of democracy that rests on two mutually reinforcing premises: (1) the supposedly linear and irreversible nature of democratic progress, something that a lucid conservative scholar like Huntington refuses to admit—once dictatorships are defeated, transition ensues and democratic consolidation seems to be just a matter of time; and (2), the belief—both historically false and theoretically wrong—that democracy is a project coterminous with the sole establishment of adequate representative and governmental institutions. The heroic enterprise of creating a democracy is thus reduced to the erection of a pure political order, that is, a system of rules and procedures allowing for the free and popular election of government authorities and unconcerned with the ethical contents of the resulting institutional order. In this conception, democracy, as a set of abstract rules, can pose only "technical" problems of governance and administrative efficacy.[6]

The Schumpeterian Legacy

One can only be astounded by the fact that something at first sight simple and reasonable was able to unleash throughout history such fierce passions and such dogged resistance, bringing about in the most diverse societies revolutions and counterrevolutions, bloody civil wars, protracted popular struggles, and brutal repressions of all sorts.[7] Was all this drama—after all, the drama of the West since the times of Cleisthenes and Pericles—just the result of a simple *malentendu*? Wouldn't it be more reasonable to think instead that the implantation of democracy reflects a particular outcome of social struggles, and as such is well beyond being a simple and innocent procedural arrangement? Looking at the historical experience of Latin America, in Brazil, for instance: how can one account for the fact that it was much easier to abolish slavery—and the empire that rested on slave labor—than to achieve bourgeois democracy?

This is not the place to explore in detail the deleterious practical consequences of the belated triumph of Schumpeterian ideas, which exhaust the scope and limits of democracy to the procedural arrangements by which "individuals acquire the power to decide by means of a competitive struggle for the people's vote."[8] This political method for arriving at decisions is "incapable of being an end in itself, irrespective of what decision it will produce under given historical conditions."[9] This is the reason Schumpeter considers it reasonable to propose a mental experiment in which a given polity may decide, by democratic methods, the persecution of political dissidents, the burning of witches, the slaughtering of Jews. His hopeless formalistic and "minimalist" theoretical approach reduces democracy to a political method, and as such this method is indifferent to the practical performance of the political regime. Thus, a Schumpeterian "democracy" can persecute, torture, and slaughter without losing its "democratic" condition, because in this fallacious argument democracy is unrelated to any notion of the good society, or to any idea of good or wrong at all.

No wonder that Schumpeter's theory of democracy is afflicted by a strong conservative bias: it not only chooses to ignore anything but procedures but, in addition, in its theoretical formulation it mirrors the narrow scope and limits of capitalist democracies. Similarly, Schumpeterian-based theoretical formulations of democracy tend to disregard both the ethical contents of democracy—as a crucial aspect of any discourse dealing with the organization of the good society—as well as the practical-historical processes of constitution of "really existing democracies" and the social basis on which they rest.

It is important to realize that the "procedural" theory of democracy implies a radical departure from the classic argument developed by the Western political tradition from Plato to Marx. For authors as diverse as Plato, Aristotle, Machiavelli, Rousseau, Marx, and Tocqueville, democracy meant something completely different from what the remote disciples of Schumpeter imagine today. This is why in *Democracy in America,* for instance, Alexis de Tocqueville portrays the epic nature of democratization with these moving words: "This whole book has been written under the impulse of a kind of religious dread inspired by contemplation of this irresistible revolution advancing century by century over every obstacle and even now going forward amid the ruins it has itself created."[10]

Democracy: Political and Social Dimensions

Despite the compelling force of Tocqueville's portrait, today's mainstream political science regards democracy in Schumpeterian terms: as the sole method aimed at the formation of a government and no longer as a condition of the civil society. Yet democracy is in fact a unique amalgam that binds together three inseparable components. On one hand, a complex set of unambiguous institutions and rules of the game that guarantee the relatively uncertain outcomes that characterize policymaking in democratic states[11] is the "political condition," a necessary condition—although not a sufficient one, because democracy cannot stand alone as a political regime embedded in a society characterized by structures, institutions, and ideologies antagonistic and hostile to its spirit. Therefore, democracy requires social and economic structures that support a minimum level of fundamental equality, allowing for the full development of unique individuals and the plurality of expression of social life; and for the effective enjoyment of freedom by all individuals—a freedom that ought to be not only a formal entitlement (which in Latin America has been beautifully written in tons of dead-letter constitutions) but a living and practical day-to-day experience. These two "social conditions" of the democratic state are, like the political condition, necessary but not sufficient to produce by themselves a full-fledged democracy. Democracy exists only when all three conditions are simultaneously met. In practical terms capitalist democracies, even the most developed ones, barely meet these standards: the institutional and procedural deficits of advanced democracies are well known and serious doubts are raised when minimum levels of equality or the effective enjoyment of freedoms are taken into consideration.[12] Dahl's classic distinction between democracy and polyarchy rightly acknowledges this incompleteness of "really existing democracies," thus revealing the inadequacies, at the theoretical level, of a conceptualization artificially confined to the boundaries of the political realm.[13]

The classic conception of democracy not only allows for a better understanding of the historical process of constitution, crisis, and recomposition of modern democracies, it also provides a valuable policy guideline for citizens, political actors, and democratic governments. If democracy is going to take root and become the common sense of the masses in Latin America—a region of the world in which the authoritarian and oppressive imprints of capitalism assert themselves with unmatched strength—the new democratic regimes must carry out policies of social reform aimed at the reconstruction of our societies along the egalitarian and progressive features congenial with the consolidation of the democratic state. Are Latin American governments doing that? Democracy calls for institutions as well as for citizens. The neoliberal capitalist restructuring under way in Latin America these days is actively dismantling states, weakening political institutions and the public sphere at large, and destroying the citizenry through the endless curtailments of rights and entitlements. Unbounded commodification, the supremacy of markets, and the degradation of the citizenry can hardly be regarded as conditions that favor the consolidation of new democratic regimes. The homeless, beggars, children of the street, people living in extreme poverty, the chronically unemployed—who today make up a sizable fraction of capitalist societies (not so much at the core but especially in the peripheral countries)—are not the right stuff out of which the citizen is made. It is usually taken for granted that Latin American democracies do have "citizens"; but, as Guillermo O'Donnell has suggested, this assumption should be tested against the data of empirical experience.[14] Ignoring the practical conditions of democratic life in our region, many abstract theorizers seem to assume that democracy functions in Argentina, Brazil, and Chile, not to mention Guatemala and Haiti, as it does in Scandinavia or in the Benelux countries. It is not by chance that crucial concepts for the study of advanced democratic capitalism—such as "governmental accountability" or "responsiveness," for instance—lack corresponding words in either Spanish or Portuguese. They have been, until very recent times, unnecessary words: the practical experience of governance in Latin America did not require such terms even under "democratic" governments.

In the democratic wave of the late 1940s in Western Europe, replacing authoritarian, despotic regimes insured large sections of the working classes the benefits of welfare and political representation, and a substantial improvement in their material conditions of existence. In Latin America, on the contrary, democratization came hand in hand with the unprecedented pauperization of wide sections of the population brought about by the economic crisis of the 1980s and the consequent orthodox neoliberal policies. The democratic state, therefore, is put into question as the effective locus of justice and equality, and as the instrument for the correction of the so-called market failures when the state apparatuses and social policies are dismantled or canceled in order not to interfere with the Darwinian selection of the fittest made by the market. It would hardly be an exaggeration to argue that the economic correlates of democracy and the economic performance of the democratic regimes are as important for the democratic consolidation as the adequate design of the political system and the institutions of popular representation.

In other words, class polarization and growing social inequality hardly could be regarded as favorable to the consolidation of democracy. Even a capitalist democracy—that means a democracy that is ingrained with the complex structures of domination of capitalist societies and that considers the existing social relations and the ensuing distribution of societal resources as invariable and permanent parameters—requires a minimum level of social and economic homogeneity that is badly missing in Latin America today. Can democracy take root and grow within the rapid extension of poverty, which undermines the social and economic citizenship of the newly enfranchised masses just in the moment in which their political citizenship is discursively exalted? Since Aristotle, we know that democracy cannot live with extremes: the generalization of poverty and its necessary counterpart, the rise of a lavish plutocracy, are incompatible in the long run with the sustainment of a democratic regime. When the poor become indigent and the rich turn into magnates, democracy—as well as freedom—are likely to succumb:

> If you would have a solid and enduring State—Rousseau observed—you must see that it contains no extremes of wealth. It must have neither millionaires nor beggars. They are inseparable from one another, and both are fatal to the common good. . . . Where they exist public liberty becomes a commodity of barter. The rich buy it, the poor sell its.[15]

Rousseau helps us understand why the prognosis regarding the consolidation of democracy in Latin America—and other areas of the world as well, like Eastern Europe, for instance—must be taken with a grain of salt to avoid the traps of unwarranted triumphalism.

Democratic Embeddedness in Capitalist Social Relations

Thus, the problems of democratic transition and consolidation vastly exceed those of political engineering. The careful design and well-oiled working of the public institutions of political representation and government are indeed very important factors; so are the democratic pacts and compromises made by collective actors as long as they are popularly scrutinized and plebiscited. But only by the caprice of the concept would it be possible to erect—in the sphere of intellectual representation, of course—a wall dividing society, economy, and politics. The penetrating critique offered by the young Marx concerning the fetishist nature of the capitalist state, founded on an artificial separation between bourgeois and citizen, and the compelling criticism made by Gramsci regarding the rigid liberal opposition between public and private, and political society and civil society, have already made clear the need for a more integrated theoretical approach in dealing with democracy.[16]

Unfortunately, the indispensable revaluation of democracy that has taken place in postauthoritarian Latin America has in many cases been based on the Schumpeterian concept, which not only is quite formalistic but also tends to foreclose the new theoretical and practical developments experienced by democracy since World War II. Agustín Cueva rightly warned against the dangers involved in considering democracy in a Schumpeterian fashion. Democracy is not an exclusively political category, which refers to a specific type of relationship between state and civil society—characterized by public freedoms, political competition, periodic elections, rule of law, and so on—and whose effectiveness appears to be a priori taken for granted regardless of the particular conditions of existence prevailing in civil society. It is for this reason that Cueva argued that "the democratic rules of the game are in themselves positive, save that they never work in an undetermined manner, independent of their insertion in a more complex social structure that provides them with one or another 'orienta-tion.'"[17]

Cueva's observation is particularly important if one recalls a common feature in Latin American redemocratization: the pervasive impact of the belief—shared by both elites and masses—that once democracy is achieved the structural problems and inequities of dependent capitalism will melt into thin air. The long-cherished triumph of democracy was misconstrued as the defeat of the economy at the hands of politics. In fact, the initial years of the democratic restoration witnessed the bankruptcy of "economicism" in all its variants ("vulgo-Marxist" and mainstream political science alike), as well as the unbounded exaltation of democratic voluntarism. This costly underesti-mation of economic factors created formidable obstacles shortly afterward, and politicians and the general public paid a high price for this negligence and naive optimism. Many rulers and policymakers sincerely expected that democratic governments would hold the magic key to open the iron gates of international investment and bank loans. Top governmental officials of new democratic regimes voiced their disillusionment in front of the inflexible position of the creditor countries, insisting on the so-called technical treat-ment of the external debt, thus immutably upholding the policies imple-mented during the years of dictatorship. The surprise and indignation of democratic leaders in the region were enormous when they realized that after the heartfelt salutations to the reborn democracies and the renascent public liberties in Latin America the same cold-blooded policies were applied, in some cases even with renewed toughness, to the fragile govern-ments of the area.

Of course, this concern with the "social conditions" of democracy does not mean that the themes traditionally highlighted by mainstream political science are irrelevant. Quite the contrary: political competition, majority rule, pluralism, political representation, division of powers, unbounded pub-lic freedoms, checks and balances, and rule of law are necessary compo-nents of the popular sovereignty, although at the end of the twentieth centu-ry ever more participatory forms of decisionmaking are an essential part of a democratic project. In spite of all their shortcomings, these individual free-doms, rights, and guarantees, as well as their institutional crystallizations, continue to be necessary conditions for any form of postcapitalist democra-cy. This was early recognized by Rosa Luxemburg, who never made the mis-take, so common among the left, of scorning bourgeois democracy for its procedural and formalistic biases. Her criticisms of the incongruencies of capitalist democracy—the egalitarian and democratic claims of which are contradicted by the structural features of capitalist societies—are still today irrefutable. A simple glance at fragile Latin American democracies, precari-ously standing over structurally unjust societies that condemn large seg-ments of the popular classes to extreme poverty, would be sufficient to prove the point. Nevertheless, Luxemburg's argument in favor of a socialist democracy has no connection whatsoever with the "Marxist-Leninist" vulgate according to which supposedly "formal" freedoms have an irreducible bourgeois character, as if the habeas corpus, freedom of speech and association, or majority rule were alien to the theory and political praxis of the workers. As Norberto Bobbio correctly poses the question, does a worker's assembly choose its leaders using unequal suffrage, or the theocratic principle?[18] Luxemburg rightly contends that socialist democracy requires that these "bourgeois" freedoms—formal only in their external appearance—must be confirmed and extended by means of the substantial democratization of the factory, the school, the family, and the entire social structure.

> We have always distinguished the social kernel from the political form of bourgeois democracy; we have always revealed the hard kernel of social inequality and lack of freedom hidden under the sweet shell of formal equality and freedom—not in order to reject the latter but to spur the working class into not being satisfied with the shell, but rather by conquering political power, to create a socialist democracy to replace bourgeois democracy—not to eliminate democracy altogether.[19]

In sum, the problems besieging the long march of Latin America toward democracy exceed those exclusively circumscribed to the mechanics of the political regime. These matters are extremely important, but to remain locked in a procedural and minimalist conception of democracy would cloud our vision and is the surest road to producing a new round of democratic frustrations in the region. What fulfilled the democratic ideal of classic Greece, or the free towns of medieval Europe, or industrial and modern society is nowadays just the historical platform from which the peoples all around the world struggle for new and more fruitful forms of participation and construction of political power. For instance, if at the beginnings of the twentieth century a polity could be regarded as democratic even though women were not allowed to vote; at the end of the same century no democracy can aspire to that name without the full participation of women in political life. Therefore, the democratic form "protective" of individual rights and freedoms, or of the "possessive individualism"—to use the felicitous formulation of C. B. Macpherson—requires today new contents of economic and social nature that, like women's suffrage, are an inevitable part of the very democratic idea. These contents tend to be incompatible with capitalist society, and from them spring a participatory conception of democracy without which the modern image of the citizen is deprived of all dignity and efficacy.

By the end of the 1970s some scholars started to express their support for a more ambitious and comprehensive, clearly postliberal, democratic program.[20] In a book written in the mid-1980s Robert Dahl, a leading U.S. political scientist, argued for the complete overhaul of the "liberal-pluralist" model of democracy. One of the components of such badly needed theoretical renovation was the extension of democratic ideas and principles to areas other than the state or the public space, like the modern capitalist enterprise. In one of the most revealing passages of his book Dahl made an important argument:

> It is not true that self-governing enterprises would violate a superior right to private ownership. It is not true that the assumptions justifying the democratic process in the government of the state do not apply to economic enterprises. Nor is it true that democracy in an economic enterprise would be a sham. . . . Of course, we do not expect that the introduction of the democratic process in the government of economic enterprises will make them perfectly democratic or entirely overcome the tendencies toward oligarchy that seem to be inherent in all large human organizations, including the government of the state. But just as we support the democratic process in the government of the state despite substantial imperfections in practice, so we support the democratic process in the government of economic enterprises despite the imperfections we expect in practice.[21]

From another perspective, Brazilian president and distinguished political scientist Fernando H. Cardoso, had reached also by the mid-1980s similar conclusions. After brilliantly summarizing the challenges beleaguering Latin American democracies Cardoso acknowledged that even if democracy is a self-justifying value, which stands on its own, it is nonetheless true that in the region's countries there exists "the experience of social inequality and the opinion that without effective reforms in the productive system and the forms of distribution and appropriation of wealth neither the Constitution nor the rule of law will be able to suppress the farcical smell of democratic politics."[22]

The tasks Latin American democrats face go beyond the sole restoration of political forms congruent with the fundamental principles of democratic theory. There is a lot more to be done, and this is the message behind Dahl's and Cardoso's words. In addition to the purely political job, the new leaders have to ensure that democracy is also an effective tool to promote social transformation and the construction of a "good society." This being the case, a reflection on Latin American emerging democracies cannot be done on "democracy in general," pretending that the type of society on which these particular democratic experiments take place, namely, peripheral dependent capitalism, is a neutral scenario deprived of any significance. Quite the contrary, in order to understand the travail of Latin American democracies it is necessary to have a keen awareness of the structure and dynamics of capitalist economies and, more specifically, of the nature of the current processes of structural adjustment and economic restructuring going on in the region. It does not make any sense to talk about democracy in its abstraction when what is needed is to examine the conditions, forms, and limits of concrete processes of democratization in capitalist societies whose constitutive structures and typical social relations are profoundly antagonistic to it. Being a value in itself, it is impossible to ignore that in its historical incarnation democracy has always been embedded in a rather inflexible structure of class domination that severely curtailed its potentialities. Democracy in classic Athens did not dissolve the relations of domination between master and slave typical of the ancient world, and the rise of Pericles did not work the miracle of transmuting the slaves into masters and vice versa. Likewise, the democratization of capitalist societies through universal suffrage, political representation, welfare policies, and so on was unable to dismantle their deep-rooted structures of domination. The adequate assessment of these relationships is threatened by the Scylla and Charibdis that cause many analyses to wreck: the economicist reductionism, which dissolves the specificity of politics in the "laws of motion" of capital. In this view capitalist democracy and bourgeois dictatorship are essentially the same, and Olof Palme is coarsely equated with General Augusto Pinochet. On the other hand, a symmetrical error prevails in mainstream social sciences, which fragment and breakup the inseparable totality of social reality in autonomous and self-sustaining "parts," each one studied in its splendid but wholly artificial isolation.[23] Economists talk about "the economy," sociologists talk about "the society," anthropologists speak about "the culture," and political scientists talk about "democracy," when what really exists is a society that has to produce, that has a given social structure and pattern of social relations, and where power is distributed within the narrow limits allowed by the prevailing social relations. What is the meaning of talking about "democracy in general" when confronted with a "democratic capitalism," where the noun is capitalism and democracy is the adjective.

Lessons from the Past and Contemporary Problems

The remainder of this chapter will examine some of the major problems threatening the course of Latin American democratization. These questions seriously challenged the optimistic hopes that flourished during the early phases of democratic reconstruction and sobered the naive expectations of both leaders and masses. A new look at the arduous historical enterprise of establishing democracy is in order. The following reflections are a contribution to this task.

The Instability and Weakness of the
Correlation of Forces Sustaining the Democratic Regime

First, it is important to remember that always and everywhere the democratization of the political institutions was a process marked by heartening progresses and sad regressions, by some encouraging leaps forward followed by big and unexpected relapses. In no case was democratization an uninterrupted and linear ascent toward the high summits of polyarchy, liberalism, and toleration. Not only did the process fail to be smooth, peaceful, and continuous, but in addition, not even advanced capitalist democracies can boast of being immune to regressive trends that may cancel democratic progress through a variety of procedures and strategies. Only a naive individual could support the thesis of the irreversibility of democratic development.[24] The well-known experiences of the Weimar Republic in Germany and post–World War I Italy speak for themselves, as do the histories of Europe and Latin America with their multiple examples of modest democratic developments violently interrupted by the restoration of despotic rule. Furthermore, the "neoconservative" experiments of the 1980s—mainly "Thatcherism" and Reagan's so-called conservative revolution—seem to have eroded the democratic performance and accomplishments of governments in advanced capitalist nations. The forceful privatization of state enterprises and large sections of public property, the consistent weakening of the "public spaces," the abandonment of the instruments and procedures used in the past to correct the inequities of markets, and the growing importance of the executive branch (at the expense of a corresponding decline in the role of the congress) have undermined the strength of democratic institutions and practices in the United Kingdom and the United States.[25] In addition, the neoconservative recomposition of capitalism has accentuated the tendency toward the creation of a highly polarized type of class structure that the grand tradition of political theory considers inhospitable to democracy. This emerging "dual society," which in peripheral nations means a handful of super-rich existing side by side with a large mass of very poor people, is hardly compatible with democracy at all.

These regressive trends are far from being just occasional relapses expressing the ephemeral predominance of neoconservative governments or ideologies. On the contrary, they take root in the deep modifications of modern industrial societies, for which the negative impacts on democracy were precociously perceived by several authors.[26] Even though this diagnosis could be challenged by those who fail to perceive these worrisome facts and their implications, the argument carries enough weight as to discount the optimistic belief that democratic progress in Latin America is irreversible. History teaches that the survival of democratic regimes, or their inaugurations in other cases, have been the outcome of the ascending impulse of the popular classes. It has been those classes' ceaseless and long-run struggles for equal rights, material well-being, and political freedoms and not the nebulous benevolence of the upper strata that have caused the democratization of capitalist states. As with any other social change, democratization depends on the stabilization of a favorable correlation of forces and on the capacity of the subordinated classes to crystallize these delicate and unstable equilibria in political institutions likely to sustain their achievements. It is necessary, therefore, to place the whole question of democratization under a historical and structural perspective. This means to conceive of bourgeois democracy not as a suprahistorical entity, floating above the social conflicts of its time, but as a result of the antagonisms, passions, and interests inherent to modern civil society. To consolidate, democracy requires social actors whose projects of domination, interests, and ideologies are compatible with the creation of a democratic political order, something that is not always the case. It is for this very reason that capitalist democracy is marked by tensions and contradictions and that its achievements are always provisional, having the potential to be canceled by a new authoritarian coalition.[27]

The New International Ideological Climate: The So-Called Crisis of Democracy and the Rise of Neoconservative Doctrines

Another obstacle facing the current wave of redemocratization in Latin America as well as in some parts of Asia and Eastern Europe is the pervasive skepticism, in some cases unrestrained pessimism, regarding democratic governments. The sudden shift of the political pendulum of the West toward the right and the ensuing modification of the present ideological climate brought to the foreground the so-called crisis of democracy. The effects of this conservative mood have been the rekindling of ancient and bitter residues of suspicion and mistrust in light of the negative impacts that democratic activism and popular mobilization and participation have supposedly had on economic life. Overwhelmed by the crisis of the 1970s, neoconservative theorists such as Samuel P. Huntington did not hesitate to point out that the problem was democracy, not capitalism.[28]

The collapse of Keynesianism in the early 1970s opened a vast political and public policy void that was soon filled by the rise of a new, neoconservative "common sense." Whereas in the 1950s and 1960s presidents and prime ministers could safely describe themselves as Keynesians, since the late 1970s the new orthodoxy has had a distinctly conservative (and, at times, reactionary) flavor. This sea change was undoubtedly favored by the work of a host of outstanding intellectuals—many of them disillusioned communists and Trotskyists, "reconverted" to neoconservatism—generously funded through an impressive network of foundations and think tanks that succeeded at articulating a neoconservative blueprint for policymakers and rulers.

The neoconservative discourse offers a novel "reinterpretation" of the causes of the economic crisis and political disorders besieging advanced capitalist societies in the 1970s. It is interesting to notice that, in some cases, neoconservative scholars and publicists made use of a peculiar reading of classic Marxist analysis to support this argument. As everybody knows, Marx was aware early on of the tendency toward incompatibility between the capitalist mode of production and the functioning of bourgeois democracy. According to his interpretation, the reproduction of the social relations necessary for the extraction of the surplus value was threatened by the expansiveness and egalitarian pressures congenital to the democratic regime, thus condemning that regime's government to a chronic propensity toward ungovernability and political instability. According to Marx, the reason for this propensity stems from the fact that, thanks to universal suffrage, democracy

> gives the possession of political Power to the classes whose social slavery comes to eternalize: the proletariat, the peasantry, the petty bourgeoisie. And the class whose old Power upholds, the bourgeoisie, is deprived of the political guarantees necessary to perpetuate its power. Democracy encloses the political domination of the bourgeoisie within democratic conditions that at all times are factors for the victory of the inimical classes, thus jeopardizing the very foundations of bourgeois society. Democracy demands that the workers not advance, passing from political to social emancipation. Democracy also commands the bourgeois not to regress, passing from social to political restoration.[29]

A transitory solution to this contradiction, adopted by the capitalist state in what Gramsci calls its "economic-corporative" phase, was to limit the political game to the classes and groups integrated into the capitalist hegemony and whose participation in public life would not pose any danger to the dominant classes. Thus, citizenship was restricted to property owners and their social allies, while the overwhelming majority of society was condemned to an increasingly contested political exclusion. As a result, some capitalist states embraced liberalism while remaining blatantly undemocratic. Only the wealthy and powerful enjoyed political rights, thus achieving an unstable compromise between the imperative of preserving the bourgeois domination and the need to ensure for the wage earners a minimum of civil and political rights. *Censitaire* democracy was the institutional form of this compromise that legally denied suffrage to the subordinated classes, thus freezing the democratic process within the narrow limits of oligarchical liberalism. Consequently, such a liberal state appeared a monstrous Janus-headed leviathan. Within the social space of the dominant classes and their allies, the liberal state showed its democratic face, granting freedom and representation to the beneficiaries of the capitalist hegemony. For the rest of the society, mostly constituted by what in the language of the times were regarded as the "dangerous classes," the liberal state presented its other face, dictatorship.[30]

As argued earlier in this book, World War I, the Russian Revolution, and the Great Depression of 1929 caused in just fifteen years the definitive demise of the liberal state. Capitalist politics became a "mass story," which prevented the perpetuation of the exclusion of the lower classes. Citizenship, previously a privilege of the rich and not a right of all adults, was extended by force to the popular classes and strata. It is not by chance that those who had been summoned for the supreme sacrifice of war would forcefully demand, once the hostilities ended, full-fledged political representation. In this way the old liberal exclusionary state was replaced, through a number of roads and paths (each profoundly influenced by local and national traditions of popular struggles and by the prevailing political institutions) by a new form of capitalist state that incorporated the masses. In this way, bourgeois hegemony reached new heights, but also it came to rest on the potentially more threatening terrain of mass politics.

The result of these epochal processes was the rise of the mass Keynesian state. This new form of the capitalist state no longer rested on the exclusion and disorganization of the masses. On the contrary, it actively promoted the organized inclusion of them within the framework of its expanded set of agencies, apparatuses, and formats of representation, although in such a manner that the irresistible presence of the plebeian components could not harm the continued domination of the capitalists. This profound mutation of the state found its major theorists in John Maynard Keynes and Antonio Gramsci, although the class horizon of them was located in each other's antipodes. In any case, this new "enlarged state" demanded a thorough reconstruction of the bourgeoisie's networks of political domination, but the prize was attractive enough: an adequate processing of the chronic contradictions between capitalism and democracy. The accomplishments of this Keynesian formula can be measured by the unprecedented period of economic growth, social peace, and political stability that lasted from the end of the 1940s until the mid-1970s. Amidst this jubilee it was announced to the world that class struggle is dead, suffocated by the opulence and abundance of the West. In addition, the ideologies that expressed—and fueled—these conflicts were dead too.[31]

Once this golden epoch reached its limits, however, many voices began blaming mass democracy for the perverse combination of inflation and recession that paralyzed the industrialized economies in the mid-1970s, and started proposing broad redefinitions of political democracy to guarantee the continuity of the process of capitalist accumulation. "Capital becomes Marxist," to use the felicitous expression of Antonio Negri, and fully assumes the class struggles in its search for a new, conservative, solution to the crisis.[32] The strategy of capitalist recomposition rested on two pillars. On the one hand was a ruthless "euthanasia," but this time not of the rentiers, as Keynes had suggested, but of the segments of the bourgeoisie unable to adapt to the changing circumstances of the world market and the scientific and technological revolution unleashed in the 1970s. This purge of the bourgeoisie took place in the market and within the bureaucratic articulations that link this class with the state apparatus, so it did not much affect democratic life. But the capitalist recomposition also rested on a second type of "euthanasia" applied to large segments of the working classes—including wide sections of the white-collar population—who were rendered superfluous in the new economic model, as well as on the strengthening of discipline over the subordinated classes, which was needed to neutralize and control the demands of the working classes.

Democracy thus appears, to the eyes of the neoconservative politicians and scholars, as the final cause of the crisis. Accordingly, the remedy was simple enough: the "overload" of the state and the "overheating" of the economy should be stopped through neo-Malthusian self-restraint, now applied to political matters and no longer to sexual ones. The state overload engenders fiscal deficits and undermines the legitimacy of the authority; the overheating of the economy closes the circle with inflation and stagnation. As such, neoliberal policies emphasize the resolute privatization of welfare problems, the withdrawal of the state, and the growing relocation of issues previously regarded as "public" to the market and the realm of the private. Neoliberalism also fosters the "reprivatization" of political life. That corresponds to an exaltation of political apathy and high levels of indifference vis-à-vis public affairs, features of a political culture that, in a not too distant past, were regarded as barbarous anachronisms of backward societies, now timely rediscovered as precious assets for the preservation of capitalist hegemony in times of crisis.

This attack on democratic "excesses," which supposedly paralyze the vitality of the market, almost imperceptibly winds up in a subtle apology for authoritarianism: democracy tends toward ingovernability and has to be tamed in order not to interfere with the "iron laws" of capitalist accumulation.[33] Whereas Marx suggests democracy should move a step forward in order to free itself from the structural restraints of the capitalist economy, the neoconservative ideologists propose exactly the contrary: the subordination of democracy to the imperatives of the economy. The realm of production shows little affinity with the principles and practice of democracy: the factory is the sanctuary of despotism, sublimated and rationalized as a "technical" necessity and protected by the bourgeois right under the sacred mantle of the private. The sole mention of the word *democracy* provokes the strongest reactions in the firm. The term assumes a "subversive" character that makes it unbearable to the owners of capital. Viewed in this light democracy is tolerated to the extent that it does not constitute a dysfunctional element in the process of capitalist accumulation. The bourgeoisie's delayed recognition of the contradiction pointed out early on by Marx ends up in a quasi-Hobbesian argument: "democratic self-restraint" and its counterpart, a government with low levels of responsiveness in the face of civil society, are transformed into a miraculous cure for the maladies of bourgeois civilization. This pessimistic diagnosis of the future of democracy becomes much more somber when projected onto the background of peripheral societies. It was precisely in these backward areas where the popular sectors, spurred by secular misery and oppression, showed less propensity to political moderation. But it was also in those parts of the globe where the elites were more irresponsible and demagogic, while the representative institutions were traditionally unable to restrain the rich and powerful and channel the wild impulses of a tumultuous citizenry.[34]

As mentioned before, this neoconservative approach has become the predominant "common sense" among the ruling circles of mature capitalism and in society at large as well. The fact that this unfavorable climate of opinion has been a powerful obstacle in Latin American democratization cannot pass unnoticed. The direction and rhythm of the region's historical movement seem not to coincide with the direction and pace of events in metropolitan capitalism. Therefore, Latin America's democratic reconstruction has to deal with a world market and an international system in which the great powers and the leading nations are much more skeptical about the virtues of democracy in the North, and indifferent (and sometimes hostile) regarding democratization in the South. It is precisely for these reasons that a recent report of the Trilateral Commission holds that "the fundamental political objective shared by the Trilateral countries and the peoples of Latin America and the Caribbean is to obtain and preserve stable and functional [*sic*] democracies in the region."[35]

One does not need a deep understanding of political issues to imagine in what sense Latin American democracies should be regarded as "functional." Not surprisingly this report ends up repeating the fundamental theses of "global neoliberalism" and praising President Bush for his Americas Initiative. Therefore, the region's democracies should be "functional" with respect to structural adjustment policies and the wild recomposition of the capitalist economies. In the concrete domain of the international political economy, the main democratic governments of advanced capitalism— regardless of whether they are conservative, liberal, or "socialist"—have shown a marked lack of concern for the fate of Latin American democracies. There is a total lack of sensibility on the part of the North regarding the impact of the foreign debt on the lives of the peoples of the periphery. The resurgence of protectionism in international trade and the very low levels of international aid are other painful examples of the indifference of the advanced democracies on these matters, as is the very low priority assigned in their foreign policy agendas to the future of democracy in the world.

Problems of Governability

A third problem besieging democratic transitions in Latin America is the question of the eventual ungovernability of new popularly elected governments in the area. Despite the conservative bias of the traditional way in which the problem is usually posed, the issue has enough substance not to be ignored. As a matter of fact, ungovernability is an endemic threat to any complex and bureaucratic society. If this potential anomaly causes concern in mature democratic capitalism, its dangers are much more serious in peripheral capitalist nations. It is impossible to deny that the increasing complexities of modern social life and of the processes of capitalist accumulation on a global scale require the ever-growing presence of the state, a fact against which even diehard free-market advocates stumble. As discussed in earlier chapters of this book, modern capitalism has become profoundly "statist" not as a result of an ideological preference of capital owners but as an unwelcome consequence of the objective needs arising from the process of accumulation. An unavoidable corollary of this process is the proliferation of intrusive bureaucratic structures, the coordination and effectiveness of which cannot always be taken for granted.

If bureaucratization is combined with the high levels of demand aggregation and popular mobilization fostered by democratic regimes, the problems of socioeconomic, political, and administrative coordination are hard to underestimate. Without reaching the Weberian fatalistic extremes—bureaucracy as the iron cage on which modern civilization depends—the tensions among democracy and bureaucracy and state hypertrophy engender innumerable problems in the functioning of modern societies. The formidable public repercussions of the so-called Bobbio debate in the West, which confronted Weberian and Marxist arguments regarding the economic and political contradictions of contemporary capitalism, are a clear signal that the menace of ungovernability is not illusory. In metropolitan and peripheral capitalism alike, it is easy to prove the decadence of the representative political institutions and the growing concentration of decisional powers in the executive and bureaucratic-administrative branches of the state. A variety of authors as different as Sheldon Wolin, Herbert Marcuse, Gino Germani, and Nicos Poulantzas share this diagnosis.[36]

Latin American history proves that the vitality of civil society and the overwhelming character that popular movements can assume in their ascending phases may pose serious dangers to the governability of nascent democracies. These hazards can be aggravated by two other complicating factors.

On the one hand is the rigidity of Latin American presidentialism. The region's constitutions place disproportionate political and administrative prerogatives in the hands of the presidency, depriving the nascent democracies of the necessary flexibility and adaptative capabilities to face unexpected challenges successfully. Therefore, emergency situations—like investment strikes, foreign intervention, runaway inflation, capital flight, political sabotage, destabilizing campaigns, and so on—that may call for the building of a new governing coalition stumble against the anachronistic rigidity of a constitutional norm that makes no room for swift maneuvers and rapid reactions at the helm of the state. Because of this impossibility, a social and political crisis may well paralyze the entire state system and the political process, opening the gates to the forceful "resolution" of the stalemate by way of a military coup d'état that restores the bourgeois dictatorship back to power. The history of Latin American countries in the 1970s clearly reflects this vicious pattern for which a crisis of governability leads, via constitutional paralysis, to the collapse of the political regime.[37]

The second factor to reckon with is the persistent role played by diehard authoritarian actors or by parties and organizations only halfheartedly loyal to the democratic rules of the game and always ready to impede the stabilization and consolidation of the new regime. In the complex political chessboard of the Latin American democratic transition, there are many social forces and political actors of this sort. If they accepted the new political regimes, they did so only because there was no other alternative. It would hardly be an exaggeration to argue that for many in this camp the establishment of democracy in Latin America was regarded only as a transient defeat. If the opportunity arises, they will not hesitate to "kick the chessboard" to restore their traditional representatives to power. This means that Latin American transitions are besieged by the dangers of an impressive host of powerful actors whose loyalty to democracy is dubious. Depending on the peculiar features of each country, this coalition includes wide sections of the bourgeoisie, the bulk of the traditional landed upper classes, the military, imperialist capital, an ultraconservative church, and so on.

Two major factors are responsible for this situation. On the one hand is the weakness of the institutional structures of the region's nascent democracies, which reinforces the social, economic, political, and cultural weight of the authoritarian enemies. On the other hand is the extreme vulnerability of Latin American economies to the political initiatives of the capitalist class, over which the fragile and heavily indebted national states lack any effective instrument of mediation and control. Nowadays the objective dependence of the state from the bourgeoisie is such that it is the market forces that regulate the state, not the state that regulates the economy. The mere skepticism of the business class with respect to the new democratic government can unleash an acute decline in private investment or prompt massive capital flight, both of which undermine the political and economic stability of the country far more severely than the most militant labor strike. As the case of President Mitterrand in the initial years of his mandate, when he attempted to carry out a radical macroeconomic policy, eloquently proves, even a strong state and a consolidated democracy like France cannot stand the ferocious impact of investment strikes on the stability of the governing coalition. The cases of Salvador Allende in Chile and, more recently, the disciplining "market coups" through which the dominant classes asserted themselves in Alfonsín's Argentina are other instances of the same phenomenon.[38]

The foregoing picture will not be complete unless it accounts for the impact that the protest and mobilization of the working classes may have on the governability of the new democracies. Popular disillusionment with the mediocre performance of democratic governments, unable to improve their lot, is likely to unleash ever louder protests. It would be unrealistic to expect from these people—frustrated, desperate, and impoverished—the phlegmatic self-restraint and moderation that most theorists deem necessary for the normal functioning of the democratic institutions. The living conditions of these people, in some cases truly appalling, push them in the opposite direction, thus creating an extremely volatile political environment during the democratic transition. In light of such high levels of class polarization, a friendly gesture from the government in favor of either the capitalists or the workers could be immediately construed by the other as a declaration of war, prompting extreme or unreasonable responses that could well bring the democratic experiment to a sudden end.

The policies of structural adjustment synthesized in the set of policy recommendations known as the Washington Consensus are cherished by the businesspeople who praise the "pragmatism and realism" of the new democratic rulers. However, neoliberal policies intended to ensure payment of the foreign debt tend to produce recession, increase unemployment, and reduce real wages, all of which aggravate the social contradictions of the postauthoritarian regimes and undermine the popular legitimacy of the nascent democracies. The popular riots in Argentina in 1989, in Brazil during all these years, and especially in Venezuela and Peru in 1992 clearly show the dilemmas facing the governments of the region. Little wonder that situations like these show a great propensity to engender periodic crises of governability, ready to be capitalized upon by reactionary coalitions to stop democratic progress and restore dictatorship.

In sum, it is impossible to neglect the threatening challenges posed to democratic governance by the defensive or offensive strategies of the ruling classes, the turbulent mobilization of a frustrated and angered citizenry, or the inevitable bureaucratization of modern states. Yet, it is inappropriate to view these problems from a conservative perspective, which assumes the immutability of capitalist society as an unspoken analytical premise. Ungovernability is the projection, on the political scene, of either the upsetting strategies of the upper classes hostile to democracy or the profound expectations and hopes of the popular classes, who believe that democratic citizenship should make a difference in their vital chances. If the popular classes' modest exigencies cannot be met, thus making the system "ungovernable," the reason is that democratic ideals surrender to the cold profit-making logic of the market. The stability of a democratic political order can be founded only on justice, not on an improbable well-being resulting from the myriad of egoistic rational choices made by the capitalist class. This means that, at least in poverty-ridden peripheral nations, either democracy resolutely pushes an audacious program of social reforms or its cause may be lost.[39]

It is beyond any reasonable doubt that democracy, in all its types, has to be governable. The worn-out argument of some "romantic left" extolling the historical productivity of social chaos, anomie, and anarchy must be strongly rejected. It is not only false; it is irresponsible as well. Dramatic lessons from the past show that situations of this sort have invariably resulted in a defeat of the popular classes and the violent recomposition of political despotism. Ungovernability facilitates a reactionary response and chastises the democratic forces and the subordinated groups in society. Of course, the need to preserve the governability of the system cannot be used to postpone sine die the satisfaction of popular expectations, especially in Latin American societies, which have shown a total disrespect for the most elementary values associated with human dignity and welfare. Democracy has to show not only its capacity to govern but also its efficacy as a type of political regime able to build a better society. The historical evidence points out that, in developed capitalism, social reform and the betterment of the poor have been done not *with* the market but *against* the market, through correcting the market's endemic failures and modifying, from the democratic state, the injustice inherent in its structure and function.[40]

The Economic Framework of Latin American Democratization

The problem has been not only the crisis but the particular strategy to fight the crisis that was pushed forward by Latin American governments. Neoliberal economic reforms have become a major obstacle in the process of democratic consolidation. Accepted as an unchallenged dogma by the ruling elites, the moral and intellectual hegemony of neoliberal ideas have reached reform-minded groups and political forces, even those supposedly identified with socialism and the cause of the poor. Economic crisis, and especially the problem of foreign debt, was instrumental in the almost swift abandonment of time-honored ideological tenets and developmentalist policies, prompting the more or less intense adoption of the neoliberal blueprint in diverse countries of the region. As has been shown, contemporary Latin America is that part of the globe in which the influence of the Washington Consensus is felt with greatest intensity. Some governments have embraced neoliberalism with the furor of the converted: this is the case of Menem's Argentina and the ill-fated Salinas governments in Mexico. Others, like the Chilean, seem to have adopted a more instrumental approach resulting from unwillingness to put into question some of the "accomplishments" of Pinochet—even at the cost of having to ignore the most flagrant shortcomings and inequities derived from his policies.

The case of Chile is particularly instructive. By 1988, after fifteen years of neoliberal restructuring, the per capita income and the real wages of Chilean workers were not much higher than they had been in 1973, amidst the chaos brought about by the boycotts and sabotages against the Allende government. This poor performance took place in spite of the immense social costs brought about by an average unemployment rate of 15 percent between 1975 and 1985, with a peak of 30 percent in 1983. Between 1970 and 1987 the percent of homes under the poverty line increased from 17 percent to 38 percent, and in 1990 the per capita consumption of the Chileans was still inferior to 1980.[41] Accordingly, between 1979 and 1988 the top 10 percent of Chilean distribution of income augmented its share in the national income from 36.2 percent to 46.8 percent, while the bottom half of the population declined its participation from 20.4 percent to 16.8 percent.[42] As was rightly pointed out by Luiz C. Bresser Pereira, "The Chilean society probably would not have tolerated these transitional costs if the regime had been democratic."[43]

In Mexico, the other "success story" of the World Bank and the International Monetary Fund, the social and economic involution after more than a decade of orthodox adjustments is unconcealable. Official data show that per capita national income fell 12.4 percent between 1980 and 1990 despite the reformist rhetoric used by PRI governments to promote neoliberal policies.[44] Similar data indicate that in those years poverty increased significantly: between 1982 and 1988 real wages went down by 40 percent, and have remained very close to that level since then. On the other hand, the traditionally high level of Mexican unemployment went up while per capita consumption in 1990 was 7 percent lower that in 1980. According to Castañeda, when the Mexican government made public in 1992 (for the first time in fifteen years) the first statistical accounts of income distribution, the data were alarming. However, the official optimism was not disturbed by these revelations. It took the outbreak of the peasant and Indian insurrection in Chiapas, two political assassinations, a huge trade deficit and, finally, the collapse of the Mexican peso in late December to make the local elites and their advisers aware that things were running out of control. The new emergency package of President Ernesto Zedillo will impose, as usual, renewed hardships on the poor: governmental officials anticipated that the purchasing power of salaries is likely to decline another 32 percent, bringing much more personal suffering and deprivations to most of 90 million Mexicans.[45]

Monetary stabilization, opening up of the economy, balanced budgets, deregulation, privatizations, downsizing of the state, and free rein to markets do not seem to have been enough to ensure self-sustained growth or a more equitable distribution of income. As Western European experience since World War II clearly shows, and as the most recent experience of Japan and Southeast Asia convincingly proves, capitalist development requires an appropriate set of public policies, and this calls for a strong—not big, but strong—state, endowed with effective capacities of intervention in and regulation of the markets. In this regard, the performance of the Chilean economy, much praised by ideologues of the Washington Consensus despite looking rather unimpressive when compared with Southeast Asian countries or China, has had as one of its most eccentric features the preservation of the strategic copper industry in government's hands—to say the least an embarrassing socialistic relic for the apostles of neoliberalism. Nationalized during the Allende years, state-owned copper firms account for about half of all Chilean export revenues. This significant amount of cash goes directly to the fiscal treasury (not, as in Argentina, Brazil, and most other Latin American economies, to the pockets of private exporters), thus strengthening public finances and the capacities of the state apparatus to formulate and execute public policies. This "deviation" from the orthodox is not the only one: the fact that in Chile the international financial flows are carefully regulated in order to prevent short-term fluctuations detrimental to the balance of payments also has been usually overlooked by neoliberal economists, who tirelessly preach that all forms of public property or state intervention are inefficient or inflationary. If the lessons of the Chilean "economic success" were to be extrapolated to Argentina and Brazil, the World Bank or IMF missions would find themselves in the uncomfortable position of having to recommend to their "clients" the nationalization of the *pampa húmeda* and parts of the modern agrarian export sector of Argentina, and the *paulista* industry in Brazil. It is perhaps for this very reason that Sebastián Edwards, one of the chief economists of the World Bank, has preferred to ignore these peculiarities of Chilean economic restructuring, even at the risk of severely damaging the credibility of the Bank as an institution. In an official document—in which there is a section called "Chile as a Model"—Edwards does not even mention the fact that the copper industry in Chile has remained in state hands, that it has been very successful in world markets, and that nobody in Chile is asking for its privatization. As if it were a completely insignificant and minute anecdote, this major feature of the Chilean economy does not deserve in his supposedly "rigorous and objective" economic analysis even a modest footnote. The same applies to the regulation of the international financial transactions.[46]

The results of this "free-market fundamentalism" have been quite uniform throughout Latin America. Both what the World Bank and the IMF used to regard as the "success" stories—Chile and Mexico, the latter being now quietly removed from the list—as well as the rest of the "economically reformed" countries show the same results: the application of neoliberal policies has vastly increased the numbers of the poor and widened the gulf separating rich and poor.

> Poverty is the greatest challenge for the economies of Latin America and the Caribbean. Between 1980 and 1990 it worsened as a result of the crisis and the adjustment policies, wiping out most of the progress in poverty reduction achieved during the 1960s and 1970s. Recent estimates place the number of poor at the beginning of this decade, depending on the definition of poverty, somewhere between 130 and 196 million. . . . Recession and adjustment in the 1980s also increased income inequality in most of the region.[47]

The impoverished and fragmented societies resulting both from the crisis and the response to it—the neoliberal policies of economic restructuring—do not offer the most fertile soil for the flowering of democracy. Nor are they factors in the upgrading of the quality of democratic governance, unless "democracy" is understood as just the liturgical fulfillment of certain routines and rituals deprived of any substantive meaning. It should not be forgotten that national elections were held on schedule under the dictatorships of Somoza and Stroessner, and that the legislatures in Nicaragua and Paraguay used to be the scenario of fierce, if inconsequential, verbal disputes between government and the "opposition."

Neoliberal policies have augmented the share of the very rich in the national income—not only in Latin America but also in the United States and the United Kingdom.[48] On the other hand, policies aimed at deregulating markets, at privatization and liberalization, have had as one of their consequences the extraordinary reinforcement of the bargaining power of a handful of privileged collective actors, whose demands gain direct access to the upper echelons of the government and the central bureaucracy. Therefore, the quality of the democratic governance is not only impaired by the deterioration of the material foundations of citizenship: these fragile democratic experiments are also endangered by the fact that, deaf to the reasonable and legitimate expectations of the underlying population, they tend to magnify the strength of the dominant classes and, as a result, to further reinforce the role of naked, noninstitutionalized power relations, in the face of which the state (and not only the president) becomes increasingly impotent.[49]

This unprecedented empowerment of private interests at the expense of everything "public" places Latin American democracies under the Damoclean sword of the bourgeoisie and its allied classes and social forces, which can easily and at almost no cost destabilize the political process when they see fit. A weak democratic state can only produce a feeble and ineffective government that, in due course, will tend to aggrandize the social, economic, and political weight of very rich, small, and well-organized private collective actors. To make things worse, the capitalist economy is extraordinarily sensitive to the initiatives of the entrepreneurs, and the weakened national states have very few instruments of mediation and control, especially if the irresistible globalization of economic and financial transactions is duly taken into account. The dependence of democratic states on the capitalist classes and their "confidence" in the ability of local rulers to maintain a favorable atmosphere for the investors have become so acute that market forces are the ones that "regulate" the state policies and not the other way around, as was the case after the Great Depression. The entrepreneurial elites' skepticism regarding a newly elected democratic government usually triggers the adoption of a set of strategic moves likely to have a devastating impact on the performance of the democratic state: for instance, firms may refrain from making new investments, may adopt a "wait and see" policy, make selective disinvestments or capital transfers, or they may choose full-blown capital flight. Each of these moves may upset the political and economic stability of a democratic government to an extent infinitely more important that a workers' general strike. The experience of Mitterrand in France convincingly illustrates the high level of financial vulnerability affecting even a powerful state. The impact of the "wildcat strike" launched by the capitalists in Chile under Allende was devastating, while the "market coups" orchestrated by the Argentinean, Brazilian, Mexican, and Venezuelan bourgeoisie were somewhat milder but still highly effective forms of "influencing" public policies in these countries. This structural imbalance among a handful of very powerful bourgeois actors and "market forces"; large sections of demobilized, disorganized, mostly apathetic or submissive populace; and a growingly impotent government make up certainly one of the most important challenges facing the new democracies in Latin America.

U.S. Foreign Policy and Democracy in Latin America

In addition to the aforementioned obstacles, which clearly show the enormous difficulties faced by democratic transitions in Latin America, the impact of U.S. foreign policy on the region's countries must be considered.

The historical importance of the United States is of course highly significant. A persistent "hegemonic presumption" has permanently colored the relationships between Latin America and the United States, creating not a few problems for previous, and fragile, democratic attempts. The superpower often used its overwhelming influence on behalf of reactionary class alliances and political coalitions south of the border. In this sense, the Bolivarian dictum that the United States seems destined by Providence to plague the Americas with miseries in the name of freedom seems particularly appropriate. During many years U.S. foreign policy hinged on the premise that U.S. national interests would be better served and protected by dictatorships of any sort instead of the turbulent democracies that, from time to time, emerged in the region. Because U.S. national interests were defined in the rather narrow terms of the handful of U.S. firms operating in the area, Washington's support for the fiercest and most bloodthirsty tyrannies became the standard policy for a long period of time. Only when the democratic wave of the 1980s engulfed the whole world did the U.S. government decide to revise its traditional orientations toward democratic regimes in Latin America.[50]

Undoubtedly, the presence and activity of imperial interests have been an objective obstacle in any process of democratization put forward in Latin America. The reasons have been manifold: the preservation of obsolete "spheres of influence"; the need to ward off the Soviets; the paranoid conceptions concerning U.S. national security, which was unrealistically perceived as being mortally threatened by distant peasant guerrillas; or the sheer defense of economic advantages for U.S. firms. The epoch-making changes that took place in the former Soviet Union and the Eastern European countries, as well as the prospects opened by Gorbachev's glasnost and perestroika, forced the United States to abandon its traditional policies. It had become increasingly difficult to support dictatorships in Latin America while the Soviets were opening up their political regime and withdrawing from Afghanistan. The "special relations" of the United States with Marcos in the Philippines; with Somoza in Nicaragua; with the Shah in Iran; with Mobutu and others alike in Africa; and with the brutal Latin American dictatorships of the 1970s were forcefully redefined, and a half-hearted support for democratization ensued.

This change has been for the good, because a simple U.S. neutrality in postauthoritarian transitions is in itself a major asset when compared with either the systematic sabotage against democratic processes encouraged by top-ranking U.S. officials in the past or the open U.S. intervention in an endless list of coups d'état, of which the cases of Brazil in 1964 and Chile in 1973 are only the most widely known. However, democracy cannot be exported, and the current U.S. "prodemocratic" stance will not by itself dispel the many obstacles in the road. Unfortunately, the United States has proved much more effective at destabilizing democracies than at stabilizing popularly elected rulers. The excessive optimism of some officials in Washington is wholly unwarranted: democracy will not triumph all around the world just because the U.S. government is now convinced that this is the correct thing to do. Of course, nobody would deny that this new U.S. foreign policy may have a favorable influence on the march of Latin American democratization. Yet the imperialist nature of the international system still persists, and despite the discourse on "interdependence," there are nations that are "more interdependent" than others and for which national sovereignty is a pious lie. Latin nations are today much more dependent than before, and no significant decision involving a major allocation of resources is made without a prior consultation with the corresponding authorities in Washington. In this regard the role played by the foreign debt in strengthening the subordination of the debtor nations is beyond any reasonable doubt. This regrettable capitulation of formerly semisovereign states is much more deplorable when one realizes that more countries have become more vulnerable to the asymmetries of the international market than ever before. Peripheral nations are today poorer and weaker than before: in 1960 the ratio between the incomes of the richer 20 percent and the poorer 20 percent of the international economy was 30 to 1; in 1989 it reached 59 to 1.[51] Therefore, it is reasonable to conclude that given these high levels of foreign dependency and vulnerability, the prospects of Latin American democratization are strongly conditioned by the initiatives, reactions, and preferences of powerful actors in the international arena, thus adding new uncertainties to the region's current problems.

Tentative Conclusions

A few tentative conclusions are in order. First, Latin American democratic transitions are taking place in a quasirecessive world economy, dominated by the ideological rise of neoliberal policies hardly conducive to the construction of a strong popular legitimacy. Yet, these "poor democracies" have so far shown themselves to be better prepared to absorb the impact of an economic crisis than their weaker predecessors. However, there are many signs warning of the chances of a rapid deterioration of these nascent regimes if poverty and exclusion are not reined in.

The new Latin American democracies have so far resisted the tough conditions imposed by economic crisis, hyperinflation, stabilization, and structural adjustment programs inspired by the Washington Consensus. Their ability to survive these unprecedented pressures has been an unexpected and welcome surprise. In a not too distant past, Latin American democracies would have succumbed to any combination of high inflation (not to mention hyperinflation), recessive trends, capital flights, balance-of-payments crises, and fiscal deficits with political unrest. The economic problems would have unleashed a typical political cycle, starting with the ever louder protest and mobilization of civil society and the intensification of class antagonisms. In due time these factors would have ended in the precipitous deterioration of the political climate, thus paving the way for a military coup to put a violent end to the critical juncture.

In recent articles U.S. political scientist Karen L. Remmer acknowledges these new developments and underlines the renewed strength and stability of democratic regimes, thus challenging the idea that Latin democracies are weak and unable to resist the weight of an economic crisis.[52] However, one need not be an economic determinist to recognize that she seems to have underestimated the factors and trends that in the medium run are likely to undermine the foundations of democracy. A democratic regime that continually increases its number of poor, widens the gap between rich and poor, and worsens the living conditions of the popular classes (i.e., by cutting social expenditures and removing welfare legislation) has little chance of stabilizing and consolidating. Its downfall may be as "unexpected" as the Berlin Wall and the Eastern European socialist regimes. In the middle term, the superficial stability of Latin American democracies may prove to be just an expression of wishful thinking, or a political mirage.

In any case, it would be unwise to think that a contradiction of this sort between an inclusionary political regime and an exclusionary model of capitalist accumulation will last forever. This has not been the case in postwar Europe, and it is very unlikely to happen now in Latin America. The events in Venezuela and Peru are sober reminders that should not be overlooked. Once the classic cycle of economic instability and military coup has been historically superseded, there will be other sources of stress and danger for the new democracies in the region. One example involves the growing "legitimacy deficits" produced by the inability of the democratic regimes to improve the lot of the citizenry. Because of the economic crisis and the neoliberal strategy of structural adjustment, which have destroyed the state's ability to regulate markets and redistribute resources, the governments of the region have lost an ever-growing number of instruments of social and economic intervention. The outcome has been to speed up the institutional decay of the new democracies and to quickly delegitimize their weak and ineffective governments.

The dangers arise from the progressive loss of content and purpose for the region's embattled democracies, transformed in their decadence into an abstract and empty set of rules deprived of much meaning for the citizenry. Therefore, the major threat now besieging Latin America's new democracies is not so much an authoritarian regression but the loss of purpose and meaning of democracy itself due to its lack of depth, its poor quality, its unfairness and its incompleteness.[53] Democracy suffers a process of ethical and substantive *vaciamiento,* or institutional decay, or it may well degenerate into "delegative democracies" (as Guillermo O'Donnell has named them) entangled in the vicious circle of messianic *caudillismo* leading to a perverse form of endurance not to be confused with a truly democratic consolidation.[54] As Anatole France once observed, it gives little comfort and consolation to the poor to know that both rich and poor are equally free to sleep under the bridges of Paris. The right to form a government, granted by universal suffrage, does certainly give the citizens a sense of dignity and value. But when democratically elected governments exhibit total irresponsibility in light of the suffering of the poor, the citizens cannot refrain from thinking that democracy is just a sham.

The democratic idea makes the citizen the ultimate sovereign of the political community, but the actions of democratic governments show that the interests of the rich are what really count. Because of this contradiction, democracy may well vanish into thin air, while society descends into the horrors of a "neo-Hobbesian" scenario, in which the privatization of violence and the alienation produced by wild capitalism give birth to all sorts of aberrant behaviors. The increases in the indices of violence and crime, the destruction of networks of social solidarity, the growing sense of anomie, the lack of representativeness of parties and congresses, the impotence of the justice systems, the corruption of the state apparatuses, and the frustration of the masses are all symptoms of a dangerous institutional decay. The participatory possibilities and the freedom enjoyed by social actors, a key feature in democracies, exacerbate the societal contradictions and the lower-class unrest, while the dominant classes exert de facto undemocratic control over the state apparatuses and institutions. The result is the democratic regime's tendential ungovernability, its rapid delegitimization, and its likely destabilization. The outcome could well be the sudden reinstallation of a new type of dictatorship, brought about by the resurgence of a populist fundamentalism embodied in the figure of a demagogue. Such an individual may well promise to "take care" of the unfulfilled hopes of the masses, broken by faulty and irresponsive democratic governments, and to redeem the poor from the hell of poverty and human misery to which they were condemned by governments in search of the neoliberal paradise. This scenario is not a fatal and unavoidable outcome of the present crisis of Latin American democracies, but it is a likely one. It would thus be a tragic paradox if the victims of capitalist recomposition were pushed, out of their disillusionment and desperation, to bring back with their votes the despotic rulers ousted by the democratic renaissance of the 1980s. In this case, the circle of hope and optimism made open in the last decade would be ominously closed.

Notes

1. Cf. his *El desarrollo del capitalismo en América Latina* (Mexico: Siglo XXI, 1976), Ch. 1.

2. On Brazil, see especially Fernándes, Florestán, *A revoluçao burguesa no Brasil* (Rio de Janeiro: Zahar Editores, 1975).

3. Cf. Boron, Atilio A., "Authoritarian ideological traditions and transition towards democracy in Argentina," The Institute of Latin American and Iberian Studies, Columbia University, paper no. 8, 1989, New York.

4. Doh Chull, Shin, "On the third wave of democratization. A synthesis of recent theory and research" *World Politics* 47 (October 1994), p. 136.

5. Cf. Huntingon, Samuel P., *The Third Wave* (Norman and London: The University of Oklahoma Press, 1991); Fukuyama, Francis, *The End of History and the Last Man* (New York : Free Press; Toronto: Maxwell Macmillan Canada, 1992).

6. See, among others, Garretón, Manuel Antonio, *Reconstruir la política. Transición y consolidación democrática en Chile* (Santiago: Editorial Andante, 1987), and Flisfisch, Angel, Norbert Lechner and Tomás Moulián, "Problemas de la democracia y la política democrática en América Latina," in Varios, Autores, *Democracia y desarrollo en América Latina* (Buenos Aires: GEL, 1985). So far, the most elaborated defense of this perspective in Latin America is found in Strasser, Carlos, *Para una teoría de la democracia posible. Idealizaciones y teoría política* (Buenos Aires: GEL, 1990) and *Para una teoría de la democracia posible. La democracia y lo democrático.* (Buenos Aires: GEL, 1991). This minimalist and procedural conception of democracy is reflected in the collective volumes edited by Guillermo O'Donnell, Phillipe Schmitter, and Lawrence Withehead, *Transitions from Authoritarian Rule* (Baltimore: The Johns Hopkins University Press, 1986). This book gathers some of the best scholarly works of this tradition, although it is only fair to acknowledge that not all the authors equally accept its premises, or fail to seriously question some of its assumptions and implications.

7. On the relationship between violence and the democratic order, see Moore, Barrington, *Social Origins,* op. cit., pp. 4–39.

8. Schumpeter, Joseph A., *Capitalism, Socialism and Democracy* (New York: Harper and Row, 1946), p. 269.

9. Ibid., p. 242.

10. Op. cit., p. 12.

11. We should stress the "relative" nature of these guarantees, because in bourgeois democracies the game is played with "loaded" dice. In our opinion the degree of "uncertainty" of capitalist democracies is, in some crucial matters, much lower than what Adam Pzreworski has asserted in his highly insightful *Capitalism and Social Democracy*, op. cit., Ch. 4.

12. O'Donnell, Guillermo, "The state, democratization and some conceptual problems," in Smith, William C., Carlos H. Acuña, and Eduardo A. Gamarra, eds., *Latin American Political Economy in the Age of Neoliberal Reform* (Miami: North-South Center, 1994), pp. 157–169.

13. Dahl, Robert A., *Polyarchy*, op. cit., Chs. 1 and 2.

14. Cf. O'Donnell, Guillermo, in "The state, democratization."

15. Rousseau, Jean Jacques, *The Social Contract and Discourse on the Origin of Inequality* (New York: Washington Square Press, 1967), p. 217. See also, in the same vein, Plato's *Republic* (several editions), paragraph 552.

16. See Marx, Karl, "On the Jewish question" and "Contribution to the critique of Hegel's philosophy of right. Introduction," in Bottomore, Tom B., *Karl Marx. Early Writings* (New York: McGraw-Hill, 1963), and Gramsci, Antonio, *Selections from the Prison Notebooks*, op. cit. (New York: International Publishers, 1971). Edited and translated by Hoare, Quintin, and Geoffrey Nowell Smith, pp. 158–168, 175–185, 219–223, and 257–264.

17. *Las democracias restringidas*, op. cit., p. 12.

18. Bobbio, Norberto, "Quali alternative alla democrazia rappresentativa?" in Bobbio, Norberto, et al., *Il marxismo e lo Stato*, op. cit., pp. 19–37.

19. "The Russian Revolution," in *Rosa Luxemburg Speaks*, op. cit., p. 393. Almost twenty years before Luxemburg had posed a impassioned defense of political democracy in her classic *Revolution or Social Reform*. A contemporary re-elaboration of these theses is found in Williams, Raymond, "Towards many socialisms," in *Socialist Review* 85, January–February 1986 On the relationship between democracy and socialism in Luxemburg's thought see also the brilliant essay by Geras, Norman "Democracy and the ends of Marxism," in *New Left Review* 203, January–February 1994, pp. 92–106.

20. Cf. Carnoy, Martin, and Derek Shearer, *Economic Democracy. The challenge of the 1980s* (Armonk, NY: Sharpe, 1980).

21. Dahl, Robert A., *A preface to economic democracy* (Berkeley and Los Angeles: University of California Press, 1985), pp. 134–135.

22. Cardoso, Fernando H., "La democracia en América Latina," *Punto de Vista* (Buenos Aires), No. 23, April 1985, p. 17.

23. Kosic, Karel, *Dialéctica de lo Concreto* (México: Grijalbo, 1976).

24. Cf. Therborn, Göran, "The rule of capital and the rise of democracy," *New Left Review* 103 (May–June 1977), pp. 3–42, for a perceptive reflection on this issue. This warning is forcefully voiced by Rosa Luxemburg in her "The mass strike, the political party and the trade unions." See *Rosa Luxemburg Speaks*, pp. 153–218.

25. See, for instance, Therborn, Göran, "Los retos del estado de bienestar: La contrarrevolución que fracasa, las causas de su enfermedad y la economía política de las presiones del cambio," in Muñoz de Bustillo, Rafael, *Crisis y futuro del estado de bienestar* (Madrid: Alianza Universidad, 1989), pp. 81–99.

26. This is the message of the work of authors as different as Herbert Marcuse, Gino Germani, and Sheldon Wolin. It is worthwhile to notice the theoretical evolution of both Germani and Wolin. In an editorial in a new journal launched at the beginning of the 1980s, Wolin asserts that the most meaningful political fact in contemporary U.S. life is the steady transformation of the United States in an undemo-

cratic society. Cf. his "Why democracy?" *Democracy* 1(1) (January 1981), p. 3. Germani's pessimism on the future of modern democracy follows the same lines as Wolin's and is masterfuly summarized in "Autoritarismo e democrazia nella societá moderna," in R. Scartezzini, L. Germani, and R. Gritti, eds., *I Limiti Della Democrazia* (Napoli: Liquori Editori, 1985).

27. A sort of democratic fatalism, strongly economicist, was quite general in the mainstream U.S. political science in the 1950s and 1960s. Cf. Lipset, Seymour M., *Political Man: The Social Bases of Politics* (Garden City, NY: Doubleday, 1960). A tough criticism of this unwarranted optimism is provided by Huntington, Samuel P., *Political Order in Changing Societies,* Ch. 1.

28. See his article, "The United States," in Crozier, Michel, Samuel P. Huntington, and Joji Watanuki, *The Crisis of Democracy: Report on the Governability of Democracies to the Trilateral Commission* (New York: New York University Press, 1975), pp. 73 and 106–113.

29. Marx, Karl, "Las luchas de clases en Francia de 1848 a 1850," in *Obras escogidas* (Moscow: Progreso, 1966), Vol. 1, p. 158 (my translation).

30. Cf. Offe, Claus, *Contradictions of the Welfare State* (Cambridge, MA: MIT Press, 1985), pp. 179–206; and Therborn, Göran, *What Does the Ruling Class Do When It Rules?* (London: New Left Books, 1978), pp. 180–218. See also Przeworski, Adam, pp. 155–231, for another theoretical perspective on these issues.

31. A description of this intellectual climate is provided in Kristol, Irving, *Reflexiones de un neoconservador* (Buenos Aires: GEL, 1986), pp. 17–40.

32. Cf. Negri, Antonio, in "J. M. Keynes y la teoría capitalista del estado en el '29," in *El Cielo por Asalto* I, vol. 1, no. 2, Fall 1991, pp. 97–118. See also the brilliant essay by Gourevitch, Peter, *Politics in Hard Times* (Ithaca: Cornell University Press, 1986).

33. See two paradigmatic articles by Samuel Brittan: "Can democracy manage the economy?" in Skidelsky, Robert, *The End of the Keynesian Era* (London: Macmillan, 1977), pp. 41–49; and "The economic contradictions of democracy," *British Journal of Political Science* 5 (April 1975), pp. 129–159. An assessment of these arguments is provided in Offe, Claus, "'Ungovernability': The renaissance of conservative theories of crisis," in his *Contradictions,* pp. 65–87.

34. These theses were originally posed by Samuel P. Huntington in his *Political Order in Changing Societies,* pp. 1–92. An extreme version of this kind of thought can be found in Kirkpatrick, Jeane, "The Hobbes problem: Order, authority and legitimacy in Central America," mimeo (Washington, DC: American Enterprise Institute, 1980).

35. Landau, George, Julio Feo, Akio Hosono, and William Perry, *América Latina en la encrucijada: El desafío a los países de la Trilateral,* Report for the Trilateral Commission (Madrid: Tecnos, 1990), p. 118.

36. Weber, Max, *Economy and Society* (New York: Bedminster Press, 1968). See also, from the structuralist Marxist approach, Poulantzas, Nicos, *State, Power, Socialism* (London: New Left Books, 1978). A crucial reference on this whole issue is provided, of course, by the Bobbio debate in Italy.

37. On the fine line between bourgeois democracy and bourgeois dictatorship, an article by Perry Anderson on Latin American new democracies is especially relevant. The English scholar characterizes the legacy of the military dictatorships with respect to the working classes as follows: "You can have democracy if you respect capitalism. If you don't respect capitalism you will be left without democracy and having to accept capitalism anyway." Cf. his "Democracia y dictadura en América Latina en la década del '70," *Cuadernos de Sociología* 2 (UBA, Carrera de Sociología, 1988), p. 14. On the issue of presidentialism, see Linz, Juan,

"Democracia presidencial o parlamentaria. ¿Hay alguna diferencia?" in Consejo para la Consolidación de la Democracia, *Presidencialismo vs. parlamentarismo: Materiales para el estudio de la reforma constitucional* (Buenos Aires: EUDEBA, 1988), pp. 19–44; Nino, Carlos, "Presidencialismo vs. parlamentarismo," ibid., pp. 115–124; Sartori, Giovanni, "Neither presidentialism nor parliamentarianism," in Linz, Juan, and Arturo Valenzuela, comps., *The Crisis of Presidential Regimes* (Baltimore: The Johns Hopkins University Press, forthcoming); Centro de Estudios Institucionales, *Presidencialismo y estabilidad democrática en la Argentina* (Buenos Aires: CEI, 1991).

38. See also Chapter 4 in this book.

39. A detailed elaboration of this argument is found in Chapter 5 of this book. See also Jaguaribe, Helio, *A proposta social demócrata* (Rio de Janeiro: José Olympio Editora, 1989). For a discussion of the merits of this argument (and a general balance of the role, achievements, and shortcomings of the left in Latin America) see Castañeda, Jorge, *Utopia Unarmed: The Latin American Left After the Cold War* (New York: Knopf, 1993).

40. Cf. Miliband, Ralph, *The State in Capitalist Society* (New York: Basic Books, 1969), pp. 66–67.

41. Meller, Patricio, "Latin American adjustment and economic reforms: issues and recent experience," Working Paper of CIEPLAN (Santiago: June 1992) and, by the same author, "Adjustment and equity in Chile" (Paris: OECD, 1992), p. 23.

42. Cf. Castañeda, Jorge, *La Utopía Desarmada* (Buenos Aires: Ariel, 1993), p. 284. See also Délano, Manuel, and Hugo Traslaviña *La Herencia de los Chicago-boys* (Santiago: Ornitorrinco, 1989); Tironi, Eugenio, *Los Silencios de la Revolución* (Santiago: La Puerta Abierta, 1988), and Arrizabalo Montoro, Xabier, "Resultados económicos de la dictadura en Chile (1973–1989)," Doc. de Trabajo 1–93, Instituto Internacional del Desarrollo, 1993.

43. Cf. his "Efficiency and politics in Latin America," mimeo (Department of Political Science, University of Chicago, 1993), p. 38.

44. Altimir, Oscar, "Cambios en las desigualdades de ingreso y en la pobreza en América Latina" (Buenos Aires: Instituto Torcuato Di Tella, 1992), Appendix C-1.

45. Cf. DePalma, Anthony, "Mexicans ask how far social fabric can stretch," in *New York Times* (March 12, 1995), Section A, p. 1.

46. World Bank, *Latin America and the Caribbean. A Decade After the Debt Crisis* (Washington, DC: The World Bank, 1993), pp. 30–32.

47. CEPAL, "The fight against poverty in the hemispheric agenda," in *CEPAL News,* vol. XIV, no. 12, December 1994, p. 1.

48. Krugman, Paul, *Peddling Prosperity. Economic Sense and Nonsense in the Age of Diminished Expectations* (New York: W. W. Norton and Co., 1994), and Phillips, Kevin, *The Politics of Rich and Poor* (New York: Harper Perennial, 1991).

49. Cf. Guillermo O'Donnell, "Delegative Democracy?" *Kellogg Institute Working Papers* no. 172 (1992).

50. A good summary of the discussion on the role of the United States in Latin American development is found in Maira, Luis, ed., *¿Una nueva era de hegemonía norteamericana?* (Buenos Aires: RIAL-GEL, 1986); Maira, Luis, "La hegemonía internacional de Estados Unidos y el proceso de democratización en América Latina," in EURAL, *La vulnerabilidad externa de América Latina y Europa* (Buenos Aires: GEL, 1985), pp. 75–86; Muñoz, Heraldo, "Reflexiones sobre el orden mundial y América Latina," ibid., pp. 51–66; van Klaveren, Alberto, "Las relaciones de los países latinoamericanos con Estados Unidos: Un ejercicio comparativo," in Hirst, Mónica, ed., *Continuidad y cambio en las relaciones América Latina/Estados Unidos* (Buenos Aires: GEL, 1987), pp. 323–353; and Whitehead, Lawrence,

"International Aspects of Democratization," in O'Donnell, Guillermo, Philippe Schmitter, and Lawrence Whitehead, eds., *Transitions from Authoritarian Rule* (Baltimore and London: The Johns Hopkins University Press, 1986), Vol. 3, Ch. 1. On the specific impact of U.S. foreign policy on Latin American democratization episodes see the excellent volumes edited by Abraham Lowenthal, *Exporting Democracy: The USA in Latin America* (Baltimore and London: The Johns Hopkins University Press, 1991).

51. United Nations Development Programme, *Desarrollo humano: Informe 1992* (Bogota: 1992), p. 86.

52. Renner, Karen, "The political economy of elections in Latin America, 1980–1991," *American Political Science Review* 87 (June 1993) and also her previous "Democracy and economic crisis: The Latin American experience," *World Politics* 42 (April 1990).

53. A interesting discussion on this subject is in Agüero, Felipe, "Democratic governance in Latin America: thinking about fault lines" (mimeo: North/South Center, University of Miami, 1994).

54. "Delegative Democracy?" pp. 6–10.

8

Marxist Political Theory Between the Transformations of Capitalism and the Collapse of "Really Existing Socialism"

The debates on the different aspects of the capitalist crisis in Latin America—common tokens in a region where speaking about stagnation, hyperinflation, extreme poverty, food riots, fiscal bankruptcy, and huge foreign debt has become commonplace—have not been able to conceal the ever-growing disappointment produced by the shortcomings of the theoretical models used to decipher the riddles and paradoxes of the region's development. Briefly speaking, the most "orthodox" approaches of Western social sciences were profoundly affected by the vicissitudes that characterized recent Latin American history, which ruthlessly belied the optimistic predictions made by sociologists and economists in the 1950s. Just think what history did with the hopeful prognosis based in Rostow's stages theory; or with Hoselitz's reassuring hypothesis on the role of the middle classes; or with Lipset's inferences regarding the impact of rising levels of per capita income on democratic developments, not to mention the illusory expectations nurtured by the conventional wisdom of mainstream economics concerning the effectiveness of "trickle-down" processes to redistribute income to the popular classes.

However, dissatisfaction with the predictive shortcomings and inconsistencies of the social sciences' dominant theoretical paradigm was far from being an exclusively Latin phenomenon. It had already shaken the European social sciences, strongly "Americanized" after World War II, when it became clear in the mid-1960s that the rosy forecasts about "the end of ideology" and the supersession of class and class conflicts had been crushed by what Norberto Bobbio calls, in a felicitous expression, "history's harsh rebuttals." The resurgence of industrial conflicts, the rise in labor militancy, and the improvement of the electoral fortunes of the left opened the door to a fruitful theoretical renovation, carried out under the strong influence of what Perry Anderson persuasively names "Western Marxism."[1] U.S. and European social sciences would experience similar disappointments later on: as Adam Przeworski perceptively notices, the complete inability of political science to predict the collapse of "Soviet-style" socialism in 1989 was a dismal failure.[2]

In the United States the dominant paradigm was at first largely questioned on the basis of the lessons drawn from recent Latin American history. This scenario was not the only source of criticism, but in some disciplines, such as political science, the repercussions of the Latin *problematique* and the heated theoretical and political debates that ignited after the Cuban revolution were overwhelming. Whereas in Europe the theoretical renovation of the social sciences came as a result of the vigorous assertion of philosophically minded Western Marxists, in the United States the theoretical criticism and rejuvenation were, to a large extent, the contribution of both U.S. Latin Americanists and Latin American scholars. Among the latter many either were Marxists or were engaged in important theoretical debates with socialist thinkers, having therefore absorbed those thinkers' main themes and fundamental questions. These issues and concerns were essentially of an economic and political nature, a meaningful difference vis-à-vis the almost exclusively philosophical character of European Marxism.

The theoretical renovation of U.S. social sciences was preceded by the incorporation of some of the rather heterodox theoretical categories and themes that had dominated the Latin American intellectual scene since the late 1950s. As a result, during the last twenty-five years, one of the most crucial debates in fields like comparative political sociology, international political economy, and social and economic development (to mention just the most obvious ones) seem to have hinged on the multiple dimensions and theoretical perspectives opened by two paramount interpretative categories: state and dependence. These two themes, with their corresponding theoretical debates, were successfully "imported" from Latin America at the beginning of the 1970s, and their impact on the theoretical controversies within the United States—and therefore in all the West—has been formidable, far exceeding the realm of political science or the rather narrow province of the Latin American studies. In this regard it would not be an exaggeration to argue that the U.S. social sciences experienced an acute process of "Latinamericanization."[3]

This is a fascinating topic, a still unwritten chapter in the sociology of science, and its scope exceeds this chapter's much more specific concerns. This chapter will explore the consequences on Marxist political theory of (1) the crisis of Latin American capitalism, (2) the vertiginous decomposition and collapse of really existing socialisms, and (3) the profound and swift transformations of the international system. These epoch-making changes, which shook to their foundations the most archaic dogmas devoutly nursed by some sectors of the left, are destined to exert a long-lasting influence on Marxist political theory. In light of all this, discourse on the crisis and death of Marxism has become fashionable, and the literature on the subject has gown tremendously. Yet, the true nature of this crisis remains by and large in the shadows, hidden by the triumphant chants of those who regard this event as the victory of liberty against its most obnoxious totalitarian foe. In the excitement of the celebration nobody bothered to verify if the dead were really dead.

Given the passions aroused by the question of the so-called crisis of Marxism, it seems appropriate to start examining this matter from a comparative perspective. To start with, a glance at what happened to other theoretical models is enough to have a sobering effect on the most feverish minds: the comparison would prove—not without surprise, even for the most critical reader—the devastating dimensions of the paradigmatic disarticulation undergone by different currents inspired in the liberal tradition, the hegemony of which was uncontested in Western social sciences for several decades. Yet, unlike what happened to Marxist theory, the collapse of the dominant paradigms since the end of World War II passed almost unnoticed. It stirred up—as might have been expected—very little attention within academia and the mass media. In any event, this cover-up was insufficient to conceal the perplexity of theorists of the stature of David Easton when they verified (1) the strange and unexpected death of the behavioral revolution and the triumphant return of the concept of the state in political science, from which it had been expelled in the early 1950s in a rather unceremonious and thoughtless manner; (2) the collapse of Keynesianism in economic thought, cast out by "Reaganomics," supply-side economics, and mathematical modeling; or (3) the silent agony and subsequent evaporation of what C. Wright Mills had called sociology's "great theory" during the postwar years: Parsons's structural functionalism. The collapse of these theoretical paradigms, which had prevailed uncontested in Western social sciences, indicates that all theories—not just Marxist theory—are suffering a profound crisis.[4]

In an age such as ours, so dense and rich in historical events, it is a basic methodological rule that no theoretical corpus can be immune to history's corrosive effects. In fact, who would have thought, during the bicentennial anniversary of the French Revolution, that before the end of that year the so-called popular democracies of Eastern Europe would actually collapse like houses of cards? Who predicted the fall of the Berlin Wall, itself a painful confession of the abyss that separated Marx's project of human emancipation from the practice of the regimes erected in his name? Socialist thought, precisely for being rooted in the permanently changing world, could not be an exception to the rule and was many times belied by historical developments; so were mainstream theories, equally incapable of predicting the course of events. However, despite their dismaying shortcomings, only Marxism is said to be in crisis.[5]

It would be useful to recall that dogmas are by nature immune to historical refutations. They resist the passing of time unruffled, immutable in

the face of the changing circumstances that characterize the concrete existence of human beings. Lévi-Strauss said that myths are true machines for
suppressing contradictions; by mythologizing history and society, dogmatic
thought transforms the real world into a mere Hegelian projection of their
narration. Because they turn their back on reality dogmas do not suffer the
perplexity of crisis. The true believers pay a high price for this attitude: they
become mere witnesses of history. They are condemned to be either its
biased narrators or—the most lucid ones—its "official interpreters." Let us
specifically examine some of the central questions of Marxist theory at the
end of the twentieth century.

Social Theory: Facts, Values, Utopias

The theme of a crisis of Marxism is as old as the theory itself. The recurring
reappearance of this issue has been a constant and by no means exceptional
circumstance since Marx's death, at least among those who interpreted his
theoretical legacy as a guide for action. However, for those who view
Marxism as the unalterable revelation of a prophet, there is no crisis in
Marxism; nor can there be one. Secluded in their sect, they contemplate the
thunderous and embattled passing of history, waiting for the day when the
"scriptures" will come true, stubbornly refusing to face reality. The beliefs
of fundamentalists—be they Christians, Muslims, or "Marxists"—can never
enter a period of crisis, because a crisis presupposes an act of contrasting the
dogma's ideas with the external world, which is revolting to dogmatic men-
tality. If social reality is imagined as a simple scenario dominated by the
forces of evil until the apocalypse arrives—be it the resurrection of the dead
or the world proletarian revolution—any discourse that points out the incon-
gruence between the course of worldly affairs and the stipulations of the
dogma will serve only to confirm the eternal validity of the doctrine and to
temper the souls of those waiting for the "decisive day." The elemental idea
of "error," crucial to scientific thought, is entirely absent in this closed discursive structure: dogmas cannot be corrected, and for that very reason they
do not suffer the sudden attacks of crisis. What happens is that people abandon them. The problem of dogma is the desertion of believers, not the
dogma's inadequacy in the face of the real world.

For others Marxism is a guide for action, an ethical and political project
pointing toward a superior form of social organization, as well as a scientific theory that allows one to understand some vital aspects of the structure
and functioning of contemporary societies—especially the capitalist and, to
some extent, the "postcapitalist" ones. For this very reason, Marxism also
has the potential to be a useful instrument in the transformation and supersession of all "prehistorical" forms of social existence, including capitalism.
In this sense, the present version of the crisis of Marxism, with all its

denouncements, revelations, and alleged invalidations, contributes few new elements from a theoretical viewpoint.[6] If the most lucid and widespread works are carefully read, it is very hard to find critical formulations that introduce substantive innovations to the arsenal of objections raised during the Bernstein-Debatte against Marx's analysis of the socioeconomic structure of capitalism almost a century ago. Perhaps some loose observations are made regarding feminism, "greens," or pacifism, but that is all; the rest of the objections already have a venerable history. To be sure, this does not mean that criticisms can be ignored or disdained just for being recurrent. However, in spite of their pretenses, they are not original. This point will be discussed again later.[7]

The cyclical recurrence of announcements proclaiming a new, this time definitive, death of Marxism cannot but raise suspicion regarding the premature nature of this funeral service and the speed with which the feared deceased is dismissed. An anthropologist moved by a genuine scientific spirit would be surprised by the frenzied enthusiasm with which the officiates of this old funeral rite carry out their ceremony before an ever renewed and heteroclite audience. Among this audience one can find former true believers now disillusioned with the dogma; others come to mitigate the resentment that the disappointing experience of really existing socialisms sowed in their hearts; still others come to strengthen their new neoliberal faith, reopening the wounds of the corpse with vicious satisfaction; and there are also the temple merchants together with the scribes and Pharisees and the contented dominant classes and their political and intellectual representatives.

At first sight, it is evident that what is being celebrated is something more than the alleged death of a scientific theory. It is the burial of a utopia and its call for a radical social change, for the purpose of bestowing on the present—this capitalist society, with all its injustices and inequalities—the longed-for gift of eternity. The excitement—and in some cases the anger—of the priests and their associates is explainable: it is not just a matter of refuting a theory, but also of exorcising a resilient utopia. It is not enough to officially pronounce the death of Marx; life must be given to many Fukuyamas so that they can credibly proclaim the final triumph of liberal capitalism over communism, of market economy over the state. The uneasiness and ill-humored temper of some of the people in charge is understandable: the other side of the crisis of Marxism is nothing less than the impossible certification of the "end of history."[8]

If the crisis of Marxism has become a cultural mass-consumption good, it is due to the fact that beyond the endogenous causes of that crisis, namely the failure of the revolution in the West and the frustration of really existing socialisms, the political use of Marxism's alleged historical and ideological bankruptcy serves to foster popular resignation to the conservative policies, regarded as the only available choice. Needless to say, this significantly helps the ruling classes face the chronic need to relegitimize capitalist societies, which is considerably more serious because of capitalism's own crisis.[9] At junctures such as these, the ruling classes must seek to disqualify any proposal for social transformation. This anxiety cannot be disassociated from the fact that, as Ludwig von Mises acknowledged in 1947 (before the Chinese Revolution and the further expansion of communism in the 1950s and 1960s), the grand socialist tradition was "the most powerful reform movement that history has ever known, the first ideological trend not limited to a section of mankind but supported by people of all races, nations, religions and civilizations."[10]

The overreaction and celebration unleashed by the events of 1989–1991 are undoubtedly related to the paramount challenge posed by socialism, especially Marxism. The overwhelming spread of the crisis of Marxism in Latin American societies—themselves day by day being torn apart by neoliberal economic restructuring and the foreign debt—is unthinkable if one does not consider the urgent need of the dominant classes to divert the attention of the masses from their unpleasant daily realities and to exclude socialism from the horizon of policy alternatives.

The Dialectics of "Permanent Revisionism"

Yet beyond these observations on the conservative ideological use of the supposed crisis of Marxism, there is another series of arguments that is useful to examine, even if rather quickly. The periodic resurgence of this issue unveils, on the one hand, the persistence of old and undeniable theoretical problems and the distressing appearance of new ones; on other hand, it also reveals the vitality of the self-critical dialectics that characterize the best Marxist tradition. Both Karl Marx and Friedrich Engels, for instance, did not hesitate to declare that their famous *Communist Manifesto* had aged after the failed 1848 revolutions. Marx's analyses of Bonapartism and of the dynamics of French capitalism were also at least partially questioned by the unexpected persistence of the Bonapartist interlude and the events of the Paris Commune, and Marx himself admitted that the predictions included in his *Eighteenth Brumaire* were belied by history. In 1895 Engels spoke on this matter once again in the famous introduction to Marx's *The Class Struggles in France,* urging a continuous effort of theoretical self-criticism and practical actualization.

Such an exhortation, by the way, can rarely be found in other social sciences' theoretical paradigms, in which the faithful prefer to quote each other, ignoring both what other theories say and what happens in the real world. The true "permanent revisionism" of Marxist thought—a legacy of the relentless criticism of dialectics—does not have much place in the liberal tradition and is completely alien to the theoretical corpus of conservatism. It is also foreign to canonical Marxism, which transformed the theory into a dogma that is as pompous as it is socially and politically sterile, incapable of accounting for the concrete historical processes and of ensuring a creative insertion of progressive political forces in the social struggle of its times.

This revisionism is why, despite the dislike of the dedicated custodians of Stalinist orthodoxy, the history of Marxism—both of its theory and of its practice—is a long succession of theoretical crises and revisionist proposals. Who could deny that, throughout almost half a century, Marx and Engels revised and corrected some substantive aspects of the theory for which they had sketched out the basis in *The German Ideology* as early as 1845? How could the radical innovations introduced by Lenin—the theory of the political party and his novel characterization of imperialism as the highest stage of capitalism, both absent in the theoretical apparatus of the "founding fathers"—be ignored? How could one possibly forget the brilliant contributions of Rosa Luxemburg to the theory of socialist democracy, challenging the then-prevailing conceptions of both Lenin and Trotsky on the single party and advocating an unprecedented rearticulation between the individual freedoms—mostly developed within the liberal philosophical tradition—and the public and collective entitlements argued for by socialist doctrine? How could the early—and, for a long time, isolated—criticism made by Trotsky on the bureaucratic and authoritarian socialist experiment led by Stalin be forgotten? Was not Gramsci a profound "revisionist," who reformulated the Marxist theory of the state in accordance with the new realities brought about by the rise of fascism, the advent of mass bourgeois democracy, Fordism, and the capitalist recomposition of the 1930s? And what is to be said about Mao, who revisited—theoretically and practically—the role of the worker-peasant alliance in the socialist revolution and in anti-imperialist struggles?

All these examples reveal that each of the foremost thinkers in the history of socialism was a revisionist and that, contrary to what its most fervent critics maintain, Marxist theory cannot be the coagulation of the theoretical categories constructed in the mid-nineteenth century and ritually invoked and ruminated by simple—or obstinate—minds at the dawn of the twenty-first century.[11] This perspective is politically banal, philosophically poor, and so historically myopic that it hardly resists any analysis. Marxism is not a dogma but a living theory that has grown and been substantially modified since the moment when two young men—who were little older than twenty-five years of age at that time—gave it their first draft in *The German Ideology*. The liberal tradition has evolved since John Locke wrote his foundational *Second Treatise* in the late seventeenth century, and to discuss liberalism today one cannot but consider all the developments that took place in the last three hundred years and that modified significant aspects of the original theoretical construction. The same is true for Marxism as a secular scientific theory. These elementary observations are in order because it is not a coincidence that many staunch critics of Marxism in the past have been either zealous Stalinist inquisitors or fervent ultraleftists, who from atop a pile of dogmatic tracts blasted anyone who had the nerve not to share their sacred and infallible perspective of Marxism.[12] The same people, who previously did not manage to understand a single word of Marxism—because in their hands it became a Talmudic verse—still do not understand it because they continue to conceive of it as a dogma and not as a guide for action.

"Why such a generalized repudiation of Marxism as a theoretical paradigm?" Ludolfo Paramio asks himself. And he answers:

> The answer is simple but painful: Marxism owes its historical success to its capacity for fulfilling the functions of a secular creed. Thus, the crisis of Marxism in the last part of the 1970s is the crisis of Marxism as religion. . . . Even worse: the same unconscious conception of Marxism *as a religion,* with the ensuing definition of an unbreakable orthodoxy, is the clue that explains the inability of the Marxist paradigm to renew itself as it could do if it were a secular paradigm, a scientific theory.[13]

This way of positing the problem, which is profoundly influenced by the more rigid tenets of logical positivism, dangerously confuses several things—such as religion, science, utopia—which Paramio would do better to keep separate. As in all other political theories, in Marxism there is a conjugation of analytical and descriptive propositions, aimed at explaining what exists, with others of an axiological nature that depict the shape of a "good society," a society in which human happiness would finally reach its maximum possible fulfillment. Profoundly rooted in the philosophical groundwork of the Western tradition, Marxism could not be the exception to a rule that also applies to liberalism and conservatism. Hence arise the difficulties in perceiving the arcane reasons the "self-government of producers" is looked down upon as a utopian statement that irreparably destroys the scientific components of Marxism, though ideals that are equally explicit and important—such as a "least government" that would free men and women from state oppression; or the invisible hand of the market, which wisely distributes resources and benefits—are not perceived as undermining the scientific structure of the liberal tradition.

Perhaps anything that propounds to change what exists is labeled utopian, whereas assertions that aim at conserving and embellishing the current social order are deemed scientific.[14] It is a gross mistake to assume that the inevitable presence—be it manifest or latent—of utopian elements in scientific discourse (radically distinguishable, though, from the analytical statements) transforms an entire theoretical structure into a collection of articles of faith. One of the most resounding flaws of positivism in the social sciences has been its inability to understand that utopia and the empirical are dialectical poles of the real, and that what is real is "unity of the diverse, and synthesis of multiple determinations," as Marx writes in *Gründrisse*. Just as there are no human beings without desires nor societies without ideals, reality does not exist without utopia, without a contradiction of its own that negates reality and sooner or later will overcome reality. Utopia and reality enrich each other reciprocally. They constitute proper and different spheres of the real. However, their boundaries are permanently in motion. Some of what today is utopia will tomorrow be reality, and, in turn, reality will become history.[15]

This bond between utopia and reality is acutely perceived by Marx and Engels when they say, "Communism is for us not a *state of affairs* which is to be established, an *ideal* to which reality has to adjust itself. We call communism the *real* movement which abolished the present state of things."[16] This permanent dialectic between utopia and reality cannot but reproduce itself in the sphere of thought. It is not necessary to be a Marxist in order to assert that no social theory can limit itself to describing and analyzing what exists regardless of its judgment and its capacity to identify—sometimes implicitly or unknowingly—the good and the evil that coexist in a given reality. This is why the "factual" and supposedly "value-free" propositions of mainstream positivist social science are invariably found mixed together with others of a normative character, which either glorify or condemn what exists. The predominance of logical positivism in the social sciences is responsible for having considered this situation as a pernicious anomaly, thereby jettisoning an age-old and rich tradition of thought in which analysis and evaluation were explicitly and legitimately integrated into a unified discourse.[17] Positivism's hegemony as the "scientific ideology" of the social sciences had as its counterpart the imposition of a rigid epistemological canon that did not leave room for values, ideals, and utopias. That is the reason the images of society projected even by the finest expression of positivist social science are barren and incurably distorted, as a consequence of the barbarous disarticulation between facts and values that inform the discipline's entire philosophy.[18]

Paramio confidently relies on the tottering philosophical structures of this epistemological tradition to support a distinction between "secular" and "religious" paradigms that is clearly unsustainable. Then he places Marxism among the latter and the rest of contemporary theoretical currents—supposedly value-free and cleansed of utopian elements—under the field of "science," ignoring their unconcealable normative components. By doing so he belatedly reiterates Alvin Gouldner's unfortunate thesis according to which Marxism is a synthesis between religion and science, a true "synchretism, fusing science with Christianity's millennial promise to overcome all sufferings and to enact brotherhood."[19] Subsequently, and in consonance with positivist stipulations, Paramio radically idealizes the virtues of scientific thought (by postulating a theoretical flexibility that is as boundless as it is unlikely), its repudiation of dogmas, and its limitless capacity for self-correction and renovation, while lowering utopia to the category of a fallacious discourse, permeated with prejudices, illusions, and deceptions.

In this context it is interesting to highlight that many of Marx's critics very often fall in curious contradictions. They charge, for instance, that Marxist theory has the character of a religious creed that does not allow for the possibility of error. Thus reconstructed, the Marxist argument appears to present itself as infallible and perfect and therefore is completely alien to the most relativist and parsimonious sphere of truly scientific thought. But the same critics also reproach Marxism for its factual "mistakes," which indisputably prove the nonscientific character of its propositions. Therefore, they make a double accusation: Marxism does not admit the possibility of theoretical errors and mistakes, and therefore it is religion, not science; on the other hand, Marxism does have mistakes, ergo it is a false theory, and thus many of its critics equate it with ideology. The vicious circle of this reasoning is thus closed: Marxism is either religion or ideology, and it has nothing to offer to social science. But as Perry Anderson accurately points out, the existence of errors is one of the distinctive characteristics of science. In fact, it was the pretension of vulgar Marxism of being error-free that discredited historical materialism as a scientific theory. Referring to the usual comparison between Marx, Copernicus, and Galileo, Anderson concludes that "no one imagines today that the writings of the latter are free from any critical mistakes and contradictions. Their very status as pioneers of modern astronomy and physics is the guarantee of the inevitability of their errors, at the dawn of the development of a new science. The same must be true a priori of Marxism."[20]

That a scientific theory may consciously or unconsciously be considered a secular religion by its followers does not in the least modify its epistemological merits and the validation criteria that sustain it empirically. Nonetheless, and given that Marxism has correctly been interpreted as a guide for action, one should ask which elements of Marxist theory are responsible for producing a "religious effect" among the historical subjects involved in practical struggles. An inquiry of this type would allow one to understand more integrally not only the "canonization" experienced by Marxism in socialist regimes—leading to its theoretical liquidation, as the official "Marxist-Leninist" doctrine of the now-defunct USSR—but also the profound motivations of its most ardent critics.

Liberalism became the secular creed of U.S. society because in no other part of the world did its central premises correspond so closely with a bourgeois society—created ex novo and therefore lacking an oppressive feudal past—as the one founded by the dissenters who arrived on the *Mayflower*. Hartz's book proves this.[21] A mere secular religion would not have been so fortunate if its essential predicates had not corresponded relatively well with the objective conditions of the society in which it attempted to root itself. In fact, it was precisely this affinity between liberalism and the unique U.S. sociohistorical circumstances that transformed liberalism into a formidable historical force. It also helps one understand why liberal ideas became the "common sense" of the greatest triumph of capitalism in its entire history: the establishment of the United States of America as a bourgeois nation. The "realism" of the liberal utopia in U.S. society prevented liberalism from congealing as the dogma of an esoteric sect, as occurred in Latin America. The "unreality" of that same utopia in Latin America—land of seigniorial landowners, not of farmers; of countries founded on the reactionary alliance of the cross and the sword, not on the separation of church and state; of the Holy Inquisition, not of tolerance; of the Counter-Reformation instead of the Reform—caused the painful agony of liberalism; when liberalism sporadically revived it would do so with an authoritarian face that revealed its conservative and colonialist nature.[22]

Likewise, if Marxism became—for a certain amount of time, during the height of its revolutionary impulse—the secular creed of one-third of humanity and a fundamental presence in the constitution of the modern world, it was not exactly due to the balsamic virtues that the reading of *Capital* radiated on the tormented souls anxious to find in its pages the comfort of a religion. It seems more likely that its practical historical influence in the twentieth century can better be explained, at least in part, by the elements of "scientific truth" contained in Marxism. To the eyes of millions of men and women Marxism has appeared as a reasonable—despite its incompleteness—explanation of the nature of capitalism and the international system, and as an inspiring source for designing a socialist strategy aimed at transforming the status quo. It is evident that the workers do not seek to take the heavens by assault mobilized by the logical and mathematical elegance with which Marx proved the declining tendency of the rate of profit. In addition to a few certitudes, ultimately based on a theory that adequately explains at least some key aspects of sociohistorical reality, a whole set of beliefs, values, and utopias more or less linked with the scientific structure of Marxism is added. It is precisely this rare and unique amalgam of discourses of diverse natures—some "scientific" and others "ideological"— that has the capacity to mobilize the masses through the path of revolution. The "truth" contained in the admirable political geometry of Thomas Hobbes does not explain the English revolutionary cycle throughout the seventeenth century; Rousseau's radical democratism surely contributed to the outbreak of the French Revolution, but the revolution would not have occurred without the intervention of many other far more important factors; and in the Russian Revolution there was a confluence of multiple conditions, one of which was the significance Marx's theory held for part of the revolutionary intelligentsia. Scientific theories and ideologies, "realisms," and utopias are combined in thousands of ways in the social production of history.

Therefore, because there were several social revolutions that invoked Marx's teachings—and that, for better or worse, indelibly marked the history of our century—it seems unreasonable to assume that those revolutions were no more than a miraculous coincidence, a product of the blind and irrational trust that the exploited classes all over the world placed in Marx's "secularized millenarianism." The crucial mistake of Ptolemy's geocentric theory was neither compensated for nor corrected by the opinions favorable to his system that during almost two thousand years were held by intellectuals, the rulers who benefited from its political implications, and, in their ignorance, the underlying masses. And Copernicus's fundamental truth took a long time to become a secular creed, yet this did not in the least affect the correctness of his reasoning and the strength of the proof.

In other words, the truth and vitality of a scientific theory are independent of the social support that theory elicits in a given population. The fact that leftist parties in Argentina or the United States do not recruit more than 1 or 2 percent of the votes does not necessarily mean that Marxist theory is false, especially given that these are the countries where some of the cardinal premises of Marxism are present with almost caricatural features. The reverse is also true: in the China of the cultural revolution, Marxism became a true mass religion, yet that did not add a bit of evidence to the structure of its scientific argument. The proof of theories does not depend on volatile collective emotions.

Now it makes sense to return to Paramio's criticism of Marxism as a religion. If Paramio were correct, his reasoning would end up in absurd paradoxes: a scientifically true theory so unfortunate as to be socially accepted would inevitably become a sort of secular creed and, therefore, a religious dogma. On the other hand, a false theory that, because of its inability to interpret and change the world, caused universal indifference would possess a hardly enviable "secularism" that would enable it, hypothetically, to critically reexamine its own premises. In both cases, the validity of the theory and the objectivity of the empirical evidence that supports it vanish into the thin air of the social acceptance or public repudiation it may evoke. This reasoning constitutes a clear non sequitur that prevents one from positing the discussion of the present crisis of Marxism in appropriate terms.

However, even if one accepts Paramio's contraposition between Marxist theory—transformed into a religion because of its social efficiency—and secular paradigms, there are still other questions that cannot so easily be overlooked. Paramio argues, not without a disconcerting excess of gullibility, that secular paradigms enjoy the gift of self-criticism and renovation. Yet the history of social sciences shows that this does not seem to be the case. When theories are "successful" they continue with their initial formulation, admitting slight "retouches" in their propositional argument; otherwise they die of weakening. But only in exceptional cases do they renew themselves. Where is the theoretical reformulation of structural functionalism, the major theorctical synthesis of the social sciences since World War II? Who rearticulated the behavioral paradigm in political science? Where and how did they do this? The answer to these questions is that these secular and scientific paradigms, so admired by Paramio, were exhausted and abandoned. Neither were they able to criticize their own premises, nor did they have the capacity to renew themselves. They simply died, and in their place other theories were invented. Today they constitute museum pieces waiting for a revived Foucault to write a new chapter on the archaeology of knowledge. If we are to believe Kuhn, the same seems to happen in the "hard" sciences. Consequently, the exaltation of the self-corrective virtues of scientific paradigms asserted by Paramio seems to be more an idealization than an accurate description of how science really works.

In any case, the other part of the argument should be highlighted, the one establishing that, because of its character as a secular creed, Marxism rejects all types of revisions and questioning. Are not Paramio and a whole legion of critics confusing Marx's scientific theory—incomplete, "finite," partial, controversial as any other—with the monstrous manuals of the Academy of Sciences of the former Soviet Union, the mandatory reading of which among the leadership cadres and intellectuals of the communist parties so much harmed the theoretical and practical development of Marx's ideas? On this point, Paramio's analysis becomes completely obscure. If one cannot see Marxism as a collective enterprise, as a living and dynamic theory—critical and self-critical, partly confirmed and partly refuted by history—having an identity that has been enriched and made more complex by virtue of the plural contributions accumulated throughout more than a century, then one runs the risk of confusing a fertile and varied theoretical tradition with the *vulgatas* narrated by the officers and petty speechwriters of the bureaucracies that spoiled the realization of the socialist project. Wouldn't it be a legitimate scandal if a self-proclaimed Marxist pretended to critically examine liberalism by analyzing a collection of editorials in *Reader's Digest?*

When the point is to seriously discuss the scientific status of Marxism, critics must at least proceed with reasonable rigor and not forget that the theoretical and political tradition begun by Marx and Engels was enriched by the social struggles that unfolded in the most remote corners of the world and by the reflections of minds of the stature of Lenin, Trotsky, Bujarin, Kautsky, Luxemburg, Korsch, Lukács, Hilferding, Gramsci, Mao, and Mariátegui, to name just a few. These individuals represent different currents and developments of the same theoretical macromodel, and only an extremely obfuscated mind could maintain that their arguments are identical repetitions of the theses contained in the *Communist Manifesto*. In spite of their differences, their contributions—varied, in part contradictory, and always incomplete—preserved the main theoretical and methodological premises of Marxist thought. But beyond this initial agreement on the fundamentals, there is quite an ample space in which debate and controversy reign. To insinuate that Marxist theory at the end of the twentieth century is a frozen monolithic theoretical corpus that has remained unaltered during a hundred years is a great mistake. Doing so does not help one understand Paramio's insightful assertion that the importance of the ideas introduced by Marx "largely justified the attempt to reelaborate and update them."[23]

Crisis—or Liquidation—of Marxism?

It is necessary to point out that many questions posed by critics of Marxist theory are, without a doubt, relevant and should not be neglected. The pronouncement of the final crisis of Marxism is based on the following diagnosis: the qualitative changes produced in the structure and functioning of capitalist societies and the collapse of really existing socialisms have inaugurated a new era in the face of which Marxist theory and the political praxis inspired in it no longer have anything to say or do. Contemporary capitalism is something so different from the one that inflamed the radical criticism of Marx and Engels that the analytical model those men created has been completely superseded by the real movement of history. Postmodern capitalism has devoured the products of nineteenth-century modernity, and Marxism died along with the "grand narrative" and the notion of utopia.

At first sight the criticism seems to be reasonable, even though it arouses suspicion as to why the same accusation is not applied to the liberal paradigm. After all, Adam Smith published *The Wealth of Nations* in 1776, whereas *The German Ideology* was written between 1845 and 1846 and was published almost a century later as a result of well-known circumstances. It is surprising that many of those who heatedly question Marxism for its alleged anachronisms simultaneously adhere to a theory characterized by its scandalous idolatry of the markets, eternally balanced thanks to the wisdom of an "invisible hand." Thus, it seems that in order for one to decide on its validity, the criticism should adopt a more precise formulation. What characterizes scientific work—as opposed to vulgar knowledge—is not so much the exactness of the responses as the rigor and accuracy of the questions. The main obstacle that slows the advance of scientific knowledge is not error but rather confusion: an unclear question is more pernicious than a wrong answer, because the corrective mechanisms work much better in the second than in the first.

Thus, it is extremely important that self-proclaimed "post-Marxists," such as Paramio and others, formulate their arguments in a much more rigorous manner. For instance, instead of their nebulous ruminations regarding contemporary society—the sociohistorical nature of which is certainly not to be discovered simply through inventing attractive and allegedly original names for it—it would be much more pertinent to clearly posit some crucial questions. For example: to what extent have recent transformations in the anatomy of bourgeois society qualitatively altered the character of capitalist relations of production? Or, more specifically: has the exploitation of one person by another—the veritable "slavery of wage labor"—disappeared in mature capitalist societies of the late twentieth century? The answers to these questions would enable one to know whether today's society is a different type than that witnessed by Marx and Engels.

It seems that the answers to these fundamental questions, necessary to anchor theoretically the practical invalidation of Marxism, are negative. The disharmonious chorus of Marxism's critics carefully avoids the detailed treatment of these matters, contenting itself with an impressionist glance that in some cases is colorful and attractive yet is lacking in depth. If it is not proven that a new mode of production has arisen—given that everyone seems to regard the present one as capitalist and that Marx's critics are busy singing hymns to triumphant capitalism—in which class contradictions have been overcome through the disappearance of their structural determinant (that is, exploitation in the labor process), the entire laborious construction of the post-Marxists is automatically condemned to irrelevance. The changes undergone by the structure of modern capitalism in the late twentieth century—which only a dogmatc intellect would be incapable of acknowledging—failed to modify the profound structure of the social relations of production on which bourgeois society rests. Hence, Anthony Giddens asserts that, despite the changes that have occurred since World War II, the present society cannot correctly be characterized as "postcapitalist" but rather as "neocapitalist." The substitution of the prefix *post* by *neo* indicates that both the fundamental features as well as the laws of motion of contemporary society are clearly capitalist. Postulating the advent of a blurry and vague postcapitalism serves only to confuse things while discouraging the critics of the allegedly dead capitalism.[24]

The recent transformations were highly significant, but none had the virtue of dissolving the fundamental class antagonism that typically characterizes the capitalist mode of production. New social actors appeared, the form and intensity of the class conflicts were modified, and the political processing and regulation of social contradictions changed accordingly; yet these contradictions continue to be the unstable foundation on which the *Spätkapitalismus* is based. Or is it that post-Marxists sincerely believe that in the United States—where thanks to neoliberal policies there was a phenomenal advance of monopolies and a concomitant pauperization of large sectors of the subordinate classes—class contradictions have vanished into thin air? Or maybe they think that those contradictions vanished in Thatcher's England, or in Kohl's Germany, or perhaps in Japan? If class conflict and class contradictions are alive and well in the capitalist core, do post-Marxists want one to believe that a dazzling capitalist postmodernity does in fact exist in poverty-ridden Latin America?[25]

It would be extremely difficult to take seriously such an argument in the social sciences. It is insulting not only to the intelligence of those who hear it, but also to the most basic canons of scientific methodology. Perhaps this is the reason a true legion of post-Marxists has not produced even a small leaflet—comparable to *Wage Labor and Capital,* for example—in which the fundamental features and laws of motion of the new historical type of society are exposed. To be sure, this does not mean that Marxism has all the answers or that it has been capable of adequately explaining the totality of social life. Such a pretension would be incompatible with the theory's scientific spirit. It would reveal the persistence of erroneous ideas that confuse the scientific nature of Marxism with the infallible dogmas preached for years by the Soviet Academy of Sciences. There are so-called Marxists possessed by that religious fervor, and perhaps Paramio's criticism refers to them. However, a discussion of such a dogmatic deformation of Marxism is completely irrelevant in terms of social and political theory.

Viewed as a scientific theory and as a guide for action, Marxism proposes not only to interpret social reality but also to transform it. This dual character, theoretical and practical, has permanently challenged Marxism with crucial questions. It also makes the novelties and changes produced in a period of extraordinary dynamism such as the one we live in today acquire such importance that a full awareness of Marxism's theoretical and practical insufficiencies is not only completely inevitable but also absolutely necessary in order to eventually overcome them. But this certainly does not amount to jettisoning Marx's theoretical legacy—which despite its shortcomings is still the most fertile paradigm available in the social sciences. The baby must not be thrown out with the bathwater, and the anxious discoverers of new theoretical worlds should keep this wisdom in mind. Marx's legacy constitutes an essential synthesis for contemporary social thought: without his ideas—as well as Weber's, Freud's, and Einstein's—one would be significantly impaired to grasp even the most elementary features of the current era. That is why some of Marx's critics—some angry, others interested, and still others disappointed and repentant—find themselves in an extremely uncomfortable position: they have to relentlessly proclaim Marxism's death, but in so doing they deny the veracity of their assertions.

In no way are the observations in this section meant to conceal or postpone the urgent need to promote a profound and self-critical reflection regarding both the failure of really existing socialisms and our incapacity to understand the magnitude of the changes sweeping the capitalist system. As a modest contribution to that reflective task, the following pages will examine a problem that seems to be of exceptional theoretical and practical significance: the issue of the working class in late twentieth-century capitalism.

Neither Working Class nor Revolution!
Social Actors in Late Capitalism

There is a widespread consensus that one of the key issues in contemporary capitalism is the question of the centrality of the proletariat. The sheer magnitude of the changes unleashed by the transformations to this mode of production since World War II is of such import that it demands an urgent and thorough reexamination of certain premises that until recently were accepted without much discussion. In this sense there are few who could match the inflamed eloquence of the requiem delivered by André Gorz in the early 1980s in *Farewell to the Proletariat*. However, neither eloquence nor popularity necessarily guarantee the accuracy of analysis.[26]

The decay of the old proletariat and the complex reconstitution of the heterogeneous universe of the subordinate classes are easily observed phenomena both in the core as well as in the periphery of the capitalist system, and no serious student of these realities can ignore or underestimate their importance. As expected, these mutations were accompanied by a plethora of theories and interpretations announcing the news with a mixture of relief and satisfaction, celebrating the disappearance of the threatening classist actor of capitalism. Hence, it became fashionable to study—in some cases with an ardent, apologetic zeal—the new social movements and their role in the dynamics of Latin American societies, not to mention the amazing feat accomplished by some "postmodern" theorists who, luckier than the enterprising alchemists of prebourgeois Europe, discovered in the entrails of late capitalism the extraordinary formula that allows for the "invention" of social actors based on the dialectics of the discourse.[27]

Several years ago, in a famous interview conducted by Perry Anderson, Lucio Colleti asserted that the failure of the "revolution in the West" represented a radical refutation of Marxist theory. The reaches of this failure and the extent to which it invalidates the entirety of Marx's theory—and the associated intellectual and political tradition—are debatable issues, and Colletti's position is exaggerated. However, there is no doubt that his argument points to a serious weakness of the theory. Yet there exist some interpretations that, without breaking with the premises of Marxism, manage to offer plausible explanations of the failure of the revolution in advanced capitalist countries. In brief, there seems to be no compelling evidence to support a complete rejection of Marxism as a theory of history and society.

Because of the publicity given to the so-called crisis of Marxism, the opinion that the fundamental assertions of that theoretical tradition are belied by real-world events has very effectively been disseminated. Consequently, some "classical" themes of Marxism, including the whole issue of social classes, were perfunctorily dismissed with alarming boldness. The theoretical and practical vacuum left by this dismissal of the notion of classes was compensated for by the exaltation of new collective actors; the alleged extinction of the former became the condition that enabled the latter to come into being. But a sketchy reconstruction of the history of capitalism in the twentieth century will easily prove that even though the Western working class failed to fulfill its "historical mission" to end all forms of social oppression and to construct a classless society, it still managed to produce significant and far-reaching reforms in the structure of really existing capitalisms. Today's capitalist societies are not the same as those that existed at the beginning of the century. And if they changed in a direction congruent with the consolidation of public freedoms, democracy, and equality—thereby bringing about more democratic states and more open societies—they did so because of the vindicative efficacy of the working class and the popular movement. The market's "social Darwinism" was first neutralized and later reversed thanks to the efforts of the subordinate classes and their political and union organizations. Contemporary Western historiography—both liberal and Marxist—has produced overwhelming evidence that fully supports this assertion.[28] As Miliband persuasively argues, if in some places today there are democratic capitalisms, welfare states, more open societies, and a trimmed despotism of capital in the economy, it is due to the Western working class resisting capitalist encroachments and succeeding at reforms. It is true that the workers fell short of carrying out their own social revolution; and it is also true that the reformist projects had varying degrees of success. However, the progressive role of the laboring masses and their definite anticapitalist vocation have been undebatable, and the positive results of their struggles are evident.[29]

The possibility of inventing new social actors, themselves creatures of powerful discourses transformed into Hegelian makers of history, has recently fascinated vast circles of European and Latin American social thought. The discrediting of economicist reductionism—a distinctive feature of a certain *vulgata* that believes itself to be Marxist as well as of multiple expressions of liberal thought—caused a true stampede of specialists who went out to study civil societies in search of new social actors. To the surprise of the most phlegmatic souls, this enterprise was undertaken with a fervor worthy of the best causes. In fact, the finding of this new "grail" mobilized the strongest emotions, blocking the researchers' memories and impairing the much-needed sobriety of their analytical vision. The "movementists" believed they had discovered terra incognita when in reality they did no more than arrive late, as well as unwittingly, to a continent that U.S. sociologists had already explored quite meticulously in the early 1940s. Spurred by the proliferation of fascist regimes and social movements, the U.S. forerunners made valuable contributions to the study of the behavior and ideological orientations of social movements and political grassroots groups. However, contrary to what has happened in more recent years, those sociologists never underplayed the role of classes and their continued activism.[30] It is true that present conditions widely justify reopening that line of research, but nothing authorizes the joyful dismissal of the needed temperance of scientific work. Throwing the figures of the class heroes of the past out the window in order to replace them with mighty images of the new social actors—and bestowing upon those images an explanatory theoretical potential that concrete practice does not ratify—could be a gesture of scientific audacity, but it more likely reveals the indolence of minds too attached to the intellectual fashions of their times.[31]

Is There Any Role Left for the Working Class?

The laws of motion of a society do not disappear on a whim. The diligent medieval theologians busied themselves for centuries demonstrating that the earth was motionless and that it occupied the center of the universe. Their geocentrism not by chance maintained the worldly primacy of the pope: a motionless world required an immutable authority, which could be no other than the bishop of Rome. Nevertheless, it is well known that their tortuous reasonings did not manage to modify in the least the regularized laws of rotation and movement of our planet. Similarly, the law of universal gravitation existed before an apple fell on the shoulder of Isaac Newton. Obviously these examples cannot be mechanically applied to the social life, given that the consciousness of human beings and their transformative historical praxis do modify the course of society. That modification is precisely what happens when revolutions triumph: necessity and freedom, structural determination and transformative praxis, are poles that coexist in perpetual dialectical negation. The proliferation of new social actors does not decree the abolition of the laws of motion of a class society. It means only that the social and political scene has become more complex. But by no means does the increase in the number—as well as the diversification of the quality—of social actors presuppose the disappearance of social classes, nor the end of their conflict as the fundamental dynamic axis of capitalist societies.[32]

On the other hand, it seems redundant to have to recall that the centrality of the proletariat as a key actor of the revolution is not a matter of statistics. The working class is not called on to create a new society because of fathomless metaphysical attributes or for the banal fact of its size relative to the rest of society. Paramio is wrong when he suggests that Marx was a thinker superficial enough to have fallen in the trap of simplistic and reductionist formulations.[33] The centrality of the proletariat is a function of the role that workers play in the production process and, consequently, in the system of contradictions proper of bourgeois society. Whether the proletariat is a statistical majority or not is a consideration of second order in Marx's argument. In certain historical stages the industrial proletariat was indeed the largest social class, but this condition was never a necessary component of the Marxist theoretical understanding of the issue. The centrality of the working class is based on its unique insertion in the productive process and its irreplaceable role in the valorization of capital; thus, only the working class possesses the necessary conditions that will eventually enable it to subvert the bourgeois order. Marx and Engels made it clear since the times of the *Communist Manifesto* that the proletariat, to fulfill its "historical mission," needs the cooperation of the other groups and social classes with whom to coalesce. To think differently of the role of the proletariat would mean to postulate the inexorability of the socialist revolution made by the workers alone. This idea is completely alien to the spirit of Marxism.

It is necessary to acknowledge that the present physiognomy of the working class is far from being like the one Marx knew in his times. The fragmentation and segmentation of the labor force as a result of sweeping changes in the work process, the shrinking size of the proletariat, and the proletariat's later recomposition—with enhanced skills and qualifications—are hard evidence of this, especially in mature capitalist countries. Yet to speak without much ado about the progressive disappearance of the proletariat is at the very least a hasty guess. Nevertheless, contrary to what a dogmatic left still maintains, it is impossible to ignore that a profound revision of the concept of proletariat used by the classic Marxist tradition is unavoidable. The traditional conception, including the subsequent Leninist enlargement formulated in the thesis of the "working-class aristocracy," is now insufficient to account for the repercussions that the great technological developments of the last fifteen to twenty years have had on the work process and the wage labor universe. The radical modifications undergone by the productive process and the modalities of valorization of capital impose the need to critically rethink the nature of the working class at the thresholds of the twenty-first century and, of course, the new class structures of late capitalism.[34]

The exclusionist reorganization of capitalism, nurtured by the crisis of the 1970s, prompted the social and economic marginalization of large sectors of civil society. If to this one adds the noticeable mutations that took place in the anatomy of the subordinate classes—which caused, among other things, the crisis of their traditional structures of mediation: political parties and labor unions—then the reasons that explain the emergence of new social movements may easily be understood. These new social movements express new forms of sociability and new collective actors, organized around new issues that are not easily incorporated—much less adequately dealt with—within the traditional structures and agenda of the labor movement. Gender demands, ecological concerns, and youth problems—as well as the issues raised by sexual minorities, conscientious objectors, indigenous populations, senior citizens, human rights activists, and many others—constitute a reality different from, although not contradictory to, social class and class conflicts. The correct assessment of the transformative potential of these new social movements does not require a symmetrical underestimation of the role social classes still retain. The vindications of the residents of popular barrios, the single mothers, the unemployed youth, the ecologists, the pacifists, and the human rights groups cannot be fully understood unless integrated into the overarching framework of class conflict and bourgeois domination. But this does not mean that the new social movements' practical productivity can be "reduced" to a classist axis that inexorably determines and conditions them. These movements are not a mere mirage, an ancillary epiphenomenon of class struggle. Rather, they express new types of contradictions, cleavages, and vindications generated by the renewed conflictual nature of capitalist society.

However, the dynamics of these new contradictions would be virtually indecipherable if they were not placed in the global context of class relations and the related structural contradictions. How could one possibly understand the demands and political strategies of neighbors' associations that demand water and electricity unless one takes into account that the way the Latin American bourgeoisies have accumulated and dominated has condemned millions to live in shantytowns and *barrios de emergencia*? How can the demands of human rights organizations be adequately interpreted if one forgets that in these countries the bourgeoisie and its imperialist allies have repeatedly relied on repressive policies to preserve a scandalously unjust social order? How can the disdain the bourgeoisie feels toward the "greens" be understood if one ignores that the conservationist proposal is profoundly antagonistic to the predatory rationale of peripheral capitalism? One last example involves Latin American political transitions. Originally there was a wide consensus among specialists that underlined the centrality of the new social movements in the transition from authoritarianism toward democracy. Soon enough, however, evidence showed that those who were fulfilling the main roles in the transition were simply the old classist actors, dismissed by some "trendy" social scientists: transnational and local entrepreneurs, foreign bankers, the labor movement, landed oligarchies, etc. The new social movements soon yielded their place to class collective actors, whose death certificates had been premature.[35]

It is enough to examine the structure and functioning of contemporary societies, in the United States, Europe, or Latin America, in order to prove that neither classes nor class antagonisms have disappeared. The neoconservative 1980s can be fully understood only as an all-out assault by the bourgeoisie on the workers' positions, which produced an epoch-making retreat of labor from the citadels and bulwarks conquered during the postwar Keynesian recomposition. Nevertheless, the persistence of class conflict would never allow one to conclude that the social classes are the only relevant actors in bourgeois societies—a notion that, aside from being false, is a flagrant distortion of Marx's theory—or that class struggle is the only meaningful contradiction in capitalist societies. The unprecedented proliferation of social actors is a novelty that requires detailed and careful analysis. A significant number of these new social actors have contributed, by their demands and initiatives, to undermining the stability of bourgeois domination, and their cooperation will be highly important in enabling the present society to be superseded. The growing complexity of contemporary capitalist formations has created new fractures and lines of conflict that coexist with traditional class cleavages. And the latter continue to be, both in central capitalist formations and in the periphery of the system, the fundamental "geological faultline" of modern societies. In this context, the words of Ralph Miliband are in order:

> This does not mean that that the movements of women, negroes, pacifists, ecologists, gays and others alike lack any importance, have not practical implications or must relinquish to their specific identity. Not at all. It only means that the main (not the only) grave-digger of capitalism is still the working class. The working class is the necessary, indispensable instrument of historical change. And if, as it is currently argued, the workers refuse to do the job then the job will not be done. . . . Nothing has happened in the world of advanced capitalism and in the world of the working class to authorize such a vision of the future.[36]

In a later article Miliband insists that new social movements and postmodern intellectuals may doubt the persistence of the classic centrality of the working class. However, "all conservative forces in these societies do not doubt it. For them, the main antagonist, as always, remains organized labour and the socialist Left."[37]

To sum up, the alleged extinction of classes and their replacement by new social actors has so far been more an illusion than a reality. Neither is this claim something new, because in the mid-1950s many theories attempted to explain the "end of ideologies," the progressive disappearance of the working class, and the exhaustion of the class struggle. It is common knowledge what history did with those inflamed formulations: the social turbulences and the political upheaval of the 1960s swept them away, and they were discreetly filed away to wait for better times. Similar ideas reappear now in different guise, and sooner rather than later they will suffer the same fate. One feature that best characterizes contemporary capitalism is the multiplication of new social actors, that is, of new "grave diggers" who collaborate with the oldest and most important ones—the industrial proletariat—in undermining the structures of bourgeois society. In this way, bourgeois society confronts the negativity and criticism of a very large and diversified group of sectors—which in some cases posit specific demands, and in others diffuse vindications. Control of these sectors by the dominant classes will become increasingly problematic.

The consternation of the main theorists of "the crisis of democracy" adequately reflects the importance of this new source of challenges to the capitalist classes. In fact, aside from the eventual radicalization of these demands for autonomy and identity, of the assertion of sectoral interests, and of the propagation of specifically antisystemic ideologies, the simple proliferation of the number of excluded social groups and sectors that mobilize, organize, and demand implies, in practical terms, an increase in the levels of social conflict amidst the declining legitimacy, efficiency, and effectivity of the capitalist state. All of this stimulates the vicious circle of ungovernability, the consequences of which will exact concrete responses from both the state and civil society. There will be either a reinforcement of the structure that freezes the unequal distribution of wealth and power—that is, a reversion to the neoliberal orthodoxy—or, on the contrary, a radical innovation in terms of the contents and forms of democratic politics that, when grounded in the renewed activism of civil society, will give impetus to the gradual but significant strengthening of the tendencies toward a profound—perhaps socialist?—transformation of the system.

Meeting the Challenges of a New Century

It is essential for the left to adopt a mature position in the face of the serious challenges besieging it at the turn of a new century. If the grave harms that the neoliberal experiments have inflicted upon our societies are to be redressed, the left has to become a valid, credible, and attractive political alternative for the popular masses. To be sure this will not be attained by an underestimation of the scope and reach of the wide-ranging capitalist restructuring currently under way. Much as Marx and Engels noted in *The German Ideology,* at the present time the development of the productive forces is proceeding at such a rate that the whole ensemble of social relations—and their corresponding ideological and institutional crystallizations—long established in advanced societies are at the brink of being completely overcome. The left will have much less success if it ignores the multiple implications of the collapse of really existing socialisms. For the left to seclude itself, seeking refuge in some essential doctrinal certainties, is under these circumstances the surest path toward its complete disappearance both as a political actor and as a project of social reconstruction. If the left turns a blind eye to the changes revolutionizing the contemporary scene, the socialist utopia will become a dogma proper of an esoteric and insignificant sect. A "religious" Marxism is fatally condemned to rapid extinction, and a capitalist society without a socialist alternative is very likely to downgrade to barbaric forms of social life.

Consequently, the left must be ready to submit everything for discussion. If it believes in the ethical and theoretical superiority of socialism, it must be prepared to uphold its arguments in front of its adversaries. Yet, and for the purpose of clarifying the convulsed theoretical and ideological panorama of the present times, it seems appropriate to ask: where is the great theory that has overcome Marxism? Who produced that gigantic theoretical and practical-historical *Aufhebung* that would rationally and scientifically authorize one to speak of post-Marxism as something found in the real world? Where are this writer's books? Where are the historical processes inspired in his or her name?[38]

The answer that postmodernity is irreducible to macrotheories or to the grand narrative is no more than a vulgar fig leaf that fails to conceal the grotesque nakedness of the emperor and does not even add up to a plausible argument. Actually, if there is a theoretical and practical model that shows unmistakable signs of exhaustion, it is the liberal one, borne of the felicitous combination of the theoretical legacies of John Locke and Adam Smith more than two centuries ago, which has gradually been replaced by a highly unstable amalgam of neoliberal economics and neoconservative politics. In the mid-1920s Lord Keynes sorrowfully proclaimed the end of laissez-faire, and subsequent events supported his foresight.[39] Liberal leaders and practices became conservative, corporativist if not openly fascist and reactionary; and liberal theorizing quickly broke loose from the liberal remains—public freedoms, individual rights, rule of law, constitutionalism, etc.—and embraced a statist thought centered in the paramount defense of the new types of interests and values incarnate in the great monopoly enterprise. A quick glance at the main theoretical contributions—from Milton Friedman to Irving Kristol—is enough to measure the intensity of this involutive descent. The figures of the citizen and of the small business owner, who work with their own hands from dawn to dusk and compete in a free market. were buried by the wholesale expropriation of the independent producers and the salarization of the labor force, by the exaltation of civic apathy promoted by neoconservative thinkers, and by the virtual disappearance of competitive markets in most branches of capitalist production. In their place, the heirs of the liberal tradition now propose the far less appealing figures of the technocrat and the managers of big monopolies, and the place of small family-owned firms is occupied by huge, faceless transnational corporations. Obviously, constructing a democratic discourse and practice is much more difficult with these kinds of social actors.[40]

It is not a mere coincidence that precisely when the liberal theoretical model trips on these agonizing obstacles, the announcements that speak of the final defeat of Marxism are enhanced.[41] So profound is the crisis of liberal thought that the themes that today confront its intellectual heirs are nothing less than the great issues of the Marxist tradition: the contradiction between capitalism and democracy (that is, between monopolistic accumulation and popular sovereignty); the state and bureaucratization; the problem of the ungovernability of civil society; the ideological crises and the processes of disintegration of what Gramsci calls "historical blocs"; and the dialectics of realism and utopia in projects of social transformation. Keynes once said that people who believe themselves to be quite practical are usually the slaves of some economist who has been dead for several centuries. Most postmodern theorists appear to be operating under the same type of slavery, which keeps them ruminating on the cardinal issues of Marxist thought while they grumble against their intellectual master.[42]

The vitality of the socialist tradition may well be much greater than its critics are ready to concede, and socialism's preoccupations currently make up a good part of contemporary theoretical and ideological debate. In fact, one could say that it has been the task of the socialist tradition to rekindle some values that were born in the heart of the bourgeois mind and were gradually abandoned by monopoly capitalism. The central role of civil society, the criticism against statism, and the respect for individual rights—among which human rights occupy a privileged place—were in the past great banners of liberal thought. Now they have been recovered from the neglect they suffered in current times thanks to a variety of anticapitalist struggles inspired, to different degrees, by the realization of the socialist utopia.

Of course, all of this does not mean that Marx's complex and heterogeneous theoretical legacy is a closed universe of eternal and irrefutable truths. Marxist tradition faces many types of problems. Some are theoretical, dealing with Marxism's capacity to correctly interpret and explain the contemporary reality of resurgent conservative capitalisms and bankrupted and/or ailing socialist experiments; and some are practical, referring to the strategies and results of the various attempts for social transformation carried out in the name of Marx, the grave insufficiencies and deformations of which have caused, in many cases, a resounding and well-deserved collapse. Those are the burning questions at the end of the twentieth century. The crisis of Marxism as the "religion" of the proletariat or as a legitimizing ideology of bureaucratic dictatorships is, in the face of the enormousness of the previously mentioned issues, a matter of secondary importance that has little to do with the future of the processes of change in modern societies.[43]

However, the severity of the crisis that affects the theory and practice of Marxism can hardly be underestimated. Perry Anderson once noted, with his usual precision and insightfulness, that the crisis of "Western Marxism" was a crisis of Latin Marxism, suffocated in the circle of fire of its philosophical solipsisms. By moving to the Anglo-Saxon world, Marxism adopted both a different style and content: removed from the epistemological and philosophical concerns that had been the distinctive mark of Western Marxism, the new current was characterized from its onset by its orientation—markedly political, economic, and sociological—and by its singular drive and creativity.[44]

Yet, shortly after Marxist thought changed centers, the situation of

Marxist theory worsened considerably: the collapse of the Berlin Wall, the disarticulation of the former Soviet Union, the Eastern European stampede toward market economy and capitalist democracy, the practical dissolution of the Warsaw Pact, the strange persistence of socialism in China, and the replacement of "bureaucratic-authoritarian" socialist governments—to paraphrase Guillermo O'Donnell's well-known characterization of some Latin American dictatorships—by others of a social-Christian or conservative inspiration pose a set of grave and unprecedented problems in the history of Marxism. In fact, the crisis of Latin Marxism was rooted in the failure of the revolution in the West. The present crisis adds a qualitatively different element: the failure of the experiences of the socialist construction, a product of the aberrant distortions registered in the "leading cases," now defunct in the face of a triumphant capitalism. The sudden collapse of this first cycle of socialist revolutions, which encompassed almost all the twentieth century, has decisively modified the geography of international politics and overwhelmingly tipped the scale toward the West. The crisis of Marxism no longer nourishes itself solely from the defeats suffered by the workers' movement at the hand of the bourgeoisie—as in the two postwar periods and with the popular fronts of the 1930s—but also from the profound discredit and the political and economic decomposition that brought to an end the cycle initiated by the 1917 Russian Revolution. What is now up for discussion is not only the capacity that Marxist theory is able to retain to interpret and adequately change the neocapitalist structures, but also the effectiveness and desirability of a project of socialist transformations that, according to the history of this century, raises serious vital questions.

Does today mark a temporary twilight or the final disintegration of socialism? The verdict is in the hands of history. I am inclined to believe the former—that socialists have suffered a grave defeat, but that they will have to see the course of events in this decisive final decade of the twentieth century before being able to venture a better-documented response. I tend not to believe that the failure of the attempts to construct a socialist society could mean something as tremendous as the final eradication of such a noble purpose, or the definitive demise of our dreams.

Nevertheless, will Marxism be able to confront the formidable challenge posed by the end of the century? Marcelo Cohen poetically captures the creative, diffuse, and profound presence of Marxism in the contemporary world. He speaks of its legacies, promises, and immense possibilities, and it is fitting to close this book with his words:

> I am the unburied voice of Marxism. . . . Only some of my avatars lay under the ruins of the Berlin Wall. Others step back in the face of the Polish images of the Virgin. Yet, spiritually, so to speak, I am everywhere. My breath suffuses the life of the world, not only the Western world. . . . I have been used, like almost everything, to perpetrate social and hodge-podge nightmares of the imagination. I have been invoked to torture. . . . I have

given words to name what today continues to harm; I have nourished the nerve, the proud anger, the critical sharpness. . . . And I have supplied openings, fantastic interpretative accounts, broad theoretical hallucinations that fed rebellious fantasy and intelligent pleasure. For soccer fans: I am a refined midfielder who creates inexhaustible game. And nothing more. With me discussions will continue. I will not be the cement of perverse constructions, but instead mobility and suggestions; I have the presentiment of new metamorphosis. Whoever wants to may receive me. And he who does not, go to hell.[45]

Notes

1. Anderson, Perry, *Considerations on Western Marxism* (London: New Left Books, 1976). Bobbio's expression is found in his "Esiste una dottrina marxista dello stato?" in Bobbio, Norberto, et al., eds., *Il Marxismo e lo stato* (Rome: Quaderni di Mondoperaio, 1976), p. 9

2. *Democracy and the Markets* (Cambridge: Cambridge University Press, 1992), p. 1.

3. Some sharp observations regarding these issues, with particular emphasis on the studies on dependency in the United States, are in Cardoso, Fernando H., "El consumo de la teoría de la dependencia en los Estados Unidos," *El Trimestre Económico* (Mexico: 1977), pp. 33–52.

4. The view of David Easton, patriarch of the "systemic" school of positivist social sciences, is clearly reflected in "The political system besieged by the state," *Political Theory* 9(3) (August 1981). Regarding Keynesianism and its decomposition see Robert Skidelsky's excellent anthology *The End of the Keynesian Era* (London: Macmillan Press, 1977). The feeble foundations of the supposedly theoretical supersession of Keynesianism, like supply-side economics, for instance, are adequately disposed of in Krugman, Paul, *Peddling Prosperity: Economic Sense and Nonsense in the Age of Diminished Expectations* (New York and London: Norton and Co., 1994), Ch. 3. The fate of structural functionalism and Talcott Parsons's sociology have been brilliantly analyzed by Alvin Gouldner in his *The Coming Crisis of Western Sociology* (New York: Avon Books, 1971). See also C. Wright Mills's pioneering analysis in his *The Sociological Imagination* (New York: Oxford University Press, 1959). Finally, on the crisis of Marxism see two works by Anderson, Perry, *Considerations on Western Marxism* and *In the Tracks of Historical Materialism* (London: Verso Books, 1983) as well as Paramio, Ludolfo, *Tras el diluvio: La izquierda ante el fin de siglo* (Madrid: Siglo XXI, 1988).

5. A notable example of the difficulties experienced by theoretical models foreign to the Marxist tradition is exemplified by Zbigniew Brzezinski. In a talk given at Columbia University two years before the collapse of the Berlin Wall, Brzezinski spoke of East Germany as a monolithic fortress, a sort of unconquerable communist Prussia. In November 1989, his predictions collapsed as loudly as the crumbling Berlin Wall. See his *The Grand Failure* (New York: Collier Books, Macmillan Publishing Company, 1990), p. 249. For a very perceptive analysis of these issues see also Blackburn, Robin, "Fin de siècle: Socialism after the crash," *New Left Review* 185 (January–February 1991), pp. 5–67.

6. Cf. Blackburn, "Fin de siècle," for an excellent compilation of the successive controversies.

7. On this subject see an excellent article written by Miliband, Ralph, "El

nuevo revisionismo en Gran Bretaña," *Cuadernos Políticos* 44 (Mexico: July–December 1985), pp. 20–35; and Ellen Meiksins Wood's penetrating work, *The Retreat from Class: A New "True" Socialism* (London: Verso, 1986).

8. See Fukuyama, Francis, "The end of history?" *The National Interest* (Summer 1989), pp. 3–18.

9. On this chronic problem see Habermas, Jürgen, *Legitimation Crisis* (Boston: Beacon Press, 1975); and Offe, Claus, "La abolición del control del mercado y el problema de la legitimidad," in Sonntag, Heinz R., and Héctor Valecillos, *El estado en el capitalismo contemporáneo* (Mexico: Siglo XXI, 1977), pp. 62–87.

10. von Mises, Ludwig, *Planned Chaos* (Irving-on-Hudson, NY: 1947), p. 124. Quoted in Blackburn, "Fin de siécle," p. 7.

11. Here, it is appropriate to keep in mind Anderson's suggestive observations on the many roads through which Marxist thought traveled in this century. See his *Considerations*, Chs. 1 and 2.

12. It should be enough to recall the names of some leading neoconservative scholars, such as Seymour M. Lipset, Irving Kristol, Daniel Bell, and Manuel Castells, among others. More recently there are María Antonieta Macchiocchi, former ultra-Maoist and arch-Gramscian, now "converted" to the neoliberal religion the same as, among Latin Americans, Mario Vargas Llosa and, before him, Eudocio Ravines. See Steinfels, Peter, *The Neoconservatives* (New York: Simon and Schuster, 1979), pp. 25–48. See also Irving Kristol's memoirs and confessions in *Reflexiones de un neoconservador* (Buenos Aires: GEL, 1986), pp. 17–40.

13. Paramio, *Tras el diluvio,* pp. 6-7 (emphasis in the original).

14. When I speak of utopia I am referring to projects for the construction of a good society that, within the conditions of a certain historical period, seems unlikely although not radically impossible. The humanistic rusticity of positivism makes its followers look over their shoulders at the great tradition of Western utopic thought, which was born with Plato and two thousand years later found one of its leading exponents in Thomas More. To be sure, when More spoke of a six-hour work day, Popper's admirers—had they existed, of course—would have dismissed his ideas as fancifully utopian. However, what More posited as a distinctive feature of his utopia will be a reality in the most advanced capitalist countries at the end of this century. To the horror of positivists, utopia and reality tend to intermingle in the actual historical process.

15. On this issue it is fundamental to see Bloch, Ernst, *El principio esperanza* (Madrid: Aguilar, 1980), 3 vols. For an excellent discussion regarding the epistemological issue see Kosic, Karel, *Dialéctica de lo concreto* (Mexico: Grijalbo, 1976).

16. Marx, Karl, and Friedrich Engels, *The German Ideology,* in Tucker, Robert C., ed., *The Marx-Engels Reader,* p. 126. (emphasis in the original).

17. This epistemological current has the dubious merit of having expelled the concepts of "power" and "state" from the sphere of political science because, according to its spokespersons, those concepts lacked clear-cut empirical referents that would enable rigorous measurement. Fortunately, the success of this barbaric enterprise, launched in the early 1950s, did not last even twenty years. See Easton, David, *The Political System* (New York: Knopf, 1953), as well as his article cited in note 4. For a critique of this perspective see Wolin, Sheldon, *Politics and Vision: Continuity and Innovation in Western Political Thought* (Boston: Little, Brown and Co., 1960), Ch. 1. Needless to say, my critique does not diminish in the least the central importance of objectivity and the rigor of proof in the constitution of a theoretical argument that is worthy of being called scientific. What I reject is the positivist canon, not the need for rigorous work.

18. See Leo Strauss's blasting critique—from a perspective that is not precise-

ly Marxist—in his *What Is Political Philosophy?* (New York: The Free Press, 1968), Ch. 1.

19. Gouldner, Alvin, *The Two Marxisms* (New York: Seabury Press, 1980), p. 117.

20. See Anderson, Perry, *Considerations on Western Marxism,* p. 113.

21. Hartz, Louis, *The Liberal Tradition in America* (New York: Harcourt & Brace, 1955).

22. A more detailed study of some of these issues may be found in my "Authoritarian ideological traditions and transition towards democracy in Argentina," *Papers on Latin America* (New York: Institute of Latin American and Iberian Studies, Columbia University, 1989), paper no. 8.

23. Paramio, *Tras el Diluvio,* p. 25.

24. Giddens, Anthony, *The Class Structure of the Advanced Societies* (New York: Harper Torchbooks, 1975), p. 164.

25. Cf., on the U.S. case, Phillips, Kevin, *The Politics of Rich and Poor* (New York: HarperCollins Publishers, 1990); Hacker, Andrew, *Two Nations, Black and White: Separate, Hostile, Unequal* (New York: Ballantine Books, 1992); and the more recent book by Krugman, Paul, *Peddling Prosperity.* On the U.K. experience see Green, Francis, ed., *The Restructuring of the UK Economy* (New York: Harvester Wheatsheaf, 1989).

26. Gorz, André, *Adiós al proletariado* (Madrid: El Viejo Topo, 1981). A sharp critique of this thesis can be found in Meiksins Wood's *The Retreat,* pp. 15–18.

27. See, for instance, the writings of Ernesto Laclau and Chantal Mouffe, especially their *Hegemonía y estrategia socialista: Hacia una radicalización de la democracia* (Madrid: Siglo XXI, 1987). After rather immodestly announcing to Spanish-speaking readers that the first edition of this book, which appeared in the English language in 1985, "was at the center of a series of debates, both theoretical and political, currently going on in the Anglo Saxon world," the authors begin the task of invalidating the alleged class essentialism and reductionism inherent in classical Marxism and against which Antonio Gramsci stumbles. Therefore, Laclau and Mouffe feel obliged to go "beyond Gramsci and to deconstruct the very notion of "social class" (pp. 7–8). The flaws of their complex reasoning are adequately exposed in Meiksins Wood's *The Retreat,* op. cit. See also Boron, Atilio A., and Oscar Cuéllar, "Apuntes críticos sobre la concepción idealista de la hegemonía," *Revista Mexicana de Sociología* 45(4) (October–December 1983), pp. 1143–1177, where it is shown that Laclau and Mouffe go into a theoretical labyrinth out of which they emerge thinking they have found Ariadna's thread of neo-Marxism when in reality they have grabbed the heavy rope of vulgar idealism. A more recent interesting debate regarding Laclau and Mouffe's thesis is found in the *New Left Review.* See Geras, Norman, "Post-Marxism?" no. 163 (May–June 1987), pp. 40–82. Laclau and Mouffe's reply appears under the title "Post-Marxism without apologies," no. 166 (November–December 1987), pp. 79–106; Nicos Mouzelis replies with his "Marxism or post-Marxism?" no. 167 (January–February 1988), pp. 107–123. Norman Geras, I believe, ends the debate with a demolishing response in "Ex-Marxism without substance: Being a real reply to Laclau and Mouffe," no. 169 (May–June 1988), pp. 34–61. In this work Geras shows that the book by Laclau and Mouffe "presents an impoverishing caricature of the Marxist tradition . . . and what they offer in its place is intellectually empty" (p. 35).

28. On the meaning of the welfare state and the so-called Keynesian revolution as products of popular demand, see Gough, Ian, *The Political Economy of the Welfare State* (London: Macmillan Press, 1979), and Negri, Antonio, *La classe ouvriére contre l'état* (Paris: Galilee, 1978).

29. See Miliband, Ralph, "El nuevo revisionismo en Gran Bretaña." His conclusions are consistent with the ones reached by Adam Przeworski in *Capitalism and Social Democracy,* op. cit. See also Buci-Glucksmann, Christinne, and Göran Therborn, *Le defi social-democrate* (Paris: Dialectiques, 1981), especially their analysis of the "Swedish way" on pp. 161–264. For a different perspective see Paramio, *Tras el Diluvio,* Chs. 4–6.

30. The best-known example of this tradition is perhaps Heberle, Rudolph, *Social Movements* (New York: Appleton-Century Crofts, 1951).

31. Needless to say, this critique does not apply to those who are seriously interested in the analysis of the new forms of social intervention by collective actors. In this sense, the contributions made by Latin American social scientists in the last ten or fifteen years have allowed one to substantially enrich one's interpretive capacity regarding the economic and political structure and dynamics of peripheral capitalist formations. On this see the contributions collected in Calderón Gutiérrez, Fernando, ed., *Los movimientos sociales ante la crisis* (Buenos Aires: CLACSO, 1986), and the ones found in Calderón Gutiérrez, Fernando, and Mario R. dos Santos, *Los conflictos por la constitución de un nuevo orden* (Buenos Aires: CLACSO, 1987). Also see the following articles: Gunder Frank, André, and Marta Fuentes, "Diez tesis acerca de los movimientos sociales," *Revista Mexicana de Sociología* 51(4) (October–December 1989), pp. 21–43; Guidos, Rafael, and Otto Fernández, "El juicio al sujeto: Un análisis de los movimientos sociales en América Latina," pp. 45–76; Calderón Gutiérrez, Fernando, and Mario R. dos Santos, "Del petitorio urbano a la multiplicidad de destinos," pp. 77–91; and Zermeño, Sergio, "El regreso del líder: Crisis, neoliberalismo y desorden," pp. 115–150. All of these articles were published in *Revista Mexicana de Sociologia* 51(4) (October–December 1989).

32. In this sense, it is worth highlighting the position of Ralph Dahrendorf, an outstanding enlightened liberal. In a recent work he reasserts the central—but not exclusive—character of class conflict in capitalist societies. This attitude notably contrasts with the traditional narrow-mindedness of Latin American (especially Argentine) liberals, many of whom are actually recalcitrant conservatives. See Dahrendorf, Ralph, *The Modern Social Conflict: An Essay on the Politics of Liberty* (Berkeley and Los Angeles: University of California Press, 1988).

33. "Following Marx's reductionist vision, the proletariat organizes itself in a class party that, after having taken over the state power, must open the doors to a new historical epoch," in Paramio, *Tras el Diluvio,* p. 173 (my translation). Nothing is more foreign to Marx's dialectical thought than Paramio's syllogistic reconstruction, according to which from class there is an automatic passage to the party, and from there, inexorably to the revolution. The least that one can demand from those who decry Marxism's theoretical errors is that they should take the pain to examine some other work besides *Manifesto of the Communist Party,* which of course was a political pamphlet aimed at the dissemination of communist ideas in the turbulent months before the revolutionary outbreak of 1848. There are several texts of much greater theoretical weight—*The Poverty of Philosophy, The Eighteenth Brumaire of Louis Bonaparte,* or *Capital*—in which Marx discusses the dialectic and probabilistic nature of the sequence that his critics reconstruct in a mechanical fashion and in a reductionist and deterministic code. Is this just an accidental "mistake" made by Marx's critics?

34. On this see the clarifying works by Offe, Claus, *Disorganized Capitalism* (Cambridge, MA: MIT Press, 1985), pp. 10–79 and 129–150; as well as Sabel, Charles F., *Work and Politics: The Division of Labor in Industry* (Cambridge: Cambridge University Press, 1982). An excellent reflection on the French case can be seen in Aglietta, Michel, and Anton Brender, *Les métamorphoses de la société*

salariale (Paris: Calmann-Levy, 1984). See also Pipitone, Ugo, *El capitalismo que cambia* (Mexico: ERA, 1986), pp. 74–114. A general analysis may be found in Giddens, *The Class Structure,* pp. 198–222.

35. I have developed some of these issues in my "Clase y política en las actuales transiciones latinoamericanas," in EURAL, *Proyectos de cambio: La izquierda democrática en América Latina* (Caracas: Nueva Sociedad, 1988), pp. 39–66.

36. Miliband, Ralph, "El nuevo revisionismo en Gran Bretaña," p. 26.

37. Miliband, Ralph, *Divided Societies* (Oxford and New York: Oxford University Press, 1991), p. 114.

38. Agustín Cueva wonders, with the subtle irony that characterizes him, whether those intellectuals who proclaim themselves as "post-Marxists" have that label for having theoretically surpassed Marx or only because they used to be Marxists. See his *Las democracias restringidas de América Latina: Elementos para una reflexión crítica* (Letraviva: Planeta del Ecuador, 1988), p. 85.

39. Keynes, John M., "The end of *laissez-faire*" (1926), in *Essays in Persuasion* (London: The Macmillan Press, 1984), pp. 272–294.

40. I have examined some aspects in previous articles. See "La crisis norteamericana y la racionalidad neoconservadora," *Cuadernos Semestrales* 9 (Mexico: First semester, 1981), pp. 31–58; and with Víctor M. Godínez, "Entre Roosevelt y Reagan: Contenidos y límites de la alternativa neoliberal," *Cuadernos Semestrales* 14 (Mexico: Second semester, 1983), pp. 47–72.

41. Roughly twenty years ago, the author of *The New American Ideology* (New York: Alfred Knopf, 1975), George Cabot Lodge, profesor of Harvard Business School—which can hardly be considered an institution inclined toward Marxist exaggerations—demonstrated the complete uselessness of liberalism as an ideology that guides the concrete practice of U.S. business executives. He put forth a new doctrine capable of reconciling actions with ideas, thereby avoiding what he called the "ideological schizophrenia" of the U.S. bourgeoisie.

42. In any case, it would be prudent to keep in mind that the theoretical collapse of the liberal model does not necessarily mean the end of the efficiency of its discourse. It is well known that there are evident asynchronisms that explain the perdurability of an ideology beyond its effective correspondence with reality.

43. A discussion of the problems confronted by the contributions of the "classical trio" of Marxist tradition (Marx, Lenin, and Trotsky) can be found in Anderson, Perry, *Considerations,* pp. 113–121.

44. Anderson, Perry, *In the Tracks,* Ch. 1.

45. Cohen, Marcelo, "Una voz en las librerías," *Página/12* (Buenos Aires: June 24, 1990), p. 24.

Index

253

About the Book

Now that democratic revolutions appear to have triumphed around the world and noncapitalist modes of development are rapidly vanishing, will—can?—Latin American capitalism become democratic? Addressing this question, Atilio Boron offers a fresh look at Western political economy and political science from a perspective that starts theoretically and geographically outside of the current mainstream.

Boron points to the formidable obstacles the Latin American countries face in their efforts at democratic reform: frail political institutions, a strong authoritarian tradition, the disruptive influence of neoliberal economic policies, the shortsightedness of the Latin American ruling classes, and the hopelessness that is taking root among the poor. Turning to the international arena, he sees economic recession, massive unemployment, the resurgence of protectionism, and the increasing insecurity of the New World Order as conditions hardly conducive to fostering democratic consolidation in the periphery.

Thus, Boron concludes, the road toward democracy in Latin America is dangerous, its final success highly uncertain, and the desperate need obvious for not only enhanced statesmanship, but also fresh and challenging theoretical perspectives to help in drawing a realistic map for an epoch-making journey.

Atilio A. Boron holds the chair in political theory at the University of Buenos Aires; he has also been vice-chancellor of the university and is founding director of EURAL (Center for European-Latin American Research). Professor Boron's numerous publications include *Memorias del capitalismo salvaje* and, most recently, *The Right and Democracy in Latin America* (coedited with Maria do Carmo Campello de Souza and Douglas Chalmers).